D1569120

Is There an Optimum Level of Population?

A POPULATION COUNCIL BOOK

Is There an Optimum Level of Population?

Edited by S. Fred Singer

McGRAW-HILL BOOK COMPANY
New York   St. Louis   San Francisco   Düsseldorf   London   Sydney   Toronto   Mexico
Panama   Kuala Lumpur   Montreal   New Delhi   Rio de Janeiro   Singapore

This book was set in Times Roman by York Graphic Services. It
was printed on acid-free, long-life paper and bound by The Maple
Press Company. The designer was Christine Aulicino. The editors
were Herbert Waentig, Nancy Tressel, and Judy Duguid. Frank
Matonti and Alice Cohen supervised the production.

Library of Congress Catalog Card Number: 76-177375

1 2 3 4 5 6 7 8 9   MAMM   7 9 8 7 6 5 4 3 2 1

07-057471-5

TABLE OF CONTENTS

Part II
Optimum Population: Considering Education,
Health, and Welfare Services

Part III
The General Question of Optimum: Life Styles and Human Values

Appendices

PREFACE

This is a provocative volume. Its importance lies not merely in the carefully considered views of an impressive group of scholars on the concept of an optimum level of population, but in the broad emphasis it brings to bear on the fundamental issue underlying the concept itself.

That issue is the quality of life.

I welcome the emphasis placed on this point. In my view, it is the key to the strategy which all nations, rich and poor alike, must adopt if they are to face the population problem realistically.

Whatever may or may not be the optimum level of population for a given society, it is clear that in much of the *developing* world the greatest single obstacle to development is the rampant *rate* of population growth. Not only does this severely hinder economic advance, but more importantly, it impedes imperative social progress.

The poor nations of the world, containing two-thirds of its population, during the Sixties averaged a 5 per cent annual growth in Gross National Product—thus meeting the prime target of the United Nations Decade of Development. But annual per capita income in these same countries—because of high rates of population growth—rose on the average only 2.5 per cent. For hundreds of millions of people, this meant a yearly cash increment so small as to be virtually invisible. In relation to the people in the privileged industrialized world, the poverty of these hundreds of millions grew more abject and more degrading.

We sometimes have the romanticized notion that life in a developing country is at least calm and serene, however backward it may be. It is a dangerous illusion. Life in the developing world is an outrageous assault on human dignity. It is an existence characterized by hunger, disease, illiteracy, hopelessness, and an early death. It may be spared some of the irresponsible by-products of opulence, but its apparent calmness and serenity are more usually apathy and despair.

The search for a methodology to determine an optimum level of population, or an optimum growth rate, is a subtle and complex matter, as the contributors to this volume make clear. But there appears to be a general consensus among them that the current rate of population growth, at least in most of the poorer nations of the world, is too high. Anyone who looks at the matter rationally and responsibly must agree with them.

ROBERT S. MCNAMARA

PROLOGUE

Is There an Optimum Level of Population?

We have become so conditioned to the inevitability of population increase that almost all concern has been to decrease the rate of increase. Only occasionally has the question been raised as to whether we have attained or even passed an optimum level of population.*

To start with, is the question itself meaningful? We need to define the word "optimum" and to spell out "optimum for what?" This itself becomes a valid subject for discussion, but perhaps we can sidestep this point for the time being by redefining "optimum" as the situation in which the population, as a whole, enjoys the highest quality of life. This means, of course, that each person receives an adequate amount of food; is adequately supplied with the necessary raw materials to make the things and devices he needs (including such nonrenewable resources as metals); that there is an adequate supply of energy, as well as water and air of high quality. But, in addition to the so-called "necessities of life," there are other requirements: adequate medical care to insure good health; recreational facilities, especially outdoors; and cultural outlets. Then there are sociological and psychological requirements, including a requirement for space and privacy.

Heuristic arguments can be a guide in arriving at a meaningful

---

*J. J. Spengler, *The 99th Hour*, Daniel O. Price, ed. (Chapel Hill: University of North Carolina Press, 1966).

discussion. Take, for example, a town. If the population is too small, then it cannot provide all the necessary services which produce a good life: cultural facilities, hospitals, and so on. And we are all familiar with the consequences of too large a population in a city, or at least in the present, overcrowded city. Intuitively, then, one feels that there must be an optimum of population—perhaps a broad optimum; and one feels that this concept could also apply to a region and to a country, and perhaps to the world.

For the purposes of the present discussion, let us confine our attention entirely to the United States, since we are interested only in investigating a methodology. It is not necessary, therefore, to involve ourselves in foreign problems.

In the United States, the production of food does not really provide a meaningful upper limit to the population. In other words, the upper limit is so high that other considerations would give a lower value. (While hunger is a very serious matter, it is due to a poor distribution system and to poverty of a segment of the population, rather than to the ability to produce food.) Rather than ask the question: "How large a population can agricultural production support?" one can reverse the question by inquiring how few people it would take to feed a population of a given size, now and in the future. One would find, I imagine, that as the level of population increases, the fraction of people involved in agriculture would drop down to an asymptotic limit, all other factors being equal. One could show that economies of scale allow one to manufacture food more efficiently in larger quantities. On the other hand, there comes a point when high-quality agricultural lands are exhausted and further production has to be carried on at a lower level of efficiency. A determining factor, of course, is advances in technology and in agricultural science: the former providing such essentials as water, fertilizer, and perhaps even carbon dioxide at lower cost; the latter developing plants that more efficiently convert the essential raw materials into food.

From a similar point of view, one could discuss the limitations introduced by mineral and other resources, and by manufacturing, and by the problems of air and water pollution which depend not only on level, but also on concentration of population. Fairly well-defined limits can be set, for example, to the capacity of streams to support the acceptance of treated chemical wastes and of thermal wastes. Furthermore, costs increase rapidly with the higher degree of treatment which becomes necessary as the population density rises.

One of the most important subjects is energy, since it forms the base for many of the other considerations. For example, with cheap and abundant energy, it is possible to produce food by nonconventional means, or to purify air and water economically to a very high degree. Social and health services can also be discussed in a fairly quantitative manner. Demographic trends can be documented, such as a lowering of the average age of the population, and a relative increase in those groups who tend to have a higher birth rate. These trends, which can lead to important consequences in our society, depend not only on the absolute level but also on the rate of increase of population. Adequate educational and health services may provide a significant bound to achieving a full and healthy life for an ever-increasing population. Perhaps there arise, also, fundamental biological problems as the level of population goes beyond certain limits.

Other factors, such as sociological and psychological requirements, can probably be discussed only in a semiquantitative way. But no one can deny the existence of a human need for cultural outlets and for recreation, much of it out-of-doors, or the need for space and privacy, again with an emphasis on natural outdoor environments.

Which of the factors provide a "lowest upper limit" to the level of population? How do these various factors interact with each other? What research needs exist? Can at least portions of the problem be handled by mathematical simulation? What are some of the philosophical, ethical, and political considerations in striving for an optimum population level?

A discussion of such questions cannot do much more than open up the problem. It is clear that it will not answer the question of what is an optimum level of population. However, we can hope for at least the development of a methodology which will allow us to pursue the major question in a fruitful way. It will also lay the groundwork for the considerations of the Commission of Population Growth and the American Future which has been proposed by President Nixon to conduct an inquiry into the consequences of population growth in the United States and into the policies which the government should adopt. The time seems to be ripe for an examination of this question which is so fundamental to the well-being of the nation, and indeed of the whole world.

SFS

ACKNOWLEDGMENTS

This volume is the outgrowth of a Symposium held in Boston in December 1969 as part of the annual meeting of the American Association for the Advancement of Science. I am indebted to a large number of people who have contributed significantly. In addition to the participants, I would single out Walter Berl and Dan Thornhill of the American Association for the Advancement of Science who facilitated the organization of the Symposium and contributed many important suggestions. My secretary, Mrs. Barbara Burke, did the lion's share of the work in the organization of the Symposium, in the pulling together of the manuscripts, and in their preparation for publication. Christopher Price and his staff at The Population Council are responsible for the final version of this volume and did an extremely effective job of technical editing. I am grateful to all of them.

SFS

PART I

Optimum Population: Considering Natural Resources and Environmental Factors

INTRODUCTION

There is little dispute among the participants of the Symposium about the *existence* of an optimum population—or rather of several optima, as suggested by Garrett Hardin. There is considerable difference, however, concerning the *specification* of such an optimum. And there is wide disagreement as to whether an optimum population level has been reached or passed, say, in the United States. But then there is general agreement that prudence dictates a slowing down of population growth, reaching a zero growth rate either in the near future or in some distant future.

The differences between what might be called a "neo-Malthusian" outlook and a "cornucopian" outlook emerge most strongly in the discussion of natural resources—minerals and energy. (The terms "neo-Malthusian" and "cornucopian" are used in a slightly pejorative sense by the advocates of one point of view when they describe the other point of view.)

In his lead-off article, Preston Cloud defines "optimum population" as one that lies within limits large enough to realize the potentialities of human creativity to achieve a life of high quality for all men indefinitely, but not so large as to threaten dilution of quality, the potential to achieve it, or the wise management of the ecosystem. He enunciates a Malthusian view concerning population. "Nothing can increase indefinitely on a finite earth." His main conclusions are: 1) we will run out of most raw materials within the next thirty to fifty years; 2) even cheaper energy from nuclear sources will not help substantially; and 3) we have by far exceeded an optimum level of population.

He argues that we must limit population, limit per capita consumption amongst the already affluent nations, and introduce sensible conservation measures including the recycling of wastes and the recovery of all by-products.

This vision of the future is strongly disputed by Harrison Brown, who argues that a resource is "created" and that, if the

3

need arises, we could extract essential metals from lower quality ores without substantially affecting our economy. Of course, the basic problem is the availability of sufficient energy, and, in any case, per capita energy consumption must necessarily increase. Brown suggests that the disposal of all of this energy in the form of heat may produce an ultimate limit to the growth of population and of the economy.

Joseph L. Fisher also takes a more optimistic view of the future. Basically, he looks to new discoveries in minerals and fuels from technical advances in exploration and extraction. Secondly, he points to the fact that, historically, the standard of living has risen in spite of a growing population. The increase in population, he argues, not only increases the labor force, but also productivity and resource availability. He does not feel that any limiting or optimum level has been reached; he does, however, advocate a slowing down of population growth.

The most optimistic view is expressed by Alvin M. Weinberg and R. P. Hammond. They point out that energy is "convertible" into nearly all other resources, including food and water. With the advent of catalytic nuclear burners, either breeder reactors or fusion reactors, we will have inexhaustible sources of energy which can be freely converted into other kinds of resources. The only limiting effects they foresee are environmental side effects. They judge, however, that waste heat will not be a problem, and, on this point, disagree with Harrison Brown. (One must note, however, that catalytic nuclear burners have not yet been developed and, until they are proven to be feasible and economical, there may be serious transition problems as conventional energy supplies based on fossil fuels and on U^{235} become exhausted.)

The picture they paint is an exciting one. Even though this new energy source won't be free—in fact, it may not be cheaper—it could allow more economical desalination of water and perhaps economical production of fertilizers and of fuels.

Chauncey Starr shares this view of a bright nuclear future. He also feels that energy supply will not set an upper limit to population level. The major limit he sees arises from population concentration; local heating in high density cities produces heat islands which could cause problems. (It should be noted, however, that the atmosphere may adjust itself to increased heat production by increasing convective flow; such problems have been studied in connection with cumulus cloud production in the tropics.)

Hans Landsberg looks at the energy picture from an economist's point of view. He, too, feels that energy will not present a limit to population growth. Energy consumption seems to be roughly proportional to the Gross National Product and therefore increases faster than the population itself. He is optimistic that any environmental effects can be handled but, of course, at a certain cost. He points out that technology can introduce large changes in such a picture; for example, a more efficient use of fuels has become possible in the last decades (but also new technology has arisen, such as air conditioning, which demands more energy consumption per capita). Overall, Landsberg concludes that resource scarcity should not be used as an argument in favor of limiting population.

Interestingly enough, these views of the energy experts are not shared by the agriculturalists. For example, Lester Brown shows convincingly that food production does not set a hard limit for United States population, particularly in view of exciting prospects for advances in food technology. Nevertheless, he feels that optimum population has been exceeded, but for ecological reasons. William Paddock very much shares this point of view. He takes a broader view of agriculture as a large economical enterprise, which involves 30 per cent of the United States working population, consumes most of the water, and even plays a substantial role in earning foreign exchange. He also feels that pollution control will become too expensive, although his cost figures are not substantiated.

The global resource picture is examined by Barry Commoner who views humanity in an impending crisis of survival generated by the destruction of the ecosystem's stability accompanied by rapidly dwindling supplies of natural resources. Therefore, a stabilized population is essential. His view of what constitutes an optimum level, however, is strongly influenced by the methods of achieving stabilization. Commoner believes that a demographic

transition will occur in the developing countries only if their
standards of living are raised very rapidly, and that this reduction
in fertility by conception control will be achieved voluntarily.
(This crucial assumption, however, cannot be considered as proven.)
By assuming that this transition time is thirty years, he arrives at
a population of between 6 and 8 billion by the year 2000. This
level, which he essentially defines as the optimum level, also turns
out to be the maximum level in view of the ecosystem crisis. He
therefore breaks sharply with some of the other contributors who
believe that sufficient resources can be created, provided energy is
available in unlimited amounts. (He also takes exception to the
proposal of how to handle the world food situation advanced by
the Paddock brothers in their book, *Famine 1975.*)

An interesting theoretical contribution to the ecological problem
is the paper of Harold A. Thomas which deals with the optimum
of a primitive population: i.e., a group which cannot control the
environment and must therefore remain in ecological balance
with it. Survival is the chief imperative. The main limiting factor
is food, a situation which still applies to some primitive tribes today. From a mathematical model which describes the anthropological situation, he can deduce an analytic relationship to derive
what is an optimum population.

Historically, small population groups were not stable and have
disappeared for a variety of reasons. Using a genetic point of
view, the paper by Bentley Glass looks far into the future and
treats the problem of optimum population level in order for mankind to survive for thousands or millions of years. This requires
adaptability to major environmental changes. Therefore, a diversity
of gene pools is necessary, which calls for a large population but
split up into smaller, isolated groups.

The paper by S. Fred Singer tries to meet the environmental
problem head on by quantifying the costs of pollution control. He
points out that pollution is roughly proportional to the GNP but
that control costs rise at a faster rate. In connection with his fairly
detailed accounting of pollution control costs, he points out the
need for technological fixes to lower costs that are becoming, or
will become, excessive; in addition, pollution costs can be lowered

or even eliminated by conservation, by re-use and recycling and, above all, by a better distribution of the population. Ultimately, however, he concludes that considerations of environmental quality would set limits to the maximum concentration and maximum levels of a population in a city, region, or country.

Christian de Laet agrees that environmental quality is perhaps the limiting factor to growth and to maximum population. His discussion deals especially with the social responsibility required within a population in order to achieve a balance with the external environment.

I like to think that there is truth in all the statements and views that have been presented, including those that disagree very strongly. Certainly we will run out of oil and high-grade ores, as Cloud predicts. But I also believe that we will achieve nuclear catalytic burners which will provide an inexhaustible source of energy, perhaps even before the end of the century. This, in turn, means that the extraction of metals, the provision of water, will continue to go on in spite of the fact that we will have to go to lower grades of ore and to increasing desalination of seawater. This does not mean, however, that the cost of this energy will be substantially less than what we are paying now. If the increasing costs for raw materials become a substantial fraction of the GNP, if the increasing costs of pollution control form an ever-increasing fraction of the GNP, then there will be less left over for the amenities of life.

SFS

Resources, Population, and Quality of Life[1]

Preston Cloud

ABSTRACT

Nothing can increase infinitely on a finite earth. It is evident, more-over, if one equates quality of life with the variety and flexibility of options available, that the quality of human existence over much of the earth is threatened where it is not already nullified. In the author's view, the number of men, not only in the world at large but even in the United States, already exceeds the optimum. Yet, populations will continue to increase until the numbers of men come under the restraints of nature or of human will. It is the central thesis of this paper that food and raw materials place ultimate limits on the size of populations; that the latter must come into balance with the eco-system at lower levels if acceptable quality is to be preserved. Since, at current rates of population growth, such limits will be reached within the next thirty to one hundred years, it is essential to human welfare that we move as rapidly as possible toward zero population growth. We need a new equilibrium economy and a better measure than GNP for expressing mean amenity level.

THE DEMOGRAPHIC QUOTIENT

What is the capacity of planet Earth for people? What can we do to assure that the number of people does not exceed Earth's capability to sustain them over the long term? Is there an optimum population for the earth as a whole and for its various habitable parts, or are there threshold limits beyond which further increases (or decreases) make for a nonoptimal situation? Are such thresholds now anywhere approached or exceeded, and, if so, what are and what will be the consequences? These are among the central questions before the world today.

Let me attempt some definitions, and, in doing so, consider what constraints the availability of resources may eventually place on the proliferation of mankind. I will approach these problems primarily from the standpoint of mineral resources, but keeping in view the broader material needs of society.

An optimal population can be defined as one that is large enough to realize the potentialities of human creativity to achieve a life of high quality for everyone indefinitely, but not so large as to threaten dilution of quality, the potential to achieve it, or the wise management of the ecosystem. The quality of life may be equated with the variety and flexibility of options available, including convenient access to ample and varied material goods and amenities. Adequate diet, plentiful clean water and pure air, sufficient industrial raw materials, attractive living and recreational space, adequate health services and educational and cultural opportunities, and sufficient wilderness to buffer unforeseen imbalances are the minimal terms of the quality equation. Loss of options in any of these diminishes quality.

Clearly, however, neither optimal population, nor quality of life, nor even the threshold beyond which deterioration occurs are concepts that are easily or permanently quantified. What might appear as an optimum density of population, an ideal rate of consumption of resources, or a life of high quality for one place, time, or society will not necessarily correspond to that of others. Although this does not invalidate the utility of these concepts in assessing the state of civilization, it may be useful to think in terms of another concept, one which I will call the *demographic quotient: Q.*

We may define Q as follows:

$$Q = \frac{\text{total resources available}}{\text{population} \times \text{per capita consumption of resources}}$$

If we could place some limits on the ability of the world, or a particular part of it, to supply resources and amenities on a sustained basis without loss of ecological integrity, then, given some range of consumption considered optimal, we could calculate the limits of an optimal population. Even though we could quibble over every one of the many variables involved, and even though the limits established might vary over a wide range, I take it as self-evident that, within any finite system such as the earth, there are limits, and that optimal population bears some relation to Q.

It is also clear that Q can be kept constant by changing the variables that define it—that is, either by increasing the death rate or resources available, or by decreasing the birth rate or per capita rate of consumption. And there is hardly any doubt that, given the choice in these terms, and not being assured of an exponential expansion of productive capability without threat to global ecology, most people would opt for reduction of the birth rate. That the birth rate has not fallen to a bare replacement level, therefore, can only mean either that not enough people are able to exercise the choice or that not enough of them understand the choice to be made.

Let me say at the outset, then, that whether or not there is an optimal population, there are, in my judgment, over much of the earth, populations that now *exceed* the optimum. We are, in fact, deluged with evidence that, for current conditions, a world population of 3.5 billion already exceeds the optimum, while the more than 200 million inhabitants of the United States are also too many for its level of consumption, aspirations, and domestic resources. (It takes more space and resources per capita to circulate in a Cadillac, or a camper, than it does to circulate on a bicycle, or on foot.)

If we do not want to increase the death rate we must settle for a decreased birth rate or a decreased rate of consumption or both. Unless, of course, we are able greatly to increase production—and space available for occupancy—which will have other undesirable effects, including, in the final analysis, ecological degradation and a reduced duration for industrial society.

In a moment I will give more concrete reasons for sharing these convictions; but first let me allude briefly to the root of our problem—the meretricious illusion of growth as an intrinsic good.

THE GROWTH SYNDROME

To return momentarily to our demographic quotient (Q), we can see that, where Q is constant and resources either remain constant or increase slowly, crises will arise where other factors affecting Q increase, or increase faster than resources. Many of the crises that have arisen to plague mankind in recent years have stemmed basically from the same phenomenon—the continuing exponential increases in human populations, and their increasing consumption and waste of Earth's material resources. Among material resources I include food, pure water, clean air, living and circulating space, and the nonrenewable mineral resources whose enhancement in value through beneficiation, fabrication, and trade account for the most visible assets of industrial society.

Resources eventually limit the level of population that may be considered optimal, simply because there are finite limits to the renewability of renewable resources and to the ultimate recoverability of nonrenewable resources. No matter how discrepant or how large informed estimates of these resources may be, they must all agree that there is some annual harvest of food that cannot be exceeded on a sustained basis, some maximal quantity of each mineral and chemical resource that can be extracted and kept in circulation.

Thus, it is possible to think of man in relation to his renewable resources of food, water, and breathable air as being limited in numbers by the sustainable annual crop. His nonrenewable resources—metals, petrochemicals, mineral fuels, etc.—can be thought of, in somewhat oversimplified but valid terms, as some quantity which may be consumed at different rates, but for which the quantity beneath the curve of cumulative total production, from first use to exhaustion, is largely independent of the shape of the curve (Figure 1). In other words, the depletion curve of a given nonrenewable raw material may rise and decline steeply over a relatively short time (as is now visibly the case with petroleum, mercury, and helium, for example), or it may be a flatter curve that lasts for a longer time depending on use rates and conservation measures such as recycling. This is a choice that civilized, industrialized man expresses collectively at any specific time by a given general density of his population, his per capita rate of consumption, and his conservation ethic.

As M. King Hubbert is fond of pointing out,[2] the ultimate extraction and consumption of all useful minerals, and of mineral raw materials as a class, must eventually be limited by the quantity we can get under the curve. That quantity, of course, depends importantly on the development and intensity of mineral-exploration and extractive technology, and on economics—but it has intrinsic limi-

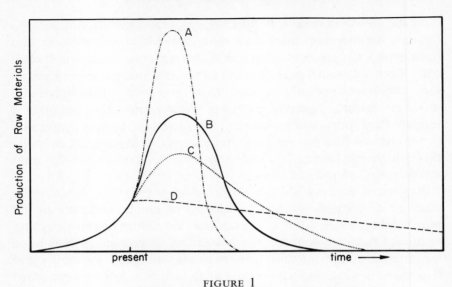

FIGURE 1
Alternate depletion patterns for a nonrenewable resource.
Efficient recycling combined with depletion curve D offers
best hope for continuing availability of industrial metals
over the long term.

tations that cannot be overridden. For any given quantity and
rate of use we can extend the depletion curve by recycling, substitution, and other conservative and innovative measures; it is axio-
matic, however, that nothing can expand infinitely on our finite
Spaceship Earth. There are not yet sufficient data available on the
ultimately accessible and extractable reserves of most mineral resources to say what the ultimate limits may be, but there are enough
data, together with current use rates and projected demands on both
food and mineral resources, to cast some sobering shadows. Among
other things, these data tell us that efficient recycling combined with
curve D in Figure 1 offers the best hope for the continuing availability of industrial metals over the long term.

Consider the limitations on ultimate human populations, and on
the quality of human life, that result from limitations of food, of
fresh water, of industrial raw materials, and of the resiliency of the
physical and biological environment.

The Committee on Resources and Man of the National Academy
of Sciences has examined the ultimate capability of an efficiently
managed world to produce food, given the cultivation of all poten-

tially arable lands and an optimal expression of scientific and technological innovation, both on land and in the sea. Its results imply that world food supplies might eventually be increased to perhaps as much as nine times the present, provided that sources of protein were essentially restricted to plants, and to seafood mostly from a position lower in the marine food chain than is now customarily harvested—and provided metal resources, agricultural water, and mineral fertilizers are equal to the task, and that agricultural land is not unduly preempted for other purposes. Given a more equitable distribution than now, such an ultimate level of productivity might sustain a world population of thirty billion, *at a level of chronic malnutrition for the great majority.* That places the maximal limit on world populations at a figure that could be reached in about one hundred years at present rates of increase—by which time, with concerted effort and luck, the maximal sustainable level of food production might also have been reached. Many students of the problem do not believe that it is possible to sustain thirty billion people—especially considering the variety and extent of demands on water supply and the psychic stresses that would arise with such numbers. I have no dispute with them. Here I seek simply to establish some theoretical outside limit, based on relatively optimistic assumptions about what could be possible and what we might do about it. More important attributes than a starvation diet would be sacrificed by a world that full!

Similarly optimistic assumptions about demographic balances that might ensue from the present wave of concern, however, led the Committee on Resources and Man to judge it possible that world population might level off at around ten billion by about the year 2050. Yet, in my view, even such a leveling off would result in a world population of about three billion more than *might* eventually be supported over the long term at a moderate level of affluence. That is the number of people—seven billion—that continuation of the current rates of population increase would place on earth by the end of this century, or very early in the next.

Granting the far-from-established assumption that a world population of seven billion can be adequately nourished, and accepting the often-expressed goal of "development" for all countries, what would it take in the way of metal resources to bring such a world population to an average level of living comparable to that which we in the United States now enjoy? It can be calculated that this would require keeping in circulation about 50 to 60 billion tons of iron, about a billion tons of lead (not allowing for battery-operated automobiles), around 600 to 700 million tons of zinc, and perhaps 80 to 100 million tons of tin—or between about 100 and 400 times present annual world production of these commodities (these figures include standing capital investment as well as annual turnover). Assuming that the metals needed could be placed in circulation and efficiently recycled, and demand stabilized, it would still take large quantities of new metals annually merely to replace those lost by unavoidable oxidation and friction—about 400,000 tons of new iron a year, for example. The needed quantities of lead, zinc, tin, and other metals, moreover, greatly exceed informed estimates of known, estimated, and inferred reserves.[3]

As it is not possible to increase metal production by anywhere near the suggested amounts by the end of the century, if ever, rising expectations among the deprived peoples of the earth that they, too, may share the affluent life are doomed to bitter disappointment without population control and eventual reduction in population—preferably to present or lower levels. We in the United States will be hard pressed to support the raw-materials needs of our own growing populations without some reduction in per capita demands for minerals, expected to triple by the year 2000! With determined effort, with a well-trained and well-staffed earth science profession and mineral industry, and with luck, domestic mineral production might also triple by the end of the century.[4] But the projected demands will by then be four and one-half times the present. The United States cannot meet such demands without ever-increasing imports *and* ever-increasing pollution—not even with the help of unlimited quantities of cheap energy from the fully breeding nuclear fission reactors and fusion reactors expected but yet to be perfected.

Thus, growing populations of Americans will be confronted with the hard choice of forgoing some of their affluence or of continuing to import, at increasing rates, the raw materials on which under-developed countries might base their own industrial growth.

At the same time, the peoples of all developed nations will have other agonizing problems. What to do about the pressures against their gates by the less privileged? How to cope with the increasing burden of biocides, nuclear wastes, mine wastes, urban and atmospheric pollution, and noise? How to endure the necessary increase of regulatory measures flowing from competition for resources, space, recreation, transportation, housing, educational facilities, and privacy?

Growth of populations, of the tax base, of real-estate values, and of the Gross National Product is thus accompanied by growth of waste, of pollution, of consumption of resources, of ecological deterioration, and of conflict. The concept of growth as an intrinsic good is a Trojan horse, but with the diplomatic privileges of a sacred cow! Those privileges need to be critically reexamined.

Among other things, we need some better measure of the success of our economy and society than GNP. As the economist Kenneth Boulding has emphasized, "The essential measure of the success of the economy is not production and consumption at all, but the nature, extent, quality, and complexity of the total capital stock, including in this the state of the human bodies and minds included in the system."[5] I suggest that rather than GNP, we must measure MAL—Mean Amenity Level—and that its proper measure must take into account not only the factors that Boulding emphasizes but also depletion rates and the state of the global ecology. No externalities should be allowed in estimating MAL.

THE NATURE AND DISTRIBUTION OF MINERAL RESOURCES

Now, since metals cannot be destroyed or leave the earth except in small amounts, why do I say that mineral resources are a limiting factor in the growth of industrial society and, therefore, of populations? To begin with, mineral resources are finite, because, for all practical purposes, the formation and differentiation of the earth is complete. The useful elements available to us, moreover, constitute only a minute fraction of the total mass of the earth. Of the quantities present, much has not been and may never be located, and much is unrecoverable by any known technology.

Copper illustrates the problem. It is a metal that is neither abundant nor in immediate jeopardy. Its abundance in the earth's crust averages about 55 parts per million, and the total mass of the crust is roughly 2.5×10^{19} tons. That suggests about 1.4×10^{15} tons of copper in the entire crust of the earth—under continents and ocean basins alike—which is a lot of copper. However, of that amount, probably no more than a billion or two tons is recoverable under likely circumstances. Of this possibly recoverable copper, about 210 million tons is represented by ore reserves now known. Thus, even with new discoveries and the working of lower grades of ore, an increase in copper eventually mined to as much as ten times current reserves is unlikely. If we then allow for increasing population and for expected end-of-century demands, it becomes clear that a limit must be reached within another couple of generations when the continuing availability of copper will depend largely on the recycling of already-mined metal. It is inevitable that the same must ultimately be true of all other metals.

Other limitations result from the geologic processes whereby minerals of interest came to be concentrated into economically recoverable deposits in the first place, as illustrated by petroleum, iron, and copper.

Crude oil originates as a product of the anaerobic breakdown of living matter into its volatile components. It is generated in quantity only in the pore spaces of sediments, and it is known primarily in marine sediments deposited during the last half-billion years of geologic time. The best source rocks, however, are commonly too fine-grained to provide permeability suitable for recovery. In order to form an oil field, the oil must migrate into suitable reservoir rocks, and it must remain trapped within such rocks until they are penetrated by the drill. Sedimentary rocks, moreover, are but a small fraction of the total crust of the earth, and only a part of these contain oil. As they show a much higher degree of regularity than most other rock types, however, it is possible to estimate, within reasonable limits, the amount of eventually recoverable oil (Figure 2). One way is to scale the quantity of oil discovered per foot of exploratory drilling against the footage of drilling necessary to explore the yet-undrilled sedimentary basins. Extrapolation from such data has pursued two modes, leading to somewhat discrepant results. M. King Hubbert of the United States Geological Survey has estimated from the observed declining rate of discovery that the total crude oil that will ever be produced from the United States and its adjacent continental shelves (excluding Alaska) is about 165 billion barrels[2]—the area under curve 1 in Figure 2. An estimate three and one-half times as large—that under curve 2 in Figure 2—is based on the hope that oil will be discovered at an average rate of 118 barrels per foot of exploratory drilling as compared to the rate of about 35 barrels per foot drilled to which discovery has now declined. Graphical analysis

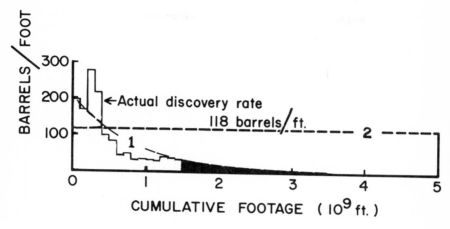

FIGURE 2

Two views of relation between footage of exploratory drilling and oil discovery (slightly modified after M. K. Hubbert[2]).

(Figure 3) of either figure shows that current consumption trends cannot be maintained, that we are near the peak of our domestic oil production at the present time, and that this production will decline to a very low figure by the end of the century. Nor is it likely that we can greatly increase the proportion of oil recovered or the quantities of imported oil. Estimates of the total recoverable crude petroleum in the world range from 1,350 to 2,100 billion barrels—a narrow gap that implies peak production between about 1990 and the year 2000, with a tapering off thereafter. Many parts of the world, of course, have no petroleum at all.

I will not here discuss the so-called tar sands and oil shales, except to mention that the estimated petroleum equivalent recoverable from the Alberta tar sands equals or exceeds the ultimate North American reserves of crude petroleum and natural gas liquids combined,[2] and that the oil shales of the world may contain liquid fuels equivalent to its petroleum reserves, but of uncertain recoverability. If recovered, therefore, and used as a primary source of energy, these materials would little more than double the output (but not the lifetime) of the petroleum family of fuels.

In contrast to oil, iron is found in a great variety of rock types and geological situations; but its largest deposits are also found in sedimentary rocks. The greatest iron deposits by far are the banded

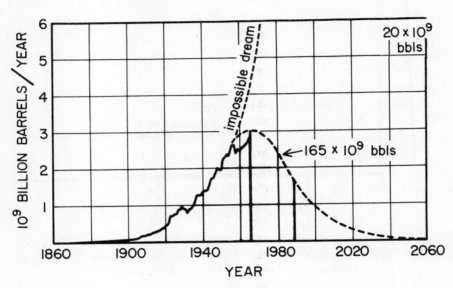

FIGURE 3

Cycle of United States crude-oil production (slightly modified after M. K. Hubbert[2]).

iron formations that occur in significant quantity only in sedimentary rocks older than about 1.8 billion years, and which formed under conditions that have not existed on a large scale since. Despite the wide distribution and local concentration of iron in crustal rocks of a wide age range, therefore, the most substantial remaining iron deposits are located in particular favorable regions. The quantities of iron in these banded iron formations and their surface enrichments, moreover, although vast, are not infinite. If we continue to produce new metallic iron, we will, over the long term, have to win it from increasingly lower grades of ore.

Copper represents a different and much larger class of ore deposits—the disseminated and replacement ores, which include not only copper, but also silver, molybdenum, cobalt, chromium, nickel, and others. The great bulk of the world's copper ore is associated with igneous activity, and such deposits were formed intermittently through geologic time. Although other types are important, the so-called porphyry copper deposits account for most current United States production and about half of world output. Such deposits are related to the working up from below of large masses of molten matter that broke up and partially engulfed overlying rocks—primarily during extensive but localized episodes of folding and silicic igneous intrusion that took place over the last 170 million years and mainly from 25 to 60 million years ago. Rising hot solutions and vapors, interacting with circulating ground water, spread the ore minerals over a large area within, and in a broad halo around, the intrusions. Subsequent alteration produced zones of enrichment within such ores, but on the whole their grade is low, and it is possible to work them mainly because their large dimensions permit economies of scale. Porphyry copper is sharply limited geographically because the essential combination of the right kinds of igneous intrusions and surrounding host rocks occur only in certain geochemically and temporally distinctive mobile belts of the earth's crust. In contrast to petroleum, copper favors igneous rocks of a limited range of geochemical composition. Rocks that are rich in petroleum are apt to be poor in copper.

Thus we see that mineral resources are products of millions or billions of years of earth history, that different mineral deposits are localized in different geochemical provinces, and that they are nonrenewable in the sense that new deposits do not form fast enough to replace those mined. Mines bear no second crop. As new discoveries decrease, there is only retreat to ever-lower grades, imports, substitutes, synthetics, recycling, and eventual exhaustion.

Some parts of the earth are relatively rich in mineral deposits and others poor. No part of the earth is self-sufficient in all critical metals (Figure 4). North America, for instance, is rich in molybdenum but poor in tin, tungsten, and manganese; Asia is rich in tin, tungsten, and manganese, but poor in molybdenum. Most of the world's essential chromium and new gold comes from South Africa. Cuba and New Caledonia possess about half the world's known reserves of nickel. Most cobalt is in the Congo Republic, Cuba, New Caledonia, and parts of Asia. The world's mercury supply is essentially limited to Spain, Italy, Yugoslavia, and parts of China and the U.S.S.R. The iron deposits of the world, basic to industrial development, are concentrated in particular old sedimentary belts of the continental cores.

Rates of consumption are critical in assessing how long a nonrenewable resource can last, and these rates tend to increase exponentially. Since the beginning of the industrial revolution each generation has consumed mineral resources equivalent to all previously

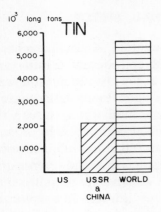

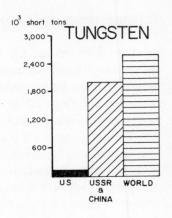

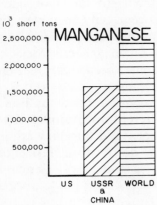

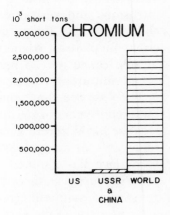

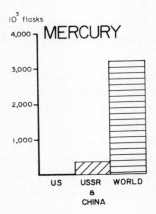

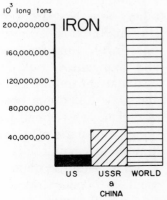

FIGURE 4

Estimated recoverable reserves of selected metals at current prices and grades (data from Flawn,[6] Sainsbury,[3] U.S. Bureau of Mines).

consumed. As industrial nations use up the accessible supplies within their own territories, they turn increasingly to recycled metals and to foreign sources—illustrated by growing United States dependence on foreign aluminum ores (Figure 5). Today, all industrial nations, except perhaps the U.S.S.R., are net importers of most of the metals and ores on which their economy depends.

The United States, long the world's largest consumer, although with only 6 per cent of its land area and people, depends increasingly on foreign sources. Among many other mineral commodities, it imports most of its manganese, chrome, cobalt, tin, and bauxite. It extensively supplements its lead, zinc, and tungsten from foreign sources. Its dependence on foreign petroleum, iron ore, and copper grows annually. Except for bulk nonmetallic materials like stone, sand, cement, and gravel, and for coal and phosphate, we are currently self-sufficient only in magnesium, molybdenum, and few other metals—although, in a real pinch, technological advances could probably supply the iron and aluminum we need. Even our readily accessible reserves of ordinary construction materials, like sand and gravel, are dwindling as the cities consume and expand over them.

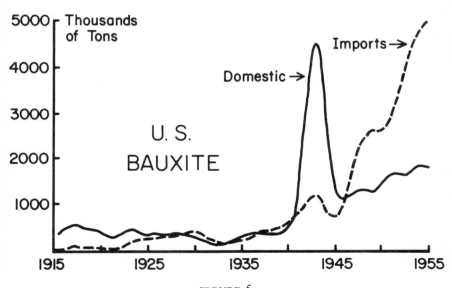

FIGURE 5
United States dependence on foreign aluminum ores (after
T. S. Lovering[7]).

Can such levels of consumption be extended world-wide or long maintained here without population control?

At what point, moreover, does exportation of their raw resources by developing countries cease to be advantageous in terms of capitalization and begin to prejudice their prospects of eventual industrialization? What kind of social and political turmoil will arise where aspiring nations discover, or think they have discovered, that exportation has handicapped their chances for development? Is universal industrialization inevitable, impossible, or even desirable—and, if not desirable, how is its limitation to be harmoniously achieved?

CURRENT RESERVES

Considering the demands for resources and their finite supply, eventual depletion is inescapable in the sense that, under projected pressures, we must eventually reach a point where significant continuing new additions to quantities in circulation either require too large a fraction of the world's productive capacity or create an unacceptable burden of pollution. But what is the time scale and real magnitude of the problem, and what can we do to defer a final confrontation with it?

Unfortunately, reliable estimates of ultimate reserves for most minerals are not available. They depend not only on the accuracy of averages for the often-sharply-varying concentrations of elements in particular kinds of rock, but also on our yet-limited knowledge of the usually concealed and highly irregular surface boundaries of mineralized rocks and their extensions at depth.

Economic factors, then—including mining, extractive technology, and transportation—determine whether a particular type and grade of mineral concentration at a particular place is or can be an ore. As we know, also, that new reserves will be discovered by geological exploration or be created by economic developments or technological innovation, and that both population and per capita demands are bound to increase for some while into the future, we have to cope with many variables in estimating the lifetimes of metals. These variables, however, tend to balance one another out,[4] so that we can roughly estimate the apparent lifetimes of secure reserves (at presently commercial grades) for the twenty best-known commodities (Figure 6). Graphs of such lifetimes show that platinum, gold, zinc, and lead are in very short supply. Of the twenty, only eleven world

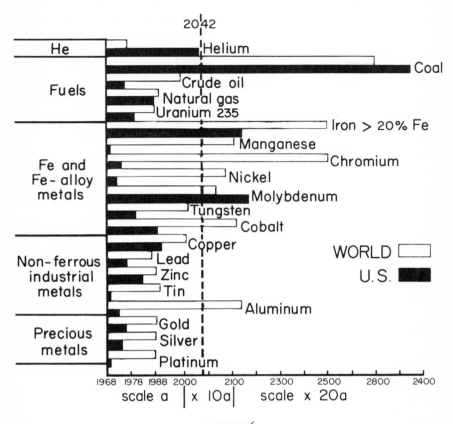

FIGURE 6

Apparent lifetimes of known recoverable reserves of 20 mineral commodities at current minable grades and rates of consumption. (Except for helium whose lifetime is estimated from U.S. Bureau of Mines data on reserves, conservation practices, and expected increases in demand. Such lifetimes tend to increase with new discoveries and technological advances and to decrease with increasing population and consumption rates; however, resources to left of vertical dashed line are in obvious danger of depletion. Data adjusted from U.S. Bureau of Mines reports and Flawn[6].)

lifetimes—four for the United States—persist beyond the end of the century. Presently commercial deposits of silver, tin, uranium, natural gas, and crude oil will be pressing their limits by then. By the year 2042, which (in 1971) is only as far in the future as the invention of the airplane and the discovery of radioactivity are in the past, we can count on only eight of the twenty commodities for the world and maybe three for the United States—molybdenum, perhaps iron, and coal (as well as, of course, magnesium, bromine, and salt from the sea). Even if assured reserves could be tripled, or even multiplied by ten, we would still be in trouble, for, in addition to the estimate that United States requirements for metals and energy in the year 2000 will be four and one-half times present demands, world demands, if raised to the per capita level of the United States, would then be more than thirty times the present.

THE FUTURE

What may be done to prolong the continuing availablity of the most critical resources?

One partial but often overestimated escape hatch is nuclear energy. The beneficent possibilities of breeder reactors and controlled nuclear fusion are threefold. First, they could provide almost "limitless" energy for the next few thousand years, permitting the "fossil fuels" (petroleum, coal, natural gas, tar sands, oil shales) to be conserved, as they should be, for the manufacture of petrochemicals, plastics and other synthetics, and for essential liquid fuels. Second, vastly increased cheap power will bring now-noncommercial mineral resources to the market place by lowering the costs of transportation and beneficiation at the mine. Third, nuclear energy can be applied to the extraction of dispersed metals from low-grade sources. Although records show little correlation between mineral production and energy input as such (Figure 7), the threat of resource scarcity requires that all possibilities be explored. Hence, we should investigate the potentialities of nuclear fracturing of sparsely metalliferous rock in place, followed by the introduction of hydrometallurgical solutions and bacterial leaching agents below ground. Such treatment involves enormous problems, however. The rock must be pulverized to the size of the dispersed mineralized particles with which leaching solutions or bacteria are to be brought in contact. Once reagents have entered the rock, they may be lost as contaminants to the circulating ground water. Bacteria of interest as metal concentrators all require oxygen, which must be supplied to them below ground if they are to work there. And, finally, there is the problem of containing the radioactive wastes—of keeping them out of contact with humans and other organisms and out of the product sought. Thus the third hope

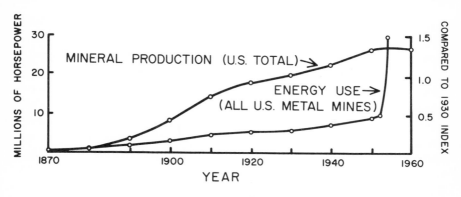

FIGURE 7

Rate of energy use compared with mineral production
(slightly modified after T. S. Lovering[7]).

of nuclear energy—drastically lowering the grade of minable rock—is a very uncertain quantity.

Substitution and synthesis through technological innovation are other ways of stretching mineral supplies: various metals can substitute for one another, and plastics can substitute for some metals; aluminum already substitutes for copper in many roles, as copper and nickel now replace silver in coinage; and synthetic crystals have come increasingly into use. Other substitutes can be created if price is no consideration. But the production of plastics consumes petroleum and coal; metals in general cannot be synthesized at temperatures attainable on a sustained and large scale outside of exploding stars; and other elements have unique properties which exclude substitution. Helium, for instance, in short supply, remains liquid at temperatures below which other substances have solidified. This, in combination with its unequaled inertness and high thermal conductivity, leaves it without good substitutes in its most important applications—in cryogenics, in oxyhelium breathing mixtures for submarine exploration, in the cooling of nuclear reactors, etc. Mercury also has no satisfactory substitutes for the many applications that arise from its unique combination of high specific gravity, fluidity at normal temperatures, and electrical conductivity. Uranium and thorium are the only elements that are suitable for nuclear fission reactors, with only the rare isotope U^{235} being usable in nonbreeding reactors. Substitution and synthesis, thus, must be exploited to the limit, but within a framework that recognizes that neither they alone nor in combination with nuclear energy are sufficient to evade indefinitely the limitations of natural supply.

A more promising means of extending resource lifetimes is to improve the technology of new discovery. We must turn increasingly to geochemical and geophysical methods to assist in discovering ore deposits that lie beneath the cover of younger rocks—including the new remote-sensing devices becoming available as a spin-off from the space program.

None of the major new mineral discoveries that have been made recently, or which will be made in the future, mean that we can relax the search for more. The discovery of a new, perhaps ten-billion-barrel oil field at Prudhoe Bay on the North Slope of Alaska, during the summer of 1968, is one of the increasingly rare discoveries of major new oil fields—few of which, probably, remain to be found, outside of remote regions and the continental shelves. The enormous new iron deposits in remote western Australia, comprising billions of tons of high-grade ore, were not studied by the right geologist until 1963, although the presence of iron in the region had been known. The fact that this iron was at the surface, yet remained long unrecognized as a major ore body, favors the institution of broad-scale remote-sensing fly-overs of the world's more isolated and geologically lesser-known terrains as an approach to selecting sites for further investigation by geologists on the ground—but few such sites remain in North America.

New techniques for ore finding should be guided by the best geological theory, which means that basic geology must be more vigorously developed. Some focal concepts that bear on exploration for new minerals invoke the ever-more-impressively substantiated models of sea-floor spreading and continental drift. The bearing of such concepts on mineral exploration is that metals may be concentrated at times and places where major segments of the earth's crust impinge on and overlap one another—especially where continental rocks drift over active zones of sea-floor spreading, or where the rising limbs of convection cells in the earth's mantle emerge beneath a continent. A related concept of value as a guide to future exploration is that of metallogenic provinces, different ones of which, having different geochemical and geological properties and histories, favor different types of mineral deposits. Examples of metallogenic provinces include the favored settings for porphyry copper and banded iron formations mentioned earlier.

In considering the discovery of new sources of earth materials, we have focused so far on the land-surface of the earth. What about the sea, which, in 1964, accounted for about 10 per cent of the value of products recovered and a billion dollar addition to domestic production of oil and gas, sulfur, magnesium, bromine, salt, oyster shells, and even sand and gravel?

Consider sea water, which is, of course, a very large and relatively accessible reservoir of materials, as well as the present source of most of our magnesium and much of our boron. The contents of that reservoir, however, are limited in variety and widely dispersed. Only sixty-four of the ninety elements that occur naturally on earth have, as yet, even been detected in sea water. Of these, only fifteen occur in concentrations of more than one pound per million gallons, and only nine of these fifteen represent 1965 values of more than $10 per million gallons (chlorine $924, sodium $378, magnesium $4,130, sulfur $101, calcium $150, potassium $91, bromine $190, lithium $36, and rubidium $125). These nine—plus boron, iodine, and fluorine, but including few important metals—are the only ones that really hold any practicable promise for direct and quantitatively significant recovery from sea water.[6]

The sea floor itself consists of two contrasting major divisions. The true ocean basins lie beyond the limits of a continental type of geology. They contrast geologically with the flooded outer margins of the continents—the continental shelves and slopes. If the current theory of sea-floor spreading is correct, the floor of the ocean beyond the continental slope will be a poor place to look for useful minerals, being mantled (beneath a thin layer of sediments) by relatively young and only sparsely metalliferous basic igneous rocks that well up along the midocean ridges and are eventually overridden by the continents. It is at best premature to visualize as an important mineral resource the mineralogically interesting but thinly dispersed manganese crusts and nodules of the deep sea floor. The nickel, cobalt, and copper in these nodules continue to attract industrial interest, but their recovery and metallurgy pose problems of enormous magnitude.

Far more likely as a source of marine mineral resources are the submerged areas that belong geologically to the continents. Here is where our exploration for new mineral resources from the sea should be concentrated. About 17 per cent of the world's petroleum and natural gas is now produced offshore and more will come—not as a completely unmixed blessing but about in proportion to the quantities produced from similar sedimentary environments on the lands. Other mineral products likely to be recovered from the sea floor in substantial quantities include heavy-metal placers formed on beaches and in streams along the coast and later submerged when the continental ice sheets melted. Submarine placers, to be sure, will be limited to heavy products like gold, tin, titanium, and diamonds, and in general to depths of 130 meters or less. They will not go far toward solving the problem of other materials in short supply.

When other inescapable limitations are taken into account, moreover, it becomes apparent that the sea, although it must be a prime target for continued intensive research, offers no panacea for resource shortages.

Finally, I must take notice of the suggestions sometimes made that we will export people to, or import resources from, other planets. Even given the unlikely assumptions of an accessible habitable planet, or the presence on a nearby planet of accessible minable resources, the impracticability of colonizing or of importing industrially significant quantities of materials from other planets is illustrated by a computation made by Garrett Hardin for the cost of colonizing the moon.[7] He calculates that if four-fifths of the current GNP of the United States were devoted to that project we could, in one year's time, export one day's increase of world population at present growth rates. The import problem is of the same dimensions.

How, then, shall we escape the constraints of resource limitation? The facts all-too-briefly reviewed here make it clear that there is only one rational way out. We must stabilize populations, limit per capita consumption among the already affluent, and introduce sensible conservation measures—including the recycling of wastes and scrap and the recovery and storage of essential by-products such as the helium in natural gas. And, of course, we must also accelerate geological research and exploration and the search for the technological innovations that will make it possible to recover and utilize larger fractions of the earth's mineral resources with minimal harm to our environment.

Although we must continue to find and to mine new metal to meet the demands of inevitable population increases yet to come, as well as increasing per capita consumption among the currently deprived, much of the metal that is now lost through dispersal and burial need not be lost. The only inevitable losses are those from oxidation and friction, and even these can be limited by a determined policy to reduce waste and encourage recycling. Provident use of our resources, including our human resources, implies sensible economies of materials and energy—utilizing no more than is necessary for the efficient performance of the task, recycling as much as practicable, and preserving for later use essential materials that are unwanted or deleterious by-products of other operations, or which we may have limited opportunity to obtain.

CONCLUSIONS

Although the adverse effects of ultimate material shortages should be anticipated by early action, such shortages need not, by themselves, become limiting factors during the current century *if* we are alert and skillful in dealing with them. The consequences of our deteriorating physical, biological, and psychosocial environment, and of inadequacies in the management and distribution of resources, may well limit the growth of populations before resource deficiencies become critical.

Eventually, to be sure, human populations will come into some kind of a balance with their environment—if not as a result of the judgment and restraints of man himself, then by the probably harsher restraints of nature. In addition to the fact that agricultural advances are now barely keeping up with world population increases, they provide little improvement of diet for the deprived two-thirds of the world. Neither the green revolution, nor food from the sea, nor bacterial production of food from petroleum, nor even wholly synthetic food production can feed a limitless population. Resources to sustain the industrial underpinning of now-affluent societies and to improve the lot of the rest of mankind will also fall short of needs if world population does not level off. If the striking of a balance is left entirely to nature, we may not know what is happening until it is too late to establish favorable terms with her.

Man, at this juncture, must choose whether or not he wishes to control his own destiny. For whether he acts or not, he makes a choice. If he chooses to come into balance with nature on his own terms, both population control and better resource management (including waste control) will be necessary and should be put into effect as soon as possible. Even were an unthinkable thirty billion to be our choice for a world population, we would have little more than another century, given current rates of increase, to establish a balance at that level. If the goal is to stabilize world population below six or seven billion, the next thirty years will be critical.

An immediate difficulty is that the populations of this nation and the world are going to get larger before they level off or become smaller, no matter what we do—short of nuclear, chemical, or biological warfare—and no matter how fast we do it. This follows from the age structure of existing populations and the inadequate understanding that many people still have of the dimensions of the problem or of what to do about it. (In the next thirty years, minimal population increase to be expected in the United States, for instance, is between 37 and 50 per cent above present levels.)

Such considerations make it essential, in my view, to recognize two new fundamental human rights:

1. The right of the fetus (and of its prospective siblings) that it not be conceived, or if conceived not born, into a world where its existence is likely to be precarious or to increase the threat to the general welfare. It seems to me in some deep sense uncivilized, not to say immoral, to consider babies as objects without rights, which people are entitled to propagate at will, regardless of the quality of life the growing child and later adult is likely to live.

2. The right of society as a whole, through democratic processes, to determine the density of population that best assures a continuing flexibility of options and access to such resources of food, clean air and water, recreation, and essential raw materials, as may be necessary for a rewarding existence.

Failure to realize these rights would jeopardize all others—either as a result of the steady growth of regulatory measures that will be necessary to assure the essentials of existence and opportunity for livelihood, or because of social and political anarchy. Delay in devising noncoercive incentives leading to population control only hastens the day when the choice may be between coercion and catastrophe. I am much more concerned that the measures designed not discriminate against the voiceless offspring than I am about whether they limit indiscriminate breeding by adults who are capable of foreseeing the consequences of their actions and, hence, have an ethical responsibility for them.

An awareness of the consequences of our actions demands that we leave some options for the future. Granted that our population is already more than large enough to assure the creative capability and creature comforts we need, the good of man in later times and other places is best served by limiting the growth of populations and reducing per capita consumption among the already affluent now and here.

REFERENCES

1. This paper is Contribution No. 2 from the Biogeology Clean Laboratory at UCSB. Its content draws heavily on *Resources and Man,* by the Committee on Resources and Man of the National Academy of Sciences (San Francisco: W. H. Freeman and Co., Publishers, 1969), and on papers by the author in *Science Year,* 1969, and *The Texas Quarterly,* Summer, 1968.

2. M. K. Hubbert, "1969 Energy Resources," in *Resources and Man* (San Francisco: W. H. Freeman, 1969).

3. P. T. Flawn, *Mineral Resources* (New York: Rand McNally & Co., 1966); C. L. Sainsbury, "Tin Resources of the World," *U.S. Geol. Surv. Bull.,* 1301 (1969); Harrison Brown, and Others, *The Next Ninety Years* (Pasadena: California Institute of Technology, 1967).

4. Hollis M. Dole, news release, United States Department of the Interior, July 31, 1969.

5. K. E. Boulding, "The Economics of the Coming Spaceship Earth," in H. Jarrett (ed.) *Environmental Quality in a Growing Economy,* Resources for the Future (Baltimore: Johns Hopkins Press, 1966), pp. 3–14.

6. *Resources and Man,* Chapter 7.

7. Garrett Hardin, "Interstellar Migration and the Population Problems," *Jour. of Heredity,* 50 (1959), 68–70.

MINERALS

Comments on the Use and Depletion of Natural Resources

Harrison Brown

I agree with much, but by no means all, of what Preston Cloud has said. Here I would like to state my belief that in our highly-industrialized technological society, we are *not*, in the long run, limited by the availability of nonrenewable resources. A resource is something we can use within the framework of our technological-economic base. Copper ore containing only a few tenths of one per cent copper would not have been looked upon by the ancient Egyptians as a useful material. We, by contrast, look upon such material as a resource because, first, we don't have adequate materials of higher grade available, and, second, we possess the technology which is necessary to isolate copper from such dilute material.

Each year each person in the United States consumes about 0.55 metric tons of steel, about 60 per cent of which is generated from pig iron produced from ore and the balance of which is generated from scrap. A variety of other metals is consumed as well, including, for example, about 9 kg. of copper, 7 kg. of zinc, 6 kg. of lead and 30 kg. of aluminum per person annually. Altogether, these basic substances—including pig iron, scrap, and all metals combined—cost considerably less than $100 per person, which represents, in this country, but a tiny fraction of the average person's income. In view

32

of this, I suggest that we can afford to spend a great deal more than we now spend on metals, and that as prices increase, vast new tonnages of low-grade ore can be processed economically. Indeed, to take an extreme case, even were our per capita expenditures for metals to increase tenfold, the effect upon our economy, although substantial, would by no means be catastrophic.

Professor Cloud has stated that at existing prices and with existing technology the reserves of copper total about 200 million tons. He suggests further that about two billion tons are recoverable "under likely circumstances," although he does not specify what he means by that expression. Yet, if we look at the earth's crust as a whole, with a copper content of but 55 parts per million, some one million billion tons of copper could, in principle, be made available were we to develop the requisite technology.

It will be a very long time indeed before we need to process ores containing as little as 55 parts per million copper—namely, ordinary rock. I am convinced, however, that, if necessary, we in the United States could live quite comfortably off ordinary rock, which could provide us with virtually all of our metals as well as our energy. One ton of average granite, for example, can yield, rather easily, the energy equivalent of fifteen tons of coal in the form of uranium and thorium. In the interim, as prices of ores and metals increase, we will process ore of steadily lessening grade and we will learn how to recover scrap more efficiently.

Our basic problem is less that of the availability of ores than it is of the harnessing and disposal of the requisite energy. Per capita energy consumption must necessarily increase with time, and the heat generated must be disposed of. I suggest that, in the long run, a basic limitation to our population and to our technological development will be the limits imposed upon us by the need to dispose of vastly greater quantities of heat than we now generate.

It seems to me that depletion of our reserves of high-grade ores confronts us with the ultimate long-range danger facing industrial society—that of getting started again following a catastrophe. The availability of high-grade mineral resources was an essential element in the emergence of civilization. Once those resources are gone, the process cannot be repeated. Once technological civilization is disrupted, as for example by a major nuclear war, it may be impossible to get it started again.

With respect to the poorer countries of the world we have a

completely different picture. One hundred dollars per year per person spent on metals would represent a large portion, if not all, of their per capita incomes. Further, the industrial countries are stripping the poorer ones of their resource heritage with increasing intensity—of course, paying for the privilege, but often not enough to accelerate development appreciably.

This is a process which, continued to its end, is bound to accelerate the widening gap between the rich countries and the poor by making it increasingly difficult for development to take place at a pace commensurate with need. This process, combined with that of population growth, creates a dismal prospect for the poorer countries.

Nonrenewable Resources and Population

Joseph L. Fisher

The subject of Preston Cloud's stimulating and comprehensive paper—resources, population, and quality of life—is one of the great subjects of all time at both the intellectual level and the practical level. Prevailing views on the matter have tended to swing from the optimistic to the pessimistic. To look back only thirty years (which is equal to the span of years ahead to the year 2000) one can recall that even as late as 1940, most of the demographers and economists were still concerned mainly about the low birth rate, the prospect that the population of the country would top out at about 180 million, and general economic stagnation. In the first years following World War II this gave way here and elsewhere to widespread concern about running short of food products, oil, numerous metals, and adequate supplies of fresh water. The extraordinary demands of World War II, the backlog of ordinary producer and consumer demands, the baby boom, the awakening of less developed countries to the possibilities of economic growth—these were the main factors giving rise to this concern about raw materials shortages.

As the world economy slowly righted itself and as technology and economic initiative turned to production to meet civilian needs, the neo-Malthusian fears diminished somewhat, especially in those

35

countries more developed economically. Statistical projections, based upon historical trends and reasonable assumptions about the future, indicated that the more than three hundred million persons expected in the United States by the year 2000 could probably be accommodated at continually higher standards of living insofar as raw materials were concerned—assuming, of course, a continued flow of new technology into this sector of the economy and continued access to supplies of certain items from other countries. The outlook in the less developed countries, according to these increasingly comprehensive and systematic projections, turned out to be far less reassuring, although by no means hopeless, especially with regard to energy commodities and technology.

However, as the 1960s wore on, concern and then alarm developed, not so much about the sheer quantity of raw materials as about the quality of the resource base itself. In the metropolitan areas of the economically advanced regions a threshold seems to have been crossed with regard to environmental pollution. The visual and health effects of air pollution in the great cities of the world became noticeable by almost everybody. Also, nearby streams, estuaries, and bays were called upon to dilute and carry away rapidly mounting volumes of waste materials. The clamor for increasing cleanliness of the watercourses became much more insistent with the growing emphasis on water-based recreation and on beautification. Rising levels of affluence, accompanied by the desire that virtually all products be sold in cans, bottles, or packages, have added greatly to the quantity of solid waste materials that have to be disposed of. In addition, noise levels, both in local neighborhoods and over entire metropolitan areas, have increased markedly; the sense of congestion, on streets and highways particularly, has risen in many places to almost unbearable levels; town and country planning has hardly kept pace with increasing construction, transportation, and incomes, with the result that large numbers of people are upset about the physical condition and arrangement of their cities. These and other factors bring us now to the point where national leaders and ordinary citizens alike agree that we are in an environmental crisis.

In his paper, Preston Cloud has combined the environmental and the population crises into one overarching crisis of resources, population, and quality of life. He is truly alarmed by the outlook, especially if that outlook extends some distance beyond the end of this century. The optimum population has already been exceeded, he believes. I find myself sharing his general views to a considerable extent; however, I am less certain than he seems to be that human beings, through the exercise of intelligence and leadership, are incapable of dealing constructively—perhaps even satisfactorily—with the rather gloomy prospect that he has depicted for us.

I don't want to refute Professor Cloud so much as I want to tell why I am less certain about the outlook. I think I can do this by examining his demographic quotient (Q) a little more deeply at several points and by placing it in a somewhat different perspective. Q, you remember, is equal to total resources available divided by population times per capita consumption of goods and amenities. In some abstract sense, population is optimum when Q is at its maximum.

The most slippery part of this equation is the numerator—total resources available. Exactly what does this mean? What does it include? If it is the existing inventory of goods and stock of capital, even including known reserves of minerals, then it is a strictly limited amount. On the other hand, looking to the future, the total resources that will become available very much depend on technological and economic trends still to develop. What amounts and kinds of new resources may be discovered as the years go by?

The location of major oil reserves on the North Slope of Alaska, plus the possibility of large additional discoveries in both Alaska and northern Canada, promises to alter considerably the outlook for this major raw material not only for the United States but possibly western Europe and Japan as well. Discovery of new sources, typically, will be related closely to advances in technology. For example, in the North Slope oil case the outlook becomes rather different if large tanker transport of oil, or submarine transport of oil, through the passages in the Canadian Arctic Islands or in the Arctic Ocean itself, proves to be economically feasible. Once the Arctic regions become opened up, then yet additional mineral deposits may be discovered and exploited.

Beyond new discoveries and new techniques in transportation lie further possibilities. To return to the case of oil, and still thinking primarily of North America, there are the immense quantities recoverable in the oil shale of the Colorado Plateau and in the tar sands of the Canadian prairies—not to mention the possibilities of liquefaction of oil products from coal. Then, of course, there are the tremendous potentialities of the breeder nuclear reactor and even the fusion process. Moving still further from the raw material developed and used in its conventional form, there are exciting possibilities for redesign of end uses. I have in mind, for example, the substitution of new kinds of engines for the conventional internal combustion engine used in automobiles, by means of which oil as the basic fuel could be utilized much more efficiently, or, directly or indirectly, the substitution of some other fuel altogether. In the final crunch, if oil and other fuel supplies become increasingly scarce and their costs of production and prices rise sufficiently, families may even give up their third and then their second cars, and take to mass transit. This, in turn, may lead city planners and community architects to design whole metropolitan complexes so as to save on fuel-consuming and metal-consuming forms of transportation.

I dwell on the example of oil to emphasize my point that the numerator of Professor Cloud's equation represents an uncertain—yet a potentially very expandable—quantity. In fact, in the United States over the years of its national history, and in western Europe during the modern period, and perhaps even in many of the less developed countries, the reserves of resources and the possibilities for making them available have, with a few short interruptions, outpaced population growth. Statistics for the United States reaching back nearly a hundred years indicate that, despite a growing population, the material level of living of Americans has risen almost continuously by about 1 per cent per year. Similar, but perhaps slightly less dramatic, results have occurred in other more economically developed countries. In some places, like Japan, the results have been even more dramatic than in the United States.

The counterargument to all this is well known: If disaster doesn't overtake us by the end of this century, it will fifty years later, or a hundred, or two hundred years later. It is simply a matter of time; any positive rate of population increase, working against an absolutely fixed ultimate supply of resources, leads sooner or later to an impossible situation.

Looking beyond the technological and economic possibilities for expanding the total resources available, another set of possibilities comes into view which could stave off calamity. I am thinking now of a wide range of behavioral responses and policy initiatives that could come into the resources–population–quality-of-life picture. With the means for effective birth control more readily available, it is by no means impossible that the desire and will to use them will so strengthen and expand that a considerable reduction in the birth rate will be achieved within a relatively short period of time. At least this is not out of the question. Perhaps one of the major contributions of the neo-Malthusian prophets of doom is, by exaggerating, to arouse people to the extent that they will actually install public policies and so alter their personal behavior as to reduce birth rates to the point that even the famous zero rate of population growth will be reached. No such result will be achieved without considerable effort through education and persuasion, through research that can develop a deeper understanding of human behavior in these matters, through a more adroit and aggressive use of public policy and incentive, and so on. Surely, long before we reach a "standing-room-only" situation, social, individual behavioral, psychological, and even biological forces will be set in motion to prevent that unhappy outcome from occurring at all. Perhaps it is mainly a matter of timing: Will the counterforces appear soon and powerfully enough to prevent losses and damages of an unacceptable or even of a devastating character?

Turning now and very briefly to the denominator of Professor Cloud's equation for the demographic quotient, I want to call attention to the obvious fact that an increase in population also brings with it an increase in the labor force that will use its skills and the associated capital and managerial factors to increase the total of resources available. For many years past, labor productivity, in the sense of output per man-hour, has been increasing in this and most other countries. This means that population increase, automatically accompanied a few years later by labor-force increase, has given rise to a net increase in Q. There is much evidence that this is now beginning to be the case in many of the less developed countries as well. Again, one has to beware of the trap involved in thinking that the population factor in the denominator of the equation increases while the total resources available in the numerator are a fixed, or relatively fixed, quantity. For many it is somehow easy to run out the arithmetic of a 2 per cent annual rate of increase in population and difficult to specify the variety of technological and economic responses—not to mention behavioral and policy responses—that can affect the situation favorably.

Finally, the denominator of the equation contains the per capita consumption factor. Most people in this country, and perhaps even more so nowadays in less developed countries, still want very much to be able to consume more and to enjoy rising levels of material comfort. On philosophical or even moral grounds I tend to agree with Professor Cloud in his fairly scathing remarks about the growth syndrome and the "illusion of growth as an intrinsic good." I have turned a few phrases on this subject myself. I wish that what I regard as an unhealthy devotion to GNP and the ever-rising standards of living in my own country could be reduced—although I certainly would not want to press this upon the 15 per cent or so of Americans living in poverty, or upon the next 15 per cent or so above that. But I think it will take more than Professor Cloud and me and a thousand others to bring about such a change, at least in the near future. However, if we in this country ever really started to run short of essential things, or even "essential luxuries," it is not inconceivable to me that individual life styles and national characteristics would change in such a way that emphasis on rising levels of material comfort would be greatly reduced. There is some evidence that a certain number of our youth want seriously to move in this direction, although there remains a measure of doubt as to the extent to which such youthful enthusiasms will be sustained into middle age. Personally, I hope their views prevail.

I would like to summarize my remarks as follows: In the next few decades, anticipated population increase in the United States is not likely to cause any serious shortages (that is, steeply increasing costs) of major resource materials, with perhaps a few exceptions for which substitutes will have to be found. For heavily populated poor countries, which contain two-thirds of the world's population, there can be no such optimistic outlook; the race between more people and the providing of more food and certain other raw materials will be hard and close.

In looking beyond the next few decades, my crystal ball becomes clouded, principally because of the uncertainties about scientific and technological advances, as these can be translated into political and economic reality, and because of the unpredictable, but considerable, possibilities for social and behavioral changes through which population growth can be reduced as a result of additional technological means, educational campaigns, and policy pressures.

The full effects of a growing population on the quality of the natural environment itself are difficult to foresee in any comprehensive way, even though some of the prospects are quite alarming. The trends in air and water pollution, pesticide damage, radioactive fallout, congestion, and landscape disfigurement, while favorable in some places, on the whole are discouraging. Certainly the trends are unfavorable with reference to rising expectations about standards of air and water quality and cleanliness of the landscape. Again, the big unknown is the response of technology, laws and institutions, and human behavior. And it is at just these points that the possibilities for constructive planning and action are greatest.

Policies and programs come into the picture both on the population and the resource-environment sides. Prudence would seem to point to a slowing down and stabilizing of the rate of population growth, and toward a continued steady increase in the production of food, energy commodities, and other materials, with much greater efforts to eliminate harmful side effects on the natural environment. Progress in these directions is especially needed in less developed regions.

It is difficult to prove that a particular level of population is the optimum except, perhaps, in a very narrow sense; the optimum population concept remains a will-o'-the-wisp which can be pursued but never grasped. The longer-run effects of a larger number of people on resources and the environment will depend on what people, and their leaders, want to do about the matter as much as on anything else, and on what policies and controls they will accept. Perhaps a more profound basis for population planning, as well as for resources development and environmental protection, is not to avoid running out of certain raw materials or even to avoid further pollution and defacement of the environment, but to bring yet another great element of the natural and social situation—that is, population itself—under human influence and conscious direction.

ENERGY

Limits to the Use of Energy

Alvin M. Weinberg and R. Philip Hammond

ABSTRACT

Energy can convert common materials—seawater, rock, air—into the materials needed by man. As we deplete ordinary resources, we estimate around 20 kilowatts (thermal) annually will ultimately be needed for each human being, if he is to maintain his present material standard. Twenty billion people would therefore require 400 billion kilowatts, or $\frac{1}{300}$, of the solar budget received by the earth. This would raise the average temperature of the earth $\frac{1}{5}$° C., which seems tolerable. However, care will have to be taken to avoid overheating of the local environment. This energy budget could be maintained indefinitely by means of catalytic nuclear burners—either fusion reactors, which use tritium as catalyst, or breeders, which use Pu^{239} or U^{233} as catalyst. Of these, the breeder seems to be entirely feasible, especially since permanent disposal of radioactive wastes by solidification and storage in salt mines is practical. We therefore conclude that the limit to population set by energy is extremely large, provided that the breeder reactor is developed or that controlled fusion becomes feasible.

Our thesis can be stated in three propositions:

1. Energy is convertible into most of the other requirements of life.

2. The energy available in nuclear sources is essentially inexhaustible.

3. Whatever limits to man's utilization of energy we can now see come not from an absolute limit on the total fuel in the earth's crust, but rather from the environmental side effects of very large-scale production of energy. The limit imposed by these side effects is probably very large.

We therefore admit to being energy optimists who see in unlimited energy a means for supporting many more people than now live on earth. In holding this view we stand with Sir Charles Darwin, the thermodynamicist, who in his grim little book, *The Next Million Years,*[1] consigned humanity to a perpetual Malthusian disequilibrium unless man discovers an inexhaustible source of energy. In Darwin's view, this inexhaustible source was fusion; in our view it is much more likely to be the burning of U^{238} or Th^{232} in so-called breeder reactors or, as we prefer to call them, catalytic nuclear burners.

No one questions that the population must be stabilized, but so far no one has found a workable, humane, and politically feasible means of doing so. Even an ideal solution will take many years to implement, so we must prepare for an interim population much larger than our present one. If the resulting burden on the earth's resources produces impoverishment, riot, and anarchy, we may never be able to get population control to work. Energy, we believe, is a possible key to ensuring a rational outcome and to buying the time needed to enforce fertility control.

What we shall outline are potentialities and possibilities. Whether we avail ourselves of these possibilities soon enough to stave off catastrophe no one can say. Nor will we try to estimate an *optimum* population. An ultimate limit set, say, by the heating of the earth by man-made energy, yes; but an *optimum* is left to others to estimate.

THE CONVERTIBILITY OF ENERGY

We list man's material needs in the following table.

TABLE 1

Man's Material Needs

Air
Food
Water
Shelter
Energy 〈 Stationary / Portable
Metals
Fibers

Aside from air, all of these can be provided with readily available raw materials and energy. This view was articulated perhaps most clearly by Harrison Brown, James Bonner, and John Weir in their book, *The Next Hundred Years.*[2] It was foreshadowed much earlier by H. G. Wells in his remarkable *The World Set Free: A Story of Mankind,*[3] which was published in 1914.

Consider water, for example. Theoretically, about 3 kwh. of work is required to separate the 300 pounds of salt contained in 1,000 gallons of seawater. Many separation processes are available; the simplest, and most highly developed, is multiple-effect distillation. If electrical energy is available at, say, 5 mills per kwh., then the thermodynamic minimum cost of desalting seawater would be 1.5¢ per 1,000 gallons. Of course, this minimum can never be attained. Current estimates suggest that fresh water can be extracted from the sea in extremely large, dual-purpose power and desalting plants at around 20 to 25¢ per 1,000 gallons. To this must be added conveyance costs, which depend on the distance from the desalting plant to the point of use. These may add perhaps 5 to 10¢ per 1,000 gallons to the price of water. Thus, our projected costs of desalted water for coastal cities fall in the same cost range as most municipal supplies in the United States. Some irrigation water costs this much; most goes for a third as much or less.

If desalted water were to be used for agriculture, the water would be purified close to the farming site so that the conveyance costs would be low. Thus, for irrigation, one could reasonably estimate water from the sea might cost 25¢ per 1,000 gallons. Can water costing as much as 25¢ per 1,000 gallons ever be used for staple agriculture? Some economists are inclined to say no. Yet agricultural technology suggests a different answer. To raise 2,500 calories (a man's daily requirement) of corn, wheat, or rice requires around 125 gallons of water, provided the crops are managed well. This means pesticide and water are available and are applied strategically. Thus, with irrigation water at 25¢ per 1,000 gallons, grain sufficient to keep a man in good health can be grown with 3¢ worth of water a day. Such culture could, in principle, be conducted in desert coastal areas not now being intensively cultivated. Israel is a good example of what can be done to convert desert lands into gardens even with expensive water: the incremental cost of water in Israel is now about 30¢ per 1,000 gallons. Cultivation of the desert is successful there because high value crops such as tomatoes are grown predominantly.

The main point made here is not that expensive water, won from the sea with energy, will be used in the short run for large-scale agriculture; it is rather that the additional cost of the water (about 3¢ per 2,500 calories) does not seem prohibitively high in the very long run. Should we run out of cheaper water, as we shall if the population increases several-fold, then we have an inexhaustible source of water in the sea, available at about 20 to 30¢ per 1,000 gallons, provided only that we have also a correspondingly large source of energy.

What about other basic commodities: portable fuel, metals, ammonia fertilizer? To a surprising degree one finds that a key to these is cheap hydrogen which is the universal reducing agent. If we have hydrogen, we can reduce metals from their ores; we can hydrogenate coal; we can manufacture NH_3 for agriculture.

Ordinary water is an infinite source of this universal reducing agent. The question is how much will electrolytic hydrogen cost? We have studied this at Oak Ridge National Laboratory, with the help of Allis-Chalmers and the Allison Division of General Motors. These organizations have developed high current density electrodes for fuel cells; we therefore asked them to apply this technology to the large-scale electrolytic production of hydrogen.

Our estimates of what hydrogen will cost if it is produced electrolytically take into consideration that the cost depends strongly on the price of electricity; if this cost is, say, 2 mills per kwh., then hydrogen costs about 35¢ per 1,000 standard cubic feet, which is within the range of the cost of hydrogen from methane reforming. If the price of electricity were 5 mills per kwh., hydrogen would cost around 70¢ per 1,000 s.c.f.; at 7 mills per kwh., 95¢ per 1,000 s.c.f. The point is not that electrolytic hydrogen is now strongly competitive with hydrogen produced from naphtha or other hydrocarbons. It is rather that, given a price of electricity, we can place an upper limit on the price of hydrogen. This upper limit seems to lie within, for example, two or three times rather than ten times the present cost of hydrogen from hydrocarbons.

Once we have hydrogen at not too high a cost, we have metals, ammonia, and portable fuel. As for iron, hydrogen is already used to reduce iron ore on a large pilot-plant scale. Arthur Squires estimates that the cost of H-iron is, again, not very far from the cost of iron produced in the conventional blast furnace.[4] As for ammonia, which makes a fair amount of sense as a portable fuel, electrolytic ammonia is already produced on a large scale, particularly in India. Experimental trucks have been operated on ammonia. This is not very surprising, since in ordinary gasoline (CH_2) 40 per cent of the energy is derived from the formation of water. Whether other more convenient modes of carrying hydrogen can be developed is uncertain. It is worth noting that liquid hydrogen has been proposed as a fuel for high-speed jet aircraft.

If we concede that energy is convertible into the basic necessities for man's future, then we can draw up the necessary energy budget for a society using energy as its basic raw material. At present, the United States consumption of energy in all forms is about 300 million Btu. per person per year, or 10 kw. thermal (kwt.)[5] per person. The present energy budget is broken into various uses and activities as follows:[6]

TABLE 2

Annual United States Energy Use per Capita (in kwt.)

	Household	Commercial	Transport	Industry	Other	Total
Space heating	1.14	.13	.03	.14	.07	1.51
Other heat	.33	.4		2	.6	3.33
Motive use			2			2
Electricity	.5	.3		1	.3	2.1
Nonenergy uses				.41	.7	1.11
Total	1.97	.83	2.03	3.55	1.67	10.05

If we assume that the entire world is brought up to this same standard of living (the present average is only 1.5 kwt. per capita) and that appropriate substitutions of energy are made for those raw materials which are not in virtually limitless supply, we can calculate the total energy budget of civilization at any population level. If our consumption of iron ore is partly replaced by use of aluminum, magnesium, and titanium, and the remaining iron is taken from inexhaustible low-grade ores, our energy budget is increased about 54 million Btu. or 1.8 kwt. per capita. If we produce half of our essential new water supply by dual-purpose desalination, we add 6 million Btu. (0.2 kwt. for 100 gallons per day). If we double the heat energy used for industrial process purposes because of recycling and lower grade sources, we add 60 million Btu. (2.0 kwt.), and if, finally, we add 50 per cent to the total electricity consumption for new uses and waste handling, it adds 30 million Btu. (1.0 kwt.). These adjustments add up to 150 million Btu. (5 kwt.), making a total energy budget of 450 million Btu. or 15 kwt. per capita. (The thermal or fuel equivalent of the electric power has been used throughout.) For safety, we shall increase this budget to 600 million Btu. (20 kwt.) per capita.

CATALYTIC BURNING OF NUCLEAR FUEL

Six hundred million Btu. per year (20 kwt.) is the equivalent of 25 tons of coal per year per person. How many people can be supplied with this energy budget with the world's fuel reserves? The most recent estimate of the world's coal supply is that of Paul Averitt in "Coal Resources of the United States," *United States Geological Survey Bulletin* No. 1275. From Averitt's estimate, M. King Hubbert calculates the world's total usable coal reserve to amount to 7.6 trillion tons. At a use rate of 25 tons per person per year, this amounts to $.3 \times 10^{12}$ man-years; if the world's population reaches ten billion, then this coal reserve would last little more than thirty years! Nor do other fossil fuels, oil and gas, alter the picture substantially.

Regardless of the precise per capita expenditure one assumes, it is clear that, as M. King Hubbert says, ". . . the epoch of the fossil fuels can only be a transitory and ephemeral event—an event, nonetheless, which has exercised the most drastic influence experienced by the human species during its entire biological history."[7]

If we discount solar energy as being too diffuse and too expensive to utilize, we shall, therefore, be obliged to turn to nuclear fuels: uranium, thorium, deuterium, and lithium. How inexhaustible are these?

As for deuterium, it is indeed inexhaustible; one part in 5,000 of the hydrogen in the sea is deuterium. Thus, if the fusion reaction

$$D^2 + D^2 \begin{cases} \nearrow He^3 + n^1 + 3 \text{ MeV} \\ \searrow T^3 + H^1 + 4 \text{ MeV} \end{cases}$$

can be made to go in a controlled fashion, we have our inexhaustible energy source. But the problems here are formidable; we shall not try to describe the current status of fusion except to say that, despite the optimism that now surrounds the project, the outlook is still very uncertain. It would be an exaggeration to say that fusion is clearly feasible; and despite recent considerable success with the Russian TOKAMAK, we are still unable to state whether or not controlled burning of deuterium is possible.

A somewhat easier process, but still one that has not been shown to be feasible, is the catalytic burning of Li^6. This process occurs in two steps:

1) Deuterium reacts with tritium (the catalyst)

$$D^2 + T^3 \longrightarrow He^4 + n^1 + 17.6 \text{ MeV}$$

2) The tritium is regenerated by reaction of a neutron with Li^6

$$Li^6 + n^1 \longrightarrow He^4 + T^3 + 4.8 \text{ MeV}$$

so that the net reaction is

$$D^2 + Li^6 \longrightarrow 2 He^4 + 22.4 \text{ MeV}$$

The D-T reaction requires the ions to be heated to about 10^4 eV, whereas D-D requires 5×10^4 eV. In this respect it is easier than D-D, but it is still very difficult.

We call this series of reactions "catalytic" burning of lithium since the tritium is regenerated. (In fact it is more than regenerated since each fast neutron produced in the D-T reaction can react with the abundant isotope Li^7 to produce a tritium nucleus and a slower neutron. This effect can be enhanced by introducing beryllium which, on reaction with a fast neutron, produces two slower neutrons and helium. These additional neutrons can then react with the Li^6 to produce additional tritium; only the lithium, beryllium, and deuterium are used up as fuels.) The ultimate amount of thermonuclear energy available if we must depend on catalytic burning of lithium is limited by the abundance of lithium and, to a lesser extent, of beryllium. The crustal abundance of Li^6 is about 2 p.p.m.; this is to be compared with the crustal abundance of Th + U which is 15 p.p.m. However, since the burning of one gram of lithium yields about four times the energy derived from the burning of one gram of uranium or thorium, the total energy content of the earth's crustal lithium is comparable to that in the U + Th. Both are immense— literally millions of times the energy content of all fossil fuels.

To release the immense reservoir of energy in U + Th, we must burn these materials catalytically. Catalytic burners of U^{238} or Th^{232} are usually called breeders. In our terminology a breeder would be a catalytic burner in which the catalyst (Pu^{239} or U^{233}) is more than self-regenerated. The amount of self-regeneration depends on the value of η. It is clear that the catalytic burner can be self-sustaining only if η, the number of neutrons produced per fissile atom destroyed, is 2 or greater. In point of fact, η must exceed 2 by a modest margin, say 0.2, to overcome the inevitable losses that must occur in an actual reactor.*

The main physical parameter that determines the feasibility of catalytic burning is η. For Pu^{239} in a fast neutron reactor, this number is around 2.8; for U^{233} in a slow neutron reactor, this number is around 2.2.

There is no question that catalytic burning of U^{238} or Th^{232} is feasible in principle. However, there are many difficult questions relating to the engineering of catalytic burners of U^{238} and Th^{232} (or, for that matter, of Li^6). Obviously, the process is rather awkward. The catalyst, Pu^{239} or U^{233} (or T^3), is burned in the reactor and is regenerated, usually in a blanket containing U^{238} or Th^{232} (or Li^6). Both reactor and blanket must be periodically reprocessed in order to recover the catalyst; unless this reprocessing is done very efficiently, some catalyst may be lost and the cycle will not be self-sustaining.

* The process in the case of thorium goes as follows:

$$U^{233} + n^1 \longrightarrow 200 \text{ MeV} + \eta n^1$$
$$\frac{(\eta - 1)n^1 + (\eta - 1)Th^{232} \longrightarrow (\eta - 1)U^{233}}{(\eta - 1)Th^{232} \longrightarrow 200 \text{ MeV} + (\eta - 2)U^{233}}$$

If $\eta = 2$, the catalytic burner is self-sustaining:

$$\boxed{Th^{232} \longrightarrow 200 \text{ MeV}}$$

If $\eta = 1 + \text{B.R.} > 2$, the catalytic burner is a breeder with breeding ratio B.R.:

$$\boxed{Th^{232} \longrightarrow \frac{200 \text{ MeV}}{\text{B.R.}} + \left(\frac{\text{B.R.} - 1}{\text{B.R.}}\right)U^{233}}$$

In the case of U^{238}, the processes are similar, though Pu^{239} replaces U^{233} as the catalyst.

In spite of these technical difficulties, there is much enthusiasm in the reactor community for development of catalytic burners. Most of the world's reactor development effort goes into the so-called Liquid Metal Fast Breeder Reactor (LMFBR), which is based on the U^{238}-Pu^{239} cycle. For reasons that we shall not go into, we find unique advantages in the Molten Salt Breeder Reactor (MSBR), based on the U^{233}-Th^{232} cycle.

There seems little reason to doubt that the world will see successful catalytic burners of both U^{238} and Th^{232} developed within the next ten to fifteen years. We hope that more effort is expended on the molten salt version, since we think—though we cannot prove—that it will be a more economical producer of electricity than will the LMFBR as presently visualized.

In principle, catalytic burners should produce very cheap electricity. Their fuel, U^{238} or Th^{232} (or Li^6), is relatively cheap: for example, at present costs for U^{238} of $8 per pound or 2¢ per gram, burn-up of the fuel adds less than .01 mill per kwh. to the cost of electricity. (Even if we have to extract thorium or uranium from low-grade rocks at a cost fifteen times higher than we now must pay, the burn-up cost of the fuel will still remain below 0.2 mill per kwh.) This number, of course, does not include all the costs associated with the fuel cycle: reprocessing, refabrication, waste disposal, inventory charges, etc. Nevertheless, fuel-cycle costs well below 0.5 mill per kwhe. appear to be achievable; and this low cost should not increase for a very long time. When such costs are achieved, it is not idle to anticipate electricity from extremely large catalytic burners costing not more than 2 mills per kwh., if they are publicly owned (and don't pay taxes), 3 mills per kwh. if they are privately owned and do pay taxes. In making this assertion, we assume that capital costs of such breeders will fall much below costs of current reactors. This long-range optimism is based upon our belief that, as the technology matures and as the size increases, reactor costs will follow the same trends as have costs of other very large pieces of industrial equipment; total costs may increase, but costs per unit output tend to fall over the long term. In any event, for the electrolytic production of hydrogen one could visualize using off-peak power. Such power should go for not much more than the operating and fuel-cycle costs.

LIMITS TO THE ULTIMATE USE OF CATALYTIC NUCLEAR BURNERS

Can we foresee limits to the use of catalytic nuclear burners? We can visualize three such limits, although there may be others that have not occurred to us: availability of nuclear fuel, dissipation of heat, and disposal of radioactive wastes. We shall discuss these in the order listed.

We have plenty of nuclear fuel, even for the very long run. At an energy budget of 20 kwt. per person per year, and a population of 2×10^{10} people, we would be burning 500 tons of thorium or uranium per day. In the Conway granites alone, there are about 30×10^6 tons of thorium, at an average concentration of 30 p.p.m. The Conway granites would, therefore, provide nuclear fuel for the entire world for about 200 years. The amount of rock to be handled, 15×10^6 tons per day, is about twice the total amount of coal now being mined in the world, the granite having almost 100 times the energy content of coal. If we run out of high-grade granites, we can eventually go to the residual granites which contain 12 p.p.m. of thorium plus 3 p.p.m. of uranium. At the energy budget contemplated here, these granites would last for millions of years.

What about dissipation of heat? Here the ultimate limit is set by the net energy the earth receives from the sun—that is, the total heat loss of the atmosphere to space. This heat loss is 120×10^{12} kw. At present, man produces 4.5×10^9 kw. or 4×10^{-5} of the sun's contribution. With a budget of 20 kwt./person, and 20×10^9 people, the total man-made energy of $.4 \times 10^{12}$ kw. would still be only 3×10^{-3} of the earth's natural rate of heat loss. This would increase the earth's average temperature by about $\frac{1}{5}$° C., which hardly seems intolerable since spontaneous swings in temperature of as much as 2° C. have been recorded in the geologic past. Thus, the total heat balance hardly would be affected until we reach a population level of several times 20×10^9. Much more serious, of course, will be local heating in the vicinity of the large catalytic nuclear burners. It seems likely that in most cases these will eventually be clustered in what are called "nuclear parks," producing perhaps 40×10^6 kwe. each, and located on the sea shore. The world would require about 4,000 such parks to produce the energy needed for 20×10^9 people. If these are located offshore, they could dissipate their heat to the ocean and thence, eventually, to the atmosphere. (It has been pointed out to us by S. R. Hanna of ESSA that local perturbations of the heat balance could indeed have a larger effect than is implied in these speculations, and great care will be needed in dispersing the heat.)

The knottiest problem, though one that is solvable, will be the disposal of radioactive wastes. With an energy budget of 400×10^9 kwt., the amount of radioactivity in wastes is very large. Each year

TABLE 3

Long-lived Activities in Wastes, 400×10^9 kwt.
Installed Capacity

Nuclide	Mean Life (years)	Megacuries Generated per Year	Total Accumulated in Steady State (Megacuries)
Sr^{90}	40.4	267,000	10.8×10^6
Cs^{137}	43.2	372,000	16.1×10^6
I^{129}	2.5×10^7	0.13	3.3×10^6
Kr^{85}	15.2	38,000	578,000
T^3	17.7	2,400	42,500
Tc^{99}	3.0×10^5	38	11.4×10^6
Pu^{238}	128	360	46,000
Pu^{239}	35,200	6	211,000
Pu^{240}	9,750	16	156,000
Am^{241}	660	620	409,000
Am^{243}	11,000	62	680,000
Cm^{244}	26.1	8,600	224,000

700,000 megacuries of long-lived activity would be generated; this activity would be distributed among the following nuclides.

Formidable though these numbers may seem, they do not present an insuperable difficulty. The general strategy is to immobilize the nonvolatile species—strontium, cesium, iodine, technetium, plutonium, americum, and curium—in ceramics and store them permanently in salt mines, and to hold up the noble Kr^{85} as a gas and T^3 as tritiated water until they decay.

At present, all high-level radioactive wastes from reactors are stored as liquids in underground tanks. However, this is admittedly a relatively temporary expedient, and in every country plans are underway to convert these radioactive liquids to solids, and to sequester them permanently, probably in salt mines. Disposal of wastes in salt was suggested in 1955 by a committee of the National Academy of Sciences-National Research Council. The main advantage of salt is that it is never in contact with ground water (though it may contain one-half per cent of somewhat mobile water occluded within the salt crystals). Experimental tests of disposal in salt in Lyons, Kansas, have already been carried out. Plans are tentatively underway to begin regular waste disposal in salt within the next few years.

Is there enough salt to accommodate wastes from reactors producing 400×10^9 kwt.? We estimate that, using currently conceived practices, the world would require about 30 square miles of salt per year. There are 500,000 square miles of salt in the United States alone; although not all of this is suitable for waste disposal, one cannot escape the impression that there is enough salt in which to sequester wastes from catalytic nuclear burners for a very long time.

DOES ENERGY LIMIT THE OPTIMUM POPULATION?

This symposium asks, Is There an Optimum Level of Population? This is a question that cannot really be answered. We have purposely taken a long-range view in our speculation. Dr. W. G. Pollard, taking a shorter view, has argued that to bring about the kind of energy-based society contemplated here, where energy replaces many other raw materials, would require so many changes in our economic and political structure as to make it all but impossible to achieve. As Dr. Pollard puts it, ". . . our present affluent society with its phenomenal standard of living has been created by abundant resources widely and cheaply available. . . . The removal of this resource base is certain to pull the rug out from under the affluent society. . . . the joy ride we have been on in this century can last not much more than another 20 years. After that . . . it will be simply impossible for us to continue to do simultaneously all of the things we want to do."[8]

Our view differs from Pollard's. Japan, for example, has become an affluent nation without the benefit of any internal resource base. The present United States energy consumption of 10 kwt. per person has a resource cost of about $100 per person per year (33¢ per M.Btu.), or about 2.5 per cent of the Gross National Product. Additional capital and operating expenses bring the cost to the consumer up to about $250. At our assumed future budget of 20 kwt., the fraction of GNP would probably remain about the same, since by that time the GNP will have increased significantly.* Therefore, since energy can take the place of other raw materials and since the ultimate cost of energy should be close to the present cost, and possibly much cheaper, we cannot see why a standard of living not very different from the present one is not sustainable indefinitely in the developed countries. We have, as noted above, taken a long-range view since the concept of an optimum population level is meaningless unless short-range problems are solved. And, in the very long run, there appears to be no clear limit to the amount of energy that man can acquire, up to, say, 400×10^9 kwt., and possibly even five times this amount. Thus, the limit to population set solely by limits to our energy production is very large indeed—considerably larger than twenty billion. Nor do we see any basic difficulties in the transition from our present state to a more energy-intensive society, at least for the developed parts of the world. For the underdeveloped parts of the world, the transition is obviously much more difficult.

We do not imply that there is no optimum population level, that twenty billion people on earth are no worse than two billion. We simply cannot say that if there were some twenty billion people on earth we would not have enough energy for them. Lack of living space, cluttering of the semantic environment, gross urbanization, loss of freedom—all these undoubtedly will make life for twenty billion people unpleasant by our standards. But we are unprepared

---

* Such expenditures for energy are, of course, greater than the total GNP for presently undeveloped countries, and the question of how that half of the human race can bridge an ever-widening poverty gap is perhaps antecedent to the question of optimum population. Investments must be found for these areas which provide a rapid increase of capital. But the poverty gap is more than anything else an *energy* gap, and it is no accident that in backward countries investments in energy can yield very high returns.

For example, the exciting "Green Revolution" in India and other parts of Asia was touched off when seed was introduced which, for the first time, showed a high response to fertilizer. Fertilizer is, of course, a form of energy input, which, under the right conditions, can yield from 500 per cent to 2,000 per cent return on its cost in less than 100 days. But this return is less if the water supply is not optimum. And water control is another important form of energy input. In the Ganges Plain, farmers have increased yields per acre three to tenfold in the monsoon season with new seed plus fertilizer, but energy for pumping water in the dry season can give two further crops, or up to 30 times the original yield per acre.

to predict that the material living standard would be catastrophically lower than that which we now enjoy in the affluent parts of the world. As for the underdeveloped parts of the world, the problem of transition to an energy-based economy will involve the same questions that underlie the transition from poverty to affluence.

The assumption underlying these views is that we shall have mastered the technology of catalytic nuclear burning. To us this is central, second only to the requirement for a more effective birth-control strategy (based, perhaps, on very simple after-the-fact contraception). We can only hope that we will devote the money and effort required to acquire this technology. Relatively little is needed to develop this art (about one day of the United States Gross National Product); yet on it the future of man may depend!

REFERENCES

1. Sir Charles G. Darwin, *The Next Million Years* (first American edition, Garden City, N.Y.: Doubleday & Company, Inc., 1952).

2. Harrison Brown, James Bonner, and John Weir, *The Next Hundred Years* (New York: The Viking Press, 1957).

3. H. G. Wells, *The World Set Free: A Story of Mankind* (New York: Dutton and Company, 1914).

4. Arthur M. Squires, "Iron and Steel with Hydrogen," *Abundant Nuclear Energy* (1969), 181–96. Proceedings of a symposium held at Gatlinburg, Tennessee, August 26–29, 1968, AEC Symposium Serial No. 14 (CONF-680810). Clearinghouse for Federal Scientific and Technical Information, Springfield, Virginia 22151.

5. *Metals, Minerals, and Fuels,* Vols. I and II, Bureau of Mines, *Minerals Yearbook 1967* (Washington, D.C.: Government Printing Office, 1968).

6. Distribution of 1967 energy use based on 1960 distribution given in "Energy R & D and National Progress," prepared for the Interdepartmental Energy Study by the Energy Study Group, Ali Bulent Cambel, Director (Washington, D.C.: Government Printing Office, 1964).

7. M. King Hubbert, "Energy Resources," in *Resources and Man.* A study and recommendation by the Committee on Resources and Man, National Academy of Sciences—National Research Council, NAS Publication 1703 (San Francisco: W. H. Freeman and Co., Publishers, 1969), p. 205.

8. William G. Pollard, "Moral Imperatives for Peace in the Remainder of this Century," presented before the Conference on Peaceful Change in Modern Society, Hoover Institution on War, Revolution and Peace, Stanford University, November 20, 1969.

FURTHER READINGS

Brown, Harrison, Bonner, James, and Weir, John. *The Next Hundred Years*. New York: The Viking Press, 1957.

Weinberg, Alvin M., and Young, Gale. "The Nuclear Energy Revolution—1966," *Proceedings of the National Academy of Sciences,* 57 (January, 1967), 1–15.

Weinberg, Alvin M. "Energy—The Ultimate Raw Material," *Science Journal* 5 (January, 1969).

Hammond, R. P. "Low Cost Energy: A New Dimension," *Science Journal* 5 (January, 1969), 34–44.

Energy Consumption and Optimum Population Density

Chauncey Starr

ABSTRACT

Energy consumption and its environmental effects do not appear to be a constraint on the projected world population growth. Energy releases might, however, pose a local problem where population density exceeds about 30,000 people per square mile.

The annual consumption of all forms of energy for the world has increased about tenfold during the past century, and will probably increase tenfold again during the next century. This is equivalent to an annual growth of 2.3 per cent. Two principal trends are involved—the first is the increased use of energy per person, the second is the steady increase in the world's population.

The energy consumption per person varies by a factor of one hundred from the most underdeveloped parts of the world to those most advanced industrially. As one might expect, the economic productivity per capita appears to be directly proportional to this energy usage per capita. Thus, the drive to improve the economic welfare of the individual—if unusually successful in a short time—could significantly boost the world energy usage.

There is, however, a slow counteracting trend which arises from the continuous contribution of technology to increasing the efficiency with which we use energy for productive purposes. If one uses the historical trends in the United States as an example, it appears that growth in economic productivity per capita results equally from increased energy usage per person and increased efficiency of conversion of energy to productive uses. Specifically, in the United States, the economic productivity per capita has grown 2 per cent per year while the energy usage per capita has grown 1 per cent per year. This is consistent with the "common wisdom" that half our economic growth is due to reinvestment of capital and half due to technological development.

Although fossil fuels (coal, oil, and gas) can undoubtedly meet the world's energy needs for the next century, they represent a finite reserve which could be severely depleted in some hundreds of years unless alternate energy sources are developed. Because of the restrictive effect on all aspects of life if energy use becomes limited, and the lead-time of about fifty years required to make significant changes in energy-use patterns, energy resource planning must truly be anticipatory in order to be effective. Fortunately, nuclear power has radically extended the limitations on energy planning by adding a new option. In combination with the breeder cycle, nuclear fuel provides an energy resource probably adequate for the next five to ten centuries. And, of course, the possible technological development of the "fusion" process could enlarge this indefinitely. The question, then, is not will energy supply foreseeably limit population growth— for the answer to that is "No."

There are two important questions relating to future energy: first, will the continued use of fossil fuels produce by-products which create an "ecological feedback" sufficient to endanger the livability of our global biosphere; and, second, will the concentration of energy use in urban areas create a practical limit to urban population density.

Let us consider the first question. Even with nuclear power, the use of fossil fuels will certainly continue to grow for the next century because of (1) the many energy devices which uniquely depend on fossil fuels (the automobile and airplane, for example), (2) the time required to expand nuclear power, (3) the continuous pressure of world population growth, and (4) the world-wide increase in per capita energy use. It is clear that local and regional environments are now unpleasantly affected by the effluents from fossil-fuel users; it is not so evident, however, that significant problems on a global scale will develop. The global life cycle of contaminants is not understood sufficiently for long-term predictive purposes. The cumulative amount of effluents so far produced are not as yet sufficient to be critical. The most measurable component addition, carbon dioxide, has increased about 7 per cent in the past half century (about half from the combustion of fuels); but the much discussed "greenhouse effect" on global climate may be offset by the balancing effect of other phenomena such as atmospheric turbidity. The influence of long-term meteorological trends on global temperatures may be much more important than either of the preceding.

Hydrocarbons are discharged into the atmosphere by natural processes—man now contributes only about one-sixth of the total. Sulfur and nitrogen compounds are of undoubted local importance, but their global effects are not detectable. The global importance of other man-made emissions is essentially minimal or unknown at the present time. In the long run, more data and global life-cycle research is needed for predictive analysis of our ecosystem.

The issue of the loading of the environment with heat—the end product of energy conversion and use—now figures in the siting of power plants. The man-made thermal load, however, is so small compared to the solar heat load as to be insignificant on a global scale—less than one-thousandth a century hence. Nevertheless, the local climatic and other ecosystem disturbances of concentrated energy conversion assemblies, such as power plants, will continue to be an important technological problem.

Nuclear power use avoids the chemical effluents of fossil fuel combustion, but does present the danger of accidental release of radioactive effluents. However, after much study, the opinion prevails in the nuclear field that such accidental releases can be made as small as needed to achieve socially acceptable levels. The design objective of nuclear plants is, of course, to avoid such accidents. During normal operation, the level of radioactivity emitted to the environment can be kept small compared to our natural background—and therefore should not be an additional health hazard. Thus, nuclear plants may truly be considered "clean air" power sources, as compared to fossil fuel plants.

In sum, therefore, energy use does not appear to be a foreseeable global constraint on the projected world population growth.

Let us now consider the second question—that of the effect of energy concentration resulting from the high population density of urban areas. There is associated with most urban areas a meteorological phenomenon known as the "heat island." This term describes a dome of warm air, covering a city, which is, both day and night, higher in temperature than that of the surrounding countryside. Solar radiation alone, in the absence of wind, can produce an urban heat island—primarily due to the small water-evaporating surface areas in the city as contrasted with rural areas. Thus, both the city's surface and air mass absorb most of the solar radiation, while in rural areas evaporation handles most of the heat. The microclimatic effect of this heat island is to significantly raise the maximum air temperature in the city as compared to rural areas—in a hypothetical case[1] by as much as 10° F. Clearly, in hot weather periods this heat island effect can make urban living only marginally tolerable—perhaps with the aid of air conditioning.

If, in addition to the solar radiation load, we now add the heat produced by energy utilization in an advanced-technology society, we can hypothesize that there may be a population density which might well make the urban heat island climatically unacceptable. For example, in a modern industrial society the total per capita energy use is about 10 kwt., all of which eventually ends up as waste heat somewhere. Assuming discharge in the city, a population density of about 30,000 people per square mile would make this waste-heat load as large as the urban atmospheric solar radiation load.

Under the occasional extreme meteorological combination of no wind and high temperatures and humidity, the resultant doubling of the maximum temperature increment between urban and rural areas (about 20° F.) might well make many of our cities intolerable in hot weather. Historically, our present urban locations were chosen at a time when summer energy use was negligible. Today, such seasonal energy variation is disappearing. One might therefore assume that for comfort the energy-use atmospheric waste-heat load should be kept a fraction of the solar load. This suggests that a population density of less than 30,000 people per square mile might be a reasonable target for a future city. This can be compared with the 1960 population densities of 77,000 for Manhattan, 16,000 for San Francisco and Chicago, 12,000 for Washington, and 6,000 for Los Angeles.

Since the urban atmospheric temperature increments due to these heat loadings is so dependent on the local meteorology, wind speed, detailed urban configuration, temporal and spatial patterns of energy use and distribution, and the social acceptance of discomfort, reasonable population density limits may vary widely in individual areas. Nevertheless, it is apparent that the concentration of energy-using devices in modern cities may set a practical limit to urban population density, or require waste-heat disposal outside the city—as with any other waste product. This may become increasingly important with time if the present trend of 1 per cent per year increase in per capita energy use (a doubling time of seventy years) continues undiminished.

REFERENCE

1. Leonard O. Myrup, "A Numerical Model of the Urban Heat Island," *Jour. of Applied Meteorology, 8,* 6 (December, 1969), 908–18.

ENERGY

Energy Consumption and Optimum Population

Hans H. Landsberg

ABSTRACT

In the traditional view, energy consumption is related to size of population in two ways: the larger the population, the higher energy consumption, therefore (1) the more rapid the exhaustion of energy resources and, at a certain threshold of consumption, (2) the more adverse the effects on the environment.

It is pointed out that population size is not in fact the major variable in energy consumption. Statistics are presented to illustrate that per capita consumption is twice as important a factor in energy consumption growth as is population size, irrespective of a country's stage of development. This effect is especially pronounced in the case of electricity.

Attention is called to the role of technology as causing significant shifts in the efficiency of energy use and thus further weakening the link between population size and energy production and consumption.

Even if it were possible to identify, in fact, that level of aggregate energy consumption at which the costs to society of an incremental unit of energy outweighed its benefits to society, there would still be an infinite number of combinations of population size and per capita consumption that would produce that particular level of energy consumption.

For the reasons given, it is concluded that in the search for an optimum population, energy production or consumption provides no useful guide. If anything, the outlook for the eventual abundance of low-cost energy opens up a supply of abundant low-cost basic commodities, a condition that would permit ever-larger populations to exist. In the light of such considerations it is suggested that the rationale for limiting population growth—or the means of defining an optimum population level—must be located elsewhere.

Thinking about the relationship between energy and population is not new. In 1910, in his book *The Fight for Conservation,* Governor Pinchot remarked, "We have anthracite coal for but 50 years and coal for less than 200. Our supplies of iron ore, mineral ore, and natural gas are being rapidly repleted, and many of the great fields are already exhausted." Calling coal ". . . in a sense the vital essence of our civilization . . ." he judged that ". . . if it can be preserved . . . if by preventing waste there can be more coal left in this country . . . we shall have deserved well of our descendants."

Sixty years later we are again concerned; but for the first time, to my knowledge, there is, at least in most of the developed countries, a greater preoccupation with what today's energy does in the process of being produced, transported, and consumed than where tomorrow's energy will come from. In other words, students of resources and conservationists are more interested in studying the effect energy has on its surroundings than in the sources of energy and their adequacy to meet future needs. In those terms one might judge that a country like the United States is even now producing and consuming more energy than the environment is capable of handling, given the technical, social, and political unpreparedness for meeting this new problem. Those who think so will make the valid assertion that the waste-assimilative capacities of the ambient air and of the water bodies that receive waste heat have been overtaxed. And so they have been in many aspects and instances. From this set of observations it is only a short step to concluding that at some level of energy consumption, alteration of water and air resources will, in simple biological terms, spell the end of a livable environment. And by analogy with similar congestion situations one is led, further, to judge that, in order to reduce or halt this trend, the pace of population growth must be slowed down and eventually brought to a halt.

This leaves out the more traditional conclusion that at some rate of growth of energy production we shall exhaust our energy resources. A great deal of light has been thrown on that proposition by Dr. Weinberg's paper, and I, for one, am persuaded that "running out" is not an issue that need concern us as a matter of urgency today. But, for reasons I will state, I have also trouble subscribing to the preceding propositions that have claimed our attention for some time now, and rightly so.

As for the "doomsday" hypothesis, I have been privileged to listen to discussions among qualified scholars and to hear them advance support on both sides of the argument. As I listened, the earth got in turn warmer and colder. I was left better educated but not better able to decide who was right and who was wrong. Let us assume, though, that persistence of present energy consumption practices and trends would eventually result in levels of pollutants in the environment that would threaten life itself. Must I then also assume that it is beyond human ingenuity technologically and, at least as important, socially, to take steps to reduce these threats? My reply is an unequivocal "No," provided that we go about it not in the simple belief that "wishing will make it so," but in the full knowledge that the cost of these steps will be large, and that the cost will include substantial interference with and modifications (if not the abandonment) of cherished customs and institutions, affecting attributes of private ownership, price levels, and traditional types of goods and services.

Hypothetical calculations of the results of long-extended trends have their uses—most of all as eye-openers of what *could* happen— but unless accompanied by a dispassionate discussion of what remedies could vitiate these far-off dire results, they are little more than devices to scare the uninformed. Of course, a slower growth rate in energy consumption would ease the waste-management task; but that is a more pedestrian issue than preventing a global disaster. Slower growth—and here I return to the traditional theme of resource adequacy—would also reduce the inroads on the world's stock of fossil fuels; however, developments of the kind envisaged in Dr. Weinberg's paper would deprive the adequacy argument of much of its weight, and while these developments are not, perhaps, within ready grasp, neither are we in dire straits with regard to the supply of traditional sources of energy among which, by now, we must count nuclear fission.

In the meantime, we have much to learn about the relationship between energy and population. What I have to say on this score will make clear why I cannot agree with the proposition that there are already too many of us for a tolerable level of energy use; or, more generally phrased, that an optimum population can be identified in terms of that population's use of energy.

What strikes me in looking at energy in relation to population, optimum or otherwise, is the very tenuous relationship between the two as borne out by a look at history. While the relevant statistics are afflicted with defects that reduce comparability (such as lack of accounting for noncommercial sources of energy), they are not bad enough to cause the enormous differences in per capita consumption that one finds (Table 1). There are today regions of the world (such as most of Africa and Southeast Asia) that consume the energy equivalent of less than 300 pounds of coal per capita per year, and others (such as North America) that consume seventy times as much. Ranked in terms of energy-consumption per capita the leading

TABLE 1

Energy Consumption and Growth Rates

	1967 Per Capita Consumption (In Kg. of Coal Equivalent)	Growth Rates 1925–67	
		Aggregate Energy Consumption (in per cent per year)	Per Capita Consumption (in per cent per year)
North America	10,162	2.6	1.3
Western Europe	3,350	2.0	1.4
U.S.S.R. and Communist Europe	4,071	7.0	5.9
Latin America	872	5.4	3.0
Asia, non-Communist:			
Japan	2,492	5.1	3.8
Other	213	4.9	3.1
Communist Asia	338	5.8	4.5
Africa	299	4.1	2.6
Oceania	3,727	3.5	1.9
World	1,730	3.3	1.9

TABLE 2

Selected Countries Ranked According to Per Capita GNP
and Energy Consumption, 1965

Country	Per Capita GNP (in U.S. $)	Rank	Per Capita Energy Consumption (in kg. coal equivalent)	Rank
United States	3,515	1	9,671	1
Canada	2,658	2	8,077	2
Sweden	2,495	3	4,604	9
Denmark	2,333	4	4,149	10
Switzerland	2,331	5	2,699	21
West Germany	2,195	6	4,625	8
France	2,104	7	3,309	16
Norway	2,015	8	3,621	13
United Kingdom	1,992	9	5,307	5
Belgium-Luxembourg	1,991	10	5,152	6
Uruguay	573	35	958	37
Libya	542	36	613	42
South Africa	535	37	2,761	20
Nicaragua	527	38	247	48
Chile	497	39	1,119	33
Panama	495	40	1,112	34
Jamaica	492	41	873	40
Mexico	475	42	1,104	35
Lebanon	438	43	770	41
Hong Kong	421	44	605	43
Costa Rica	415	45	317	47
Portugal	396	46	520	45
Peru	367	47	577	44
Malaysia & Singapore	332	48	424	46
Guatemala	318	49	188	49

countries are distinguished by high per capita GNP, the low-consumption countries by low GNP (Table 2). This tells us that energy is one of the ingredients in high levels of production—not exactly a spectacular discovery. But it also tells us something less obvious, less frequently noted, and more pertinent to the subject under consideration. Crudely formulated the statistics suggest something like this: If for some reason—such as lessening the environmental impact or warding off impending scarcity—one wished to slow down the pace at which energy consumption is rising, reducing population growth would be a poor way to achieve one's end and slowing down per capita income growth a good way (disregarding other ways of dealing with the problem). To this proposition I would then add a second one, stemming from the increased role of electricity as a source of energy: what is true for energy as a whole is many times as true for electricity, presumably because use of electricity above a very low level, at which only the need for lighting is satisfied, requires possession of a growing number and variety of expensive hardware.

A few simple calculations, based upon a recent study made at Resources for the Future, will illustrate the points made. To begin with, it shows that, between 1938 and 1965, increases in energy consumption in three widely differing areas—selected as representative of differing economic settings: the United States, the United Kingdom, and the area of Southeast Asia that in 1938 constituted India—were prompted one-third by population growth and two-thirds by per capita consumption growth.[1]

One can look at this phenomenon in a way to illuminate, especially, the population variable (Figure 1). Energy consumption in the United States rose from 670 million tons (in coal equivalents) in 1938 to 1,880 million tons in 1965, or by some 1,200 million tons. The data allow one to estimate that population growth alone, with per

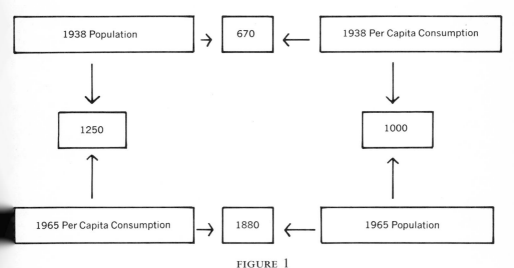

FIGURE 1
United States energy consumption in 1965 under varying
assumptions (in million tons of coal equivalent).

capita consumption constant, would have boosted 1965 consumption to about 1,000 million tons, or by only 330 million tons above the level of 1938. In contrast, under conditions of zero population growth, but with per capita consumption growth rising as it in fact did, aggregate consumption would have been boosted by nearly 600 million tons between 1938 and 1965. Thus, a policy intended to hold down energy consumption would have accomplished twice as much, so to speak, by keeping per capita consumption constant as by stopping population growth. (I omit from this calculation the joint effect of the two growth factors as irrelevant to the point of this hypothetical comparison; nor do I intend to appraise the relative feasibility of one or the other of the two growth-repressing policies.)

Another useful way of illustrating the phenomenon is to calculate— assuming current per capita consumption standards—the size of a population compatible with a level of aggregate energy consumption that might be chosen as desirable for some compelling reason. Taking again the United States, and assuming for the sake of illustration that aggregate energy consumption at the 1938 level is as high as we find desirable, then simple arithmetic shows that a population of seventy million is all we could afford. On such an assumption the United States would now have a population nearly three times the tolerable size. But, of course, the case for the 1938 or any other specific aggregate energy consumption level has not been made. Its definition would have to take into account the energy source mix as well as technologies of production, transportation, processing, consumption, and waste disposal. On a highly theoretical plane, aggregate energy consumption could probably be said to be at an optimum level when the costs of an incremental unit, including the full environmental and other external costs, would exceed the benefits of that unit. Not only, however, is this a concept that we are a long way from being able to measure, but even were we able to measure it, this optimum level could be a product of an infinite set of combinations of per capita consumption and population size.

To return to the illustrations, the significance of per capita consumption is greatly accentuated when we look at electricity rather than at total energy consumption. Thus, population growth accounts for only about 10 per cent of the rise in electricity consumption from 1938 to 1965 in the United States, less than 6 per cent in India, and a mere 2.5 per cent in the United Kingdom. In other words, per capita consumption growth is the whole show. Not surprisingly, therefore, if it were desirable to return to total electricity consumption at the prewar level, but at current levels of per capita consumption, the United States population would have to be trimmed from its current two hundred million to a mere twenty million people.

Or let us look, in an even narrower framework, at motor-fuel consumption in the United States. Consumption in 1968 was about two billion barrels, at 400 gallons per capita. Suppose we wanted to roll back aggregate use to the 1940 level, on the grounds that air pollution was then a rarity; but suppose we were unwilling to go back to the 1940 per capita consumption of less than 200 gallons. Population would then have to be shaved to no more than sixty million people, if each was to own as many cars and drive them as much as we do now.

Whether we critically eye rising energy consumption for the in-roads it is making on a finite amount of fossil fuels, or for its role in environmental pollution, the data suggest, first, that reduced population growth would affect consumption only moderately, and, second, that a country's stage of development appears to make little difference in that respect. Nor does the wide spectrum of applications of energy or the ratio of energy use to the size of population give us any clue as to an optimum population. Indeed, the high correlation of per capita GNP with per capita energy use seems to suggest an open-ended "the more energy the better." This, of course, presumes that GNP, and growth of GNP, are "good." That is an issue we shall refrain from discussing here, but it calls attention to a frequently-used technique of portraying as an impending crisis what is in fact a slowly unfolding development. I am referring to the future rise of energy consumption in the less developed countries, and to its impact on both resource availability and environmental quality. In this context it is useful to point out that it would take the continent of Africa, for example, about sixty years at an unrealistically high (as evident from a glance at Table 1) annual growth rate of 5 per cent in per capita energy consumption to reach the United States per capita consumption level not of 1970 but of 1925, and obviously much longer to attain the 1970 level. Such calculations give some badly-needed perspective to the crisis specter easily conjured up by manipulations of compound interest.

One other consideration hampers attempts to link population and energy consumption in the context contemplated by this panel, and that is changing technology. A simple example will suffice. In 1968,

United States electric utilities burned fuel in the amount of about 480 million tons of coal equivalent. At the much lower thermal efficiency afforded by 1940 technology, they would have had to burn 740 million tons to generate the 1968 amount of electricity. The one-year savings of 260 million tons are equal to the contemporary total annual energy consumption of about twenty-six million Americans; and that twenty-six million, in turn, is the net growth in the United States population in the last decade. Obviously, an optimum population becomes an elusive concept in the presence of changing technology.

At any moment, then, aggregate energy consumption is the product of population size and per capita consumption, where the latter is a function of per capita income, of the specific bundle of demands of which the consumption consists, and, in the widest sense, of the state of technology. Examination of data suggests that per capita consumption is the dominating variable.

What does all this add up to in terms of population size? If abundant, or even unlimited, low-cost energy sources, as portrayed in Dr. Weinberg's paper, is a realistic vision—and I find his exposition persuasive—then abundant availability of a large range of other resources is a legitimate second-order conclusion. In that event, it becomes clear that in the search for a convenient and widely shared, so-to-speak "objective," motivation for reducing the rate of population growth, we had better not take our stand on the conventional resource-scarcity argument—or even the more novel pollution issue, provided we learn, as we can learn, to manage the unwanted by-products of energy production and consumption.

The "green revolution" serves as an indication of how slippery a foothold a scarcity syndrome may prove for a rationale of population control. For however one may qualify the prospects and consequences of that development—and the full implications won't be in for some time—it surely has pushed back the horizon of hunger and, by providing a breathing spell, probably slowed the momentum of the effort to reduce population growth. By analogy, the prospect of abundant, low-cost energy and, based on it, of fertilizer, metals, and a host of other basic commodities, could pull the rug out from under any effort to reduce population growth that finds its principal rationale in a growing scarcity of the conventional resource commodities.

There emerges then a plausible sequence that leads one (1) to cast doubt on whether the search for an optimum population can be linked at all to energy—a field where changing technology and income are such powerful factors; (2) to insist that in the development of very cheap energy sources we must be absolutely certain to adequately consider the true costs of the new technology—by which I mean, above all, its environmental impact—lest we end up once more with low private and high social costs; and (3) to prepare for reaching decisions on population size on a quite different, and philosophically and morally far more complex, terrain—namely, that of values unconnected with material needs and oriented rather toward ultimate goals or, to use a more fashionable term, life styles. As in so many other situations, when the easy, quasi-automatic sanctions—be these disease, hunger, societal punishment, or specific material scarcities— are lifted, we are thrown back on our individual and on society's moral and ethical resources, and that is where the easy decision is hard to come by. Desirable as it would be, I see no way in which consideration of energy availability or of its environmental effects would give us an easy handle for cranking in the "right number" of people for any country or for the world as a whole.

REFERENCE

1. Source for these data and also for tables and figure: Joel Darmstadter and Others, *Energy in the World Economy—A Statistical Review of Trends in Output, Trade and Consumption Since 1925,* forthcoming (Baltimore: Johns Hopkins Press).

FURTHER READINGS

Landsberg, Hans H., and Schurr, Sam H. *Energy in the United States.* Contains guide to further reading. New York: Random House, 1968.

Barnett, Harold J., and Morse, Chandler. *Scarcity and Growth.* Baltimore: Johns Hopkins Press, 1963.

Revelle, Roger R., and Landsberg, H. H. (eds.). *America's Changing Environment.* Boston: Houghton Mifflin Company, 1970, and Boston: Beacon Press, 1970.

Effects of Population Growth on Natural Resources and the Environment. Hearings before a Subcommittee of the Committee on Government Operations, H.R., 91st Congress, 1st Session, September 15–16, 1969.

World Population Conference (Belgrade, August 30–September 10, 1965), Vol. II, *Projections, Measurement of Population and Trends.* (See Section on natural resources.) Department of Economics and Social Affairs. New York: United Nations, 1967.

Food Supplies and the Optimum Level of Population

Lester R. Brown

ABSTRACT

Food is one of man's basic necessities. Any discussion of a nation's optimum population must take into account its food supply. This paper looks at trends in food production and in agricultural technologies, and concludes that the agricultural land in the United States could support a population considerably larger than the present. Food supply, however, has other aspects that affect the quality of life in the nation. Principal among these is the danger of damage to the environment from a growing intensity of farming.

The face of the United States agricultural economy has been changing very rapidly in this century. New seeds, mechanization, and fertilizer have led to gains in yields per acre in all the important food crops. This has allowed the government to retire millions of acres of cropland from production while still feeding the domestic population cheaply and exporting nearly $6 billion worth of agricultural commodities. And it seems that the technological limit has not yet been reached. The plant breeders promise higher yields, food of better nutritional quality, and even entirely new man-made plants.

The farm population, already small, will continue to decline as larger farm units become more economical. This will aggravate the social problems of the cities.

The author also discusses ecological threats from the use of pesticides and fertilizers, along with some means of ameliorating them.

The question before us, "Is there an optimum level of population?" is forcing us to develop a methodology for determining the relationship and the tradeoff between quantity and quality of life.*

In responding to the question before the Symposium, I believe that we are beginning to redefine the population problem, moving beyond our legacy from Malthus, which was concerned almost solely with food supply as it related to population growth.† We are realizing the importance of other factors in attempting to determine what an optimum population is. This process has gone furthest in the United States, where aggregate food supply has not been a significant problem in this century, and has placed no real constraints on population size. Although we are confining our considerations in this session to the United States, our conclusions will have relevance for the entire world. The most difficult task in relating optimum population and food supply is in formulating the questions which will add to our understanding of the interrelationship of the two in the United States.

POTENTIAL IN CONVENTIONAL AGRICULTURE

Gazing into the agricultural crystal ball is an uncertain business. We do not know what the production potential of our cultivable land is, even in terms of known technologies; it is impossible to predict exactly what that potential will be after another thirty years of continuing advances in technology. Despite this, we can look at the trends in agricultural production over recent decades, and we can examine likely constraints on the continuation of these trends, together with the new technologies that are in the pipeline. The general conclusion is that the production potential of conventional agriculture as such is by no means exhausted.

---

*I am deeply indebted to Robert Shaw, my colleague at the Overseas Development Council, for many of his ideas and for his assistance in preparing this paper.

†For a more detailed discussion of the need to redefine the population problem on a global level, see Chapter 14 of the author's *Seeds of Change* (New York: Frederick A. Praeger, Inc., 1970).

Yields of the most important crops have increased markedly over the past four decades due to the introduction of new plant varieties, the enormous growth in the use of chemical fertilizers (a sevenfold increase since 1940) and herbicides, economies of scale and better management, and the greater use of machinery. The most dramatic gains have been in corn and sorghum, the two cereals for which successful hybrids have been developed. From the Civil War until the beginning of World War II, corn yields changed little. Since then, with the adoption of hybrids and the rapid increase in the use of fertilizer, yields have shot upward, going from 30 bushels per acre in 1940 to 80 bushels in 1967. Advances in sorghum yields are even more impressive, climbing from 22 bushels per acre in 1956 to 56 bushels in 1966, as hybrids were introduced (Figure 1).

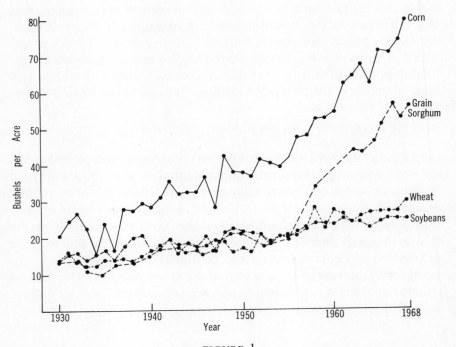

FIGURE 1

Average yields in the United States since 1930 of corn, grain sorghum, wheat, and soybeans.

It is unlikely that the rates of growth in the yields of these two cereals can be sustained. The transition to hybrid varieties is a once-and-for-all move, as is the introduction of herbicides. Yields are likely to grow at a more leisurely rate in response to even better varieties, improved management, and the greater use of fertilizer. Many scientists see this slowing in the rate of yield increases in terms of that familiar biological function, the S-shaped growth curve. It seems probable that these two cereals are approaching the middle of the S curve. Even so, the United States Department of Agriculture still projects yield increases of 2 per cent per year for sorghum and 3 per cent per year for corn, through at least 1980, as a result of the factors mentioned above. These growth rates are considerably higher than the projected rate for population growth, so that present consumption levels could be maintained by use of even smaller acreages of land.

The future for wheat and rice, and such important noncereal crops as soybeans, is even less certain. In general, the yields of these crops have not been raised to the same extent as corn and sorghum. But there are exciting possibilities on the horizon. Hybrid wheat varieties, for example, developed by one of the large seed companies, were grown on a semicommercial basis on a considerable number of farms during the past season. With improved plant-breeding techniques, and a greater collection of breeding materials, we can anticipate considerable gains in the yields of conventional varieties. Increasingly, plant breeders will develop disease resistance in their plants; they will extend the range of adaptability of their varieties; and they will work toward greater efficiency in the plants' ability to use fertilizer, water, land, solar energy, and other resources.

The prospects for conventional agriculture are further enhanced by another technological breakthrough on the plant-breeding front. The heart of this new technology is the identification of high-lysine genes (specifically Opaque-2 and Floury-2) which raise the nutritional quality of the corn plant when incorporated into it. There are still problems with yields that are lower than other varieties, and with flavor, but substantial improvements in the food value of high-lysine corn, both for animals and for humans, is evident from initial tests. Similar searches are now being conducted for wheat and rice varieties of high nutritional content.

Looking slightly further into the future, we can see the development of "man-made" cereals of high yield, efficiency, and protein content. Since 1888, plant breeders have known about Triticale, a cross between wheat and rye, with exceptionally high protein content. Until 1968, the development of Triticale had been held up by two problems: partial sterility and a high incidence of shriveled grain. Within the last two years, however, highly fertile lines have been discovered, as have other lines with superior grain types. If these two characteristics can be combined, Triticale could soon become commercially competitive with the established cereals.

It is very difficult to say how high crop yields can or will go by the end of the century. This may depend more on economic factors (such as the strength of demand and the relative costs of inputs), on the adverse impact of certain technologies (such as the use of agricultural chemicals), or on the environment than on constraints inherent in the plants themselves.

Even if the future increase in yields were to fall well below that projected, there is still sufficient slack in United States productive capacity to provide food for a considerably larger population. This excess capacity is best seen in the acreages idled as a result of the growth in yields. These could be brought back into production if acreage controls were removed and if economic incentives were strengthened. The cropland harvested within the continental United States totaled 360 million acres in 1930. By 1964, it had declined to 287 million acres. At the latter date the United States was feeding not only its own population, but one hundred million people abroad, to forestall famine after massive crop failures in India, Pakistan, and elsewhere.

The urgent need for food abroad to prevent famine has dropped markedly as a result of the gains made with the new high-yielding cereal varieties developed by the Rockefeller and Ford Foundations in Mexico and the Philippines. Nevertheless, exports from the efficient farming systems of the United States are still considerable. The exports of agricultural commodities in fiscal 1969, at $5.7 billion, were equivalent to 13 per cent of the $44.4 billion of cash receipts from farm marketings in 1968. Thus, even if we assume no increase in production, a considerably larger domestic demand could be satisfied by the existing output.

Some consideration must also be given to that share of the United States food supply which comes from the sea. Per capita fish consumption in this country has remained fairly constant over the last fifteen years at about thirteen pounds. Even though the global yearly fish catch could conceivably double by the end of the century, there is likely to be little change in United States consumption in the next few decades.

The idea of using algae as food was presented by science-fiction author Jules Verne more than a century ago. It is technically feasible to do so, but there has been little progress toward making algae a tasty commercial food product. Another food from the sea, with better prospects of success, is fish-protein concentrate. It can be processed from species of fish not usually consumed by humans, and which are, therefore, relatively inexpensive. Neutral in taste and color, it can be added directly to other dishes to boost protein intake, avoiding the difficulty of changing eating habits. But soy protein concentrate can do these things, too, and at a much lower cost with current technologies.

DEMAND DETERMINANTS

The amount of food that must be produced on United States farms depends, of course, on the effective demand for food. And that demand depends upon a number of factors, principal among which are population growth, income levels, food prices, and the evolution of new food technologies resulting in commercial production of imitation livestock products of vegetable derivation. Sorting out the individual effects of these factors is not easy. But an overall look at food consumption offers some interesting trends, and can indicate the points at which demand pressure may be greatest in the future.

In the world at large, the relationships between increases in per capita income and the consumption of grain are illustrated in Figure 2. The direct consumption of grain, as food, rises with income per person throughout the low income brackets; at higher income levels, it declines, until it levels off at about 150 pounds per year. But total grain use is closely related to income—the consumption of an additional pound of grain being associated with a two-dollar gain in annual per capita income. The excess of total use over direct con-

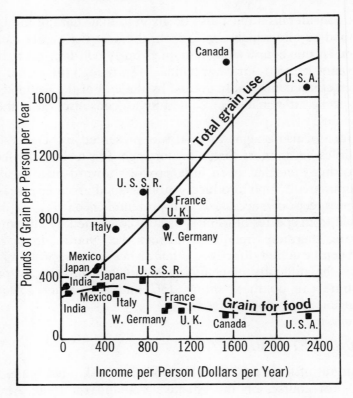

FIGURE 2

Income and per capita grain consumption, total and for
food. Source: U.S.D.A.

sumption is consumed indirectly in the form of meat, milk, and eggs.
When incomes reach a high level, other factors become very
important. Table 1 gives the per capita consumption of some major
food commodities.

Americans are eating much more beef and poultry. In the case
of beef, the reason seems principally status, since prices have risen
steadily. For poultry, it is difficult to separate out the effects of
income from those of price, since the efficient new modes of production have led to the costs of poultry being halved in a generation.

Recent history has been marked by a move from active to more
sedentary jobs, from farms to cities and from blue- to white-collar

occupations. This has had a strong effect on food tastes. In 1965, for example, the average urban dweller consumed 3,131 calories, as opposed to 3,620 for his rural counterpart. This has been associated with other trends. A man who sits down at work all day drinks less milk (milk consumption reached a peak of 350 pounds per capita a year in 1950, and has been declining ever since, dropping to 286 pounds in 1967). Consumption of eggs has declined almost 20 per cent since 1950. One reason for this is the tendency of white-collar workers to substitute a coffee break for breakfast. This hypothesis is supported by the declining consumption of manufactured cereal products.

We can expect these trends toward consumption of smaller quantities of some foods to continue for some time as the movement into white-collar jobs goes on. Poultry consumption, on the other hand, should continue to grow as chicken and turkey meats enjoy relative price advantages. But beef consumption will be dependent upon productivity in that industry. The factors likely to bear on this are discussed below.

In general, over the years, the American consumer has proved to be remarkably flexible in his eating habits, responding to price advantages and to the changing requirements of his job situation. He spends less than 17 per cent of his income on food (a smaller proportion than in any other nation). Yet he eats well—perhaps too well in the sense of being overweight.

TABLE 1

Per Capita United States Consumption of Major Food Commodities (in pounds per year)

Commodity	1940	1950	1960	1965	1968
Beef (carcass wt.)	55	63	85	99	109
Pork (carcass wt.)	74	69	65	58	65
Eggs (number)	319	389	334	314	318
Chicken (ready to cook)	14	21	28	33	36
Total milk fat solids	32	29	24	23	21
Total fresh fruit	139	109	93	81	77
Flour	155	135	118	113	109

TECHNOLOGICAL REPLACEMENTS IN THE LIVESTOCK INDUSTRY

It is helpful to look ahead at future food requirements and consequent claims against our agricultural resources in terms of per capita grain requirements. As noted earlier, the average American requires some 1,600 pounds of grain yearly, all but 150 pounds or so of it for consumption in the form of meat, milk, and eggs (Figure 2). Obtaining fat and high-quality protein in the form of livestock products is costly in terms of the resources required. Harrison Brown suggests that the United States livestock industry is a gigantic welfare society returning only 10 per cent of the energy invested in it in foodstuffs. There is, thus, a strong temptation for the food industry and the food technologist to find shortcuts.

Two of the earliest successful shortcuts were the development of oleomargarine as a substitute for butter and the commercial production of hydrogenated vegetable shortenings as substitutes for lard. The net effect of these advances in food technology was a change in the character of both dairy and hog production. High fat content in milk became less desirable and hog breeds shifted from the fat, lard-type animals to the more lean, bacon types.

Needless to say, these shortcuts have profoundly affected consumption patterns. In 1940, the average American consumed seventeen pounds of butter and two pounds of margarine (Table 1). By 1968, butter consumption had dropped to six pounds and margarine had climbed to eleven pounds. The decline in butter consumption was closely paralleled by a decline in lard consumption from fourteen to six pounds. On a national scale, the effect of this substitution of vegetable oils for animal fats has greatly reduced the agricultural resources required to meet consumption needs for this category of foods.

Food technologists are now turning their talents to the development of vegetable-derived substitutes for milk itself. Imitation milks are now beginning to make inroads into the fluid milk market, particularly in the southwestern United States. Consumption of fluid milk, declining from 350 pounds per person in 1940 to 286 pounds in 1968, will likely continue to decline for some time into the future.

Recent data indicate that 65 per cent of the whipped toppings and

35 per cent of the coffee lighteners purchased by United States consumers are of nondairy origin. The combination of declining milk consumption and rising output of milk per cow has reduced the number of dairy cows from twenty-six million in 1940, to fifteen million in 1969. The net effect of these shifts in consumption habits is a decline in agricultural resource requirements.

Thus far, most of the replacement of animal by vegetable products has been limited to animal fats. But, more recently, it has begun to shift to animal protein. A vegetable-derived product designed to substitute for bacon has met with considerable commercial success over the past year. Ironically, soybeans produced in Iowa will be converted into a baconlike product in a processing plant being constructed in Cedar Rapids, side by side with corn being converted into bacon by more conventional means on nearby farms.

One of the obstacles to the development of acceptable substitutes for beef, ham, or poultry was the difficulty in replicating the texture of these items. With the discovery of a technique for spinning vegetable proteins into fibers which can then be pressed together, colored, and flavored to simulate steak, ham, or poultry, the way has been opened for the substitution of vegetable for animal protein on a rather massive scale. How rapidly this replacement proceeds will depend, among other things, on the quality of the simulated products and their relative cost.

This technological breakthrough may mean that our grandchildren will visit a zoo rather than a farm to see cows and pigs. Should this substitution of vegetable-derived products for those traditionally coming from livestock continue, it will greatly reduce the land, water, and other resources needed to satisfy food needs.

PETROLEUM INDUSTRY SUBSTITUTES FOR FARM PRODUCTS

By far the largest single substitution of a nonfarm product for a farm product occurred when agriculture was mechanized. The replacement of horse power with tractor power resulted in the substitution of gasoline and, later, diesel fuel for oats, hay, and other feedstuffs for horses. The capacity of the internal combustion engine to release the solar energy captured by plants and stored underground in the form of petroleum for millions of years has made possible the substitution of petroleum fuels for the feed products of some ninety million acres of cropland.

What is not yet widely appreciated is that the petroleum industry may be on the verge of another technological breakthrough with even greater implications for conventional agriculture. The feasibility of using petroleum as a feedstock for single-cell organisms, such as yeast, which can then be used for livestock feed or human food, is being intensively researched by more than a score of international petroleum companies. Many technical problems bearing on both acceptability as a human food and production costs remain to be solved, but, overall, the technology appears to be advancing.

British Petroleum began construction of a single-cell protein plant in France in 1969. This plant, scheduled to come onstream in 1971, is expected to produce 16,000 tons of feed-grade protein per year. In both the Soviet Union and Japan, where feedstuffs are costly, investments are being made in production facilities. I am told the Japanese are planning to have three plants, with a total yearly protein production of 100,000 tons, in production by the end of 1971.

Whether or not this innovation will eventually provide important competition for conventional agriculture on a global basis remains to be seen. All that can be said now is that technology seems to be advancing in the field. The significant thing is that chemists have discovered another means of tapping the photosynthesis of eons ago, making it competitive with contemporary agriculture.

American cattlemen have adopted a novel compromise between traditional and unconventional technologies in the production of beef, the most popular source of animal protein in American diets. They are feeding urea, commonly used as a nitrogen fertilizer, to cattle as a means of reducing the need for protein concentrates and, thus, lowering the costs of beef production. In 1968, some 300,000 tons of urea were fed to cattle in the United States, more than is used as fertilizer in many countries. Microorganisms in the rumen combine the nitrogen and carbohydrates to form protein, which the cattle can then absorb. By feeding urea, farmers can reduce the protein content of other rations and rely heavily on low-cost roughage, such as cornstalks, corncobs, straw, and even sawdust. (To make them palatable, the roughages are combined with molasses.)

Where there is an adequate supply of roughage in the United States, as in the corn belt, feeding urea to cattle significantly reduces the cost of beef production. But this method should result in even greater economies in the tropics, where low-cost roughage can be produced easily all year round.

STRUCTURAL CHANGES IN UNITED STATES AGRICULTURE

Technological changes in United States agriculture have led to vast structural changes in the farming community, which have in turn, created stresses throughout the society. Some notion of the magnitude of the revolution is indicated by the fact that in 1934 the United States farm population reached a peak of over thirty-two million people. By 1967, that figure had fallen below eleven million. Nearly a million people a year are leaving agricultural employment, the majority of them going to the cities. Some 300 farms go out of business each day. This great trek is altering the population balance between town and country, and between the states of the Great Plains and those in the coastal areas. Social problems on a huge scale have been created by this transfer of people into urban situations for which they are unprepared either culturally or vocationally. It is these problems which are at the heart of the urban crisis.

We can expect these trends to continue, at least for some time, for obvious reasons: the incomes of farm families are far below those of the population as a whole, and there are significant returns from scale to be gained from raising the average size of a farming unit.

It is perhaps not very fruitful to speculate about the likely numbers of farmers and farm people by the end of the century. We can, however, say with virtual certainty that the number of farms will continue to decline and that the size of farms will increase significantly. More farms will enter the category of being "million-dollar-plus" sales organizations, and more will be corporations themselves or owned by corporations, in order to provide the large amounts of capital required for modern farming operations (the average value of a farm's land and buildings increased by a factor of nine between 1940 and 1964).

Nearly a third of farms are worked on a part-time basis. If land prices and the costs of farming continue to rise, it is likely that a very large number of these units will cease to exist: in the five years between 1959 and 1964, some 300,000 farm enterprises ceased to function. Of the 2.2 million commercial farms in 1964, the 60 per cent comprising the smaller ones earned only 16 per cent of the total farm income. The great majority of these farmers will be

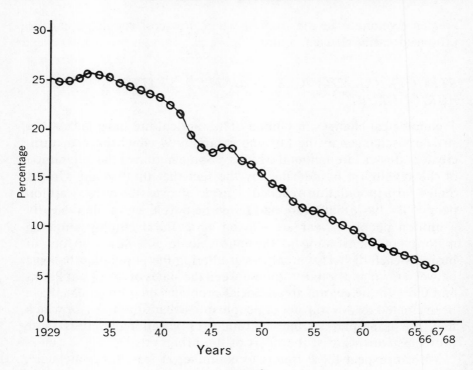

FIGURE 3
Farm population as percentage of total United States
population. Source: U.S.D.A. agricultural statistics,
1967–1968.

squeezed out of farming in the coming decades. It is essential that adequate retraining and relocation be provided for these farm people.

One interesting feature of the enlargement of farms is likely to be the slowing of the steep downward trend in hired labor on farms, and possibly even its reversal. Between 1964 and 1969, the number of hired workers fell by 50 per cent. As very big farming operations develop, they are increasingly likely to be owned by partners or by corporations, and to employ a manager and hired labor rather than to rely on family labor.

UNITED STATES AGRICULTURAL POLICIES AGGRAVATE ENVIRONMENTAL CRISES

The United States has faced two distinct types of ecological crises with their origins in agriculture. The first reached its zenith during the dust bowl of the 1930s. It was the result of overplowing. More and more grassland was cleared of its natural cover until wind and erosion of soils reached a critical dimension. Dust-laden air masses moving eastward until they blotted out the sun over Washington stimulated an alarmed Congress into action and led to the creation of the Soil Conservation Service.

Since that time, we have learned how to deal rather effectively with soil erosion. The fallowing of some twenty million acres of wheat land each year in the Great Plains, combined with the planting of windbreaks and adoption of other conservation practices, put an end to the dust-bowl era. Fortunately, we had enough slack in our system to permit this large acreage of land to be fallowed. Many over-populated poor countries today face a similar situation but cannot afford to fallow land because of population pressure.

The second ecological crisis with its root partly in agriculture is the pollution of our environment. As American agricultural production becomes more intensive and more agricultural chemicals are used, environmental pollution worsens. Pesticides, animal wastes, and compounds of phosphorus and nitrogen originating in fertilizers are all pollutants. The last two primarily affect water: both the quality of our water supply and the complex of plant and animal life inhabiting our lakes and inland waterways.

A growing problem is runoff from areas contaminated by livestock and poultry wastes, and particularly from feedlots. The overall annual production of livestock wastes has been estimated at more than 1.5 billion tons, or twenty times that of the human population. Most of this waste is disposed of by spreading on the land, which allows the nitrates to run off into local water supplies. The concern over the growing amount of nitrates in water is due, in part, to their role as nutrients for algae and other water plants in inland lakes and waterways. But at least as important is the health danger from nitrates in ground water. Both infants and livestock have become ill and sometimes died from drinking water containing nitrates, which causes methemoglobinemia in infants.

The problems of nitrate pollution are aggravated by the increasing use of fertilizers on farms. In 1940, less than two million tons of fertilizers were used in the United States; by 1965, this had risen to twelve million tons (Table 2). About half of this increase was due to the expanding use of nitrogen fertilizer; the remaining half was rather equally divided between the other two plant nutrients, phosphate and potash. Phosphates, like nitrates, also act as nutrients

TABLE 2

Quantities of Primary Plant Nutrients in United States
Fertilizers, 1940–1965 (in thousands of tons)

	Nitrogen	Available Phosphoric Oxide	Potash
1940	419	912	435
1945	701	1556	807
1950	1237	2110	1381
1955	1933	2247	1875
1960	3030	2645	2169
1965	5328	3896	3221

for water plants. In most localities it is not known precisely whether fertilizers, livestock or human wastes, or nitrates formed naturally in soils are the major sources of danger to natural water systems.

Pesticides which are not bio-degradable, and which are potentially harmful to various forms of life, including man, are the chief causes of concern. The United States production of pesticides was 1,159,-793,000 pounds in 1968, up 35 per cent from 1965. About one-third of this was exported, and the rest used domestically. Eighty per cent of total production consisted of synthetic organic compounds, which are the most important pesticides both in terms of rate of growth of use and of potential for contaminating the environment.

The long-term consequences of accumulating nondegradable pesticides such as DDT, and some of its even-more potent relatives such as dieldrin, in the biosphere are not fully known. We do know that the reproductive capacity of some predatory birds and fishes is being destroyed at relatively low environmental concentrations of chlorinated hydrocarbons. Several species are threatened with extinction. The DDT content of mothers' milk in the United States is now well above that permitted in commercial foods by the Food and Drug Administration. The pressing question here is what are the long-term effects of rising DDT concentrations in the environment on human health and well being. Until this question can be answered more confidently than at present, it would seem wise to use such potent chemicals with the greatest discretion, if at all.

What is sorely needed is greater knowledge of the effects of various agricultural chemicals now so widely used, including pesticides and nitrates, on all forms of human metabolism. And, with only slightly less urgency, we need to know how the many other species making up the complex web of life in our biosphere will be affected. Without much more knowledge than we now have, it may be difficult even to develop safe alternative practices.

Those United States farm policies that divert land from production in order to avoid overproduction are unintentionally aggravating the environmental crisis by encouraging the more intensive use of agricultural chemicals. If our farm policies were being formulated by ecologists—rather than by economists and politicians as has always been the case—one can be certain they would be quite different. Rather than diverting land from use to balance supply and demand, an ecologist would likely permit farmers to crop as much land as they wish, as long as it did not result in erosion. A tax would then be placed on fertilizers—at least nitrate fertilizers—and harmful pesticides. The tax on these items would be raised and lowered as needed to balance supply and demand. The net effect of such an approach would be to provide an adequate supply of food, as at present, while minimizing adverse effects on the environment.

The same technological capability which created the agricultural production methods that led to these threats to various life forms, including man, can also provide solutions, if given the resources. Among the possibilities in the pipeline that may help us to have our cake *and* eat it are chemical pesticides that are specific to particular insects, diseases, and weeds without affecting other organisms; other pesticides that are relatively nontoxic and bio-degradable; and, somewhat further in the future, the possibilities of extending biological controls to a much wider group of pests.

CONCLUSIONS

In considering the question of what is the optimal population level as far as food supplies are concerned, it is important that we ask the right questions. The relevant question is no longer, "Can we produce enough food?" but, "What are the environmental consequences of doing so?" Unfortunately, although, from a technological standpoint, we can produce more than enough food, the ecological consequences of doing so are only beginning to appear. If we succeed in producing more than enough food, but destroy our environment in the process, what will be gained?

At present, it seems clear that American agriculture is inherently unstable from a technological point of view. We cannot continue using current farming practices and technologies indefinitely without endangering many forms of life, including, quite possibly, man himself. Adjustments will have to be made—but exactly what adjustments or how costly they will be we do not know. Based on our lack of technical understanding of the consequences of some of the technologies used to achieve our vaunted levels of productivity, and on our unwillingness to foot the bill for correcting them once we recognize some of the dangers in pursuing them, I conclude that we have already, at some time in the past, exceeded our optimum population level in the United States. In this light, arguments for the stabilization of United States population growth, on a nation-wide basis, appear increasingly relevant.

FURTHER READINGS

Brown, L. R. *Seeds of Change.* New York: Frederick A. Praeger, Inc., 1970.

Resources and Man. Committee on Resources and Man, division of Earth Sciences, National Academy of Sciences—National Research Council. San Francisco: W. H. Freeman and Co., Publishers, 1969.

Agricultural Statistics 1968. Washington, D.C.: United States Department of Agriculture, 1968.

Farmers World: Yearbook of Agriculture 1964. Washington, D.C.: United States Department of Agriculture, 1964.

Wittwer, Sylvan. *Maximizing Agricultural Production,* journal article 4855. Michigan Agricultural Experiment Station (1969).

World Food Problem. Report of the President's Science Advisory Committee, Washington (1967).

Agriculture as a Force in Determining the United States Optimum Population Size

William C. Paddock

ABSTRACT

Agriculture is a powerful force in determining the optimum population size of the United States. In addition to its obvious contribution
of food and fiber, agriculture provides employment for over twenty-
three million Americans involved with various agribusinesses—plus
five million farmers. It is a major foreign exchange earner and will
continue to play a role in our foreign policy via food diplomacy.
Today's level of agricultural production cannot be achieved without
the use of pollutants (nitrates and phosphates from fertilizers, and
pesticides). To maintain this production, the use of pollutants will
increase in the future when there will be less land on which to farm
than there is today. Because United States agriculture cannot fulfill
its various functions without the use of pollutants detrimental to
future generations, one must conclude that the optimum population
size for the United States is *less* than its current 205 million people.

Nine blind men, each touching a part of an elephant, end up with
nine different impressions of the animal. The man feeling the trunk
decides that the elephant is like a snake; the one with the leg says
it is like a tree, etc. A Symposium on the question of "Is there an

optimum level of population?" which is broken into nine sections could well end up with the same distorted view of the problem as the nine blind men with the elephant.

We all know that the sections of this Symposium (Energy, Environmental Quality, Food, Health Services, and Educational Services) are interrelated. Similarly, this section on food cannot be considered without recognizing its source: our nation's agriculture. Agriculture is far more than just a food- or fiber-producing activity on the part of our farm community. The former head of the United Nations' Food and Agriculture Organization, B. R. Sen, used to say, "Food and water are inseparable." In the United States economy, food and industry, food and transportation, food and education, food and foreign exchange, as well as food and foreign policy are all inseparable. Agriculture is a powerful force in determining the size of our optimum population.

We are proud that today the American family uses only 17 per cent of its income for food, that our average farmer produces enough to supply agricultural products to thirty-five Americans plus over six people abroad. However, while only five million of our labor force actually are farmers, these farmers are backed up by an army of over twenty-three million Americans involved in one way or another with agribusiness—manufacturing and selling fertilizer and vitamins for chickens, exporting grain, processing food, etc.[1] Thus, our farm economy involves over 30 per cent of our working population.

One is blind if he looks only at the food-producing capabilities of our farms to determine the optimum population of our country. Our farms represent a sizable portion of our economy. They also consume an enormous amount of material and are responsible for enormous amounts of pollutants—all of which have an additional impact on our population.

AGRICULTURE AS A MATERIAL-CONSUMING ACTIVITY: WATER

America uses daily the equivalent of 1,500 gallons of water per person—of which half goes to agriculture in the form of irrigation. Industry uses a slightly smaller amount—and of this, the agribusiness industries are extravagant consumers. To produce a ton of fertilizer takes 150,000 gallons of water; to process a ton of edible oil, an industrial plant uses 35 tons of water. To grow a ton of cotton on irrigated land requires 800,000 gallons of water.[2]

Already we face a water crisis that threatens to limit economic growth, undermine living standards, endanger health, and jeopardize national security. According to a number of government reports, we live on the edge of water bankruptcy. The threat of bankruptcy will clearly affect the ability of our farm land to produce.

AGRICULTURE AS A MATERIAL-CONSUMING ACTIVITY: LAND

No commodity is of greater value in this world than *good* farm land. The United States has been blessed with more of it than any other country in the world. However, every year there is less of this valuable commodity. We take five million acres of land out of production each year for roads, airports, and cities. Unfortunately, cities use *prime* land since most cities originated as agricultural centers. Roads generally don't follow ridges but valley bottoms. It is incorrect to believe that our nation can deal effectively with soil erosion. We may have learned how, but we are not practicing enough of what we have learned. Over 60 per cent of United States crop land is today in need of conservation treatment—of which 37 per cent needs erosion control.[3]

Without additional conservation practices, the amount of cultivated land in the United States will continue to decrease annually. However, with conservation practices, the amount of cultivated land will still decrease because many conservation practices remove land from production through forestation and pasture programs. This fact becomes a concern because even if we could increase our production by 50 per cent during the next ten years—which is unlikely—the United States would still need 300 million acres of crop land for our agricultural needs. Since we now have only 335 million, the current rate of land use for purposes other than agriculture will bring us well below this 300 million figure.[4]

Do not be overly optimistic about the land in our soil bank. Much of the 47 million acres so set aside should never be put back into cultivation again because its quality is either marginal or submarginal. It represents the hills of New England and Appalachia, the poorly drained spots of Iowa farms, etc. Of course, it contains some good land, but farmers retire their poorest land, not their best.

Some have used statistics—such as those showing that the Netherlands produces seventy-one bushels of wheat to the acre while the
United States average is twenty-five bushels, or figures which show
that Canada has higher corn yields than does the United States—to
conclude that there is slack in United States productivity. This conclusion is inaccurate. Such higher yields are due to the use of *only*
prime acreage.

Agriculture is considered a renewable resource. But how renewable
is it? We are unable to stop the encroachment of the city onto our
agricultural land and it is unlikely that we will ever see a cement
slab removed so that the land stolen by a highway can be returned
to its original agricultural use.

Like it or not, any future optimum population must live on less
land than we now have available for agriculture.

AGRICULTURE AS A WASTE-PRODUCING ACTIVITY

The United States Department of Health, Education and Welfare's
first study in *Toward a Social Report* says that available evidence
suggests "that resource scarcity has not posed a threat to American
economic growth over the last 60 years, nor is it likely to over the
next 50 years." While the industrialist may take some satisfaction
from that statement, the agriculturalist must be concerned over the
report's following sentence: "The same cannot be said of the new
type of scarcity: nature's limited capacity to absorb wastes."[5]

If the outcry that has been growing steadily since the publication
of Rachel Carson's *The Silent Spring* continues, we can expect future
public reaction to depress agricultural production. Twentieth-century
agriculture pours an ever-growing number of pollutants into our
environment.

Nine hundred million pounds of pesticides are now used annually.
While 1969 saw a ban on the use of DDT, other insecticides—dieldrin, aldrin, chlordan, and toxaphen, which are twenty-
five times more toxic, and endrin, which is fifty times more toxic
than DDT—are not banned. Without today's pesticides our farmers
could not produce the food they do.

Meat production is becoming more and more of an assembly-line
operation. Consequently, many see future Americans continuing to
have steak whenever they want it. But the feeding and processing

of meat animals will, like the use of pesticides, become a matter of ever-greater public concern. A feedlot raising 10,000 head of cattle produces about the same sewage disposal problem as a city with a population of 165,000.[6] Today we have eleven million cattle on feedlots in the United States—producing a sewage problem not unlike that of fifty-five Chicagos!

Increased agricultural production will, in addition to pesticides, require greater use of fertilizers. Already there is a growing awareness and preoccupation over the runoff from farm lands of nitrates and phosphates. The large-scale use of fertilizers has, in some areas of the United States, increased the water-pollution problem, causing toxicants which have jeopardized human health.[7] The problem is already of considerable concern in the San Joaquin Valley. So far, no economical process for removing nitrates or nitrogen compounds from the water has been developed, and dissolved phosphates can be removed only at great cost by alum coagulation.[8]

UNITED STATES AS A WORLD FORCE

But back to the blind man and the elephant. To consider what our optimum population size should be only on the basis of our nation's domestic problems is to feel the elephant's tail and call the animal a broom.

The United States uses nearly one-half of the world's nonrenewable resources. She does not produce them all by any means. She buys them from the developed and undeveloped world and she is able to do so because of the size of her exports—20 per cent of which comes from her farms. To maintain our way of life, then, United States agriculture must be able to continue earning foreign exchange. Our dependence on a number of foreign-sourced minerals is remarkably high (80 per cent of the bauxite we use, 97 per cent of the manganese, 65 per cent of the potash, 36 per cent of the iron ores and concentrates) and will increase. Department of the Interior projections show that United States use of metals and nonmetal minerals will grow by 300 per cent during the next thirty years.[9] It is true that the United States has enormous reserves of certain minerals, but many are found in low-grade ores. Thus, it is cheaper to import the minerals we need.

Like our steel, aluminum, and copper industries, some of our agricultural production is dependent upon foreign imports. For example, half of our poultry industry is based on low-cost fishmeal from Peru.

Thus, in order to continue to support our affluent society—which is dependent upon these relatively inexpensive imports—United States agriculture must continue to be a major earner of foreign exchange.

But that is not all.

The years ahead will see an increase in civil unrest in the Third World of Asia, Africa, and Latin America, with anarchy, military dictatorships, and revolution becoming a way of life in much of the area because the resources of each region are not sufficient to satisfy the needs of its growing population. Where a United States presence is needed, our "surplus" food exports can act as a short-term stabilizing force in the power struggles within the hungry nations.

The much-heralded "Green Revolution" is now only a hope and not a reality, and recurrent food shortages in the developing nations can be expected—if not due to their populations being too large for their agricultural capabilities, then due to periodic poor weather or disruption by civil unrest.

Right or wrong, it is highly likely that United States foreign policy will continue to find food diplomacy useful.

CONCLUSION

Our agriculture does much more than simply feed Americans. It is a major factor in supporting not only our standard of living but our position as a world leader. America's agriculture cannot fulfill this role without relying on fertilizers and pesticides. Because these fertilizers and pesticides are contaminating our environment, America's agriculture serves today's population to the detriment of future generations.

The conclusion is clear.

Based on the limitations of our agriculture, too many people now live in the United States. Our optimum population size is, therefore, less than our current 205 million people.

REFERENCES

1. "Food for Us All," *1969 Yearbook for Agriculture,* United States Department of Agriculture.

2. Georg Borgstrom, *Too Many* (New York: The Macmillan Company, 1969), p. 159.

3. Yatt Smith, *Conservation in America* (New York: Rand MacNally & Co., 1969).

4. Based on Table 4, p. 10, of "Fertilizer Use in the United States," AER No. 92 (May, 1966), Washington, D.C.: Dept. of Agriculture, and on table, p. 433, of *Agriculture Statistics 1968,* Washington, D.C.: United States Dept. of Agriculture, 1968.

5. *Toward a Social Report* (Washington, D.C.: United States Dept. of Health, Education and Welfare, 1969), p. 28.

6. *The Cost of Clean Water,* Vol. I (Washington, D.C.: United States Dept. of the Interior, 1968), p. 36.

7. Ruth Winter, *Poisons in Your Food* (New York: Crown Publishers, Inc., 1969), p. 156.

8. Murphey O. Finbar, *Governing Nature* (Chicago: Quadrangle Books, Inc., 1967), p. 169.

9. *Conservation Yearbook No. 2* (Washington, D.C.: United States Dept. of the Interior, 1968), p. 17.

Survival in the Environmental-Population Crisis

Barry Commoner

ABSTRACT

Human society is entering a crisis generated by the coincidence of two interpenetrating crises: the environmental crisis and the population crisis, which combine to threaten its survival. At what size will the earth's population optimize the possibility of humanely averting this crisis of survival?

The term "humane" is taken to mean that population is to be controlled voluntarily. Thus, by optimizing with regard to a moral factor, amongst others, a minimum optimal population size is determined, namely that size to which population is likely to have grown by the time humane methods of population control have achieved their ends.

Sociological and demographic literature describes the demographic transition which has governed population size in industrialized countries: (a) Food production was sufficiently high to provide adequate national nutrition; (b) there was an extended period of rapid industrial growth; (c) expectations for improved quality of life were high. Given these conditions, an initial drop in death rates is followed, within the span of a generation, by a drop in birthrates bringing the nations near a stable population size. Humane survival of the dual crises requires that the demographic transition occur in the developing nations, while the industrialized ones pay the "debt to nature," resulting from environmental degradation. The latter will require an immense reconstruction of agricultural and industrial technology, in the next generation. If the economic conditions necessary for a world-wide demographic transition are achieved by then, theoretically the world population should peak at eight billion in the early twenty-first century. It is estimated that an outlay of $1,000 billion will be necessary between 1970 and 1980 to achieve the necessary world-wide economic growth for supporting the nutrition necessary for a demographic transition; this must be achieved by environmentally sound methods.

Due to the limited capacity of the earth to produce food without the destruction of the ecological cycles of the soil and the water, it is probable that the earth can only produce enough sustenance for 8 billion people if that sustenance is equitably distributed. Equitable distribution of sustenance will probably necessitate revolutionary changes in the technological, social, and political structure of the world and its separate nations. In these terms, world-wide demographic transition appears to be within the reach of the world's material and technological resources.

While the demands on the industrial nations that will result from this effort will be massive, it should be noted that the industrial nations were able to achieve their demographic transition as a result of wealth obtained in no small measure through colonial exploitation of the very nations which are now experiencing intense population pressures. If these nations had been able to retain their resources, it is likely that they would be significantly closer to the economic conditions necessary for falling birthrates. Thus the required outlays by the western nations can be viewed as the repayment of a dual debt, to a mercilessly exploited world environment and to mercilessly exploited colonial nations.

THE CRISIS: DESTRUCTION OF THE ECOSYSTEM AND THE DWINDLING OF NATURAL RESOURCES

To determine the optimum size of the human population we need to decide first what feature of human life we wish to optimize. In the abstract, the choice might be made from among a wide range of conditions of value to human beings and involve the most complex moral, social, and political questions. However, in the reality of present circumstances this choice is very considerably simplified, for the current condition of the human population is such that one value dominates all others—the survival of human society.

In my view, human society is now entering a crisis of survival. This crisis is generated by the coincidence of two interpenetrating crises: the environmental crisis and the population crisis.

The immediate evidence of the environmental crisis is the widespread and rapidly intensifying pollution of the environment. In almost every case it can be shown that such pollution is indicative of self-perpetuating instabilities induced by the effects of modern technology on major segments of the ecosphere—the complex of physical, chemical, and biological processes which comprise the environment. Major problems of environmental pollution arise not out of some minor inadequacies in new technologies but because of the very success of these technologies in accomplishing their designed aims. A modern sewage-treatment plant causes algal overgrowths and resultant pollution *because* it produces, as it is designed to do, so much plant nutrient in its effluent, Modern, highly concentrated, nitrogen fertilizers result in the drainage of nitrate pollutants into streams and lakes because they succeed in the aim of raising the nutrient level of the soil. The modern high-compression gasoline engine contributes to smog and nitrate pollution *because* it successfully meets its design criterion—the development of a high level of power. Modern synthetic insecticides kill birds, fish, and useful insects *because* they are successful in being absorbed by insects, and killing them, as they are intended to do.[1]

Thus, technology is enormously successful in producing material goods, but too often it is disastrously incompatible with natural environmental systems. Yet, the survival of all living things (including man), the quality of life, and the continued success of all human activities (including technology, industry, and agriculture) depend on the integrity of the complex web of biological processes which comprise the earth's ecosystem. And what man is now doing on the earth violates this fundamental requisite of human existence. We are, in sum, in a crisis which threatens the suitability of the ecosphere as a place of human habitation—a crisis which threatens the survival of human society.

The population crisis is expressed, in its most general terms, by the growing disparity between the rate of increase in world population and the rate of increase in available food. As this divergence worsens we approach the possibility of widespread famine that threatens to engulf the greater part of the world's population. Moreover, there is the danger that hunger and starvation will, at some point, become self-perpetuating as they engender large-scale social disruptions and reduce the capability of the population to produce more food. Estimates of the time of this catastrophe vary; one observer sets the time as early as 1975[2] and others predict some point in the 1980s. Others expect increased food production and widespread introduction of contraceptives to avert the catastrophe completely.[3]

While it is also uncertain how much time remains before the environmental crisis brings major segments of the ecosphere past the point of no return, most estimates cover the same range as those given for world-wide famine. My own estimate is that we are unlikely to avoid environmental catastrophe by the 1980s unless we are able, by that time, to correct the *fundamental* incompatibilities of major technologies with the demands of the ecosystem. This means that we will need to put into operation essentially emissionless versions of automotive vehicles, power plants, refineries, steel mills, and chemical plants. Agricultural technology will need to find ways of sustaining productivity without breaking down the natural soil cycle or disrupting the natural control of destructive insects. Sewage- and garbage-treatment plants will need to be designed to return organic waste to the soil, where, in nature, it belongs. Vegetation will need to be massively reintroduced into urban areas. Housing and urban sanitary facilities will need to be drastically improved. In my view, unless these actions are taken in the 1980s, large-scale environmental disasters are likely to occur—at least in the highly developed regions of the world.

In sum—and probably within the next generation—we are in grave danger of a dual world-wide catastrophe which threatens to destroy the stability of the ecosystems on which we depend for food, oxygen, pure water, and suitable temperatures, while a rapidly growing population places increasing demands on the earth's dwindling and degraded natural resources. The two crises not only coincide but interpenetrate in a complex way; together they confront mankind with the threat of extinction or, at the least, with a gross deterioration in the level of human society.

POPULATION SIZE IN BALANCE WITH
THE ECOSYSTEM

In view of these considerations, I believe that we are required to state the basic question to which this symposium is addressed in the following terms: At what size will the earth's population optimize the possibility of averting the crisis of survival?

It is useful to begin a discussion of this question with purely biological considerations. Human beings are constituents of the world ecosystem, in which they represent a species of omnivorous animal. Considered only in these simple biological terms—i.e., devoid of the effects of technology and other features of advanced human societies—the size of the human population becomes rigorously determined, and is not subject to any such voluntary control as optimization. This situation is approached most closely in primitive hunting and gathering societies; here, the population size is determined by the relations between man and the ecosystem and by the effects of physical environmental factors. However, social controls on population growth intervene as well.

Food required by human beings is generated by ecological systems in the soil, fresh waters, and the ocean. In each of these systems there exists a natural cycle of biological processes: green plants absorb solar energy and convert inorganic nutrients (principally carbon dioxide, nitrates, and phosphates) into organic matter; the latter serve as the original nutritive source for a food chain of animal species; organic waste—the bodies of plants, animals, and man, and excreted products—is returned to the soil or water; in turn, a series of microorganisms convert organic materials to inorganic products (in the soil, organic matter is stored in a slowly degrading form as humus); the inorganic products are nutrients for plants, thereby completing the cycle.

The dynamic properties of such a cycle determine the rate at which nutrients can be passed through the human population which participates in it, and in a primitive system this rate fixes the average size of the population that can be sustained by a given ecosystem. The overall cyclical rate is largely regulated by the rate of the slowest process in the sequence. In soil, this is usually the rate of release of inorganic nutrients from humus; since this is a rather slow process (the half life of humus is of the order of one hundred years) compared with the rate of organic degradation in aquatic systems, the latter have a larger intrinsic rate constant.

It is also relevant that these cycles are subject to complex feedback processes which maintain the stability of the system as a whole. Hence, a stress delivered to any given point in the system, if too severe, will destroy the stability of the whole system. For example, in aquatic systems, an overburden of organic materials will consume the available oxygen (microbial degradation of organic materials is an oxidative process and the organisms require molecular oxygen), so that the microbial organisms of decay cannot survive, and the cycle as a whole breaks down. In the same way, an overburden of nutrients causes an overgrowth of algae which quickly die, releasing excess organic material, again causing the system to break down. Similar feedback mechanisms govern the stability of soil ecosystems. These effects mean that there is an intrinsic limit to the rate at which these fundamental food-producing systems can operate—a limitation which places a major constraint on the human population that can be sustained by the earth's ecosystem.

In a primitive system the human population is also directly subject to the negative effects of animal predators, pathogenic organisms, and the rigors of the physical environment. The overall size of the human population is the resultant of the nutrition derived from the ecosystem and of the foregoing negative agents. The rate of change in the population is given by the difference between the birth rate and the mortality rate; these rates are based on the intrinsic fertility of the species, its natural life span, and by the effects of available nutrition and the intensity of negative environmental influences. It should be added that the environmental factors which influence a population are subject to variation in time (for example, the outbreak of a microbial epidemic or of unusual weather conditions). Fluctuations in the intensity of these factors, and in the natural productivity of the ecosystem, induce variations in the constituent populations of the system, including man. Hence, the stability of a population will also be determined by its genetic heterogeneity, for this is the source of unusual genetic endowments which may be important in surviving strong excursions in environmental conditions.

In the last few thousand years, nearly all human populations have departed from the primitive, ecosystem-determined condition, through the development of agriculture and other forms of productive technology. As a result, the ecological base available for the nutrition of most human populations has been greatly enlarged. Cultivation has replaced wild, nonnutritive plants with food crops; domestication has enhanced the yield of animal food; fishing vessels have extended the photosynthetic base of human nutrition into the sea. At the same time, technology has protected the species from the ravages of the weather and from many of the assaults of pathogens. These effects have also minimized fluctuations in human population in response to environmental factors. The general result is well known—the vast, exponential rise in the human population of the earth.

POPULATION SIZE TO OPTIMIZE SURVIVAL

We can turn now to the specific task of estimating the changes in the size of the human population which might optimize our possibility of surviving the massive threat represented by the dual environmental-population crisis. The problem involves a wide range of processes and effects—all of which interact to influence population size—in several major areas: the biology of agricultural systems, human biology, technology, productive economy, sociology, and politics. As we face this complex net of interrelated processes, the operational question which arises is: At what point can we introduce the resources and effort available to us with the best hope of preventing the impending catastrophe?

One possibility is to attack the problem on its basic biological ground—human fertility—and to direct the primary effort toward an immediate reduction in birth rate through the use of widespread contraception. A rationale which supports this view is that the growing excess in population relative to available food and other necessary resources debilitates the capability of the human population to increase the necessary food and resources, so that this feedback cycle needs to be interrupted directly at the point of the birth rate.[4]

This approach has already been tested, at least in some parts of the world. In recent years, campaigns designed to popularize various methods of birth control and to make available acceptable contraceptive methods have been undertaken. Generally, they have failed to bring about a significant decline in birth rate, so that, in the less developed nations of the world, the gap between the growth of the population and the increase in available food continues to widen.[5]

On the other hand, it is evident that a number of populations have passed through a period of rapid growth, based on increased agricultural and industrial productivity, and have proceeded through a demographic transition to a relatively stable population size. This has occurred in most of the populations of western Europe, Hungary, Rumania, Poland, to some extent in the United States, and most recently in Japan. In these populations, the following conditions prevailed: food production was sufficiently high to provide adequate nutrition for most of the population; industrial productivity grew rapidly over an extended period of time; expectations of an improving quality of life were, therefore, also high; the availability of contraceptive methods was quite variable and in the earlier demographic transitions did not include modern techniques such as hormone pills and intrauterine devices.[6]

Analysis of these experiences has led a number of observers to conclude that the accomplishment of the demographic transition from a rapidly growing population to a stable one is not achieved by the *direct* intervention of birth control, but through a far more complex series of processes.[7] The detailed data which support this conclusion are based on experience in highly- or moderately-developed nations. However, less complete evidence indicates that a similar process has occurred in Ceylon, Mauritius, British Guiana, and Puerto Rico. (In any case there is as yet no evidence of a nation which has achieved a stable population by some other means.) In all of these cases, it appears that the decline in the rate of population growth is *not* due to an increased mortality rate, but is, in fact, *always preceded by a decline in mortality rate*. In general, the pattern of the demographic transition has been characterized by: an initially high rate in both births and mortality; a subsequent decrease in mortality rate—due to improvement in medical services and the greater availability of food and other goods and social security—and a consequent rise in population; a later decrease in birth rate sufficient to counterbalance the reduced mortality rate and thus stabilize population size.

Analysis of the factors involved in these events indicates that a willingness to reduce the birth rate is predicated on living conditions sufficiently good to enhance the expectation of the survival of children, family size being determined by the desire for sufficient surviving children (especially sons) to ensure the family's security.[8] Because of this factor—and the added effect of social security systems which lessen the need for surviving children to support aging parents—most sociologists are convinced that the voluntary desire to limit births is dependent on a high and stable standard of living, which is necessarily accompanied by a low mortality rate. Thus Fredricksen concludes, from a detailed study of fertility and mortality in a number of populations in both developed and developing nations, that: ". . . a reduction in death rate would seem to be a necessary, if not sufficient, condition for a deliberate reduction in the birth rate, whether by spontaneous family planning or national population policy, regardless of economic system, political ideology, or religious doctrine." [9]

Similarly, Spengler concludes, from an analysis of the motives behind restriction of fertility, that: "A first step to the effective control of fertility in underdeveloped countries is the gradual introduction of a social security system for those over 65 years of age, for instance."

According to Spengler it is the failure to take this initial step that accounts for the pessimistic assessment by the United Nations Secretariat of recent efforts to limit births in underdeveloped countries.

"The launching of new countries upon the transition from high to low fertility seems to have been temporarily halted; with a few possible exceptions, there is little sign of decided downward trends having been begun in the remaining countries of high fertility." [5]

If, as indicated by initial evidence, these considerations are applicable to demographic transitions in underdeveloped nations, we can now specify more precisely the conditions which would need to govern the stabilization of the world population—an event which is essential to survival, given the intrinsic limitations of the earth's ecosystem to support human life. If it is assumed that reduction in fertility within any national group ought to be *voluntary,* and not imposed on it from without (the significance of adopting this assumption is discussed below), then this process must proceed through steps which sufficiently enhance the standard of living and social security so as to motivate the use of available contraceptive methods. At the same time, of course, contraceptive methods must be made available, and the population sufficiently educated to use them. The last requirement, again, leads to the conclusion that a high standard of living must be attained.

If this course is followed, there is a necessary delay before the changed motivation of families for large numbers of children can influence the overall size of the population. The delay is occasioned by two factors: the time required from the inception of a program to improve living standards until it begins to have a noticeable effect on the motivation of individuals for reduced fertility; and the delay between the effect of a falling mortality rate and improved social security on the mores of the generation which first experiences them and the time at which these individuals reach reproductive age and begin to govern their fertility in accordance with this experience.[10] In effect, this means that a sociologically-determined (i.e., voluntary) reduction in population growth can only be accomplished after a delay of perhaps twenty to thirty years. Thus, if world-wide steps along these lines were taken now, population size would become stabilized, on the average, only at about the year 2000. It follows, then, that to avoid catastrophe the world population will need to be sustained—at a sufficient level of nutrition to avoid widespread famine—at the size that it will inevitably attain, given the present rate of growth, in approximately the year 2000.

These considerations help further to define my use of the term "optimum population." If one accepts, as the criterion for optimization, survival through the environmental-population crisis, then clearly there is some upper limit to the population, a limit established by the necessarily limited rate of turnover of the basic ecosystems that provide human beings with food and a suitable environment. On the basis of the considerations just described, there is, paradoxically, also a *lower* limit to the size of the world population which is likely to enable us to avert the crisis of survival. If the population is to be limited by the process characteristic of the demographic transitions which have thus far occurred in human history, then this lower limit is the size which the population will attain in twenty to thirty years following the initiation of the process—i.e., at about the year 2000, if it begins now. Since it may be considered to be unlikely that the earth can support a viable population above the level which would be attained, under the foregoing conditions, in the year 2000, the optimum population is also the maximum population. In effect, this viable level is dictated by the time involved in achieving a voluntary demographic transition—in other words it is too late to avert a population level lower than that which will probably be reached in the year 2000.

Estimates of the population in the year 2000 have been made by a number of authors;[11] the general conclusion is that if widespread starvation can be avoided the world population in 2000 will be between six and eight billion. This compares with an estimated world population of 3.3 billion in 1965. This, then, is the population we shall need to accommodate on the earth, for the sake of human survival, before voluntary control of the birth rate is likely to stabilize the size of the population.

On these grounds, the answer to the original question—What population size will optimize the possibility of surviving the crisis of survival?—is: six to eight billion, or about twice the present world population.

CAN WE SUPPORT AN "OPTIMUM" POPULATION?

This conclusion forces us to return to a consideration of the basic biological problem: Can the earth's ecosystem support a population which grows from its present size to six to eight billion before—hopefully—it begins to level off? The primary problem is, of course, food. If we consider only the total world food supply and ignore the gross disparity in food available to developed and developing nations, then, given that the *total* supply in 1965 was apparently sufficient to provide the world population with nutrition at approximately the FAO standard, the total world food supply will need to be at least doubled by 2000. However, if it is assumed that the present disparity between food available to populations in developed and developing countries is maintained (in the United States, for example, we produce about 11,000 calories of basic food per capita, whereas only about 2,000 to 2,500 calories per capita is needed to meet nutritional standards) then total world food production will need to be appreciably more than doubled.

Can the earth's ecosystem support at least twice the present food production without catapulting us into an ecological disaster through fatal stresses on the ecosystem? Unfortunately, no definite answer to this question can be given at this time. As I have indicated elsewhere,[12] even the present system of agriculture in the United States, and probably other countries as well, has already taxed the soil ecosystem so severely (through feedlots and the excessive use of fertilizer) as to cause major problems in water pollution. However, we are still poorly informed on the basis of the *natural* fertility of the soil, and it is probable that, at the expense of certain major economic readjustments, we could find ways to maintain and perhaps even improve present productivity without incurring further environmental degradation. Without taking into account such environmental problems, some observers have concluded that it should be possible for overall world food production to keep pace with population growth to the period 1985-2000.[3] Others have concluded that a doubling of world food production cannot be anticipated from an extension of present or foreseeable methods of food production, given the economic constraints which govern agricultural productivity and the oversupply (in biological terms) of food in the advanced nations.[13]

If most nations are to accomplish the demographic transition and if the world population is to become stabilized, the present disparity in the *availability* of food in developed and developing countries must be drastically reduced. At the same time, overall world food production will need to be brought as close as possible to twice its present level and the food available in developing countries increased by a much larger proportion (by a relatively large increase in their own food production and through the diversion of food and agricultural resources from the developed countries). Moreover, all of this must be accomplished by means of agricultural techniques which do not strain the ecosystem to the point of collapse, if we are to survive the *environmental* crisis.

On balance, it would appear that all these accomplishments lie within, but perhaps close to, the limits of the overall productivity of the world ecosystem. However, it is clear that if food actually *available* where it is needed—in the developing nations—is to be sufficient to these needs, major changes in the technology of food production and in distribution and economic constraints must occur.

Despite the uncertainties, a sense of the magnitude of the effort required to prevent famine during the necessary doubling of the world population can be gained from some isolated data. For example, Ehrlich and Holdren[13] calculate that, assuming that the proposed nuclear-powered "agro-industrial complexes" actually meet design specifications (which the authors seriously doubt), the initial investment cost for the construction of sufficient units to keep pace with the growth of the world population would be about $41 billion per year. This investment, together with operational costs, would need to be met during the total period, perhaps 20-30 years in which the population increases—a sum probably in excess of $1,000 billion in all. Revelle[14] estimates that a total investment of $25 billion in the next fifteen to twenty-five years is needed to sustain the population of India alone; extrapolated to the total expected increase in world population in that period, this would represent a total required investment of about $125 billion. (The President's Science Advisory Committee on the world food problem[3] estimates a twenty-year investment of $17 billion. However, since United States aid to agriculture in underdeveloped countries was already operating at the rate of $.6 billion per year in 1967, with the population-food gap still widening, this estimate would appear to be excessively low.)

While costs of some hundreds of billions of dollars were being met in order to avert catastrophic famine, the developed countries themselves would simultaneously need to reorganize major segments of their own productive systems, along the lines indicated earlier, in order to avert their own environmental catastrophies.

These estimates, rough as they are, nevertheless suggest to me that in a nation such as the United States, a considerable fraction of the total productive capacity will need to be devoted to the task of averting the environmental crisis at home and of providing food abroad in the next twenty years. This will mean, in turn, a major reorganization of our national priorities; for example, it is difficult to see how the United States could maintain a $70–80 billion dollar per year military budget and also meet the aforementioned demands. It is also likely to require fundamental changes in the organization of our system of productivity. In particular, it seems likely that the dependence of our economy on constantly increasing environmental exploitation will need to be drastically reduced. In addition, if the economy is to be brought into harmony with the ecosystem which supports it, it will be necessary to accommodate the rate of economic exploitation to the natural turnover rate of the ecosystem itself. This means that the rate of return of economic investments into different sectors of the ecosystem will need to vary with their natural turnover rates—a principle which will probably generate considerable difficulty for our economic system.

I have introduced the foregoing observations in order to emphasize that the cost of averting the crisis of survival represents a huge accumulated debt compounded of our past follies in recklessly exploiting the natural ecological system which must sustain us. That this is true of environmental deterioration is almost self-evident, for environmental pollution clearly represents hidden costs imposed on the natural environment for the sake of an advantageous balance in the books of industrial and agricultural production enterprises.[15] As we now approach the probability of irreversible damage to the ecosystem which supports productivity, the huge accumulated debt must be paid, or we forfeit survival.

In the same sense, the cost we now face in stabilizing the world population is also an accumulated debt incurred over the last century through the exploitation of the human and natural resources of the underdeveloped world by the technologically advanced nations. This is the conclusion recently reached by Keyfitz[16] from an analysis of the effects of colonialism on the present population explosion in the developing nations. He argues that the development of industrial capitalism in Western nations in the period 1800–1950 resulted in the development of a one billion excess world population, largely in the tropics, as a result of exploitation of these areas for raw materials (with the resultant need for labor) during the period of colonialism. He argues further that after World War II modern technology replaced tropical raw materials with synthetic ones so that the technologically developed world ". . . again with no one's intention, rendered functionless in relation to its further self-enrichment almost all the populations of the tropics." Finally Keyfitz asserts, "In disregard of this change in their status, the tropical populations formed themselves into sovereign states and, benefitting from modern medicine, especially insecticides, further accelerated their increase in numbers."

These observations, whether or not accepted in detail, are sufficient to remind us of the intimate, functional connection between the development of modern technology and both the enrichment of the developed world and the population crisis of the underdeveloped world. In effect, the population crisis is the huge hidden cost of the wealth accumulated in the advanced nations as a result of the industrial revolution. If the advanced nations are now confronted with the urgent need to pay this long-delayed debt, there is at least the moral consolation that it is their own.

Thus, while I have been concerned in this paper with the consideration of an apparently biological question—the optimization of the size of the human population of the earth—I am led to conclude that both the causes of the present environmental-population crisis and the process that must be used to avert it are in the realm of political economy. The cause of the crisis is the massive technological, social, and political revolution which has built the modern advanced nations of the world. The cure, in my view, will necessitate equally revolutionary changes in the technological, social, and political structure of the world and its separate nations. This essential sym-metry between cause and cure is not complete. Whereas both the environmental and population crises are the largely unintended result of the exploitation of technological, economic, and political power, their cure must clearly be based on a conscious understanding of the limits of this power and on a thoughtful, designed program of action. This task, in its size, complexity, and urgency, is unprece-dented in human history.

Confronted by this enormous task it is natural to seek for easier solutions. Since the basic problems are themselves biological—the limitation of population growth and the maintenance of ecological balance—there is a natural tendency to short-circuit the complex web of economic, social, and political problems and find direct biological solutions, particularly for the population crisis. I am persuaded that such reductionist attempts would fail.

Suppose, for example, we were to adopt the solution to the popu-lation crisis urged on us by Paddock and Paddock.[17] They propose the application, to famine-threatened nations, of "triage"—a practice in military medicine which divides the wounded into three groups: those too seriously wounded to be saved, those who can be saved by immediate treatment, and those who can survive without treat-ment regardless of their suffering. The United States, for example, would decide which nations are too far gone along the road to famine to be saved and which are to be rescued by American aid. Apart from its, to me, abhorrent moral and political features, this scheme is a certain road to biological disaster. Famine breeds disease, and in the modern world, epidemics are rarely confined by national boundaries; the Paddock scheme would condemn the earth to a kind of biological warfare. Nor can we ignore the political consequences. What nation condemned to death by the very society that has, albeit blindly, brought it to its tragic condition would willingly refrain from retribution? The Paddock scheme would condemn not merely the "hopeless" nations, but the whole world to political chaos and war. And the first victim of this political degradation might be the United States itself, for to quote the authors of the triage scheme: "The weakness of triage lies in its implementation by a democratic gov-ernment like that of the United States." How long would this "weak-ness" last if the scheme were to be adopted?

Another biological attack on the population crisis is the proposal for enforced contraception, usually by means such as the introduction of chemical contraceptives into food. Apart from the moral issues involved in this approach and the huge risks involved in mass medical intervention into the complex physiology of reproductive hormones, there are other serious problems associated with it. If adopted in the absence of a massive, concerted effort to raise living standards, the scheme requires that a nation condemn itself to continued poverty—an unlikely event. If, on the other hand, the scheme includes the elevation of living standards, then it becomes reasonable only if it can be shown that there are literally insufficient resources on the earth to provide support to the developing nations adequate to sustain a voluntary demographic transition. However, the position that the total world resources are in fact inadequate is usually based on the assumption that many present economic and political constraints on the *distribution* of resources will be maintained. That these restraints are significant can be seen from a single example. At the present time the huge Peruvian fishing industry sends to advanced nations enough fish meal to provide for the total protein deficiency of Latin America. If nations, such as the United States, were willing to forgo the use of this fish meal to reduce the price of their poultry and livestock, it could be used to support voluntary demographic transition in Latin America. Thus, the enforced contraception scheme implies a choice which avoids the acceptance by the advanced nations of their long-delayed debt to the developing nations. Once the scheme is seen in this light, it is likely to become, if only for this reason, politically unfeasible not only on the part of the developing nations, but perhaps in the view of the citizens of the advanced nations as well.

These considerations suggest strongly that human society is capable of generating an internal process of population control; the process is based on the biological well-being of the population, and leads to the regulation of a basic biological factor, fertility. However, between the biological initiation and the biological end result, the process is mediated by a social factor, the awareness by the society of a satisfactory future, which motivates control of fertility. This intrinsic process of population control has been operative in the advanced nations, based on their rising standard of living. However, in the underdeveloped regions of the world, population has been regulated, not by internally controlled events, but by the intervention of an outside force—the advanced nations. This intervention has introduced into the underdeveloped areas of the world those factors which have a large positive effect on population growth, but the advanced nations have thus far failed to permit the development of the crucial factor which leads to a reduction in fertility—economic and social well-being.

The world is now confronted with a vast crisis of survival generated by the reckless way in which mankind has used the power of technology. The task of averting this crisis is, in my view, the gravest issue in human history. The immediate danger is that we will, even now, fail to grasp its nature, and will attempt to rectify the population crisis by perpetuating the very process which has generated it: external control of underdeveloped nations by advanced ones, this time by enforcing control of fertility. I am persuaded that we can avert the crisis of survival only if the huge debt incurred by the blind use of technological power—a debt which advanced nations owe to the integrity of the ecosystem and to the plight of the developing nations—is paid in terms which are consistent with the processes that control the stability of the ecosystem and with the processes that control the size of human populations. But time is rapidly running out.

REFERENCES

1. B. Commoner, "The Ecological Facts of Life." Paper presented at the Thirteenth National Conference sponsored by the United States National Commission for UNESCO, San Francisco, November 24, 1969.

2. P. R. Ehrlich, *The Population Bomb.* p. 36: "The battle to feed humanity is already lost, in the sense that we will not be able to prevent large-scale famines in the next decade or so." p. 44: "If the pessimists are correct, massive famines will occur soon, possibly in the early 1970s, certainly by the early 1980s. So far most of the evidence seems to be on the side of the pessimists, and we should plan on the assumption that they are correct" (New York: Ballantine Books, 1968).

3. The President's Science Advisory Committee, *The World Food Problem* (Washington, D.C.: Government Printing Office, May, 1967) Vol. II.

4. Ehrlich, *op. cit.*

5. J. J. Spengler, *Science,* 166, (December, 1969), p. 1234. Quoting *Population Bulletin of the United Nations,* No. 7 (1965), 1, 135, 150, 151.

6. H. Frederiksen, *Science* (November 14, 1969), pp. 00–00.

7. G. E. Immerwahr, *Demography,* 4 (1967), 710; T. Schultz, *A Family Planning Hypothesis: Some Empirical Evidence from Puerto Rico,* Agency Int. Develop. Mem. RM-5405-RC/AID (1967).

8. D. M. Meer and D. O. Smith, *Demography,* 5 (1968), 104.

9. H. Frederiksen, *Public Health Reports*, 81, 8 (August, 1966), 724.

10. S. Enke, *Quart. Jour. Economics*, 71, 1 (1957), 19.

11. Harrison Brown, *The Next Ninety Years* (Pasadena: California Institute of Technology, 1967); R. Revelle, in *Prospects of the World Food Supply* (Washington, D.C.: National Academy of Sciences, 1966); The President's Science Advisory Committee, *The World Food Problem*, Vol. II (Washington, D.C.: Government Printing Office, 1967). The highest estimate, 8 billion, is obtained by extending the 1965 results of the President's Science Advisory Committee. adding all their self-estimated errors to their figures. They admit a possible 200 million underestimate of 1965 population. Thus, starting from a population of 3.5 billion and assuming for 1965 to 2000 an intrinsic growth rate of 0.024, use of natural logs and the exponential population growth assumption yields a [year] 2000 population of 8,080 million. By comparison, Harrison Brown estimates as many as 7.5 billion.

12. B. Commoner, "The Ecological Problems Related to Public Policy." Presented at the Symposium on Public Policy Aspects of Environmental Improvement of the American Chemical Society, New York, September 9, 1969.

13. P. R. Ehrlich and J. P. Holdren, *BioScience* (December, 1969).

14. R. Revelle, "Population and Food Supplies: The Edge of the Knife," *Prospects of the World Food Supply* (Washington, D.C.: National Academy of Science, 1966).

15. B. Commoner, "The Social Significance of Environmental Pollution," *Jour. of Nat. Assoc. of Business Economists* (1970). Address to eleventh annual meeting of the National Association of Business Economists.

16. N. Keyfitz, *Journ. of Social Issues*, 23 (January, 1967), 62–78.

17. W. Paddock and P. Paddock, *Famine—1975!* (Boston: Little Brown, 1964).

Genetic and Evolutionary Considerations

Bentley Glass

ABSTRACT

The point of view adopted toward optimal size of population is long-term survival of the human species. This requires adaptability to changes of the environment, which in turn requires a wide diversity of gene pools. To achieve this diversity, it is necessary to have a relatively large population, but one divided into more or less isolated groups. A danger arises from our advanced technology which, by weakening the action of natural selection, is supporting an increasingly large pool of defective genes in the human population.

The question "Is there an optimal size of population?" poses, to a geneticist, the immediate need for definition of several terms. First, of course, one must ask, optimal for what? Second, precisely what is meant by "population" and "size of population"? Third, is one to be concerned chiefly with the welfare of man in the immediate present or in the distant future? Finally, if the optimal size of population is related to changing parameters of the environment, can we expect to preserve an environment sufficiently buffered against change that any prescription made today will have any validity whatsoever for tomorrow?

114

A biologist must examine these questions in the light of "mankind evolving," to use Theodosius Dobzhansky's apt phrase.[1] The human gene pool possesses a certain constitution which may best be characterized in terms of the relative proportions of alternative genes (alleles) and coadapted gene complexes. These are what they are because of the evolutionary processes of the past: mutation, genetic recombination, natural selection, geographic isolation, and migration (or gene flow) between populations, and the arbitrary effects of chance (random genetic drift) occurring when isolated groups are small or founders of new populations are few. The product of the evolutionary process is the adaptation of the human species to the environments in which it has evolved, and includes even the minor genetic differences between relatively isolated populations evolving in different parts of the world. The primary characteristic of *Homo sapiens,* in contradistinction to other mammalian species and in particular his closer primate relatives, is the high order of intelligence he possesses, a quality that enables him to adapt his environment increasingly to his own desires in place of awaiting the far slower genetic adaptation of himself to his changing environment. Man's own adaptability, including his power to learn from experience, and through science and technology to enlarge his power to exploit and modify the environment, depends on the considerable diversity of the human gene pool. It seems to me that although a "brave new world" is conceivable—one in which man is artificially constrained to become genetically homogeneous or is reshaped into a few genetic castes—it is unlikely to develop within a democratic society, nor is it as optimal as a continuance of extensive genetic diversity. Evolutionary history has repeatedly witnessed the downfall of once dominant and abundant creatures whose genetic adaptations were insufficiently flexible to permit readjustment to radical alterations in their terrestrial environments—including the appearance of more adaptable competitors. If there is any paramount law of evolutionary history, it is that rigorous adaptation to a particular environment is successful only while that environment still persists, and that, in general, highly adapted lines die out and successful new types arise from the more generalized, more flexible types that were not irrevocably committed to the old conditions. For mankind, therefore, a continuance of his adaptability and a maintenance of the diversity of his gene pool would seem to be optimal, at least for the remote future.

A Mendelian population is not to be taken as equivalent to the total number of individuals in a species; in a sexually reproducing species it is defined as a group of interbreeding individuals. In a species such as ours, there are twice as many genes at each chromosomal locus in the gene pool of the population as there are breeding individuals, since each person carries both a paternal and a maternal set of chromosomes and genes. The genetic differences in the gene pool exist because different forms of a particular gene can arise by mutation; and these different forms of a gene, these alleles, as they are called, undergo competition and consequently exist in particular frequencies, which in different populations may differ either by chance or because of natural selection. According to Sewall Wright,[2] the situation most favorable for progressive evolution is that which is provided by a relatively large population alternating between homogeneity and subdivision into many local, fairly isolated populations, at least some of which are medium or small in size. In that case, the small isolates will come to differ both in concealed genetic variability and in their visible characteristics (or phenotypes) from one another, and natural selection may discriminate between them. This view is generally accepted by population geneticists. Because so many mutant genes are recessive in their effects—that is, do not in single dose produce phenotypic changes that may be acted on by natural selection—most of the genetic variability in a very large uninterrupted population is hidden. Only in relatively small and isolated populations, because of inbreeding, do we find genetic variability forced into expression and thus made subject to selection. On the other hand, if the total population of the species consists of only a few small isolates, there is too much danger that none of them can provide a phenotype permitting preservation in the struggle for existence. Here, both chance and adverse selection will combine to magnify the likelihood of extinction.

In the one or two million years of existence of the human species, the total population was at first undoubtedly small; it was broken up into small, local breeding units that might be designated as bands, or extended families. Inbreeding was high; diversification among the isolates was probably great. The risk of extinction of the species was overwhelming until after the total population of the species had risen to one hundred thousand or so, when there would have been many troops or bands. Later, as methods of group hunting developed and the usefulness of fire as a protective weapon was discovered, larger tribes succeeded the small troops or bands. Ever since, we have moved steadily toward larger and larger Mendelian populations, with always a higher proportion of the variability lying hidden in the gene pool, and with less and less diversity of isolates and racial groupings. The human melting pot came into being. The melting pot has not yet eliminated all racial distinctions, but it is rapidly doing so. Genetic variability now chiefly differentiates individuals of the same breeding population, and a greater proportion of it is concealed in the recessive state. Populations have grown so vast that sheer distance, both geographic and social, has become a primary factor in offsetting a purely random breeding pattern. Evolutionary change has thus slowed down, even without considering what diminution of the rigor of natural selection has also taken place because of better standards of health and nutrition throughout the world. As the population structure of man has thus changed, his evolutionary prospects have altered.

EFFECTIVE SIZE OF POPULATION AND THE BREEDING STRUCTURE

Let us now examine some of the parameters of the problem more quantitatively. We must first distinguish between size of population, obtained by a census at a particular time, and *effective* size of population, which depends upon its breeding structure. First, the total population at a given time comprises persons of different ages and overlapping generations, roughly three in number. The relative proportions of successive age groups may be quite different in populations of the same total size. From a genetic point of view the effective size of population is the number of actual parents per generation—that is, the number of individuals in the current breeding generation who will ever become parents. This number, N, excludes from the census count all children, all persons past the reproductive age, and all persons within the reproductive period who never produce offspring. The remainder is very different in populations of different structure, for example, one that is characterized by a high birth rate and a high death rate, especially a high infant death rate, such as India, and a population like that of the United States, which has a relatively low birth rate accompanied by a low death rate (Figures 1 and 2). The age pyramid for a theoretical population that has attained a steady state with no infant or childhood mortality and

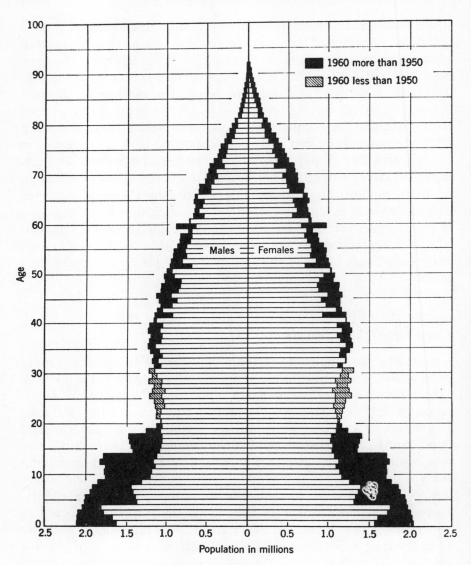

FIGURE 1

Population of the United States, by single years of age and
sex: 1960 and 1950. Source: Department of Commerce,
Bureau of the Census.

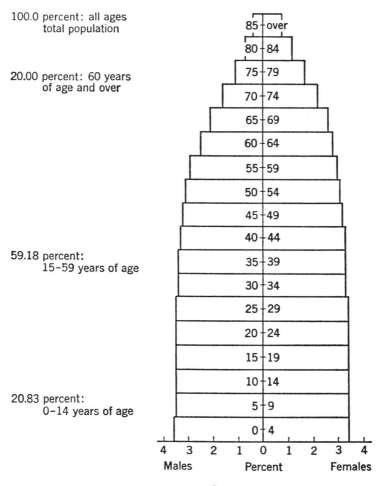

100.0 percent: all ages
total population

20.00 percent: 60 years
of age and over

59.18 percent:
15–59 years of age

20.83 percent:
0–14 years of age

| 85 over |
| 80 84 |
| 75 79 |
| 70 74 |
| 65 69 |
| 60 64 |
| 55 59 |
| 50 54 |
| 45 49 |
| 40 44 |
| 35 39 |
| 30 34 |
| 25 29 |
| 20 24 |
| 15 19 |
| 10 14 |
| 5 9 |
| 0 4 |

4   3   2   1   0   1   2   3   4
Males   Percent   Females

FIGURE 2
Life-table population of the United States, by age and sex:
1960.

no total increase is very different from either of the foregoing examples (Figure 3).

For the United States in 1960 (total population, 180 million) N was about 76 million, since 68 million persons were either under age 20 or over age 50 and between these age limits 16 per cent of women (and presumably an equal proportion of men) were childless. For 1970, the effective population size of the United States must be about

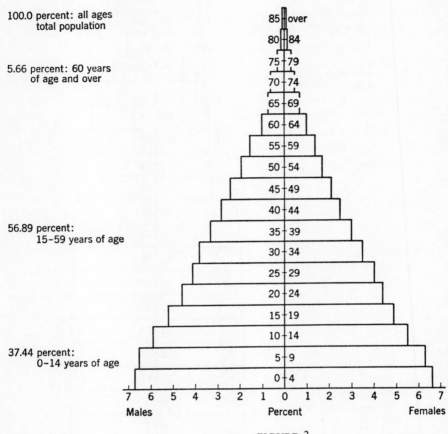

FIGURE 3
Population of India, by age and sex: 1951.

85 million. The effective population size must be less than 1,000 for local differentiation to occur on a geographic basis, by virtue of distance alone. Clearly, a population such as that of the United States will approach total genetic homogeneity unless other factors set up barriers to random breeding.

There are of course many social factors that do operate. My own studies of a religious isolate of German Baptists in southern Pennsylvania[3] showed clearly that in a small community, isolated from the surrounding population by very strong tenets of mating within the sect, genetic differentiation can produce sweeping changes within even one or two generations. Certain alleles once present may become eliminated. Distinctiveness from both the ancestral character and the surrounding population may become great. The Dunkers, in some genetic respects, proved to be as unique as Eskimos or Hottentots, although, of course, in the majority of their traits they remained like Germans of the Rhineland and like the native white population of the United States. Similar studies on other groups have fully confirmed the generality of these conclusions.[4] The barriers to interbreeding with outsiders may have social bases other than religious preferences. They may be rooted in social customs, racial origins, or professional ties and status. The phenomenon is, one might say, a residue of the social forces that existed in the earliest days of the human species, and that promoted breeding within the troop or tribe in place of mating with any outsider.

On the other hand, there is an aspect of the breeding structure opposed to the foregoing—emphasized by many anthropologists, and most recently by C. D. Darlington[5]—the taboo against incest. This taboo has been interpreted to include not only immediate members of the same family but even members of the same lineage or clan or subcaste. This practice of exogamy has undoubtedly been of great importance in human evolution because it has tended to keep much of the genetic variability in a concealed, recessive state, from which a small proportion in each generation emerges and becomes exposed to selection.

THE HUMAN GENE POOL AND MUTATION

Most mutations of genes and most chromosomal alterations are harmful when present in an individual in the double dose (homozygous state), that is, when inherited from both parents. The percentage of harmful mutations among all mutations may run as high as 80 or 90 per cent—although there is a caveat to acceptance of such statement: harmful mutations are more easily detected! In any case, in the single dose (the heterozygous state), when inherited from one parent only and consequently accompanied by a normal allele transmitted from the other parent, many mutations may actually be neutral or even advantageous by promoting increased viability or fertility on the part of their possessors.

Evolution cannot proceed without a supply of mutations to provide hereditary variation in the populations of the species. The spontaneous mutation rates of the genes and the size of the population

together determine the initial supply of these mutations, which provide the concealed variability and also the manifested variations upon
which natural selection acts. For example, the estimated rates of
mutation of human genes range from one in 20,000 gametes as a
maximum to rates of less than one per million.[6] If N, the effective
population size, is 100 million persons produced from 200 million
gametes, each kind of mutation will occur from 100 to 10,000 times
per generation. But if the effective population consists of only 1,000
persons, each kind of mutation will occur only once in 10 generations
to once in 1,000 generations. Inasmuch as the probability of chance
loss of a new mutant gene from the population, even in the absence
of selection, is approximately 98 per cent by the hundredth generation, recurrent mutation is required to maintain the gene in the gene
pool. It follows that unless the mutation rate of the gene is very
high—and most are not—a small population simply cannot attain
a high level of concealed variability by means of the mutation
process.

The alteration of a mutant gene's effect from one that is detrimental or neutral to one that is advantageous depends on some
change in the environment. This change may, in the first instance,
be merely a change in the assemblage of other genes with which
a particular mutant gene is associated, since genes commonly work
together. The genes, provided they can undergo recombination from
generation to generation—and that is the normal and primary outcome of the sexual aspect of reproduction—become coadapted; that
is to say, they tend to become locked into semipermanent groups
that are exposed to natural selection. Those groups that survive are
the ones which produce harmonious developmental effects. A gene
thus comes to be known by the company it keeps.

Alterations of the external environment are equally important. If
the external environment changes radically, there will be a compelling need to have an abundant supply of gene combinations
already present in the gene pool. Mutation rates are too low to be
depended on in an emergency. By chance, $\frac{1}{4N}$ genes are lost in
every generation, balancing $\frac{1}{4N}$ genes that reach fixation through
elimination of their alleles. In a large population, these fractions are
small; that is, most of the variability remains and mutation can
adequately replace it. In a small population, most of the genetic

variability is lost by chance at a greater rate than mutation can replace it. Hence, small populations tend to be fixed in genotype; they are very unlikely to survive a drastic change of environment. Only when a great many small or medium-sized populations exist within a great total population may we expect that at least one or two of the isolates will happen to present favorable characteristics for survival under radically altered circumstances.

THE HUMAN GENE POOL AND SELECTION

The presence of selection is also related to population size. In a small population (e.g., $N = 1,000$) a selection pressure, s, of $\dfrac{1}{4N} = \dfrac{1}{4,000}$ has little effect. That is to say, a difference allowing the favored type to produce 4,000 offspring to 3,999 for its competitor is of little consequence. But in a population four times as large, e.g., one of 4,000, even $s = \dfrac{1}{8N} = \dfrac{1}{32,000}$ has considerable effect. Actual selection pressures may often range from 0.04 to 0.4 and will generally determine the genetic outcome even in populations of less than 100. What is most surprising, perhaps, is that even very small differential advantages can lead to the establishment or elimination of particular genes in populations we would regard as very modest in size.

THE HUMAN GENE POOL AND MIGRATION, GENE FLOW, AND ISOLATES

Isolation between breeding populations is rarely total. Migrants commonly interbreed with members of the populations they enter. Obviously, it will take enormously more intrusion of foreign genes to modify the character of a large population of a million individuals than a small isolate of a few hundred. The slowness of the process of genetic assimilation is shown by the fact that after the passage of some ten generations of intermixture since the African Negro slaves were first brought to North America the present admixture of genes from white ancestors in the present socially defined urban black population is about 22 per cent and the rate of introgression of foreign genes into the black population has averaged about 2.5 per cent per generation.[7] An extrapolation of that rate into the future indicates that about 100 generations, or 2,750 years, will be required to bring about a complete genetic assimilation.

THE HUMAN STATE

The present rate of change in the human condition is exceedingly great. No genetic change can occur fast enough to cope with it even under conditions of maximum mutation rates and rigorous selection. As we have seen, mutation rates are in general low, although the great size of present human populations ensures that many mutations, of each and every gene, will occur in every generation. The new genes will also undergo extensive recombination, so that many different coadapted gene systems will exist. But, at the same time, our large populations ensure that most genetic variability will be concealed in the recessive state. Selection will consequently act mainly on the heterozygous effects of genes, which are commonly smaller in extent than the homozygous effects. Selection has been further slowed down by the advances in medicine and nutrition that now guarantee every child born alive, and some that previously could not have been born alive, a good chance of reaching the reproductive years. The reduced rigor of selection is increasing the abundance of once detrimental genes in our population, for these genes no longer lower their possessor's chance of reproduction. Dominant genes that are reduced from $s = 0.5$ (elimination of half the genes in each generation) to $s = 0.01$ will tend to increase fifty times in frequency. Recessives undergoing a similar moderation of selection will increase ten times in frequency. Thus, in anomalous fashion, we have found a way to increase our genetic variability without requiring any alteration of the mutation rates—though these, too, may become greater in the modern world, through greater exposure to ionizing radiations, chemical mutagens, and increased temperatures.

This genetic variability, however, is of little advantage to us in producing adaptation. We now modify the environment around us by technological means and create for ourselves a novel and artificial world in which our defective genes, even though active, fail to impede us in reproduction. The man of tomorrow will clearly need many more pills and prosthetic devices. That need not worry us so long as the social cost is not too great and so long as we can maintain our artificial environment unimpaired. By natural standards we may become degenerate physical beings, but we will not wish to apply natural standards any more.

CONCLUSION

What is the optimal size of population? Man has achieved his present status chiefly through intelligence and adaptability. That evolutionary process occurred in populations very much smaller, and much more broken up into breeding isolates, than we see now. Evidently, the great size of our present populations is not needed for progressive evolution and the maintenance of diversity. Our new condition provides us with added genetic diversity, but at a considerable cost: the social repair of genetic defects. This diversity seems neither necessary nor advisable.

There is, I believe, only one condition under which diversity may actually save our species. Were we to blunder into a nuclear war and thereby eliminate nine-tenths of the human lives on our planet, the scattered survivors would find themselves once more in the population structure of early Pleistocene man. Those who survived the direct effects of heat and blast and radiation and who were later spared by the fallout might, nevertheless, perish in large numbers because of their inability to provide themselves with the special foods, drugs, and devices on which they now depend for life itself. Among the others, in some remote inbreeding isolate, there may chance to be the appropriate phenotype to enable *Homo sapiens* to make a wiser fresh start—provided that enough genetic diversity exists through the preservation of a sufficient number of such small, isolated populations.

REFERENCES

1. T. Dobzhansky, *Mankind Evolving* (New Haven and London: Yale University Press, 1969).
2. S. Wright, "Physiological Genetics, Ecology of Populations, and Natural Selection," in S. Tax (ed.), *Evolution after Darwin*, Vol. I (Chicago: The University of Chicago Press, 1960).
3. B. Glass, Milton S. Sacks, Elsa Jahn, and Charles Hess, (1952) Genetic drift in a religious isolate: an analysis of the causes of variation in blood group and other gene frequencies in a small population. *Am. Naturalist*, 86: 145–59; Glass, "The Genetics of the Dunkers," *Scientific American*, 189 (1953), 76–81; Glass, (1954) Genetic changes in human populations, especially those due to gene flow and genetic drift. *Advances in Genetics*, 6: 95–139; Glass, (1956) On the significance of random genetic drift in human populations, *Amer. Jour. Phys. Anthropology*, 14 n.s.: 541–55.
4. A. S. Steinberg and Others, "Genetic Studies on an Inbred Human Isolate," in *Proceedings*, Vol. III, International Congress Human Genetics (Baltimore: The

Johns Hopkins Press, 1967); V. McKusick, (1964) The distribution of certain genes in the Old Order Amish, *Cold Spring Harbor Symposia Quant. Biol.,* 29: 99–114.

5. C. D. Darlington, *The Evolution of Man and Society* (London: George Allen & Unwin, 1969).

6. Glass, (1954) Genetic changes in human populations, especially those due to gene flow and genetic drift, *Advances in Genetics,* 6: 95–139.

7. ———, and C. C. Li, (1953) The dynamics of interracial mixture—an analysis based on the American Negro, *Amer. Jour. Human Genetics,* 5: 1–20; Glass, (1955) On the unlikelihood of significant admixture of genes from the North American Indians in the present composition of the Negroes of the United States, *Amer. Jour. Human Genetics,* 7: 368–85; T. E. Reed, "Caucasian Genes in American Negroes," *Science,* 165 (1969), 762–68.

Population Dynamics of Primitive Societies

Harold A. Thomas, Jr.

ABSTRACT

The approach chosen is both anthropological and mathematical in that the author constructs a model which describes the demographic processes of a primitive human society. This model expresses in mathematical form the interaction of a species with various ecological and environmental parameters. The model is actually checked by applying it to an anthropological study of the Kalahari Bushmen. General, as well as specific, conclusions can be drawn from such a model, particularly on the relationship between an optimal population and a Malthusian population.

New data from the investigations of a new breed of anthropologists have tempted me to try to model some of the demographic processes of primitive societies. Field work on living archaeology in Australia, in the Kalahari in Africa, and elsewhere is beginning to provide foundations for a new quantitative science that hopefully will improve our knowledge of the patterns of life of early man. The new records contain detailed demographic information, precise measurements of the layout and spacing of villages and camp sites, food consumption and other dietary information, and quantitative descriptions of production processes. Even at this early phase it is clear that some of our conventional views of paleolithic life need to be revised. One of these beliefs has been stated recently by J. K. Galbraith:

"The natural tendency of man, as manifested in primitive societies, is almost certainly to work until a given consumption is achieved. Then he relaxes, engages in sport, hunting, orgiastic or propitiating ceremonies or other forms of physical enjoyment or spiritual betterment."[1]

I think this view is wrong. Probably the tendency did not become effective until quite recently, perhaps not until the end of the Riss-Würm interglacial when it appears that a major breakpoint in the rate of expansion of the human population occurred.

From the viewpoint of mathematical analysis the tradeoff between labor and leisure and the elasticity of demand for food and other necessities are important parameters of the potential for survival of any species. Until the spate of technological jumps that started during the last glacial period and peaked in the neolithic, mankind did not have sufficient mastery of his environment to afford an inelastic food-demand function. Increasing evidence indicates that hominids have been tool-users for perhaps as long as ten million years. During this time, our predecessors in savannas and rain forests practiced artificial population control to maintain local population densities consonant with the properties of their various environmental niches. Actual densities varied markedly in different places depending upon the fertility of the region surrounding each focus of production and, of course, with the regnant level of technology. Technical innovations were extremely rare and genetic progress was slow. Over an area as large as Africa south of the Congo River during a period from say 600,000 to 500,000 B.C. the net reproduction rate perhaps did not exceed 1.0001. But, probably, in a region as small as that of the present tsetse swamp of the Okavango River, over short periods measured in centuries, much larger and much smaller net reproduction rates occurred. In response to ecological perturbations local populations waxed and waned in a complicated manner with fluctuations in the numbers of other species—prey, predators, and competitors. At times, as in recovering from a century-long drought, our species would turn on its full power of reproduction in order to meet the competition. At other times—say, following a long period of unusually favorable climate or possibly in the decades following the invention of the blow-gun—tribes would have to apply population brakes with an artificial control as rigorous as any practiced since urban life began in Eridu and Mohenjo-Daro. Control included abortion, infanticide, long lactation, and migration. The size of tribal communities oscillated between limits fixed by the material conditions of life in the cluster of environmental niches in each region. At the focus of each of the niches, near caves, waterholes, islands, thickets, mesas, and oases, man's productive and reproductive enterprises were organized and implemented. Throughout the Pleistocene epoch, production in each niche was conditioned partly by the current level of technology and partly by the density and areal distribution of game and edible plants. Leopards, locusts, and leprosy, among many other natural agents, made production a stochastic process. Local hydrological, geological, and meteorological conditions as well as world-wide climatological shifts determined the quality of life. This varied widely in different niches at any given point in time, and in any particular niche from millennium to millennium as we know from the famous cave near Peking. Like variable stars, some niches, such as those east of the Caspian Sea and in the Arabian peninsula, exhibited remarkable properties. They were powerful but sporadic people-breeders. They have generated countless population explosions that altered life in the more quiet and placid places. A series of related eruptions in late prehistorical times caused the widespread propagation of Indo-European peoples and production techniques with a major impact on the course of history.

I am going to assay a modest mathematical description of the interaction of species and ecological niches, but first it would perhaps be pertinent to remark on the relevance all this may have for the population problems of our time. The group of anthropologists who are reconstructing life in the Pleistocene—J. B. Birdsell, I. Devore, R. B. Lee, R. A. Gould, and L. R. and S. R. Binford to name a few of the pioneers—point out that human behavior and physiology are the outcome of several million years of selection for the hunting-gathering mode of living. Agriculture, pastoralism, not to mention industry, are much too recent to have produced any significant genetic shifts or fundamental physical changes. Human modes of aggression, patterns of emotion, reactions to stress, and habits of working and nesting were all imprinted in the hunting-gathering era which lasted until 10,000 years ago. Psychiatrists associated with the paleo-anthropologists have been interested in certain aspects of the new data. David Hamburg, at Stanford University, has directed attention to questions relating to the appropriateness of man's biological behavior and genetic endowment—as conditioned in the Quaternary period—to modern urban life. Hunters alternate between times of intense exertion in hunting and long periods of sustained labor in treks between campsites or from dust bowls. In modern society the body may mobilize for such activity under emotional stress. When the sequel is inactivity, the consequence may be psychic strain. Much more research is needed to elucidate these problems, but it is of manifest interest to modern man to learn how primitive man reacted to affluence and adversity and how the response was shaped in economic, social, psychological, and reproductive behavior.

THE MATHEMATICAL MODEL

The model I shall describe has a limited scope. The approach is more akin to Marshall's partial analysis than to Walras' attack on the problem of general equilibrium. The model pertains to a folk society with a simple and unchanging technology. Through age-long experience a high level of folk wisdom and social control is prevalent. And within their lights a high degree of economic acumen is manifest. The factors of production (including reproduction) are intimately known and deployed in patterns of allocation that shift with environmental changes from year to year and from niche to niche. The model treats the "harvest" fluctuations as exogenously determined, partly random, events that form a stationary time series. Thus, while long-term climatic trends are not possible in the model, more or less random land fertility fluctuations about a constant mean constitute its driving force. Similarly, while economic and reproductive behavior vary in response to ecological signals, the model in its present form does not accommodate significant mutations, either genetic or technological.

Despite its modest scope I believe the model helps to illuminate some of the darker areas of our current understanding of population dynamics. Incidentally, it rather agrees with the most renowned of all population models; it accords with the Malthusian model in predicating that primitive man lived at the margin of subsistence. But I hasten to say that marginal subsistence interpreted stochastically and dynamically is a very different mode of life from the static gray existence envisaged by the great classical economists. And it differs considerably from the low-level income traps modeled by respected modern economists. For example, my model has it that in a harsh environment subject to severe climatic changes, people eat more, work less, and live longer than they do in many more fertile and friendly environments. Prior to the investigations of the new anthropologists this conclusion would have been hard to sustain. However, accumulating evidence tends to corroborate the model. Human distaste for population pressure and abhorrence of a population vacuum have equal status in the model, and an important control parameter is the elasticity of the demand function of food in response to annually changing supply functions offered by nature. Equally significant is the parameter relating human fertility changes to land fertility changes. The main feature of the model, however, is the embodiment of a pervasive principle of ecology.

A successful species or subspecies is one that has undergone selection so as to "ride its niches" that is, to change its population levels in close reference to more or less random shifts in climate and land fertility. By behaving thus it prevents competing species from obtaining an ecological foothold on the niche. It is perhaps worthwhile to try to state this population principle in economic language. A natural species with a high potential for survival has a high evaluation of food and a low evaluation of leisure. The higher the ratio of the shadow prices corresponding to these evaluations relative to the price ratios of other species that compete for the same food supply, the greater will be its ecological thrust. Moreover, selection will operate in such a way that a surviving species evolves physiological characteristics and reproductive behavior that cause it to "harvest" its set of niches in different environments and years at the same level of marginal productivity. This theory, which determines the spatial and temporal variations in population density, is the ecological counterpart of the much-discussed competitive model of economic theory. By having a high price ratio the species is an *effective* competitor, and by distributing its members in space and time to produce at the same marginal rate it is an *efficient* competitor. An effective and efficient species will deny ecological entry to rivals. Of course, objections and reservations associated with the model of perfect competition in economics can be anticipated with its application to ecology and evolution. It surely is an oversimplification from many viewpoints. But one argument may be made in its support. During the vast stretch of the Pleistocene epoch there was much time for alleviation of "market" imperfections and dissipation of large diffusion gradients in the areal density of useful tools and superior genes.

ECOLOGICAL PERTURBATIONS

A brief listing of the categories of natural phenomena and agents that affected the economic activities of the hunter-gatherers is as follows:

I. Physical Factors
   A. Hydrological: floods, damaging rains, hail, droughts, waterlogging, and salinity.
   B. Meteorological: temperature extremes, high winds, tornadoes, and hurricanes.
   C. Geological: land erosion, silting, volcanic action, earthquakes, and landslides.
   D. Forest and prairie fires.

II. Biological Factors
   A. Large predators.
   B. Competitive herbivores and carnivores.
   C. Pathogenic microorganisms.
   D. Plant pathogens and pests.

In preliminary model studies a stochastic variate representing the annual potential yield of plant foods and animals was defined as follows:

$$g_{i+1} = \bar{g} + \rho(g_i - \bar{g}) + t_{i+1}\sigma_g(1 - \rho^2)^{1/2} \qquad (1)$$

where g_{i+1} is the potential yield (calories per square meter) in year $i + 1$, and t_i is a random variate with zero mean and unit variance. This simple autoregressive series is stationary when $\rho < 1$. The stationary distribution of g has a mean $\bar{g}$ and variance σ_g^2. The serial correlation coefficient ρ reflects the tendency of years of poor yield to be followed by poor years, and for good years to be followed by good years. A variety of factors can cause statistical persistence of this type. For example, during years of abundant rain, soils and groundwater aquifers are saturated and this may allow good growths for a period of time even though subsequent precipitation is subnormal. With high values of the serial correlation coefficient, the values of g tend to remain above or below the mean value for long periods; with $\rho = 0$ the mean crossover interval is two years. Long-term fluctuations of areal fertility of plant food cause long-term fluctuations in species of the higher trophic levels. The reproductive characteristics of a species tend to be selected to accord with the parameters $\bar{g}$, σ_g, and ρ of its ecological niches.

Areal productivity varies not only with climate, soil, and rain but with species. In typical nonarid terrestrial ecological communities, natural rates of photosynthesis vary from 1 to 4 grams of carbon per square meter per day, or 2,000 to 8,000 kilogram calories per year. In lakes and swamps, mean production rates may range from 2 to 7 grams per square meter per day, or 4,000 to 14,000 calories per year. Unlike gorillas, man did not ordinarily consume stalks and leaves, and the edible portion of plants usually constituted only a small fraction of the foregoing production. The net productivity of mice, rabbits, and squirrels ranges from 200 to 1,000 calories per square meter per year—about 10 per cent of the rate of plant production. The density of Neanderthal man in the valleys and plains of Europe has been estimated at 2 to 5 square miles per person. On deltas and coasts higher densities were maintained. Indians of the prairies of North America and aborigines of the Australian bush required 8 to 14 square miles per person. In more humid zones and on the littoral, higher densities were supported.

The annual variation in productivity varies with fluctuations in water supply, temperature, and solar radiation. The standard deviation of the annual flow of the Nile River is about 15 per cent of its mean annual flow. The standard deviation of annual rainfall of coastal California is about 30 per cent of the mean. In Figure 1 a historical trace of rainfall at a station in the Indian subcontinent is shown. In arid regions, such as the lower Indus plain, the variability of rainfall may be very large. The coefficient of serial correlation of annual runoff of the Indus River is 0.4, an unusually high value for a great river. The average wind speed in August in Sioux Falls is 9.5 miles per hour and the standard deviation is about 25 per cent as large. On some islands of Polynesia the standard deviation of the number of typhoons per decade is larger than the mean number. These miscellaneous items of climatology and ecology illustrate the range of man's environments; his evolutionary progress in the Pleistocene can be gauged by his ability to live in them.

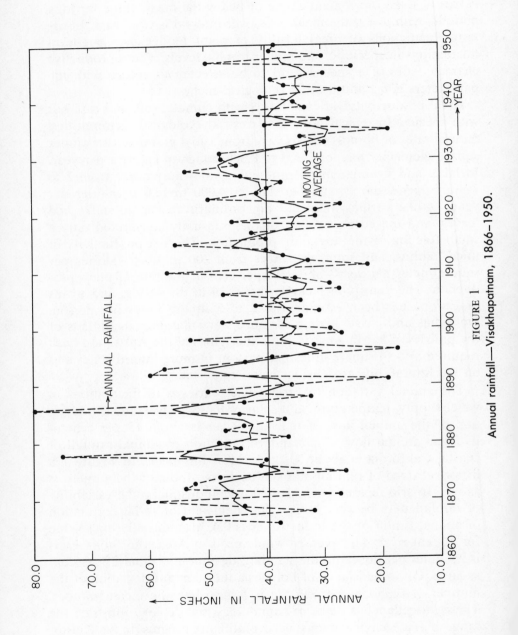

FIGURE 1

Annual rainfall—Visakhapatnam, 1866–1950.

THE PRODUCTION FUNCTION

The production function for hunter-gatherers formulates the rate of work input and food output, and embodies the law of diminishing returns. In fitting scatter diagrams of field data or time-motion analyses, the Cobb-Douglas function appears to be generally suitable, at least over limited ranges. But so do a number of other two-parameter families of curves that exhibit diminishing returns. (See Figure 2.) There is little to choose from among them on the basis of data presently available. For hunter-gatherer production with fixed capital stock and unchanging technology the Cobb-Douglas function is

$$X = \alpha W^\beta \qquad (2)$$

where X is the rate of food production in megacalories per day or week and W is the work of collection, transportation, and preparation performed by the effective adults of the band or tribe occupying the niche. I have defined it as the number of man-days per day or week worked by men in hunting and women in gathering.

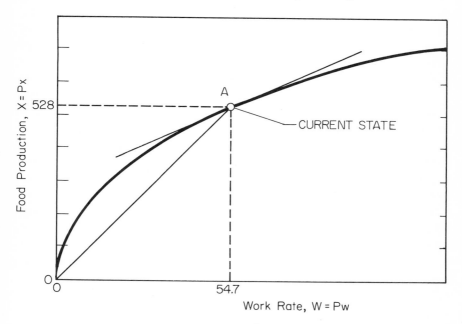

FIGURE 2
Production function.

Equation (2) may be written in another form,

$$x = \alpha w^{\beta} P^{\beta-1}$$

where
    P = number of effectives in the tribe;
    x = X/P, food produced per effective per day; consumption rate
        per head;
    w = W/P, work rate per effective.

The parameter α reflects the general level of fertility of the region; β is the ratio of marginal productivity to average productivity, which for the Cobb-Douglas function is constant over the entire range of the independent variable.

It will be useful, perhaps, to outline briefly the results of anthropological studies by Dr. Richard Lee of Harvard University.[2]

Lee is making a sustained study of the ecological base of a hunting-gathering community of Bushmen in the harsh environment of the northern Kalahari Desert by means of an input-output analysis of work and consumption. The Bushmen have only a very simple technology but live quite comfortably in a severe and unsparing place. The mode of life is of a type that may have been characteristic of early man. Their economy is centered around eight waterholes that are bounded by dry barren terrain. The extreme isolation and marginal environment probably account for the persistence of the tribe to the present. The boundaries of the region are not precise and to the west and southwest the range merges with vast, empty, waterless desert. Game is not abundant, although there is a considerable variety—big antelopes, including eland, gemsbok, and hartebeest, and smaller animals such as warthogs, duikers, and various birds. The women forage for nuts, berries, beans, bulbs, tubers, melons, and truffles. Mongongo nuts from the mangetti tree (*Ricinodendron rautanenii*) are an important component of the diet. Dr. Lee tabulated eighty-five plant species and fifty-four animal species that were eaten. The people keep no domestic animals, except a few hunting dogs, and have no technology for storing food.

Food is gathered on routine trips from the waterholes through the surrounding country. Usually these are made within a six-mile radius of each waterhole. Toward the end of the dry season the trips are long and everyone must carry out as much water as possible and bring back as much food as possible. Food is consumed by each subgroup of the tribe near the waterholes within two days of its collection. Therefore, level of work effort is closely related to food requirements.

Although the Bushmen use poles and nets for carrying food they have no large containers for storing food or water. Travel over waterless regions is precarious because the only vessels they have for carrying water are the fragile shells of ostrich eggs. On long trips to nut forests during the wet season parents carry their small children and all their possessions. The father carries weapons and loads of foodstuff in skin bags balanced on a pole while a three- to six-year-old child may ride on one shoulder. The mother carries all her household goods, including a dozen ostrich eggs full of water, in the pouch of her kaross. Her infant is suspended in a little leather sling above the egg shells. Children over six years old walk along with the adults. Journeys of fifty miles or more are not uncommon.

The parts of Dr. Lee's data relevant to my model are the following:

1. Total population, 248 persons: 30 per cent, 0 to 15 years; 62 per cent, 16 to 59 years; and 8 per cent over 60 years.

2. The population of effectives (16 to 59 years) consists of 72 males and 80 females. The other groups do not contribute significantly to the food supplies of the camps.

3. Birth control is rigidly practiced and the population is thought to be in a nearly steady state. Ten of the fourteen camps at the time of Dr. Lee's most recent trip had members over 60 years old, and one person was thought to be over 82 years old.

4. Over a period of several weeks Lee compiled data on the amount of food brought into the camps and calculated that the daily allotment amounted to 2,140 calories and 93 grams of protein per person. Taking into account the heights and weights of the adult males (average: 157 centimeters and 46 kilograms), together with corresponding measurements of the other members of the tribe and using the formulation of Taylor and Pye[3] that takes account of basal metabolic requirements and the appropriate activity regime, Lee estimated a mean daily energy requirement of 1,975 calories per day. Thus, food output exceeded energy requirements by 165 calories per person per day. Part of the caloric surplus was given to the hunting dog population (five to eight animals per band).

5. Dr. Lee's diary records the work activities for a twenty-eight-day period in August, 1964. From this the number of man-days of work by the effectives was calculated. This period was chosen because it was neither the best nor the worst time of the year for the collection effort (distance walked on the round trip to gather edibles). It covered the period of transition from better to worse conditions. At each point of time during the year the people prefer to collect and eat the most desirable foods to be found at the shortest distance from the water- holes. Thus, the work rate varies from month to month in an annual cycle. The over-all results showed that 65 per cent of the people worked at food collection 36 per cent of the time and that 35 per cent of the tribe did not work at all. The study demonstrated that a relatively small subsistence effort was more than enough to provide an adequate diet for the !Kung Bushmen. They do not live in priva- tion, and they do not suffer from population pressure.

In fitting Dr. Lee's data to the production function [Equation (2) and Figure 2], the current state of the society is represented by a point, $X = 2.14(248) = 3.48(152) = 528$ megacalories per day, and $W = 152(.36) = 54.7$. The effectives worked 36 per cent of the time (36 days per 100 days). With the aid of large-scale maps showing distances between waterholes and the food-producing regions in different directions, I estimated the additional amount of food that would have been produced annually if the effectives had worked an additional hour each day. The calculation indicated that the ratio of marginal productivity to average productivity was about 1 to 3. The Cobb-Douglas function that incorporates this information is

$$X = 139W^{1/3},$$
$$x = 139w^{1/3}P^{-2/3},$$
$$P = 1640w^{1/2}x^{-3/2}.$$

From the last equation it is evident that a 2.5 per cent $(1.05^{1/2} - 1)$ larger population could be sustained if everyone worked 5 per cent longer, or if everyone's caloric intake were reduced 1.7 per cent $(1 - .983^{3/2})$. Other combinations of the factors within physically and physiologically possible ranges could be selected by the society. The feasible region for social choice is indicated by the shaded area in Figure 3 in which Equation (2) is plotted for different levels of population density. The horizontal dashed lines represent upper and lower bounds for consumption as fixed by metabolic and other physiological requirements of our species. The dashed vertical line indicates the upper limit of the work rate per head which is also fixed by human physiology. As the curved lines show, the food supply

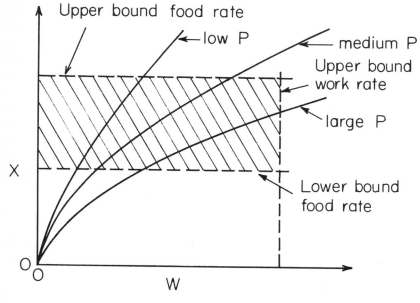

FIGURE 3

function can be made to intersect the feasible region in different zones by maintaining the population at different levels. At a low population density, the food supply function rises steeply in the left side of the feasible region in which the work rate is low and high consumption is possible. At high population densities, the supply function is constrained by the upper limit of the labor rate per head.

If Equation (2) is solved for P,

$$P = \alpha^{1/(1-\beta)} w^{\beta/(1-\beta)} x^{-1/(1-\beta)}, \qquad (2a)$$

the largest possible population in a niche with a production function with a given α and β is that in which the work rate is as large as possible and consumption as small as possible:

$$P_m = \alpha^{1/(1-\beta)} w_m^{\beta/(1-\beta)} x_m^{-1/(1-\beta)}. \qquad (2b)$$

Here w_m represents the maximum (sustainable) work rate and x_m the minimum (sustainable) rate of consumption. Dividing Equation (2a) by Equation (2b) the following relationship is obtained:

$$\frac{P}{P_m} = \left(\frac{w}{w_m}\right)^{\beta/(1-\beta)} \left(\frac{x_m}{x}\right)^{1/(1-\beta)}. \qquad (2c)$$

For any specified value of β, Equation (2c) may be plotted as in Figure 4. The area for social choice again is indicated by the shaded region. The upper curved line shows the relationship of Equation (2c) plotted with $x = x_m$; it defines the minimum diet constraint. The lower curve is plotted with $x > x_m$ at an adequate diet level. All physically and physiologically possible choices lie in the shaded region between the curves. Any point in the region, such as point A, represents a possible choice for the economy. The point M represents a Malthusian population with the greatest possible population density. Maintenance of this state requires maximum work and minimum consumption. Points representing actual populations lie below and to the left of point M. Carr-Saunders[4] and others have advanced a theory of optimal population for human communities, stating that populations adjust (or should adjust) to their environment to densities at which income per head is maximized. For our model, in which the only goods are food and closely related necessities, points satisfying this criterion would fall somewhere on the lower curved line. Tribes with economies represented by points above this line are "overpopulated." From the viewpoint of the present model two criticisms of the Carr-Saunders theory may be made. (1) Actual populations in fact do plot above the line, and this suggests that primitive societies do not maximize income per capita as this concept is ordinarily defined. (2) In addition to food, two other sources of satisfaction or utility apparently are operative: there is a tradeoff between goods and leisure; and people themselves are a public good from the viewpoint of each member of the group. Unless shadow prices can be specified for these components of utility, the Carr-Saunders criterion is not operational. It does not uniquely define the state of the system. Evidently, further analysis must proceed in the domain of the welfare economist.

If a primitive society persists for a long time at or near a given point on the diagram of Figure 4, it may be inferred that the equilibrium involves the balance of three forces or drives: sex, hunger, and leisure. Leisure is an aggregate for all activities and proclivities that are neither productive nor reproductive. Most of these are subsumed in Robert White's concept of "competence." Other language to describe the three motivations may be more appropriate, depending on the location of the vector representing the state of the economy. For example, for points lying near the lower curve, it would perhaps be more appropriate to speak of partiality for tasty foods and com-

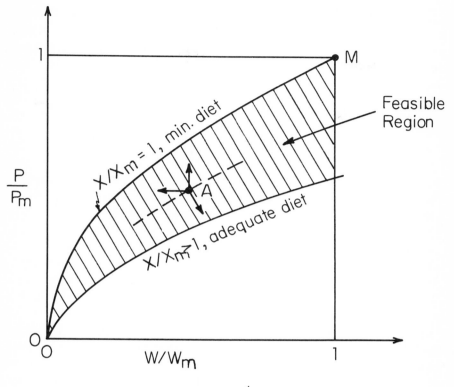

FIGURE 4

fortable caves rather than aversion to hunger. And in some cases the utility of an increment of population may derive from tribal defense requirements and the need to resist aggression rather than from the utility of coitus and other short-run benefits associated with reproduction.

Mathematically these ideas may be expressed by defining a utility function, $U(P,x,w)$, in which the independent variables denote the three aggregated motivations. For a small three-dimensional region about the equilibrium point $(\overline{P},\overline{x},\overline{w})$ the utility function may be approximated by the first terms of a Taylor's series:

$$U(P,x,w) = U(\overline{P},\overline{x},\overline{w}) + b_1(P - \overline{P}) + b_2(x - \overline{x})$$
$$+ b_3(w - \overline{w}) + \cdots, \quad (3)$$

where b_1, b_2, and b_3 represent the partial derivatives, $\partial U/\partial P$, $\partial U/\partial x$, and $\partial U/\partial w$ evaluated at the equilibrium point. Assuming that the utility function is continuous and otherwise "well behaved," the b's are related to shadow prices or preference coefficients for the components of utility. These prices may be evaluated by Lagrangian analysis if the coordinates of the equilibrium point are given and the production function specified. The Lagrangian function is

$$L(P,x,w) = U(\overline{P},\overline{x},\overline{w}) + b_1(P - \overline{P}) + b_2(x - \overline{x}) + b_3(w - \overline{w})$$

$$- \lambda(\log P + \frac{1}{1 - \beta} \log x - \frac{\beta}{1 - \beta} \log w - \frac{1}{1 - \beta} \log \alpha), \quad (4)$$

where λ is a multiplier. By setting to zero the partial derivatives $\partial L/\partial P$, $\partial L/\partial x$, and $\partial L/\partial w$ and eliminating the multiplier, the following expressions for the price ratios are obtained:

$$\frac{b_2}{b_1} = \frac{\overline{P}}{(1 - \beta)\overline{x}}, \quad (5)$$

$$-\frac{b_2}{b_3} = \frac{\overline{w}}{\beta\overline{x}}.$$

In mathematical language, a Malthusian population is one in which the state variables pertain to a point in a part of the feasible region where b_2 is large relative to b_1 and to $-b_3$. That is, the equilibrium point is located in a region where the marginal utility of an increment of food is very large—a further reduction in consumption would involve high cost (starvation). Moreover, a further increase in the work rate (to increase P or x or both) would be expensive (death by exhaustion). The price ratios b_2/b_1 and $b_2/(-b_3)$ computed for actual primitive societies are smaller than those of a Malthusian population. This implies a higher utility of leisure and of consumption than limned in the indelible first essay.

An intriguing application of the foregoing theory is to calculate the shift in equilibrium (or the direction of the shift) from vector (P_1,x_1,w_1) to a new position (P_2,x_2,w_2) that results from a technical innovation which changes the parameters of the production function. The theory predicts how the ecological bonus will be distributed to the different components of utility. Depending on the amount that the particular invention changes each parameter of the production function, consumption and population will increase and labor will decrease. New reproductive behavior will develop with added longevity. It is of interest that the theory defines "positive" and "negative" inventions based on the direction of the change in survival potential. Like the history of foot races between men and gorillas, conventional texts of technological history are biased in that only positive results are recorded. In another paper I have discussed an application of the theory underlying Equations (4) and (5).[5]

The present goal is to investigate the implications of impermanent changes in the production function due to weather and other exogenous agents rather than the permanent effects of inventions. Before analyzing the perturbing effect of rainfall and other factors on primitive production, it will be useful to derive a particular form of production function which is helpful to a comprehension of the mechanics of primitive production. Consider a circular range with the camp or home base of production at the center. Let G(r) denote the areal density of foodstuffs (in calories per square meter) at radius r from the home base. Let r_m denote the maximum radius of the area harvested during the year. Then, in accord with the notion previously used,

$$365X = 2\pi \int_0^{r_m} rG(r)\, dr. \qquad (6)$$

Next, consider a special family of possible areal distributions of foodstuffs for which

$$G(r) = gr^{h-2} \qquad (7)$$

where g is the areal density at $r = 1$. The parameter h reflects the rate of variation of areal density of edibles in the radial direction. Thus, for uniform fertility, $h = 2$; in an oasis or a mountain valley, fertility decreases with r, $h < 2$. If the productive zone is along the banks of a stream or the ridge of a long hill, $h < 2$. If fertility increases with r, $h > 2$. From equations (6) and (7)

$$X = \frac{2\pi}{365h} gr_m{}^h. \qquad (8)$$

The amount of labor required to transport the foodstuffs from an annular ring, $2\pi r\, dr$, to the home base is

$$dW = \frac{2\pi\eta g}{365} r^h\, dr, \qquad (9)$$

where η is a conversion factor reflecting the ease or difficulty of transport. In rough, uneven terrain or dense jungle η is large; in smooth, open country it is small. Integrating:

$$W = \frac{2\pi\eta g}{365} \int_o^{r_m} r^h \, dr = \frac{2\pi\eta g}{365} \frac{r_m}{h+1}^{h+1} \tag{10}$$

and

$$r_m = \left(\frac{365(h+1)W}{2\pi\eta g}\right)^{1/(h+1)}.$$

Substituting in Equation (8), a production function of the form of Equation (2) is obtained,

$$X = \left(\frac{2\pi g}{365}\right)^{1/(h+1)} \left(\frac{h+1}{\eta}\right)^{h/(h+1)} \frac{1}{h} W^{h/(h+1)} \tag{11}$$

where $h/(h+1) = \beta$.

Equation (11) is appropriate when the dominant component of production is transport. Before the agricultural revolution this was often the case. If other components of work effort such as assembly (picking a berry patch, or digging up a gopher tortoise) or food preparation (cleaning, cooking, etc.) require substantial effort, then the exponent β will differ from $h/(h+1)$: usually it will become smaller. In all normal cases, the law of diminishing returns will obtain. In terms of the variables $w = W/P$ and $x = X/P$, Equation (11) may be written as follows:

$$x = Kg^{1/(h+1)}w^{h/(h+1)}P^{-1/(h+1)} \tag{12}$$

where

$$K = \left(\frac{2\pi}{365}\right)^{1/(h+1)} \left(\frac{h+1}{\eta}\right)^{h/(h+1)} \frac{1}{h}.$$

Equation (12) indicates not only the strong effect that the parameter h may exert in the relationship between the state variables during any particular year, but also the impact of weather fluctuations and other ecological perturbations on production in different years.

In the stochastic process to be outlined, the state of the economy in successive years can be depicted as a cluster of points about an equilibrium point such as A on Figure 4. At all times equilibrating forces will operate. These correspond to motivations associated with the state variables and are shown schematically on Figure 4 as vectors radiating from point A. The vertical vector indicates the "pull" of utility associated with P; the horizontal vector pertains to leisure, and the third vector to consumption.

It will be convenient to use a linear approximation of the production function (Equation [12]) which is valid in the region of the equilibrium point $(\bar{P},\bar{x},\bar{w})$:

$$\frac{x - \bar{x}}{\bar{x}} = \frac{h}{h + 1}\frac{w - \bar{w}}{\bar{w}} - \frac{1}{h + 1}\frac{P - \bar{P}}{\bar{P}} + \frac{1}{h + 1}\frac{g - \bar{g}}{\bar{g}}. \quad (13)$$

In Equation (13) g is a stochastic variate as defined in Equation (1). I shall derive moments of the distribution of P, x, and w from Equation (13) by introducing two parameters pertaining to economic and reproductive behavior. The moments of the stationary distributions of the state variables provide a rough but useful description of the size and shape of the cluster of points in the space about the equilibrium point that represent the state of the system from year to year. The constrained random dance in this three-dimensional space, defined by the physical parameters of the niche and by the physiological and behavioral parameters evolved by the species in the process of surviving, constitutes the basic dynamic of life of the community. It is the diapason delimiting the range for tribal harmony and dissonance. What remains is orchestration.

The first of the two behavioral parameters is defined in the following deterministic relation between work rate and food production rate:

$$\frac{w - \bar{w}}{\bar{w}} = -\delta\frac{x - \bar{x}}{\bar{x}}. \quad (14)$$

This, in effect, is a specification of a Marshallian demand function defined for the vicinity of the equilibrium point. The elasticity of demand for food at the equilibrium point is $1/\delta$. Figure 5 shows (with reversed axes) the supply and demand functions for primitive production in Marshall's conceptualization. The supply curve fluctuates from year to year with changes in land fertility and population density, and therefore the point of intersection of the supply and demand curves moves about. During lean years the effectives of the group must work harder to obtain food; in good years less work is done. If δ is large, the variation in x about $\bar{x}$ will be small. But this can only be achieved by a large variation in the work rate. Alternatively, with a small value of δ, the variance in work rate will be small and time for leisure fairly constant. This, however, will involve a large variance in food consumption. The food demand elasticity of early hominid societies represented a compromise between social

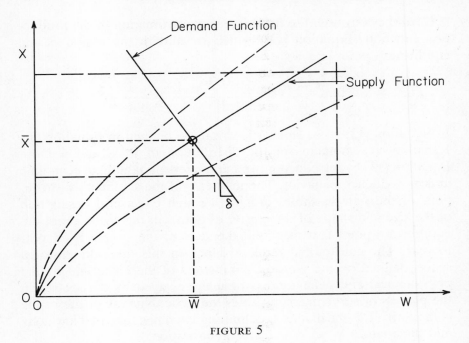

FIGURE 5

objectives, including survival, and private desires. Consumer sovereignty applies but to one species and is meaningful only with high technology.

Eliminating w from Equation (13) by use of Equation (14), the following relation is obtained:

$$\frac{x_{i+1} - \overline{x}}{\overline{x}} = \frac{1}{c}\left[\frac{g_{i+1} - \overline{g}}{\overline{g}} - \frac{P_i - \overline{P}}{\overline{P}}\right] \qquad (15)$$

where $c = 1 + (1 + \delta)h$.

The second behavioral parameter is introduced in the following difference equation that relates the state of the economy in two successive years:

$$P_{i+1} = P_i + \frac{a\overline{P}}{\overline{x}}(x_{i+1} - \overline{x}) \qquad (16)$$

or

$$\frac{P_{i+1} - \overline{P}}{\overline{P}} = \frac{P_i - \overline{P}}{\overline{P}} + a\frac{(x_{i+1} - \overline{x})}{\overline{x}}.$$

Equation (16) states that the population will increase during good times and decrease during hard times. The sensitivity of the response is determined by the parameter a. The level of a is fixed by tribal patterns of income distribution to the various demographic components during lean and fat years, and to tribal customs of birth control and death control including infanticide and parricide. Group extinction could be averted in extreme crises with the lump sum transfers of cannibalism.

Eliminating x from Equation (16), using Equation (15), and rearranging,

$$\frac{P_{i+1} - \overline{P}}{\overline{P}} = \left(1 - \frac{a}{c}\right)\frac{P_i - \overline{P}}{\overline{P}} + \frac{a}{c}\frac{g_{i+1} - \overline{g}}{\overline{g}}. \tag{17}$$

Equation (17) formulates the demographic impact of environmental perturbations and incorporates the behavioral parameters δ and a, $\overline{w}$ and $\overline{x}$, and the physical parameters h, $\overline{g}$, σ_g, ρ, and η. The model will be completed with the introduction of two physiological parameters discussed in connection with Figure 3 and Equation (2). However, before putting these last two bricks in place, it will be worthwhile to consider briefly a refinement of Equation (17) that is needed to formulate correctly the demographic processes of very small bands of people.

Consider a small band with, say, twenty effectives for which the probability of survival to age 15 is 0.70 and to age 45 is 0.52. During this thirty-year interval the average probability of death during any year is 0.006 and the mean survival probability is 0.994. The expected number of deaths in this age range in a stationary population is $0.006(20) = 0.12$ persons per year. If the actual number of deaths accorded with a Bernoullian frequency distribution, the variance would be $0.006(1 - .006)20 = 0.12$ and the coefficient of variation $\sqrt{.12}/20 = .017$. However, in real life the variance is likely to be considerably larger than Bernoullian, because of accidents not necessarily associated with the current state of the economy. Random encounters with Bengal tigers, coral snakes, and malaria-carrying mosquitoes occur in good years and in bad ones. Another component of variance derives from variable fertility—birth control has always been a stochastic process. All these accidental effects may be aggregated in a single term.

Using standard theorems of expected value theory, the variance of the stationary distribution of P from Equation (17) may be derived:

$$V(P/\overline{P}) = \frac{(a/c)^2 V(g/\overline{g})}{1 - \left(1 - \dfrac{a}{c}\right)^2}. \tag{18}$$

To include the effect of accidents, Equation (18) is modified as follows:

$$V(P/\overline{P}) = \frac{(a/c)^2 V(g/\overline{g}) + d^2 p(1 - p)/\overline{P}}{1 - \left(1 - \dfrac{a}{c}\right)^2} \tag{18a}$$

where p is the mean death rate per effective per year, and d is a Lexis ratio. The added term is significant only for small groups. For nuclear families living by themselves, the term may be very large—too large, perhaps, in many niches, so that this form of social organization may have been rare. For the sake of simplicity, in the remaining analysis it will be assumed that the populations are sufficiently large that the difference between Equations (18) and (18a) is negligible.

Given the variance of both g and P, the variance in food rate may be derived from Equation (15):

$$V(x/\overline{x}) = \frac{2V(g/\overline{g})}{c(2c - a)}. \tag{19}$$

Also from Equation (14):

$$V(w/\overline{w}) = \delta^2 V(x/\overline{x}). \tag{20}$$

Equations (18), (19), and (20) provide a description of the stationary distribution of the state variables in terms of their variances. A wide range of states is possible, depending on the magnitudes of the exogenous and endogenous parameters relating to environment and behavior. There are, however, physical and physiological constraints that must be honored. They determine the boundaries of the feasible region for social choice within each environmental niche. These constraints, therefore, are important determinants of economic, social, and demographic behavior. In the present model the constraints are defined stochastically—that is, the frequency of violations is maintained at a low level.

Let x* denote the minimum permissible level of food supply per head defined stochastically so that

$$\bar{x} - 2\sigma_x \geq x^*. \tag{21}$$

Thus, the proportion of years during which the food supply is less than the 2-sigma level would be .025 or one year in forty if the stationary distribution of x were normal. Probably many frequency distributions of annual food supply during hominid evolution were near normal and violations of the 2-sigma quantile occurred two or three times each century. If the constraint (Equation [21]) is binding then the following relationship may be derived from Equation (19):

$$\frac{x^*}{\bar{x}} = 1 - \frac{2\sqrt{2}\,q}{\sqrt{c(2c-a)}} \tag{22}$$

in which $q = [V(g/\bar{g})]^{1/2} = \sigma_g/\bar{g}$.

Analogously, w^* is defined as the upper 2-sigma bound for the work rate on a sustained basis with due allowance for maintenance and replacement of capital stock (searching for a new rock of the right shape or repairing a footbridge). Thus:

$$\bar{w} + 2\sigma_w \leq w^*, \tag{23}$$

and if this constraint is binding, it follows from Equations (19) and (20) that

$$\frac{\bar{w}}{w^*} = \frac{\sqrt{c(2c-a)}}{\sqrt{c(2c-a)} + 2\sqrt{2}\,\delta q}. \tag{24}$$

If P^* denotes the upper 2-sigma quantile of the stationary distribution of population,

$$\bar{P} + 2\sigma_P = P^*, \tag{25}$$

it follows from Equation (18) that

$$\frac{\bar{P}}{P^*} = \frac{\sqrt{c(2c-a)}}{\sqrt{c(2c-a)} + 2\sqrt{ca}\,q}. \tag{26}$$

Finally, it is of interest to compare the mean level of the population with the Malthusian level, which is defined by the production function, Equation (12), with mean land fertility, maximum work rate, and minimum consumption.

$$\bar{P}_m = K^{h+1}\bar{g}\,\frac{w^{*h}}{x^{*h+1}} \tag{27}$$

The mean levels of total food supply and total work may be derived from expected value theory.

$$\bar{X} = \bar{x}\bar{P}\left[1 - \frac{1}{c}V(P/\bar{P})\right] \tag{28}$$

$$\bar{W} = \bar{w}\bar{P}\left[1 + \frac{\delta}{c}V(P/\bar{P})\right] \tag{29}$$

If

$$\bar{X} = K\bar{g}^{1/(h+1)}\bar{W}^{h/(h+1)} \tag{30}$$

then, from Equations (27), (28), and (29),

$$\frac{\bar{P}}{\bar{P}_m} = \frac{\left[\dfrac{\bar{w}}{w^*}\left(1 + \dfrac{\delta}{c}q^2\right)\right]^h}{\left[\dfrac{\bar{x}}{x^*}\left(1 - \dfrac{1}{c}q^2\right)\right]^{h+1}}. \tag{31}$$

The right-hand side may be evaluated with Equations (22) and (24).

DISCUSSION

The model is now complete and its implications can be examined. But before proceeding to numerical analysis it would be useful, perhaps, to affirm that *Homo sapiens* is an exceptional species and that, unlike other species, our demographic behavior today is not greatly constrained by natural environmental controls. The point of this investigation, however, is that, initially, our uniqueness was not marked and, for a long time, while technology was primitive, our species, like all others, coped with incessant environmental change. Hominid instinctive and learned behavior was selected primarily for survival. "Consumer preferences" were strongly conditioned for social ends. In the language of the model, the prices or preference coefficients of Equation (5) were determined by the physiological and environmental parameters rather than by arbitrary consumer tastes as predicated in modern economic theory.

By degrees, as technology improved and our control of the environment and other species increased, our demographic behavior was less constrained by natural environmental changes and more responsive to other factors. At the present time, and for the past few millennia, the feasible range for demographic control has increased. In terms of the model, the permissible range of the parameters a and δ has been widened and now can be quite different from those of other primates. With highly evolved technology, we are no longer obliged to control production and reproduction so as to follow closely the fluctuations in the natural environment. But here an important question arises. The inventions that have had the greatest impact on human ecology—such as the canal, the horse collar, and the modification of wild wheats—are recent inventions. The duration of the food-gathering era was more than a thousand times that of the current food-producing era, and the question arises as to whether our species as a species has had time to learn new demographic behavior appropriate to new conditions.

To provide a frame of reference, it would appear to be useful to attempt to identify by mathematical analysis the demographic behavioral patterns appropriate for primitive societies. Even with our severely simplified model, it is manifest that a very wide range of types of environment could be occupied by the hominid food-gatherers. In riding their niches, in expanding and contracting population density in response to perpetually changing conditions of food supply, the various groups evolved demographic response patterns, partly instinctive and partly learned, that were suitable for each locality, and which were in harmony with the physiological realities of the species (x^* and w^*) at each stage of biological evolution. Mathematically, the problem can be stated as follows: Given a niche specified by a set of environmental parameters, $\bar{g}$, σ_g, ρ, η, and h, and given a set of physiological parameters, x^* and w^*, what ranges of the parameters of demographic control, a and δ, will be feasible and appropriate for species survival? In preliminary studies the inverse problem has been investigated. That is, various levels of a and δ have been assumed for various types of environment and the demographic and economic response has been calculated in terms of $x^*/\bar{x}$, $\bar{w}/w^*$, $\bar{P}/P^*$, and $\bar{P}/P_m$. This computation surfaces a number of implications of the model that are not obvious from its premises.

Tables 1a, 1b, 1c, and 1d summarize calculations pertaining to the stationary frequency distributions of the state variables with levels of the behavioral parameters, δ and a, and the environmental parameters, h and q. In each table the first row is the "standard" system and in the other four rows one parameter is varied at a time so as to ascertain its influence on the ecological balance. For example, in Table 1a, by comparing the first and second rows, it is seen that a reduction of h causes an increase in mean food consumption $\bar{x}$, a decrease in the work rate $\bar{w}$, and an increase in the magnitude of

TABLE 1

Ecological Balance with Various Levels of
δ, a, h, and q

Number	δ	a	h	q	$\dfrac{x^*}{\bar{x}}$	$\dfrac{\bar{w}}{w^*}$	$\dfrac{\bar{P}}{P^*}$	$\dfrac{\bar{P}}{P_m}$
				a				
(i)	1	.6	.5	.2	.783	.822	.856	.604
(ii)	1	.6	.25	.2	.702	.770	.833	.578
(iii)	1	.6	.5	.3	.675	.755	.799	.440
(iv)	2	.6	.5	.2	.829	.746	.871	.627
(v)	1	.3	.5	.2	.792	.828	.898	.616
				b				
(i)	.5	.3	.5	.2	.761	.893	.891	.603
(ii)	.5	.3	.25	.2	.692	.866	.877	.585
(iii)	.5	.3	.5	.3	.641	.848	.845	.433
(iv)	1.0	.3	.5	.2	.792	.828	.898	.616
(v)	.5	.15	.5	.2	.766	.895	.922	.610
				c				
(i)	.5	.3	.25	.2	.692	.866	.877	.585
(ii)	.5	.3	.125	.2	.640	.847	.868	.570
(iii)	.5	.3	.25	.3	.538	.812	.826	.400
(iv)	1.0	.3	.25	.2	.719	.781	.882	.598
(v)	.5	.15	.25	.2	.701	.870	.912	.595
				d				
(i)	2	.6	.25	.2	.749	.666	.846	.605
(ii)	2	.6	.125	.2	.671	.603	.826	.576
(iii)	2	.6	.25	.3	.623	.570	.786	.440
(iv)	4	.6	.25	.2	.809	.567	.864	.639
(v)	2	.3	.25	.2	.761	.677	.891	.619

fluctuations of population density. In both cases the mean population level is well below that of the Malthusian population (.604 $\bar{P}_m$ and .578$\bar{P}_m$). From row iii it is seen that if environmental perturbations are increased, with q going from .2 to .3, people eat more and work less. Population density fluctuations are increased. The mean population density in this case is reduced to about one-half the Malthusian density (0.440 $\bar{P}_m$). In row iv of Table 1a it may be noted that a reduction in food-demand elasticity (δ going from 1 to 2) reduces mean food consumption and the mean work rate; population density increases and is less variable. In the last row it is seen that the reduction of the parameter a decreases food consumption and increases work, and the population density moves closer to the Malthusian density. Tables 1b, 1c, and 1d summarize similar sensitivity studies in other ranges of the behavioral and environmental parameters. In Tables 1b and 1c, δ and a are reduced by a factor of 2 relative to the values in Table 1a. This has the effect of raising mean food consumption and work rate with a slight reduction of mean population density relative to the Malthusian level. In Table 1d, δ is increased by a factor of 2 and h decreased by a factor of 2. Relative to results in Table 1a, food intake is increased and work rate is reduced. Population densities do not change significantly from those in Table 1a.

CONCLUSIONS

The principal conclusions from these computations are the following: (1) As food demand becomes more inelastic (δ increased), food consumption and work rate are reduced, and the population density is increased and becomes less variable. (2) If a is reduced (so that human fertility changes are less responsive to food-supply changes), the effect is to reduce food intake and increase work rate; population density is increased and becomes less variable.

These conclusions are compatible with the fact that, as technology gradually improved and production became more capital intensive, man could increasingly afford a more inelastic demographic and economic response to changes in the supply function. He could get enough food with less effort and, at the same time, his niches could carry higher population densities. Moreover, with his increased dominance over other species, there was a diminishing need to follow land fertility fluctuations since competitors could be eliminated by methods other than by out-eating them. These developments, however, were slow in coming. Anthropological evidence indicates a very long stage in the use of simple tools by small-brained bipeds and, eventually, an increase in the rate of growth of technology with the evolution of the genus *Homo*.

If the serial correlation coefficient of Equation (1) is set at values greater than zero, then the interrelations between the state variables and the parameters of the model become more complex. In general, as shown in the Appendix, the effect of an increase in ρ, with other parameters fixed, is to increase $V(P/\overline{P})$ and decrease $V(x/\overline{x})$ and $V(w/\overline{w})$, as given by Equations (18), (19), and (20).

It is evident that many combinations of input parameters are possible and that a wide variety of system states can occur. In continuing research, systematic studies are being made of the response surface of this preliminary model as well as of those of more sophisticated models. The more comprehensive population models are being investigated by computer simulation. In these, the linear approximations of the preliminary model are eliminated and various refinements are incorporated. The principal objective in this stage of the investigation is to ascertain the relationship between species "operating policy" parameters, a, δ (and their analogues in more elaborate models), the environmental parameters, and the frequency distributions of the state variables. Of particular interest in the simulation studies is a ranking of the survival potential associated with each set of behavioral parameters for various specified environments, based on the relative degree of constancy of marginal productivity in the niches achieved from year to year.

REFERENCES

1. J. K. Galbraith, *The New Industrial State* (Boston: Houghton Mifflin Company, 1967), p. 270.
2. R. B. Lee, "What Hunters Do for a Living," R. B. Lee and I. Devore (eds.), *Man the Hunter* (Chicago: Aldine Publishing Company, 1968).
3. C. M. Taylor and O. F. Pye, *Foundations of Nutrition,* 6th ed. (New York: The Macmillan Company, 1966).
4. A. M. Carr-Saunders, *The Population Problem: A Study in Evolution* (London: Oxford University Press, 1922).
5. H. A. Thomas, Jr., "Human Ecology and Environmental Engineering." Conference of the Department of Demography and Human Ecology and the Center for Population Studies, Harvard University, February, 1968.

APPENDIX

If there is statistical persistence in the time series of the land-fertility variate, g, of Equation (1), as will be the case with non-zero values of the parameter ρ, then P_i and g_{i+1} of Equation (17) will not be statistically independent as was assumed in the text in deriving Equations (18), (19), and (20). Application of the standard theorems of expected value theory, however, is straightforward, and the following modified versions of these equations are obtained.

$$V(P/\overline{P}) = \frac{a}{2c - a} \left[\frac{1 + \rho\left(1 - \frac{a}{c}\right)}{1 - \rho\left(1 - \frac{a}{c}\right)} \right] V(g/\overline{g}) \tag{18a}$$

$$V(x/\overline{x}) = \frac{1}{c^2} \left[1 + \frac{\left(\frac{a}{c}\right)^2}{1 - \left(1 - \frac{a}{c}\right)^2} \cdot \frac{1 + \rho\left(1 - \frac{a}{c}\right)}{1 - \rho\left(1 - \frac{a}{c}\right)} - \frac{2(a/c)\rho}{1 - \rho\left(1 - \frac{a}{c}\right)} \right] V(g/\overline{g}) \tag{19a}$$

$$V(w/\overline{w}) = \delta^2 V(x/\overline{x}) \tag{20}$$

In a series of papers in *Water Resources Research,* a journal of the American Geophysical Union, starting in October, 1968 (*4*, No. 5, pp. 909–918), Mandlebrodt and Wallis describe a generalized family of autoregressive functions that are useful in modeling long times series of natural phenomena, such as hydro-meteorological events. The limitations of the series represented by Equation (1), which is the simplest member of the family, is discussed.

FURTHER READINGS

Lee, Richard, and Devore, Irven. *Man, the Hunter.* Chicago: Aldine Publishing Company, 1968.

Pfeiffer, John. *The Emergence of Man.* New York: Harper & Row, Publishers, 1970.

Wynne-Edwards, V. C. "Self-Regulating Systems in Population in Animals," *Science* 147 (March 26, 1965), 1543–48.

Birdsell, Joseph B. "On Population Structure in Generalized Hunting and Collecting Populations," *Evolution* 12 (June, 1958), 189–205.

Birdsell, Joseph B. "Some Environmental and Cultural Factors Influencing the Structuring of Australian Aboriginal Populations," *American Naturalist* 87, 834 (Supp. to May–June, 1953), 171–207.

Bartholomew, G. A., Jr., and Birdsell, J. B. "Ecology and the Protohominids," *American Anthropologist* 55 (1953), 481–98.

Kindleberger, Charles P. *Economic Development* (2nd ed. "Economic Handbook Series."). New York: McGraw-Hill Book Company, 1965.

Dorfman, R., Samuelson, P. A., and Solow, R. M. *Linear Programming and Economic Analyses.* New York: McGraw-Hill, 1958.

Environmental Quality— When Does Growth Become Too Expensive?

S. Fred Singer

ABSTRACT

Environmental quality is a necessity, not a luxury. Polluted water and air not only increase the cost of various economic operations, but ultimately imperil human survival. In turn, it costs money to achieve and maintain a desirable level of environmental quality. As the population expands, and more particularly as general affluence rises, the level of pollution increases roughly in direct proportion to the Gross National Product; but the cost of control increases more rapidly. Thus, it can be shown that an ever-increasing fraction of the GNP must be used in order to maintain environmental quality. Certain technological fixes can achieve a dramatic lowering for some of these costs, but they do not affect the general upward trend. Redistribution of population would also lower these costs and postpone by some years or decades the day when an unacceptably high fraction of the GNP is used to abate pollution. Ultimately, considerations of environmental quality set limits to the maximum concentrations and levels of a population in a city, region, or country.

Environmental quality is not a luxury; it is an absolute necessity of life. Pollution increases the costs of various economic operations. In a manufacturing plant, if the intake water is not pure, then money must be spent in cleaning it before it can be used. In an electric power plant, if the intake water is too warm, then it will not provide adequate cooling and the thermodynamic efficiency of the power plant goes down. Air pollution causes economic losses, including sickness and loss of productivity, as well as direct damages to crops, equipment, and buildings.

I would like to organize this paper as follows:

First, I would like to discuss the current and planned costs for various pollution control programs and put these in some meaningful relationship.

Second, I want to mention the need for technological fixes to overcome some major pollution problems. This need becomes quite obvious when one begins to examine the cost figures. But not all problems can be solved by technology and, in many cases, technology only alleviates the immediate problem and postpones the inevitable.

Third, I would like to discuss the need for basic changes in the attitudes of people, corporations, and governments: (1) avoiding waste by inherent reliability and long life of products; (2) improving the fundamental efficiency of products rather than merely and regularly changing their appearance; (3) the need for recycling and reuse, especially of water and metals; and (4) the need for real dispersion of a population to remove the high concentration in urban areas and megalopolises.

Finally, I want to discuss a trend which appears to be inevitable; namely, the lowering of environmental quality as the level and affluence of the population rise. In fact, there appears to be a fairly direct correlation between pollution and the GNP. And, since the costs of achieving and maintaining environmental quality go up faster than the GNP, it follows that a larger and larger fraction has to be spent in order to maintain environmental quality. It is difficult to say at what point such costs become unacceptable, whether at 1 per cent, 5 per cent, or even 25 per cent. But wherever the fraction becomes unacceptable, it is at that point that we have passed the optimum level of population.

This is the general plan of my presentation. Let me turn now to look at the cost figures for pollution control of land, air, and water.*

LAND POLLUTION

§ MUNICIPAL WASTES

A recent survey shows that it costs $4.5 billion a year to dispose of the 360 million tons of solid wastes created annually in the United States (or 10 pounds per person per day). Even though only half this amount is regularly carted away, the collection and disposal problem has become critical. Current estimates show that public and private agencies in the United States collect an average of 5.3 pounds per person per day of solid wastes, or more than 190 million tons per year. By 1980, this figure will have risen to 340 million tons per year and costs, too, will have doubled.[1] In addition, about 7 million passenger cars, trucks, and buses are junked annually in the United States.

Waste disposal ranks right after education and road construction in cost to municipalities. A new HEW report indicates that it will take an additional $4.2 billion over the next five years just to develop a satisfactory national waste-disposal system.[2]

Mining and agriculture produce the largest amount of waste, approximately ten times that of municipal refuse.

§ MINING WASTES

Solid wastes from mining and processing are accumulating at the rate of 1.5 billion tons per year from mine wastes, mill tailings, washing plant rejects, processing plant wastes, and smelter slags and rejects. This figure will rise to 2 billion tons by 1980 and will go higher as lower quality ores are developed.[3] There are additional special pollution problems associated with mining; for example, the widespread problem of acid mine drainage, in which water pollution is

---

* It should be realized at this point that the various pollution problems are interrelated and that, in solving one kind of pollution, one may only shift it into a different part of the environment. For example, the burning of solid waste produces air pollution. Chemicals released into the atmosphere will eventually wash down in rain and pollute rivers. The ultimate sink, however, appears to be the ocean which covers three-quarters of the earth's surface and, through its general circulation, carries water, waste materials, and pollutants over the whole globe. Nevertheless, it is useful to discuss each form of pollution separately, while keeping in mind the interrelationships.

produced by water seeping through abandoned and operating mines and leaching acids into streams; the problem of brine disposal of oil fields; and future problems in the retorting of oil shale and in underground nuclear retorting.

Even were there no increase in population or in the GNP or in the demand for minerals, the lower quality ores required just to satisfy the continuing demand will result in increased pollution.

§ AGRICULTURAL WASTES

Agricultural wastes constitute the largest solid waste problem in the United States, exceeding even that created by mining wastes. They consist primarily of animal manure and other organic material which can either be burned, or oxidized more slowly by bacteria. In addition, there are 2 billion tons of sediment which are washed down from farmlands into rivers and streams every year.[4]

Adding up all these numbers, we arrive at a total figure per person of 32 tons of solid waste per year. If all this material had to be disposed of, at about $25 per ton, this would be about $800 per person per year, or 20 per cent of the GNP. The actual expenditures are probably less than 1 per cent of GNP, but are rising.

There is a form of land pollution which is the complement to the types of pollution just discussed. I have in mind here the continual destruction of forest areas, grasslands, and even producing farms and orchards, in order to make way for more housing, more highways, and more factories at the rate of 5 million acres per year.* This is

---

* The situation can be alleviated but not entirely eliminated by proper land-use planning. It should be possible to arrange land uses so as to minimize needless destruction and so as to accommodate competing uses to the largest extent. One example of such accommodations is given in a piece of legislation recently introduced by the Department of the Interior dealing with estuarine and coastal zone management. The coastal zone is probably one of the most valuable, but also one of the most endangered pieces of land in the United States. Here the population pressure is greatest and, at the same time, the amount of shoreline and estuarine land is limited. What has been proposed is a joint federal-state endeavor in which the states prepare a long-range comprehensive plan for the management of the coastal zone, with guidance and support from the federal government. After this plan has been examined and accepted, the state then carries out its development in the coastal zone, for all purposes, in accordance with such a plan, and uses the plan to determine land-use assignments at the local government level. State authorities make sure that zoning proposed by local governments is consistent with the plan.

directly related to an expanding population and, more particularly, to an expanding GNP. The cost to the nation in terms of loss of recreational resources is difficult to quantify. Like the slag piles that are not removed, the strip mines which are left unfilled, the silt which fills up lakes and estuaries—these are all costs which we pass on to the next generation.

For solid waste pollution, a partial answer lies in technological fixes and in recycling. One place where a technological fix is needed is in packaging, which contributes about 46.5 million tons, about 13.3 per cent, to the nation's annual refuse burden. This includes cartons and paper wrappers ($\frac{2}{3}$ by weight), about 25 billion glass bottles and jars, and some 50 billion metal cans.[5]

Recycling of wastes is another necessity, one with considerable economic potential. The ordinary household and commercial refuse collected annually contains more than 11 million tons of iron and steel scrap, almost 1 million tons of nonferrous metals—including such valuable materials as aluminum, copper, lead, zinc, and tin. In addition, 15 million tons of glass and lesser amounts of other worthwhile materials are recoverable from these two types of municipal wastes alone, and the energy value of this waste is equivalent to the heating value of 60 million tons of coal. The total scrap and energy value that could be derived annually from these wastes approaches $1 billion. The potential scrap value of the iron and steel alone is nearly $200 million.[6]

The principal problems in metal recovery are to remove copper from iron pieces and tin cans so as to get high-grade ferrous scrap, and to separate and recover the aluminum, copper, lead, zinc, and tin values from the nonferrous fractions. Other efforts should be directed at reclamation of cobalt, nickel, and chromium from high-temperature or superalloy scrap, and at the recovery of these metals from waste electroplating solutions (which, incidentally, also eliminates a major water-pollution hazard).

Vast quantities of precious metals, such as gold, silver, and platinum, are presently lost from electronic equipment in commercial and defense applications because of a lack of effective recovery techniques. But electrolytic methods are being developed to transform contaminated aluminum into commercially pure metal.

A tremendous potential in recycling and recovery lies in the 7 million automobiles junked every year. A major problem, however, is to eliminate copper, which is a troublesome impurity. The eventual answer may lie in educating our automobile manufacturers, and indeed all manufacturers, to pay attention to the ultimate fate of the articles they manufacture and to design them so that they can be easily recycled. Various positive and negative tax incentives could be used to accelerate the educational process.

AIR POLLUTION

Air pollution has become mainly the problem of the cities, with the major contributors the internal combustion engine, fossil fuel power plants, industry, and the combustion of various materials—from leaves to refuse. The major pollutants are carbon monoxide (51 per cent), sulfur oxides (18 per cent), hydrocarbons (13 per cent), nitrogen oxides (9 per cent), and particles (9 per cent). Of the 142 million tons of pollutants released into the atmosphere annually, about 60 per cent comes from automobiles.[7] Carbon monoxide is produced almost entirely by automobiles. Sulfur oxides come mainly from the combustion of fossil fuels in electric power plants, while hydrocarbons, nitrogen oxides, and lead come mainly from the gasoline-powered internal combustion engine.

There are also some rather specialized problems: hydrocarbons evaporate from cleaning fluids, and other volatiles leak into the atmosphere (e.g., nitrogen oxides from the excessive use of artificial fertilizers); asbestos particles have been recognized as presenting a severe health hazard; carbon dioxide is produced in vast quantities by the combustion of fossil fuels, but is not generally considered as a pollutant although it may have long-range effects on the climate. [As far as we can tell now, even though the percentage of carbon dioxide in the atmosphere has risen by 15 per cent and will continue to rise, the heating produced is small (less than 1° C.) and may be overpowered and neutralized by the radiating effects of particulate material introduced into the atmosphere by pollution.]

Another point of long-range concern is the heat energy released to the atmosphere by human industrial activities. In the United States, the average electric power generated at the present time is 1.5×10^{12} kwh per year, or 1.7×10^{11} watt. This works out to 180 milliwatts per square meter, about 0.1 per cent of the value of solar heat contribution of about 220 watts per m². Total energy consumption in the United States in 1970 comes to 2.2×10^{12} watts, or nearly 1 per cent of solar heat contribution. On a world-wide basis, energy consumption is about 6.6×10^{12} watts, area is 5.1×10^{14} m², giving an energy release of 1.3×10^{-2} watt/m², or 0.06 per cent of solar heating.

Another specialized problem is the air pollution produced by aircraft. We are concerned here not only with the combustion products but also the emitted water vapor which causes high-altitude contrails. If they occur frequently enough, the artificial cirrus clouds which are thereby produced can have substantial effects on local weather and on world climate generally. With the tremendous increase in high altitude jet travel, this is a distinct possibility.

§ TECHNOLOGICAL FIXES

Air pollution problems are amenable to technological fixes, but at a cost. Sulfur can be removed from fossil fuels and, in some cases, the sulfur extracted has commercial value. In any case, sulfurous fuels can be and should be burned as far away as possible from populated regions so as to eliminate the synergistic effects of different types of air pollutants. Particles and most industrial air pollutants can be eliminated either by process design or by properly designed pollution control devices which are added at the end of the process. It is clear that we should provide positive incentives to industry to develop processes so that pollution will not be produced in the first place.

The pollution abatement costs are not excessive. For example, the additional annual cost of reducing human exposure to sulfur oxides and particulates by 60 to 75 per cent in all metropolitan areas (containing 70 per cent of the population) was estimated to be about three quarters of a billion dollars. Of this, manufacturing and electric power companies would likely bear about one-half the cost or $350 million—the equivalent of one-sixth of 1 per cent of the value added by industry to the production of goods and services in the United States in 1967. In contrast, another industry cost, labor, rose by 5 per cent, or thirty times as much, in 1967. Service and distributive firms and households would bear the balance of the abatement cost, averaging about $3 per person in cities.[8]

Other estimates, however, lead to higher costs. A major midwestern electric utility company prefers to import 6 million barrels of low sulfur residual oil (which produces 6.5 million Btu. per barrel) at a cost of 45¢ per million Btu.; this oil would replace high sulfur local coal (which produces 26 million Btu. per ton) at 30¢ per million Btu. If we were to apply this differential of 15¢ per million Btu. to the

400 million tons of coal used annually by utilities, the total national cost would be $1.5 billion per year. (Or $15 billion over a ten-year period, which is a reasonable time scale for new technology development; it is against such costs that one must judge the desirability of expending funds for new technical approaches, such as sulfur removal during the burning of coal in fluidized beds.)

But the chief polluter, as mentioned earlier, is the internal combustion engine, which accounts for nearly all the carbon monoxide, most of the hydrocarbons, nitrogen oxides, and nearly all of the lead. It is instructive to look at this example in more detail because it illustrates the great value of a national investment in technology to get rid of pollution.

Today, the total vehicle pollution emission into the atmosphere is close to 90 million tons per year. By 1980 this will have been reduced to nearly 60, or about one-third less. However, from then on, in spite of ideal maintenance and with the use of the latest California standards, the emission load will reach 70 million tons by the year 2000 when the total registered vehicles in the United States will have climbed from 100 to 220 million.[9]

But can we afford this ideal control program? Over a fifteen-year period, say 1975 to 1990, the total costs to the public for emission control devices and maintenance has been estimated by one industry source as between $96 and $141 billion, without any essential improvement in air quality.[9] In fact, since it must be assumed that these devices will not work perfectly between inspections, the air quality will probably deteriorate. It is against costs like these that we have to weigh the importance of making major technological investments in low-pollution engines or of devising other alternatives for mass transportation.

WATER POLLUTION

Water pollution in some sense seems to be more fundamental than either land or air pollution: it tends to persist and accumulate—especially in lakes; and there are no technological fixes to biological waste production by human beings. Water pollution itself, however, is due to the use of water to transport these wastes; it was the invention of the water closet over a hundred years ago in England that gave rise to the serious problems of river pollution which are only now being overcome by appropriate treatment plants.

In our discussion it is well to keep in mind that there are conservative pollutants, such as chlorides and other inorganic salts which dissolve in water, and nonconservative pollutants, such as heat, or organic waste materials which are oxidized naturally by biological action.

§ DOMESTIC WASTES

What one would like to do is develop a method for determining the per capita cost to supply and clean up water to a certain degree of purity, as a function of population level and concentration. Into this model we would feed the fact that there is a certain natural rate of disappearance of a nonconservative pollutant and that there is also a critical level of pollution above which many undesirable things take place. This critical level may be either a legal criterion incorporated into water-quality standards, or it may be a physical-chemical level such as the eutrophication threshold for a lake: i.e., the critical concentration levels for nitrogen and phosphorus above which we get prolific growth of algae.

Some simple considerations will illustrate how such a methodology can be constructed:

10^{12} gallons of water flow to the ocean in the continental United States each day;

(18 per cent flows into the Pacific, 21 per cent into the Atlantic, 50 per cent into the Gulf of Mexico, 11 per cent into the Gulf of California.)

To oxidize one gallon of raw sewage requires 140 p.p.m. of oxygen (or 0.0011 pounds of O_2 per gallon).

It has been estimated that per capita contribution is 135 gallons of sewage per day; this would demand 0.167 pounds of oxygen or $135 \times 140 = 19,000$ p.p.m. of O_2 demand per person per day.

Water at $10°$ C. contains about 10 p.p.m. of O_2 when saturated. In order to bring the O_2 content to a minimum value of 5 p.p.m., 4,000 gallons of water are required to self-purify the sewage per person per day.

These simple considerations show that there is not enough fresh water in the United States to self-purify the sewage of more than 250 million people, even if these people were perfectly distributed. As a matter of fact, the amount of waste water from various manufacturing industries came to 46 million gallons per day in 1965 and will be probably of the order of 75 million gallons per day in 1980. The biochemical oxygen-demanding material (BOD) in the industrial waste water came to 60 million pounds per day, which is just about three times as much as that of the 120 million people served by sewers in the United States.[10]

It is therefore clearly necessary to treat waste water discharged into fresh water streams and lakes. In the case of ocean outfalls, it may also be necessary to apply treatment, particularly if the dispersal is not adequate. In 1962, about 20 per cent of the waste water in communities served by sewer systems was untreated, 30 per cent received only primary treatment, and 50 per cent some kind of secondary treatment.[11] This situation is now changing rapidly, largely because of national water-pollution-control legislation and the federal funds which have become available to spur the construction of treatment plants.

Primary treatment, which is basically mechanical removal of solids, costs between 3 and 4¢ per thousand gallons and removes about one-third of the BOD and only small amounts of the nitrogen and phosphorus. Secondary treatment is an accelerated and controlled form of natural oxidation by bacteria. When done in a properly designed plant, as much as 90 per cent of the BOD can be removed, about half of the nitrogen, and a third of the phosphorus. The total cost (including primary treatment) is about 15 to 20 cents per 1,000 gallons.[12] However, nitrogen and, especially, phosphorus are very troublesome, particularly in lakes and estuaries where the flushing rate may be very low. These nutrients can give rise to the growth of blue-green algae and other noxious phytoplankton which can cause fish kills and deplete the lake of oxygen.

Various types of tertiary treatment are now available which can purify water to any desired extent. In fact, purification can be carried to the stage where the water can be directly reused for drinking purposes, at an additional cost of 15 to 20¢ per 1,000 gallons.[13] Currently, complete re-use of waste water is practiced in Windhoek, South Africa; other communities are cleaning up water to an extent where it is available for many domestic uses other than drinking.

One of the exciting possibilities coming out of the laboratory research program, and now in the pilot-plant stage, is the complete elimination of secondary (biological) treatment; primary treatment can be followed directly by physical-chemical methods which remove nearly all of the phosphorus and nitrogen, and more than 99 per cent of the BOD as well. It is clear that advanced waste treatment methods will be required where the population concentration is very high.

§ THERMAL POLLUTION

A similar analysis can be performed for thermal pollution. One starts with a level of electric energy production, which for the United States in 1965 was about 5,000 kwh. per capita. This production is conservatively assumed to have a doubling time of ten years. Since the thermal efficiency of power plants is approximately one-third, the energy which has to be rejected in the form of waste heat is 10,000 kwh. per capita, a figure which will double every ten years. This heat has to be carried away, at least partly, by cooling water.

Predictions indicate that in 1990 between 92 and 94 per cent of the power generated in the United States will be produced thermally, with almost two-thirds of this produced by nuclear plants which require 40 per cent more cooling water than fossil-fueled plants.[14]

In principle, rivers may be re-used over and over for cooling water since they dissipate the heat to the atmosphere as the water flows downstream. But the establishment of water temperature limits, in order to protect water quality, markedly reduces the number of available river sites and, in addition, requires the installation of supplemental or alternative cooling methods such as cooling ponds or cooling towers. This, again, increases costs and also loss of water by evaporation. It is becoming clear that a growing number of power plants will have to be located along the coasts where the waste heat can be efficiently discharged into the oceans.

By 1980, electrical needs will require the use of one-sixth of the total available fresh-water runoff in the entire nation for cooling purposes. Now, if we discount flood flows which usually occur about one-third of the year and account for two-thirds of the total runoff, it becomes apparent that the power industry will require about half the total runoff for the remaining two-thirds of the year. More recent projections of the waste-heat load by the year 2000, which take into account probable technical improvements, indicate that the requirements for cooling water will equal two-thirds of the total national daily runoff of 1,200 billion gallons.[15]

It is clear, also, that maintenance of environmental quality in the face of increasing demands for energy means an increase in costs, but not an excessive one. The increase in production cost normally would not exceed 0.3 mill per kwh., which adds about $300 million to the total national cost, an increment of the order of 1 per cent to energy costs for consumers.

§ AGRICULTURAL POLLUTION

Even if municipal and industrial waste discharges can be controlled at a reasonable cost, the discharges from agricultural and other diffuse sources will continue to plague us. The chief problems in this area come from the improper, and excess, application of fertilizers, from pesticides which wash into rivers or vaporize into the atmosphere, and from organic wastes, particularly from feedlots, which are allowed to wash into rivers. Ten thousand cattle produce as much waste as a city of 164,000.[16]

The answer here lies in stricter control and conservation methods. Full waste treatment may be necessary for feedlots; the application of fertilizers and pesticides will have to be strictly controlled and their excess or unnecessary uses prevented; and soil erosion will have to be reduced by proper conservation methods. This is an expensive but necessary program.

WATER CONSERVATION

There are a few essential steps which will alleviate the immediate situation and postpone the inevitable, and chief among these is water conservation.

In the United States, water is used in excessive quantities and for many unnecessary purposes. Other countries which are water-short are leading the way in experimentation to reduce water consumption.

Irrigation, our chief consumer of water, will have to be made much more efficient than it presently is: for example, by automatic sprinkling devices which respond to the actual water need of plants or which do not operate unless the meteorological conditions are proper; or by trickle irrigation which supplies water, nutrients, and occasional pesticides directly to each plant rather than spreading it over the whole field.

In domestic use, great savings are possible by properly designed baths, showers, and toilet facilities. In a number of locations throughout the world there have been installed so-called vacuum toilets, in which toilet wastes are moved by pneumatic pressure rather than solely by water. This system also has the advantage that the sanitary wastes are highly concentrated and can be treated apart from other wastes which do not contain such large amounts of BOD as well as bacteria and viruses.

Another remedy is re-use of water. Waste water can be cleaned up to drinking-water quality and reintroduced into the water-supply system. Three or four cycles are possible before chlorides build up to excessive values. (Parenthetically, we might remark that waste water which is often completely untreated is re-used naturally, but in diluted form, from rivers and lakes.) Even without re-using waste water for drinking purposes, it is possible to set up a hierarchy of water supply and waste-water uses in which the cleaned-up waste water is used for laundry, gardens, golf courses, etc.

WATER TREATMENT COSTS

The cost of remedial measures to abate pollution is high, of course. Studies performed by the Federal Water Pollution Control Administration for their report *The Cost of Clean Water* indicate the following with respect to certain waste sources for the five-year period from 1968 to 1973.

Municipal Wastes: Costs for construction of new treatment facilities, replacement and expansion of existing facilities, removal of phosphates by the Great Lakes communities, operation and maintenance expenses, and construction of sanitary sewer lines range from $17.4 to $23.4 billion. (About $10 billion of this construction is eligible for federal grants on a cost-sharing basis.)

Industrial Wastes: Acceptable treatment of industrial wastes, including thermal effluents from power plants, will cost from $8.5 to $10.9 billion for both capital costs and for operation and maintenance.

To achieve complete cleanup, the following programs will have to be carried out—necessarily on a longer time scale.

Overflows from Combined Storm and Sanitary Sewers: The cost of total separation of lines handling storm water and sanitary sewage is estimated to amount to approximately $49 billion, $30 billion of which would be applied to public sewers. Effective alternate solutions to this problem, other than complete separation, might reduce the cost to perhaps $15 billion.

Erosion and Sedimentation: The total cost of controlling erosion is difficult to estimate since it is not entirely a pollution problem, but the range extends from a minimum of $300 million to perhaps as much as $10 billion.

Acid Mine Drainage: Estimated total costs range from $1.7 billion for a 40 per cent reduction to as much as $6.6 billion for a 95 per cent reduction. Actual costs will depend on the amount of neutralization necessary for each specific area to meet the water quality standards.

There are other pollution problems—such as pollution from vessels, oil spills, agricultural wastes, and radioactive wastes—for which the costs cannot yet be well defined.

THE COST-POPULATION RELATIONSHIP

It is clear from the preceding pages that the physical environment has the ability to assimilate a limited amount of pollution. The atmosphere can disperse local pollution concentrations, and rainfall can clean the atmosphere—up to a certain point. Rivers, lakes, and the oceans can assimilate varying amounts of BOD and dissipate a certain amount of waste heat, before becoming overloaded. Therefore, pollution abatement becomes necessary only when the population concentration—and therefore the waste inputs—exceed certain limits. For man living in ecological balance with his environment, the cost of pollution control is zero.

If we view the human-population/water-pollution situation, we can see the following picture: As the level of population increases, the degree of treatment must be constantly increased in order to keep the level of pollutants below a critical value. However, the cost of treatment rises quite rapidly as we increase the degree of purification. We are therefore back to a kind of Malthusian equation: The cost of maintaining environmental quality increases at a faster rate than the population. Inevitably, therefore, at some point in the future, a major fraction of the GNP would have to be devoted to maintaining environmental quality. Everyone would agree that spending more than 50 per cent of the national income on pollution control is unrealistic. On the other hand, 1 per cent does not appear unreasonable. Perhaps the right level is of the order of a few per cent, which is very close to what is being contemplated now.

In conclusion, there are a number of points, all of them important, which should at least be mentioned:

1. What should be our goal for environmental quality? How do we measure the benefits, including those which are difficult to quantify, so that we can gauge the extent of our national investment?

2. How do we distribute the costs of maintaining a quality environment so that each sector of society pays its fair share? For example, groups that pay for abatement, such as municipalities and industries, do not favor a very high standard of quality; groups that benefit but do not pay directly, such as fishermen and outdoor recreationists, are likely to demand very high standards.

3. Finally, we must face the question of passing along environmental problems to future generations. To what extent should we invest our current income so that future generations, which will have a higher income, will be able to spend less? To what extent can we leave a legacy of pollution? Do we have the moral right to do so?

SUMMARY

It is clear that the present costs of maintaining environmental quality are huge but not yet excessive when measured in terms of other public expenditures. It is also clear that we cannot continue in the same manner since the costs are rising faster than either the population or the GNP. Various technological fixes are possible which will alleviate the present situation and postpone the inevitable confrontation. These include re-use and recycling to overcome some of the problems of solid wastes (particularly junk automobiles), industrial wastes, mining wastes, and agricultural wastes. Re-use of water by chemical-physical purification or its desalting will become increasingly important, as will better and more economical ways of using water.

Another mandatory requirement is a more adequate spreading out of the existing and, especially, of the future population. We simply cannot let our present cities expand without limit; nor are satellite cities located within the megalopolis belts a real long-term solution. They just diffuse the problem a little bit. What we need are brand new cities in areas of the country that have not hitherto been settled. We have many areas where the geology and the climate are highly desirable; with transportation available and with communication established they only require water to support an economic base of industry and population.

A partial answer to the Malthusian problem might be to spread out the population so that each river basin has its appropriate number of people. In a sense, this is an ecologically beneficial solution, since the water supply also has to be in balance with the population level and density. Perhaps this should be our aim, for both short-term and longer-term solutions.

Ultimately, however, the general upward trend in the cost to maintain environmental quality must set a limit to a population in a city or in a region. This limit can be established fairly accurately locally, and even applied to the country as a whole, with the optimum range established less accurately since that depends on the distribution of the population.

R E F E R E N C E S

1. R. J. Black, A. J. Muhick, A. J. Klee, H. L. Hickman, and R. D. Vaughan, *An Interim Report: 1968 National Survey of Community Solid Waste Practices,* 1968 annual meeting, Institute for Solid Wastes, American Public Works Association, Miami Beach, Florida, October, 1968. Bureau of Solid Waste Management, Department of Health, Education and Welfare (Washington, D.C.: Government Printing Office, 1968), p. 47.

2. *Ibid.,* p. 51.

3. W. A. Vogely, "The Economic Factors of Mineral Waste Utilization," *Proceedings* of the symposium: "Mineral Waste Utilization" IIT Research Institute (Chicago: Illinois Institute of Technology, March, 1968), p. 7.

4. C. H. Wadleigh, *Wastes in Relation to Agriculture and Forestry.* Department of Agriculture, Miscellaneous Publication No. 1065 (Washington, D.C.: Government Printing Office, March, 1968), p. 6.

5. Orsen Darnay, and William E. Franklin, *The Role of Packaging in Solid Waste Management, 1966 to 1976.* Department of Health, Education and Welfare, Public Health Service Publication No. 1855 (Washington, D.C.: Government Printing Office, 1969).

6. Carl Rampacek, "Reclamation and Recycling Metals and Minerals Found in Municipal Incineration Residues," *Proceedings* of the Symposium: "Mineral Waste Utilization" (Chicago: IIT Research Institute, March, 1968), p. 124.

7. *The Sources of Air Pollution and Their Control.* Department of Health, Education and Welfare, Public Health Service Publication No. 1548 (Washington, D.C.: Government Printing Office, 1966).

8. Jack W. Carlson, "What Price a Quality Environment," *Jour. of Soil and Water Conservation* (May–June, 1969).

9. Private communication from William P. Lear, Chairman of the Board, Lear Motors, Reno, Nevada, February, 1970. In addition to the control devices themselves, the figures include the cost of semiannual inspection and an allowance for adjustment of faulty control devices.

10. *The Cost of Clean Water: Vol. 1, Summary.* Department of the Interior, Federal Water Pollution Control Administration (Washington, D.C.: Government Printing Office, January, 1968), p. 21.

11. Andrew C. Glass, and Kenneth H. Jenkins, *Statistical Summary of 1962 Inventory of Municipal Waste Facilities in the United States.* Division of Water Supply and Pollution Control, Department of Health, Education and Welfare, Public Health Service (Washington, D.C.: Government Printing Office, 1964).

12. *Cleaning Our Environment: The Chemical Basis for Action.* Subcommittee on Environmental Improvements, Committee on Chemistry and Public Affairs, American Chemical Society (Washington, D.C.: American Chemical Society, 1969), p. 108.

13. *Ibid.,* p. 125.

14. *Industrial Waste Guide on Thermal Pollution* (rev. ed.). Department of the Interior, Federal Water Pollution Control Administration (Washington, D.C.: Government Printing Office, September, 1968), p. 7.

15. R. W. Holcomb, "Power Generation: The Next 30 Years," *Science,* 167 (January 9, 1970), 160.

16. Wadleigh, *op. cit.,* p. 41.

FURTHER READINGS

Ernst and Ernst. *Costs and Economic Impact of Air Pollution Control, Fiscal Year 70-71.* A report prepared for the Department of Health, Education and Welfare, Consumer Protection and Environmental Health Service, National Air Pollution Control Administration (Washington, D.C.: G.P.O., October, 1969).

Jarret, Henry (ed.). *Environmental Quality in a Growing Economy.* Published for Resources for the Future, Inc. Baltimore: The Johns Hopkins Press, 1966.

Landsberg, Hans. *Natural Resources for U.S. Growth: A Look Ahead to the Year 2000.* Published for Resources for the Future, Inc. Baltimore: The Johns Hopkins Press, 1964.

Perloff, Harvey S. *The Quality of Urban Environment.* Published for Resources for the Future, Inc. Baltimore: The Johns Hopkins Press, 1969.

Restoring the Quality of Our Environment. Report of the Environmental Pollution Panel, The President's Science Advisory Committee, The White House. Washington, D.C.: Government Printing Office, November, 1965.

Waste Management and Control. Report to the Federal Council for Science and Technology by the Committee on Pollution, National Academy of Sciences-National Research Council, Publication 1400. Washington, D.C.: 1966.

Environmental Quality as a Determinant for an Optimum Level of Population

Christian de Laet

ABSTRACT

Because of our failure to operate on the basis that private interests and the common good of the world are identical, the optimum level of population must already have been exceeded. The human population may be classified into three groups: "natural" man who is in unconscious balance with nature; "industrial" man who exploits the natural resources to raise his standard of living; and "post-industrial" man who is aware of the relationship between environmental quality and the quality of life. In a system whose environmental resources are being used to the limit, the behavior patterns of post-industrial man are the only ones compatible with survival and with suitable rewards and punishments, and we must induce such responses in all groups.

Man's continued presence on earth in ever-growing numbers is largely dependent on the dislocation and volume of waste the natural environment can tolerate. Further rates of technological development will require that we institutionalize innovation. Our greatest obstacle is our unwillingness to change our habits in order to take the steps we know to be in our interests.

INTRODUCTION

Naturae enim non imperatur nisi parendo. (Bacon)

The question implied in the title is essentially a problem of human ecology which is rising to the fore at an increased and unforeseen rate. This paper could have considered the relationships of man and each of his natural resources on principles of environmental quality. The earlier papers in the Symposium and in this series will likely have done so; rather, I shall look for a few keys to the problem and their critical understanding in terms of systems thresholds. The mode of argument will be pragmatic and nonnumerical.

Too little attention has been given to the relationships between resources and contemporary society. Are they to be used merely for the tangible physical growth of the human species as such? Are they the basis for affluence? Are they to be considered in terms of aesthetic or other abstract rewards? In order to focus on the work at hand we must reconsider man and nature and its "meta"-implications. As a species we are dependent on the natural environment, but as civilizations we are dependent on the wholesale alteration, exploitation, and transformation of natural resources; there are basic conflicts here and we are coming to realize that there are no absolute and unique solutions to what are universal dilemmas. Such is the basic premise in dealing with the relationships between environmental quality and an optimum level of population. It would not be helpful to begin with the nature of man, yet we must look at very long futures and with the utmost detachment from the day-to-day affairs of our planet. In that framework, it is reasonable to state that environmental quality is ultimately the only nonresolvable constraint on population numbers.

THE TERRESTRIAL CONTEXT

Life on earth is not self-generating and self-sufficient. It has been totally shaped by, and is still largely dependent upon, the terrestrial environment in which it has evolved.

Before life began on earth, the geophysical environment on which all existing forms of life depend was evolved: conditions of matter, atmosphere, temperature, light, etc. combined to provide the precarious framework for the evolution of life as we know it. But the narrow range of conditions favorable to life will endure for only an instant in the ongoing evolution of our solar system.

The basic elements of the terrestrial environment which have made possible and shaped the evolution of life are air, water, and the fertile combination of organic and inorganic matter known as soil.

In one sense, biological evolution can be viewed as a process whereby living organisms become less and less dependent on their immediate environment. While always restricted to the narrow range of life-supporting conditions, higher forms of life are generally more resistant to small variations in their environment.

A turning point in this process occurred with the emergence of animal life. Plants are at the mercy of their environment, which they can hardly choose or change. But animal life has a new characteristic: mobility. To some extent, all forms of animal life can alter their environment as a result of this particular attribute and many higher land animals can, to some degree, control their environment by transforming it, thus becoming increasingly independent of the natural environment.

When man lived in caves, without clothes, tools, fire or weapons—when he was merely a hunter and a berry-picker—he was not significantly different from many other forms of life, and had no greater effect on nature. In this early stage he was very much a part of the natural system, competing for essential resources in an intricately balanced and interconnected life system, the growth of which was governed by the rate of natural increase that the existing resource base would support.

However, when man began to manage his environment to an unprecedented degree, beginning his cultural evolution to our present stage, he stepped outside the existing natural system and created a new one of his own.

All life is based on carbon, oxygen, nitrogen, and hydrogen, and our contacts with these occur through air, water, and soil. These basic resources must be free to complete their respective cycles. If they are impaired or altered by pollution or otherwise, the pattern for survival can be changed with a speed far exceeding man's ability to evolve or adapt. Until man began to transform the environment on a massive scale the living world changed fairly gradually, without violent upheavals and dislocations. Man is unique in his ability to alter the environment, which means he is unique in his ability to create imbalances.

Within a balanced system there is no such thing as waste, for what is waste in one process in the system is food or fuel for another phase of the cycle. There are two ways in which this balance can be upset. One is by vastly increasing the proportion of one type of matter, which has the effect of overloading the system, at least temporarily. The second is by the introduction of material that does not occur naturally within the system. In this situation the system generally cannot absorb and integrate the foreign matter. Besides the obvious impairment of efficiency, a reaction may be set up with matter already present to form new products, resulting in spectacular and sudden effects.

Industrialization and urbanization have caused a revolution in the quantity and quality of our wastes, and social structures have not undergone the necessary parallel transformations to cope with the situation. (Air and water are often still foolishly used as reservoirs for indiscriminate waste disposal.)

The city is not in balance with its surroundings; it may be on the way to destroying itself as a viable environment for mankind. Its own wastes accumulate in and around it, contaminating its air and water supply and too often contaminating also the sense of responsibility of its inhabitants. All this renders it unsuitable for providing food, shelter, and leisure, and, possibly, even for industry. Man as the maker of his environment and man as the product of his environment are engaged in a conflict that could become deadly. Either way, man stands to lose.

THE QUESTION OF NUMBERS

Whatever the nature and the strength of the arguments to the contrary, we must feel that if such a large proportion of the world population lives below subsistence levels, the optimum level of population* must already have been exceeded. (It is largely a matter of social efficiency.) It is intuitively clear, and nonetheless an acceptable argument, that this state of affairs exists because of our failure to accept an aggregate responsibility for the species, because of our failure to recognize the problem at a level of global strategy, and also because of our unwillingness to operate on the basis that in the

---

* No specific reference need be made to developing countries: a good fifth of the "Western" world is in a state of poverty.

long run (and in the not-so-long run) private, local interests and the common good of the world are identical.

We need a functional understanding of the question of numbers (and its relations to environmental quality). Since a philosophical approach is not useful here, it is proposed to classify the human population into three broad groups and to sketch out some of their relevant characteristics with respect to reproduction and their environment* (see Table 1).

In a balanced system, where man is no more disruptive than any other animal and external factors such as "death control" have not been introduced, the Class I way of life belongs. In a world of apparent plenty, the attitudes of Class II man may appear to be justifiable. However, in a system whose limited supply of environmental resources is being threatened with overuse, the behavior patterns of Class III man are the only ones compatible with survival.

These three classes are striving simultaneously to use or control overlapping and nonseparable segments of the environment. The problems related to finding compromises between these classes are enormous. They are not made any easier by the lack of any real awareness by any one class of the existence and nature of the other classes' demands on the environment.

Within our finite system, the spaceship earth,† we may deem the human species to represent a capital value which can increase in quantity and in quality, the two aspects being inversely related beyond a saturation point. We cannot afford any downward shift in overall human quality without declaring open bankruptcy for the species.‡ We must raise the quality of man, or at least the quality

---

* The characteristics are absent of jargon: they are not designed as entry points into the disciplines concerned, merely as broad situational guides to the argument. In different societies and life settings, the boundaries between the classes will be different; they are thresholds related to dynamic forces. Such thresholds cannot be specified numerically because their causal factors are not numerable, and, even if they were, it would not be in the interest of the relevant decision-makers to act overtly on their knowledge.

† Kenneth Boulding must by now accept that his phrase has become common property and feel recompensed in that he has thereby contributed significantly to our awareness of global problems.

‡ In particular, I do not consider valid the thesis that the quantity of environmental quality is unlimited on the strength that there is always a lower level of quality which permits everybody to have enough of it; there is a threshold below which the benefits of environmental quality are mere survival.

TABLE 1

Relevant Characteristics of Human Population

	CLASS I Homo Homo *the natural man*	CLASS II Homo Faber et Artifax *the industrial man*	CLASS III Homo Sapiens et Sentiens *the post-industrial man*
GOAL	survival, freedom from hunger	high standard of living, freedom from poverty	high quality of life, freedom from constraints
OBJECT	to secure food, clothes, shelter	to produce, trade, and transform economic goods and services	to know, to enjoy living
TOOLS	instinctive responses, learned skills	specialized skills, social cunning	knowledge, social service, intelligence
SOCIAL UNIT	the individual, the tribe	the community, the corporation, the association	the family, society at large
ATTITUDE	atavistic, innate: "Be fruitful and multiply"	egotistic, self-centered: "Fill the Earth and subdue it, have dominion . . ."	humanistic, social-orientation, the "good gardener"
REWARD	an irrelevant notion; transient satiety	the means: profit, economic, efficiency	the end: a purpose to life and to living
POPULATION	defensive urge to reproduce	numbers determined by economic and social status	self-regulated numbers: social responsibility
ENVIRONMENT	use; space is to be occupied	transformation and abuse; space is to be owned	conservation; space is to be utilized
ITS QUALITY	not a meaningful concept; no specific value	postulated as a free good; non-marketed value	an absolutely meaningful concept; of critical value

of his societal awareness and responsibility, to the point where the urge to multiply will cease to be an atavistic defense mechanism or an index of achievement and will become reasoned.

In other words, not only must we do all we can to raise the world population above Class I, but we must also find alternatives to the standard patterns of Class II. Hopefully, we can attract people to some appreciation of Class III before they are satiated in their appetites for the apparent comfort of Class II.

In parallel, Class III must strengthen its purpose and its action on Class I, in an attempt to remove its most turbulent anxieties and to de-fuse its potential revolt. Most so-called civilized societies have large segments of their populations in Class I, but its Class II population is creating compounded pressures by their demand for ever higher unit-cost goods and services that only benefit a small number.

The impossibility theorem is proved here in that we cannot reconcile individual and collective choices without violating someone's preferences, but we need not go to the other extreme and satisfy indiscriminately the infinite expectations of those who supply us with the prolific progeny of unbridled technology.

Biological advances which could be used to man's evolutionary advantage are soon in contravention of our comfortable, if inoperable, concepts of individual rights. Such rights, which often are perceived by the majority only as a fiction, prevent us from taking actions which are essential to our survival.

Society as a whole is a generic device intended to advance (and protect) all its members; but it should not be foolish and fail to recognize that man's continued, if not improved, survival as a species is solely related to the achievements of a very small percentage of its numbers in each generation.

If individual freedom and life have to be curtailed for the good of the majority, the decision to do so rests with an intricate machinery which diffuses the responsibility for the decision and seldom allows it to be identified with any one individual or small recognizable group. The decision to control the levels of human population rests largely with a small group of "social" servicemen of Class III. Considering the essential necessity for this control, we must carefully weigh the implications of a persistent attachment to the conventional verbalizations about "our" way of life. This imperative may regretfully ring the death knell of conventional democracy in spite of its evident attraction.

ENVIRONMENTAL QUALITY

There is no absolute definition of environmental quality. Many philosophical statements may be understandable without lending themselves to easy quantification. In a specific problem area, any absolutely defined levels of environmental quality may be above or below acceptance levels.

There are two levels of urgency regarding appreciation of ecological balances and the environment: survival of the human species, and valuation of the long term benefits of environmental quality in terms of quality of life. Until recently, these concepts have been understood only abstractly, resulting in a "nonattitude" toward the conservation of the natural environment.*

One thing is incontrovertibly clear: man's continued presence on earth in ever-growing numbers is largely subject to the amount of wastes the natural environment can tolerate. With the possible exception of war, the greatest threat to man's survival is his propagation of himself and his wastes beyond the ability of the environment to cope.

It is unrealistic to think we can eliminate waste entirely, for it is a condition of life. From man's point of view—and it is reasonable to be anthropocentric—the conversion of natural resources to his own ends is the basic operation. However, this operation must be as efficient as possible so that the regenerative powers of nature are not taxed beyond their capacity in the global long run.† We just cannot go on living off our environmental capital. Our interventions in the environment should be tentative, incremental, and experimental, particularly as any abuse of the environment is likely to cause long lasting and unforeseen side effects. We must hold back on nonessential changes until there is a well-informed consensus.

The rise of urbanization and industrialization has been foreseen for a long time; the compounding effect of a parallel increase in mobility and leisure is going to affect our environmental values

---

* This condition is possibly worse in Canada because of its low densities: only twenty-one millions are inhabiting the second largest country in the world.

† The environment can only supply a limited number of inputs and can only tolerate a limited amount and mix of outputs. Optimally, the gross production of net outputs (i.e., nonrecyclable, durable wastes) must be nil. In this sense, the population level will be determined by the level of inputs which can be provided without causing a net long-run increase in outputs.

fundamentally. As a society we have failed to recognize the "social" role of the environment and to program this role (if only, at the beginning, as a check and balance), introducing it in our traditional "economic" equations. We need compatible scales for social values and a mechanism to introduce them into our marketing system. It is clear that the notion of a Gross National Product relating only to the economic goods and services produced is frivolous if not suicidal: we will have to include social progress and environmental retrogress if we want a national product to have any meaning at all.

Environmental quality control will demand a continuous upgrading of our "behavior" thresholds; the relative merit of our individual and collective activities will have to be rated as to the durable damage they inflict on the environment. The burden of proof of the innocence of any environmental change must be placed on he who initiates. Traditional burden shifting, if not obfuscating, poses a danger to our collective survival.

For the population to become self-regulating, the externalities represented by excessive wastes and residues will have to be internalized so that each segment automatically takes such matters into account. A system of rewards and penalties should be established to match the particular attitudes and responses of the three population classes suggested previously. In terms of environmental quality, the three classes could be described as follows:

Class I: the natural man has a rising awareness of the role and existence of the environment—his object could be *non-pollution:* to prevent avoidable damage.

Class II: the industrial man considers environmental quality measures an unavoidable nuisance—his object could be *anti-pollution:* to control and manage his wastes and residues.

Class III: the post-industrial man desires the enhancement of environmental quality—his object could be *de-pollution:* to recover from the damage done in the past.

RELATION BETWEEN NUMBERS AND ENVIRONMENTAL QUALITY

In the long run, we may well be capable of satisfying our physical needs, at any level of population, by developments in technology and science; but continued survival as a species will depend also on the satisfaction of our inherent nonphysical needs, which are directly or indirectly related to environmental quality. There are already clear indications of this in advanced societies where the quality of life is the main concern, at whatever standard of living.

A preliminary conclusion is that a search for a lowest upper limit to numbers is essentially related to an agreement on the quality of life which, for the human animal, is in its very essence related to environmental quality.

We should explore the nature of S curves which might be drawn showing the relationship of environmental quality and satiety of physical and nonphysical human needs, to time (and rate of change), to spatial density of use, and to resource uses and their attendant sets of conflicts. These relationships should be examined for each of the three classes of man described earlier.

The second law of thermodynamics and the whole concept of entropy are crucially important to understanding these problems. The natural laws governing local and global transitions between organization and randomness must become of direct concern to our social planners. Our attitudes toward pollution depend on our own individual and highly subjective feelings about "excess," "disorder," "disharmony," which in themselves are breeders of decay and decadence.

CONCLUSION

In the perspective of technological advances, scientific discoveries, and improved management, the limited supply of natural resources, renewable or not, does not define an absolute limit on population numbers. The rates of resource conversion and of population growth may be in conflict at certain levels of expectations but this does not necessarily vitiate the statement that environmental quantity can only set relative upper limits to numbers. Environmental quality, however, is probably the limiting factor, since, hopefully, we will agree on the optimum population we want before we are forced to accept the maximum population we can have.

Optimum implies judgment. If we can agree on an adequate standard of living, that at best can only be relative, can we agree as easily on the quality of life, its length, its productivity, and more generally on our rate of progress toward still largely undefined goals for humanity?* An optimum level would likely be reached in terms of national or local criteria, and large discrepancies which could only be settled by aggressive conflicts would have to be avoided.

There is no comfort in the thought that war is not reducing our numbers very much any longer, since modern warfare is likely to hasten biological demise, a worse peril to the species. Aside from man-man conflicts, man-environment conflicts are the gravest. We are unable to define and program for peace, beauty, and health whereas we can for war, ugliness, and sickness. But even if we have to price beauty as the cost of removing ugliness—that is, by using strictly a negative approach, let us find comfort in that the means justify the end.

We are at a point in the development of our world where, if we look behind us, tomorrow's exponential take-off curves still look relatively "flat." There is no comfort to be found in this: tomorrow will require quantum jumps that are more usually associated with catastrophes and revolution than man's usually low individual sense of evolution. We must innovate and we must institutionalize innovation.

Every aspect of the problem displays a social component which far outweighs the technological factor: we are able to solve the problem, we indeed have an interest in doing so, but we must become willing to do it. This will involve an incredibly large number of habits to be changed, of systems to be redesigned, of criteria to be modified. They will touch on every facet of our lives and on many of our "rights" in urban settlement, land tenure, *abus de droit,* community laws, and the like.

It is indeed a problem of human ecology which will require wartime approaches in terms of desperate urgency, unswayable purpose, and global vision and commitment.

An alternative to bungling and collective suicide might be to reach agreement on a likely date at which our species will disappear and work back from that point to at least program and enjoy the good life ahead of it.

---

*Some subgoals are implied in the methods proposed for the management of this problem.

ACKNOWLEDGMENTS

As a person who owes his precarious living to working simultaneously for eleven governments, I also benefit from a wide variety of viewpoints and can count on support in most of the natural and social sciences. Many of these friends have been particularly helpful: some like Albert Breton in terms of their early and lasting contribution to my intellectual sanity; some like Sonia Stairs and Susan Singh of my staff by their analytical backup to many audacious tangents. Particularly, to my wife, Susan, goes a large measure of gratitude for her patience and steadfastness in putting up with almost constant widowhood.

This paper was written for the purpose of eliciting discussion and controversy. Since it was not my intention to present a tightly argued and fully referenced construction, there are no explanatory notes or footnotes as such. References to other authors, implicit or explicit, have not been singled out and identified with their original source. While it is intended to develop the argument in a more rigorous fashion elsewhere, I wish to acknowledge at this time indebtedness to friends and colleagues.

PART II

Optimum Population: Considering Health, Education, and Welfare Services

INTRODUCTION

As we have seen in Part I, natural resources as well as environmental considerations give fairly tight upper limits to the size of the population, and also to its concentration, with the optimum, of course, well below the maximum. But from the point of view of educational services and medical services, the situation is rather different. Both require investments on a fairly large scale in hardware (buildings, laboratories, libraries, instruments, etc.) and in software (research, textbooks, training films, computer programmed instruction), all of which involve economies of scale. Therefore, the cost per capita goes down as the number of users increases. For example, the heavy cost of developing new drugs and new methods of treating diseases can be better justified when it is spread over a larger population.

This argument applies, of course, to the ideal situation, where there is perfect communication and interchange within a population. As a practical matter, we do not have such communication; and then, as is shown by Werner Z. Hirsch, the concept of optimum population is not meaningful at a national level but does have meaning at the lowest level at which effective communication is possible. For public education, this may be a school district with an optimum size of perhaps 25,000 students. (In this context, it would be interesting, for example, to study the problem of the optimum size of a university which also requires certain fixed capital facilities in library, laboratories, etc., independent of the number of students.)

The paper by Norman Glass and colleagues raises the point that the *rate* of population increase is an important parameter. It turns out that the rate of increase affects the population age structure, and therefore fixes the proportion of young people who require education to the proportion of people who pay taxes to support educational services. For example, with a population growth rate of 2 per cent, the average taxpayer must pay 2.33 times as much taxes as compared to zero population growth. From that point of view, any positive rate of growth of population is suboptimal.

This same kind of demographic analysis could be made for medical services as well. It would not give such clear-cut results since every age group requires medical services; but with the costliest services required by the very senior age group, a population structure which gives the smallest ratio of retired people to younger people would be optimum.

The outstanding feature of John H. Knowles's paper on medical costs, which sets the stage for a discussion of the economics of health services, is that national health expenditures doubled between 1961 and 1968, thus rising at a faster rate than all other services. Medical care accounts now for about 6.2 per cent of our GNP with a per capita expenditure of about $200 per year for the population under 65 and $600 for those over 65. These costs are the highest in the world. Yet, although we spend more money than any other country, the quality of care is very uneven and our health statistics are quite poor compared to many other countries. The highest benefit-cost ratio comes from keeping people healthy—by education, early diagnosis, and disease prevention. It would be premature to discuss the subject of optimum population before we rationalize and improve the nation's health services.

The problem is approached more directly by Victor R. Fuchs who contends that geographic distribution of population is more important than the total size; that is to say, in many parts of the United States, the population density is too low to permit adequate medical care. On the other hand, where the population density becomes too large and exceeds an optimum value, health suffers primarily because of the impact of pollution and other environmental factors.

A different aspect of health services is discussed by Philip R. Lee: namely, their contribution to our present population problems and their potential role in the solution of these problems. The application of sanitary measures, and more recently of modern medical practices, has greatly reduced the death rate. Health services, however, can also contribute to the solution of the population problem by fertility control and by developing methods for making these controls easily available.

A somewhat different demographic analysis is required in connection with social services. Ezra Glaser points out that differential fertility, specifically the higher fertility of low-income women, can lead to a great expansion of the poverty sector and therefore welfare costs, unless the population is moved rapidly out of the poverty sector by adequate social measures. (There is no assurance, of course, that the present higher fertility of low-income women will continue into the future; yet this problem deserves more careful analysis.)

Philip Hauser takes a much more serious and pessimistic view of urban problems, particularly in the United States. Four developments have suddenly transformed us from an agrarian to an urban society: the population explosion; the implosion, i.e., the extremely rapid growth of metropolitan centers; the population displosion, which refers to the great heterogeneity of people who share not only the same geographic area but similar social-economic-political activities; and, finally, the accelerating tempo of technological change. Hauser feels that it is necessary to add a new "Urban Bill of Rights" to the Constitution in order to keep our society viable.

S.F.S.

Population and Education: Meeting Change with Change

Werner Z. Hirsch

ABSTRACT

This paper investigates the levels and kinds of educational achievement in relation to the size and growth of population. Useful analyses have been made of the educational requirements needed to satisfy minimum physical and social needs, but the analytical means for determining the optimal levels of education are not presently available. The question of an optimum level of population makes little sense at the nationwide level, but it is relevant at the school district level.

INTRODUCTION

We face today a serious education crisis in several dimensions:

Rising population is producing many associated monster problems such as pollution and hunger that threaten our future; education, traditionally our strongest shield and sharpest sword against these problems, now appears less effective in their solution.

The promise of equal opportunity is unfulfilled, and minority groups are losing patience; education, the traditional means for bringing minorities into the mainstream, seems to work too slowly, if at all.

More people are seeking education, and ever more extensive or new education is demanded by our technological style of life. The education system seems ill prepared to meet these demands.

The rising demands for and rising costs of education are imposing great financial burdens at a time when our citizens seem increasingly reluctant to provide the required financial support; a reluctance created in part by a perception that the education system is failing to meet the challenges we face.

These great issues cannot be solved only by educational improvements. But such improvements are needed, and if they are to be made then two paths must be followed: education must be made more efficient so that the financial burden is less pressing; and the public must become more willing to support education. I focus on these paths partly because I am an economist but primarily because the financial crisis is already serious and all signs point to its becoming more so.

I think we need to start moving along both paths and I will make some specific suggestions for providing more effective incentives to do so. A particularly promising step is modification of the uniform salary scale that basically rewards teachers' seniority rather than being based upon performance and the demand for special skills and services. I make such a recommendation in spite of my awareness of the political implications, especially the strong opposition which would arise from teachers' organizations.

In the following sections I first look more closely at what we mean by education. I proceed from a general definition to consideration of the outputs provided by education and the inputs needed to produce these outputs. The education production function so derived is essential to consideration of efficiency and evaluations of the effectiveness and equity of the education system.

Next I consider whether the level and kinds of educational achievement are related to the size and growth in the nation's population. I find that useful analyses have been made of the educational requirements needed to satisfy the minimum physical and social needs of the population. However, the analytical means for determining the optimal levels of education are not presently available. Much of the discussion of this and the following sections emphasizes primary and secondary education.

I next reverse the question and ask whether there is some optimal population which can be related to a known education budget. It turns out that such a question makes little sense at the nationwide level. However, if the population is separated into segments, then useful statements can be made about improved environmental conditions under which the population can more effectively and efficiently attain its education objectives. Also, it is shown that considerations of optimal population size are particularly relevant at the school-district level, and I discuss issues of decentralization and efficiency in these terms.

In the final section I raise questions about the future and how the education process itself must change to meet the larger changes in society.

WHAT IS EDUCATION?

First, I would like to make clear what I mean when I say education. We hear the term often, used in different ways: the educated man is the man with the most school degrees, or the man who has learned to adjust to life, or the professional man who has a special skill, or the person who has achieved self-fulfillment, and so on.

A person learns from contact with his *total* environment—his home, neighborhood, school, job—and, of course, TV. What do I mean by education? I mean the various deliberate efforts, under the guidance of education officials, which aim to control a part of the environment in a way intended to bring about certain learning experiences which result in the acquisition of a new stock of knowledge by certain segments of our population. Thus, I do not include street-gang brawls, TV commercials, or casual dinner conversation with educated parents, all of which can account for much learning. I do include schools, educational television, and on-the-job training programs.

Thus, one characteristic of our education is that it accounts for only a part of a person's learning. Another characteristic of education is that it operates in a feedback manner: what is presented and how it is taught is in large part determined by the values, "needs" (or goals), and resources of society; and what is learned feeds back to reinforce or to change the structures and processes of that society as the educated perform their roles. There are, of course, discontinuities and outside interventions in this feedback process: what educators intend to teach in school and what students actually learn in school may be different; in fact, students often seem to learn the opposite of what socially sanctioned education intends; also, what students learn in school and what they learn outside of school may conflict, and the outside "lessons" may triumph; values and motivations of students and instructors may differ, and so on. In any case, if one views the individual, or the country, as an "equilibrium system"—a balance of diverse forces—then education may lend stability by passing on traditional values and knowledge from one generation to the next. Or education may take another turn; it may work to tilt the system off balance, as appears to be the case in some schools today. In some cases, this may be what is required to meet the anticipated changes in conditions, for though education acts as a partial control unit in a feedback circuit, it is a unit with a long built-in time delay, and as such it is often a reflection of past needs rather than present or future ones.

More specifically, we can relate education to a production function. A production function represents the relationship between inputs of productive factors and outputs per unit of time, subject to certain constraints. Ideally, a production function shows what each set of physical inputs, service conditions, and technologies will produce in terms of specified outputs—e.g., education. Education output has certain implications which have been expressed in such general terms as: preparing individuals for adequate income and rewarding employment, productive use of leisure, effective family membership, fulfillment of civic and social responsibilities—all of which are difficult to measure in terms of quantity and quality. Economists have made good progress in identifying such surrogates as incremental lifetime earnings and in measuring them.

Input factors can be divided into labor, capital, and materials, as well as management. Management can be divided into managerial services, which may be treated as an input, and entrepreneurial capacity, which is a residual claimant in the production process. In this view, a school superintendent furnishes managerial services in terms of internal coordination, supervision of external services, and supervision and assignment of other resources. Entrepreneurial activity involves decisions by an owner of resources. In the private sector, the owner can be the stockholder of a corporation. In the public education sector this function is carried out by voters who are represented by elected members of the legislature and school board. The voter's success as a resource owner expresses itself through the level of educational services and corresponding property taxes on the value of land.

If dissatisfied, the voter can move away from the community or vote officials and programs out. In theory, vigilant voters, and in turn able school board members and legislators, can exert pressures on education officials to run education in an efficient way. In fact, this process is constrained by law, by relatively low salaries, and by the rough and tough of politics.

Service conditions refer to the environmental constraints placed on the production process and the environmental and native factors bearing on the quality of inputs. Thus service conditions differ from physical input factors in that they are less under the ready control of education decision makers. Service conditions include a variety of physical, human, financial, legal, and political factors which can make it easier (or more difficult) for effective education to be provided: a child's native ability and his motivation to learn, and population density, which affects crowding and teacher-pupil ratios, are examples.

Technology concerns the way in which inputs are combined. Like a cake recipe, technology specifies ingredients as well as sequence of operations. A technological change, be it an improvement in knowledge or in technique, results in an alteration of the productivity of inputs; a new production function results. New technologies being explored today include new organizational structures—nongraded classrooms and flexible scheduling, for example—and new teaching techniques, such as the use of teacher assistants, teaching machines, and TV. So much for what I mean by education.

IS THERE AN OPTIMUM EDUCATION?

What is the optimum education level for any given level of population? We must specify "optimum" with respect to certain education goals and standards,—i.e., define an objective function.

In spite of popular old mottoes and the constant flow of new studies, blue ribbon commissions, and public opinion polls, no solid agreement on clearly defined goals and standards for education has yet been found. Some shifts are visible, prodded by the realization of the future we face, where perhaps the only thing of which we can be sure is change itself. Thus, one hears such general goal statements as: learning to learn, learning to make decisions, learning to adapt to change, learning to handle the information explosion, and so on. In a few instances, uncoordinated attempts are being made to translate some of these into classroom practice.

There is some agreement. It has been said over and over again that the goals of education are twofold: first, to enable the individual to fulfill his potential; and, because the individual must always operate in a group or "society," the second goal is to help us build and maintain a healthy society. The two are symbiotic. But such formulations have little utility when stated at this level of generality. Can we break these two general goals down into operational terms, find some measures, specify limits, and see what education is required to meet these limits, and thus set up some reasonable set of standards? To some extent, this is already being attempted, in fragmented ways.

We can say, for example, that an individual has certain biological needs in the sense that if they are not met, he will perish: he must have, say, 1,100 calories a day, X cubic feet of air, clothing and shelter enough to keep from freezing, medical attention at certain times, and so on. This means he and his compatriots must produce, which means he needs knowledge and skills, which implies standards of education if he is to survive, and higher standards for better living conditions above survival.

Psychologists, social workers, and urbanologists, armed with case histories, tell us there are also certain conditions required for the mental survival and health of a self-sustaining individual. Though these are "soft" concepts difficult to measure, when such qualities as emotional stability, ability to adapt, strong self-image, and freedom from excessive fear remain undeveloped, people for all practical purposes are "crippled" or "dead," buried on welfare rolls and in mental institutions. Suicide rates and crime rates are measures of unmet psychological needs. Education can play a major role in emotional development and in providing for required mental health services, etc.

We might look at the second general educational goal—maintenance of society—in the same way by asking: What is needed as a minimum for a group of individuals—a society—to survive and, beyond this, to remain "healthy"? Clearly, we can specify some requirements. Perhaps the most fundamental requirement for the survival of a society is the ability of individuals to communicate with each other; so language skills are among the first things taught, and communications are the first targets of enemy forces who seek to conquer.

Communication, in turn, forms the basis for other survival requirements of society: shared goals and values that hold individuals together; an efficient economic system of production and distribution that takes care of biological needs; structures and processes for orderly decision making and administration and coordination of the group; some system for communicating knowledge about the state of the society to its various members and to the new generation—so the group may make the required adjustments to survive in the face of internal and external changes.

Such minimum survival needs for societal groups are dramatized by the new nations of Africa, many of which are now in life and death struggles to meet these minimum requirements. Our own country is feeling the strain of the lack of shared values and of the communication gap between large groups—such as black and Mexican-American communities and youth groups clamoring for change—and the body of conservative middle-class citizens.

Our ability to meet these individual and societal survival requirements comes not from instinctual drives, as in the birds and the bees, but almost completely from learning. And so these survival requirements should be, almost by definition, a basis for agreed-upon educational goals. For if we don't survive, then more subtle questions about what is "good education," what is "the good life," etc., will be unimportant. Survival requirements, broadened to what we establish as better living conditions, over an extended period, can give at least some meaning to the concept of optimum education. There is much evidence that our education today is far from "optimum" in this survival sense.

IS THERE AN OPTIMUM POPULATION IN RELATION TO EDUCATION?

In terms of the shape of the education production function, a country with a small population may not generate sufficient demand (or have sufficient resources) to produce efficiently the desired type of education output. So some minimum population may be required to meet, efficiently, certain education goals. This is a problem for higher education in some of the developing countries, but not in the United States.

What is the optimum population for any given society with its education budget? Economies of scale for larger populations may improve resource use in some cases, and diseconomies may work the other way. Clearly, this would depend, among other things, on the design and conditions of the education system itself. For example, one would expect different results for a system of small, locally controlled classes than for nationwide television-size classrooms.

One can say, in principle at least, that there is an optimum population with respect to a given education budget. Of course, for this to have any meaning, one must specify "optimum" in relation to the goals and performance of a certain educational program. And as already mentioned, education goals and standards beyond the basic skills of the three Rs continue to be debated, so they do not give us a firm basis for answering the question of optimum population. The question is academic anyway, since, for all practical purposes, a nation's population size will not follow the dictates of education, but rather the other way around.

It is more useful to look at the specific segments of our population in which we encounter serious education problems. For example, many Americans in rural areas and city ghettos are far from getting an adequate education in terms of the survival standards already mentioned. They cannot get jobs to feed themselves and their families; they are being psychologically crippled; they cannot communicate or take a useful, active part in society. If we are to improve education in America, this is where to start. Improvement will require more than additional monies. Ways will have to be found to increase the efficiency of education for these disadvantaged populations. I would like to put forth three suggestions along these lines.

We have for a long time talked about equal opportunity for all in relation to primary and secondary education. But we have been slow to define "equal opportunity." Implicitly, we have looked upon equal opportunity in terms of providing for each child an equal amount of money for his education, or equal opportunity in terms of *inputs*. Rather, our concern should be to provide more nearly equal opportunities in terms of *output*. Because great differences exist in the environment within which education takes place—that is, differences in the service conditions of the education production function—equal input does not result in equal output. To overcome unfavorable service conditions, education for a ghetto child might need many times more educational inputs than education for a middle-class suburban child. To come close to accomplishing such a goal of equal output, we might want to shift state and federal grants-in-aid from a per capita basis to an output performance basis.

Recent research is beginning to make it possible for us to define differences in service conditions for different populations in the country, and to begin to establish the costs to overcome them—that is, to achieve specific educational outcomes. Our knowledge has been increasing about the frequency, duration, and intensity of the particular educational activities needed to produce definite types of behavior in students of different ages, aptitudes, and interests. Analysis is reaching a stage where we can begin to determine cost-effective means to accomplish specific educational objectives. To the extent that this is possible, state and federal funds allocated for educational improvements should take into account the specific service conditions associated with a given population, so as to produce more nearly equal outputs in terms of learning.

Secondly, I suggest we improve the efficiency of our large school districts by doing away with the uniform salary scale. This is an albatross around the neck of our public schools because it prevents schools from paying teachers in line with changing demand and supply conditions, in terms of school location, subjects taught, etc. Without financial incentives, ghetto schools in large school districts continue to suffer from a decisive lack of qualified personnel; and schools throughout the country suffer from shortages of science and mathematics teachers in the midst of a surplus of art and physical education teachers.

My third suggestion concerns the problem of centralization. This has been a concern as far back as the days of Alexander Hamilton and Thomas Jefferson. Hamilton called for centralization of power in the interest of efficiency and order, and Jefferson demanded diffusion of power and the right of the citizen to be close to government and to participate in decisions, even at the price of inefficiency. Jefferson warned, "If ever this vast country is brought under a single government, it will be one of the most extensive corruption, indifferent, and incapable of a wholesome care."

The postwar period has seen much consolidation and growth of school districts. However, recently, gains from decentralization may have been on the increase, especially because of modern technology, size, and affluence. Modern technology has stripped us of the protections of distance and time, which once mitigated the effects of others' actions. Furthermore, political decisions increasingly bear on our economic, social, and personal lives. In the late 1960s we find a widespread feeling of powerlessness among many citizens, produced by the sheer size, complexity, and rapid change of society. Feelings of powerlessness, in people who have a fundamental, instinctive desire for a degree of personal mastery of their lives and environment, are greatly aggravated by our lethargic and often unresponsive institutions. The desire to be close to government and to have a responsive government has been further intensified recently because of the many untouched problems and many uncertainties of our own private and public lives. While this desire appears common to most Americans, it is strongest among members of minority groups who today are aggressively seeking, through education and other devices, to rapidly improve their economic and social positions.

Thus, the old principle of federalism—to have responsibility assumed by the smallest unit consistent with the scale of the problem—is still sound. To determine the proper size of governmental units, gains and losses of centralized authority need to be traded off. In this we must use, as criteria, resource allocation efficiency through scale economies and orderly planning, equity in financing and distributing education, consumer choice, and distance of government from people and the feeling of powerlessness that goes with it.

First, let us make clear that decentralization of resource use by schools can be separated from the issue of who finances the school activities. Thus, although the rendering of services can be diffused and carried out by middle-size school districts, rigorous standards for the use of federal and state aid can be maintained.

What is the evidence relative to these criteria? Empirical studies indicate that while very small school districts are likely to benefit from scale economies, very large school districts are likely to suffer from major diseconomies. An empirical study I did many years ago estimated the type of education production function mentioned earlier. It shows that there are very few scale economies once we go beyond a district size of 10,000 to 20,000 students in average daily attendance, and that, in overall terms, school districts serving from 20,000 to 30,000 students in average daily attendance might be the most efficient.[1]

There are reasons for these empirical results. The conditions which help private industry to benefit from scale economies—lower factor costs, larger and more efficient plants, etc.—do not exist for school districts. Schools, except for labor, purchase a diversified array of inputs, few, if any, in large enough quantities to secure major price concessions. Unionization of teachers is unlikely to produce economies; location considerations—only relatively small distances from home to school are acceptable—tend to keep plants relatively small. Legal restrictions on permissible debts retard technological economies.

The evidence seems to be in the same direction in relation to the effect of school district size on coordinated planning for orderly growth. Large school districts appear able to internalize certain spillovers, an advantage which, however, is counteracted by size—leading to a sacrifice of freedom of schools to act independently. Very large districts appear to suffer from a geometric increase in the difficulties of successfully communicating intentions and procedures, establishing a harmonious system of incentives, and achieving adequate cohesion among personnel in subunits with sharply conflicting wills.

Large school districts reduce consumers' choice with regard to educational services. The existence of many middle-size school districts, compared to one huge school district, makes it possible for people to select their place of residence according to their tastes in education. In very large school districts, most parents are far removed from the central administration of the school. Under such conditions many parents feel disenfranchised and frustrated. They have no way of affecting school decisions, although such decisions directly and heavily affect them.

Before we can propose ways to bring into better harmony school-district population size and education, we should take a brief historical view of some of the issues. In the United States, there exists a long-term cycle in which values favoring centralization alternate with values favoring decentralization. Herbert Kaufman speaks about ". . . a succession of shifts . . . each brought about by a change in emphasis among three values: representativeness, politically neutral competence, and executive leadership."[2] The early postwar period saw strong central government being advocated, both in terms of the consolidation of local governments and emphasis on categorical grants—i.e., earmarked for specified functions—from higher levels of government. In the middle sixties, a reversal began, and in the late sixties and early seventies, we find that government decentralization and block grants are being sought.

However, the present desire for decentralization, noncategorical grants, and local control have built into them forces which generate change. Providing more noncategorical grants and greater local influence on public programs is likely to result in disparities among the numerous small units, brought on by differences in human and financial resources. These disparities can stimulate calls for central intervention to restore equality and balance, and thus, once again, bring forth the forces underlying categorical grants and consolidation. Intensive decentralization will tend to interfere with racial integration in schools, to enlarge educational inequalities, to reintroduce the spoils system and thus lower the quality of some vital services, and to bring about diseconomies of scale.

A variety of decentralization patterns can be pursued to strike an improved balance between school population size and education services. Some involve evolutionary steps while others would be revolutionary and require major legislation. Moving in the first direction would require the central administration to assign major responsibilities to assistant superintendents in charge of geographic clusters of schools. Moving in the second direction would call for breaking up very large school districts into a number of entirely independent smaller ones.

I would suggest that careful consideration be given to the possibility of reorganizing very large school districts into a number of separate local school districts—each containing perhaps 100,000–250,000 residents—while retaining the central district for select functions. Each local district could be governed by a local school board composed of parents and local residents. Some board members could be elected locally and a few could either be elected at large or appointed by the central school district. Each local school district could have its own budget and, within limits, determine its own educational program. It could hire its own superintendent who, in turn, would be responsible for hiring principals and teachers subject to agreed-upon areawide conditions. The central school board and its superintendent would then become a coordinator for the separate local districts, with responsibilities for setting areawide standards, for areawide planning, collective bargaining, raising local funds, etc.

These, then, are three suggestions for matching education and population: focus on output rather than input; do away with the

single salary scale; give closer attention to the question of centralization. These can bring about improvements while we are working
to find answers to the many intricate questions related to other
education changes.

WHAT OF THE FUTURE?
WHAT STEPS SHOULD WE TAKE TO MORE
CLOSELY APPROACH "OPTIMUM"?

Should we change physical inputs, service conditions, or technologies
in our education production function? How?

In principle we know that there are obvious and subtle relationships among these many elements; that is, there are many different ways independent variables may be substituted and recombined.
Some combinations will yield more efficient education than others.
Take a long-term example: It is said that there are millions of hungry
children in this country, and research suggests that malnourishment
may impair a child's intellectual capabilities for his lifetime. It is
conceivable that we might improve education output in certain cases
by taking funds from a category such as classroom construction and
spending them on an expanded free-food program for school children.

Because of the delayed feedback nature of education, whereby
education directly affects so many facets of society, many other
long-term relations exist which suggest possibilities for substitution:
the relation between education and population control (all the birth
control devices will do little unless people are educated to family
planning); the effects of education on technological development and
the effects of technological tools on education output; the relation
between quality of education and school dropout, and between school
dropout and crime, etc. These suggest that many possible combinations of input factors, service conditions, and technology exist which
might bring greater efficiency in education. The growing use of many
different system analytic techniques should help us to reduce these
to constructive operational innovations.[3]

For the more immediate future, we seem to be blessed with what
appears like an almost endless supply of ideas for innovations—many
of which are already being explored. Some involve new technologies
which require large additional capital inputs (such as educational
television, home-study consoles, and computer-based teaching ma-

chines). Others, such as use of student and parent tutors, self-directed learning programs, and nongraded classes, may be virtually cost free. Many of these innovations are being tried on an experimental basis.

Two major challenges continue to face such efforts. The first is evaluation, to enable us to choose among alternatives. Evaluation involves a number of steps: measuring inputs; measuring outputs; comparing outputs to established educational objectives; revising and making substitutions; recombining elements into better, more efficient educational programs.

Progress on evaluation is being made, but there are many difficulties, and results are coming slowly. We can measure the costs of certain inputs, such as capital and technology, but it is still difficult to measure service conditions, such as the characteristics (inherited or culturally developed) which are built into the student and which influence the efficiency of a given educational program. The Coleman study and others have recently dramatized the importance of such conditions. Moreover, measuring educational output has many pitfalls, though certain trends, such as the establishment of behavioral objectives, may make these easier to avoid. But again, there is not yet agreement on a set of standards, expressed in operational terms, for a large share of the educational effort, particularly for that part outside the sciences.

The second challenge, the ability of education to adapt to change, includes the evaluation problem and many others with which we are well acquainted: the slow response time of education, political realities, competing demands for resources, etc.

While we cannot predict the future, certain changes seem fairly certain. For example, many have suggested that increasing technology will bring more leisure and greatly increase life span; many people may go in for multiple careers, and so on. Such changes could mean entirely new types of demands for education, and could bring radical changes to the lifetime budget of most citizens.

An even more dramatic change will be the population itself. As the President's science advisor noted, speaking before the recent Thirteenth National Conference of the United States Commission on UNESCO, ". . . by far the most critical change man faces is the problem of overpopulation; this will require an unprecedented education program to avert catastrophe."

Studies are beginning to confirm how our quality of life may change unless dense populations are countered. Philip Zimbardo's experiment of abandoning a car in a metropolis and another car in a small town offers us a grisly hint.[4] The car left in the city was completely stripped within twenty-four hours and was rubble in three days; most destruction occurred in the daylight hours and was led by well-dressed white adults. The car left in the small town was not only untouched, but a thoughtful passerby sought to protect it from the rain! The repeated cases of individuals looking on while serious crimes were being committed (e.g., the Genovese murder) are even more dramatic reminders of the extent to which individuals retreat from social responsibility in the face of high-density population.

Can education be mobilized to meet such superproblems as population, pollution, control of resources? Education is not the only means, but in view of the alternatives—government controls, starvation, war—it is certain to be the most agreeable.

REFERENCES

1. Werner Z. Hirsch, "Expenditure Implications of Metropolitan Growth and Consolidation," *The Review of Economics and Statistics,* 4 (August, 1959) 232–41.
2. Herbert Kaufman, "Administrative Decentralization and Political Power," *Political Administration Review,* 29 (January–February, 1969), 3.
3. For an extensive annotated bibliography of writings on such techniques, see "Organization for Economic Cooperation and Development," *Systems Analysis for Educational Planning* (Paris: OECD, 1969).
4. From an invited address by Stanley Milgram to the American Psychological Association, Washington, D.C., on September 2, 1969.

FURTHER READINGS

Benson, Charles S. *The Economics of Public Education,* 2nd ed. Boston: Houghton Mifflin Company, 1968.

Hirsch, Werner Z. *Inventing Education for the Future.* San Francisco: Chandler Publishing Company, 1967.

Schultz, Theodore W. *The Economic Value of Education.* New York: Columbia University Press, 1963.

Vaizey, John, *The Costs of Education.* London: George Allen & Unwin, 1958.

Human Ecology and Educational Crises:

One Aspect of the Social Cost of an Expanding Population

Norman R. Glass, Kenneth E. F. Watt, and Theodore C. Foin, Jr.

ABSTRACT

One aspect of population growth, the change in population age structure, attendant to high rates of increase in populations, is examined as a fundamental process which affects a number of social processes, including education taxation and funding. At relatively high rates of population increase, the proportion of the population in younger age groups is high. At the same time, the proportion of the populace comprising older age groups declines. These changes in population age distribution occur in response to population growth and alter both the demand for education tax dollars generated by young age groups and the ability of older age groups in the population to generate education tax revenue. Since changing proportions of people in different age groups couples an increase in the proportion of tax consumers with a decrease in the proportion of the population which constitutes tax producers, population growth and attendant age-structure shifts cause a two-edged problem for education funding. In general, any institution, service, or function which differentially derives its operating revenue from an older age segment of the population and serves a younger age segment of the population is expected to be similarly affected.

INTRODUCTION

Upon initial consideration, ecology and public education do not appear to be closely linked by even the most tenuous of threads. However, closer examination of several principles which have emerged from ecological investigations in the past two or three decades reveals that, in fact, some phenomena which are reasonably well known to ecologists have important implications for, and could have made possible the prediction of, several aspects of the current crises in education. Such bodies of ecological theory as those treating the principles of diversity, stability, organization, and energetics in communities of lower animals can, in a more general way, be extended to encompass some aspects of the human community. It is, of course, very obvious that theoretical constructs such as these cannot be indiscriminately transferred from simpler communities to the highly complex human system with its many and varied environmental manipulations and dependencies. On the other hand, there are some theoretical and observational pieces of information from population and community ecology which can be applied to the human system with minimum risk and very little modification and extension. Below is given a comparatively simple example which shows how human population growth and change affect both educational needs and the ability of the populace to produce funds to pay for those needs.

All levels of public education are in the midst of serious crises of several kinds and varying degrees of gravity. However, there does seem to be some doubt about what the root causes of these crises are. In higher education, the underlying causes appear to be—at least—political, philosophical, and budgetary. All major groups which have a vested interest in higher education, particularly in California, are dissatisfied about one aspect of the educational system or another. Many college students are dissatisfied because of political control and interference and the conviction that their education is not relevant to the society in which they will live as adults. Faculty members, on the other hand, appear to be primarily concerned with political control of the universities and state college system, and the failure of a financially parsimonious legislature to face up to the fact that a burgeoning student population requires an increased rather than a decreased budget. The general public and its elected representatives are disenchanted with higher education because the goals and values of present-day students appear not to coincide with the goals and values of those people who now constitute the electorate. They therefore object to paying increased tax dollars to support an institution which seems to espouse philosophies sometimes seriously discrepant from their own. At the intermediate level, the high schools, political and monetary problems appear not to be as grave as they are at the college or university level. At the elementary-school level there seems to be virtually no serious philosophical or political problem—with a few obvious exceptions such as sex education. At this level, budgetary considerations are paramount.

While the various crises and their roots, either combined or singly, may be obscure or moot, one aspect of the current crisis in California's educational system which has not received sufficient discussion is that of the stress placed upon the system, particularly at the elementary level, by a relatively high yearly rate of population increase. The *rate* of increase is probably more important in determining the level or magnitude of the crisis which will confront education than either the absolute size or the density of the human population. This is due to the fact that as the rate of population increases varies, the age structure, the proportion of people in each age group, changes.[1] At high rates of population increase, i.e., rates of increase in the neighborhood of 1 to 3 per cent, the proportion of the total population in the younger and youngest age groups rises dramatically. At the same time, the proportion of people comprising older age groups declines. These changes in the population age distribution alter both the demand for education tax dollars and the ability of the population to generate tax revenue. Unfortunately, changing proportions of people in different age groups couples an increase in the proportion of tax consumers with a decrease in the proportion of tax producers. This phenomenon is well known to demographers and population biologists, but largely not understood by the general public or by educators. In general, the only attributes which most lay people ascribe to a high rate of population increase is simply that there are more school-aged children and, perhaps, that the average age of the population declines. Both of these statements are true. However, they do not in themselves constitute the whole story or even a very significant portion of it. The process of population growth itself is such that a series of corollaries or consequences to education (or, for that matter, a host of other social or cultural institutions) result to varying degrees from different rates of population increase. This paper discusses the implications of different rates of population growth and their theoretically attendant stable age distributions for education-tax-revenue production and consumption.

MODEL ASSUMPTIONS, STRUCTURE, AND OUTPUT

As part of a larger research effort concerned with the social costs of an expanding population,[2] a simple computer model using data on California was devised to describe several relationships which exist between the rate of population increase and the supply of and demand for education tax dollars.

Three vectors to describe a population were read in as initial input information. The first of these was a vector of numbers of people by single years of age from age 1 to age 75. The population of California in 1965, exclusive of those individuals 76 years of age and older, was used for this purpose. The two other vectors consisted of an age-specific birth rate and an age-specific death rate. These were obtained from census information for the California population in 1960. It was assumed that all births and deaths occurred on the same day and that the net age-specific migration was zero. In other words, a simple population where all newborn babies enter at age 1 and all surviving individuals die at age 76, having the age distribution of California's 1965 population, was used as an initial population. It should be noted that whether or not any or all of these vectors are precisely correct, the processes involved in population growth rate and their effects on related phenomena are not materially altered. Furthermore, the assumption of no net migration would be expected to result in an underestimate of the rate of increase in younger age groups and an overestimate of the proportion of the population in older age groups. This is because there is differential migration by age into California. Actual California population characteristics were used because they were readily available from the literature, but assumed or generated vectors for a population and its characteristics could have been developed and used as initial input. This probably would not have resulted in any substantive changes in output since the model was designed to simulate the process of population growth and change at various levels of population growth rate, rather than predict or project actual population size.

A second type of initial input information based upon an assumed probability distribution for the proportion of people by single year of age in elementary school, high school, and college was then provided for the model (see Figure 1). All children 5 years of age and younger were assumed not to be in public school and were not considered as either educational tax consumers or educational tax producers. Children from age 6 to age 15 were all assumed to be in elementary or high school and were assigned a probability of 1.0 of being lost as educational tax producers. Young adults 16 years and older and adults were assumed to be enrolled in high school or college according to the probability distribution in Figure 1, and the remainder were assumed to be gainfully employed and, therefore,

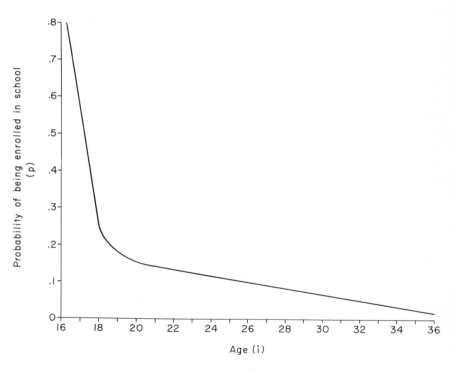

FIGURE 1

Probability distribution of being enrolled in school (p) for different ages. All children between the ages of 6 and 16 have p = 1.0 of being enrolled in school; those from ages 1 through 5 have p = 0.0 of attending school.

educational tax-revenue producers. The simplifying assumption that
all people in school were full-time students and not able to produce
any tax revenue was also made, but if a wage and salary bill for
high school and college students were either available or assumed
it would be very easy to incorporate the minimal tax-revenue production of students. The number of educational tax consumers could
therefore be determined by summing over all age groups, above 5
years, the number of people of the age i times the probability (p)
that they were in school,

$$\text{Total consumers} = \sum_{i=6}^{75} N_i p_i = C \tag{1}$$

where N is the number of people in age class i, and p is the vector
of probability of being enrolled in school at age i.

A third major data input to permit computation of the educational
tax revenue produced by the population was also made. Figure 2
shows the proportion of the total education tax produced by each
age. This distribution was normalized so that the sum of all proportions of the total for all age groups equaled 1.0. That is, the implicit
assumption was made that all necessary education tax revenue was
produced by California's 1965 population after the age-specific
birth-rate vector was adjusted to yield a zero rate of population
growth, given the age structure at that time. Whether or not the
education tax revenue generated in 1965 was sufficient is beside the
point; this assumption was made to provide a baseline value for tax
production which could be compared with tax production under
different population-growth conditions. It was then possible to compute the number of education tax producers in each age class by:

$$\text{Producers}_i = N_i - N_i p_i; \sum_{i=16}^{75} \text{producers}_i = T \tag{2}$$

for all ages greater than fifteen. Assuming the proportion of the total
education tax paid by each age group in the population (PT_i) from
Figure 2, and the number of producers in each age class, the tax-
generating capability of the population was calculated. That is, by
multiplying the vector of producers—Equation (2)—for any generated population times the vector of contributions to the total education tax revenue shown in Figure 2 it was possible to compute the

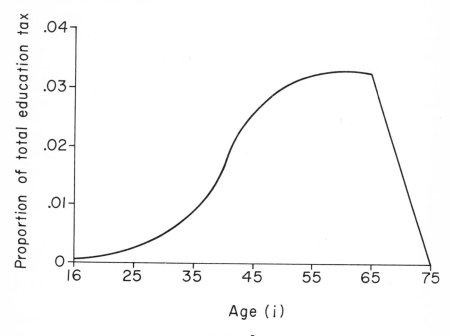

FIGURE 2

Proportion of the total educational tax assumed to be paid
by producers in the population for each age. California
population age characteristics in 1965 yield a baseline
tax-generating capacity assumed to be adequate to fund the
educational system.

total tax-revenue-producing capacity of the population under different age structure conditions, so that for each relevant age group:

and $$\text{Tax generated}_i = \text{Producers}_i \cdot PT_i \qquad (3)$$

$$\text{Total tax production} = \sum_{i=16}^{75} \text{producers}_i \cdot PT_i . \qquad (4)$$

Futhermore, it was assumed that all education tax revenue was
generated from personal income and that no funds for education
were provided by industrial, state, federal, or other sources. This
might appear to be a gross oversimplification, but these other revenue
sources would only change tax-revenue income, as it is affected by
population growth, by some constant.

We feel that these assumptions do not seriously distort the relationship between population growth rate, the resultant numbers of people enrolled in school, and the numbers of people able to support the educational plant financially. Moreover, individual school districts are not under consideration but, rather, all of California.

Flexibility in model design was maintained so that if additional information, such as net age-specific migration, income distribution by age, etc., were to become accurately known in the future, they could be readily incorporated. Greater complexity could be built into the model with relative ease if objectives broader than the relationship between population growth rate and the concomitant changes in tax producers and consumers were desired. For example, the authors have extended part of the model to explore the consequences that California's populace might anticipate in the future for the availability and general costs of physicians and other components of the health-services industry under different rates of population growth and with varying assumptions about the future development of medical-school facilities.

The general model was designed for use on a time-sharing terminal so that an operator could enter, in appropriate places, any decisions built into the model and then immediately see the results attendant to those decisions. For present purposes, the only operator information which will be considered is that pertaining to the rate of growth of the population from one year to the next. After the population growth rate is provided to the model, the population is allowed to grow through a hundred-year period. Despite the relatively long generation time of the human population, one hundred years was found to be sufficient to achieve an approximately stable age structure, so this time period was used for all population growth rates. The resulting age classes were assumed to be stable and were compared with the proportion of people in each age class under zero rate of population growth conditions. Model output information includes: the separate proportions of the total population enrolled in elementary school, high school, and college for the particular population growth rate entered by the operator; the proportion of the population which are producers; the proportion of the population classed as consumers; the ratio of producers to consumers (T/C); the tax revenue available per consumer; tax revenue produced per producer; tax revenue produced per capita; and the ratio of tax revenue per consumer to tax revenue per consumer under zero rate of population growth conditions.

Figure 3 shows graphically the consequent changes in the proportion of people in elementary school, high school, and in college when the age structure shifts downward under progressively increasing per cent growth rates in population size. Clearly, the elementary school age group experiences a phenomenal rise in the proportion of the total population it represents. Figure 3 gives no indication of the absolute size of the population, but it does provide a scenario of the magnitude of the cost which could confront society and the possible changes in tax structure that would be required to provide adequate facilities and funding. In the extreme, it is obvious that if the human population were to grow at a sustained rate of 10 per

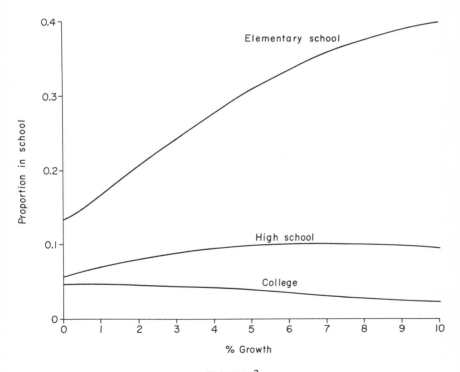

FIGURE 3

Model output showing the proportion of the total population enrolled in school at all educational levels as a function of the rate of population growth.

cent per year, over half of the citizenry would be attending school—
assuming sufficient teachers, administrators, classrooms, etc., existed
to serve their needs. Even the comparison of proportions in school
under 0 and 2 per cent growth rates gives some idea of the extra
burden taxpayers must carry as their reward for even a 2 per cent
annual increase in population.

Changes in the producer and consumer fractions of the population
under different rates of increase are shown in Figures 4 and 5.
In Figure 4, the growth rate beyond which the number of tax
consumers exceeds the number of tax producers is in the neighborhood of 4 per cent. Bearing in mind the assumption that *all*
people over age 15 who were not in school were considered tax
producers, the 4 per cent rate must be deemed very liberal. Indeed,

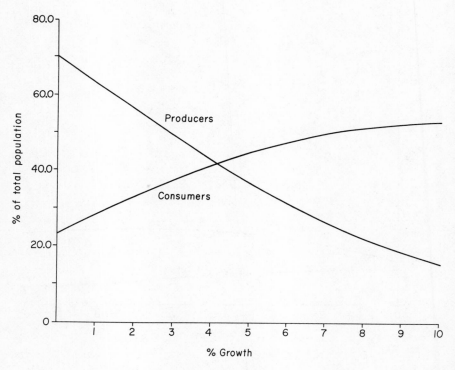

FIGURE 4
Per cent of the total population producing tax revenue and
consuming tax revenue at different rates of population
growth.

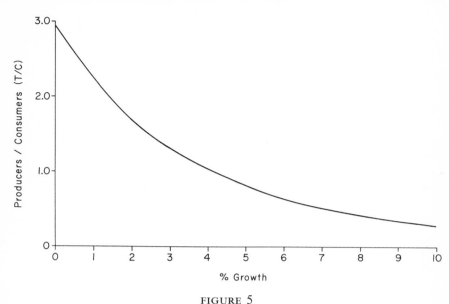

FIGURE 5

Model output which shows the change in the ratio of net
educational tax producers to net educational tax consumers
for different population growth rates.

if housewives and others earning essentially no income were not
included in the number of producers in the population, the rate of
growth at which consumers exceeded producers would be lowered
considerably—probably down to the 2 to 3 per cent range. Another
way of viewing the producer-consumer relationship is given in Figure
5. Clearly, as the ratio of net education-tax producers to net education-tax consumers diminishes—and the decline is definitely not
linear—producers must dramatically increase their output to maintain a level of funding capable of supporting an educational system
at least equal to the system required under conditions of no population growth. To place the producer/consumer ratio in an ecological
perspective, most natural communities have vastly more producers
than consumers. Charles Elton's pyramid of numbers or a thermodynamic comparison of energy production and utilization for non-
human communities reveals that, in general, orders of magnitude
differences between producers and consumers exist.

Figure 6 illustrates the nature and relative seriousness of different
rates of population growth from the standpoint of the student, and,

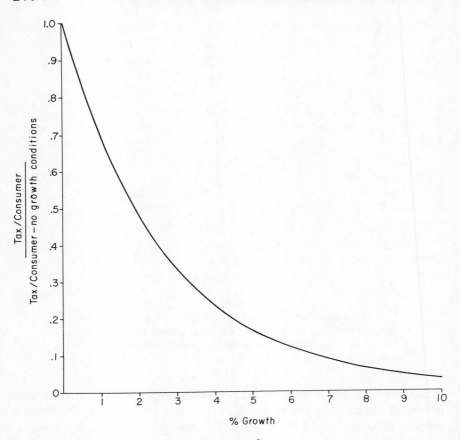

FIGURE 6
The tax-generating ability of the population per student
under zero rate of growth conditions as a function of varying
population growth rate.

by implication, indicates why the tax-producing fraction of a population must increase its per capita output to meet the increased need
for tax revenue to support an expanding population. Even if population growth is as low as 2 per cent, then tax-revenue producers must
provide funding which is approximately double that required under
conditions of no population growth. It should be pointed out that
not only must the level of funding double, but the revenue must be
generated by fewer producers than would be extant if the population
were not growing. In other words, if growth were as seemingly low
as 2 per cent, the tax revenue required from each producer would
actually be more than double. More precisely, the taxes produced

per producing citizen at a 2 per cent population growth rate must be increased to about 2.33 times the taxes paid by each taxpayer under conditions of no population growth to maintain the same level of services.

It comes as no great surprise that an incipient "taxpayers' revolt" is being widely proclaimed by newspapers and other media. What is surprising is that the tax loopholes of advantage to the very wealthy are touted as the prime cause of this revolt. It seems more reasonable to suggest that these loopholes have only provided a spark to ignite public furor over higher and higher taxes, and that an expanding population is the real culprit. Furthermore, it also appears reasonable that institutional timidity and inertia will delay any effective remedial action directed at the root causes and that population policy (or some other euphemism for birth control) will remain conspicuous by its absence. Clearly, it is not merely the educational system which suffers from population growth and change, virtually every other social or institutional service or function serving younger age classes of the population and deriving its operating revenue from older age classes faces a similar fate.

It is important to point out that the process discussed in this paper is only one small component of an extremely complex system; the total array of consequences of high rates of population increase resulting from the effects of the process discussed are exacerbated by two other processes occurring simultaneously: increased cost per person for all services due to demands for a higher level of service, and decreasing real value of financial support derived from interest or other returns on invested capital due to inflation. The three processes together are producing a taxpayers' revolt with respect to all services—educational and govermental—and are leading to serious future problems to the whole system for delivering educational, medical, and hospital services (among others).

Also, the final effects of shifts in age distribution go much further than indicated here, because they lead to chain reactions and progressively more violent oscillations in the human ecosystem. For example, suppose that professional salaries rise to excessive levels, with the consequence that the total cost of services is unbearable for the taxpayer, and there is a taxpayers' revolt against education taxes. This means that there will be an even greater shortage of professionals in the future, and the cost of their services will rise even higher—if, in fact, the services are even available.

This type of simulation quickly exposes another interesting phenomenon. Figure 3 shows that the principal response to high rates of population growth is at the elementary-school level; the proportion of the population in college actually declines with growth rates over 1 per cent and the proportion in high school declines with growth rates over 8 per cent. Society is currently faced with an excess of Ph.D.'s in some fields and a shortage of elementary-school teachers. This would appear to be an instance where two problems are each other's solutions.

By fusing some assumptions, principles, and information from elementary ecology, population biology, and demography into a relatively simple model of those processes expected to influence a social or institutional function, it is possible to anticipate and approximately measure a cost which society must be prepared to pay for varying rates of population growth. Particularly in the area of education there has been too little emphasis on the sword of Damocles poised above our heads by current population growth rates. Increasing numbers of people implies a general downward shift in population age structure; greater numbers and proportions of the population will have to be educated, with financial responsibility ultimately resting upon the shoulders of individuals who comprise an ever-decreasing proportion of that population. Since the question asked by this symposium—"Is there an optimum level of population?"—is relatively general, a broad answer upon which decisions could be based would appear to be in order. In general, the conclusion dictated by consideration of population growth and shifts in age structure would have to be that *any positive rate of growth is suboptimal*.

REFERENCES

1. There are numerous books and articles on this area of population biology. An early example is a book by A. J. Lotka written in 1925 entitled, *Principles of Physical Biology*.
2. K. E. F. Watt, N. R. Glass, T. C. Foin, and staff, *A Model of Society*. Environmental Systems Group, Institute of Ecology, University of California, Davis, Report Number 1, April, 1969 (Davis: University of California Drafting and Duplication Department, 1969).

Quality of Health Care and Medical Costs*

John H. Knowles

ABSTRACT

Medical care accounts now for about 6.2 per cent of our GNP with a per capita expenditure of about $200 for the population under 65 and $600 for those over 65. These costs are the highest in the world. Yet, although we spend more money than any other country, the quality of care is very uneven and our health statistics are quite poor compared to many other countries. The highest benefit-cost ratio comes from keeping people healthy—by education, early diagnosis, and disease prevention. It would be premature to discuss the subject of optimum population before we rationalize and improve the nation's health services.

Expenditures for the national health rose from 24.7 billion in 1961 to 46.7 billion in 1968, and the 1968 figure represents a rise of 13 per cent over 1967. By all economic indicators, the rise in cost of medical services has outstripped all other services with the rise

* Based on testimony before the Subcommittee on Fiscal Policy, Joint Economic Committee, Congress of the United States, October 14, 1969.

particularly rapid over the past three years since the advent of Medicare. We now spend around 6.2 per cent of our Gross National Product on medical care and our per capita expenditures of $195 per year for those under 65 years of age and $590 per year for those over 65 years of age are the highest of any nation in the world. These facts are cause for great concern for several reasons:

1. Although we spend more money than any other country on health, the quality of care produced remains uneven, and our health statistics in certain areas are frankly embarrassing. The health of some thirty million poor people is abysmally bad and almost totally neglected. In 1965, we ranked eighteenth of the countries of the world in infant mortality. The mortality of middle-aged men is a source of concern. We rank seventeenth in male and tenth in female life expectancy. In Sweden, ninety-five of one hundred males age 45 will reach age 55. In America, only ninety will.

2. With rapidly rising costs (recently, 12 per cent annually), medical indigency increases as wages have been rising at only 3 to 4 per cent annually and retirement income has withered under inflationary forces. Medicare, for example, covers 46 per cent of the total medical costs of the aged, Veterans Assistance and Public Assistance (Medicaid) covers 13 per cent, and 41 per cent remains the private responsibility of elderly individuals, nearly half of whom live in or border on poverty.

3. With increasing tax monies and employer-employee funds being used to pay for medical services, a collective and very powerful responsibility now exists in the hands of third-party payers and the government to serve the public interest in health more effectively. What was piece work, individual and private in 1930, is now organized and collective, public and private. Public scrutiny of medical care is increasing along with demands for improved quality, accessibility, comprehensiveness, and cost controls.

The three largest demands on the national health expenditures are made by hospitals, doctors, and drugs. Hospital care consumes 19.5 billion, physician services 10.9 billion, and drugs 5.7 billion of the 46.7 billion dollars spent. Of the total, 66.5 per cent (31 billion dollars) are private and 33.5 per cent (15.7 billion) are public expenditures. In 1961, 78 per cent was private and 22 per cent was public expenditure, the large change to more public funds coming with the advent of Medicare and Medicaid in 1966. The following table illustrates the breakdown of public and private monies for the three largest demands on the health dollar (in billions of dollars):

The Year 1968	Total	Private	Public
Hospital care	19.5	10.1	9.4
Physician services	10.9	8.7	2.2
Drugs & sundries	5.7	5.4	.3

Note that the private sector far outweighs the public in the purchase of physician services and drugs. At the present time, 70 per cent of hospital costs, 21 per cent of the cost of privately practicing physicians, and 17 per cent of drug costs are paid by prepayment mechanisms. It is quite clear where the leverage will be applied by collective action.

The increase in personal health expenditures between 1961 and 1968 has been due to the following three factors:[1]

Population increase	15 per cent
Price increase	36 per cent
Other (quality; utilization; additional services; and increased numbers of health workers)	49 per cent
Total	100

As can be seen from the table, only 49 per cent of the increase in personal expenditures has been used to improve quality and provide new services.

The rise in hospital costs has aroused the most interest and consternation, and justifiably so. The *causes* for the increase are easily identified:

1. Increased wages and fringe benefits which consume between 62 and 70 per cent of the operating budget;

2. An absolute increase in the number of "employees per bed" required by the doctor and the patient to carry out their work; and

3. Increased costs of construction, equipment, and supplies due both to inflation and to the development of new facilities and technology required for the best medical care.

REFERENCE

1. Secretary of Health, Education and Welfare Wilbur Cohen before the Ribicoff Subcommittee, 1968.

Some Notes on the Optimum Size of Population, with Special Reference to Health

Victor R. Fuchs

ABSTRACT

The principal conclusion is that in the United States the question of the geographic distribution of population is much more important than that of total size. In terms of both health and general economic considerations, the population is probably too large in some parts of the country and it is surely too small in other parts.

GENERAL REMARKS

Why does population size matter? From an economic point of view population size is of relevance primarily because the costs of carrying on certain activities and of achieving certain satisfactions are likely to vary with the size of the population to be served. Some of these activities involve the production of goods and services for sale in the market, such as the manufacture of steel or the provision of telephone service. Others are partially nonmarket in character, such as the achievement of good health or the finding of a suitable mate. All involve the use of scarce resources (including time) and fall within the domain of economic analysis. When costs decrease as size increases, we say that this activity is experiencing economies of scale. When costs rise as size increases, the activity is experiencing diseconomies of scale. The terms increasing and decreasing returns to scale are also sometimes used.

It is obvious that the optimum scale differs among activities. The economies of scale for barber shops, for instance, are probably exhausted with a population of a few thousand, but automobile manufacturers may still experience decreasing costs while serving many millions. It follows, therefore, that the optimum population size will be different for different consumers depending upon their preferences among goods and services.

Although there is potentially a different optimum size for each activity and each person, it may be possible to define an optimum population for a society in the following way. At any given size there are likely to be some who wish it were smaller and some who wish it were larger. We can define the optimum as that size where the amount that people in the society would be willing to pay to have the population reduced by, say, 10 per cent is exactly equal to the amount other people in the society would be willing to pay to have it increased by that amount. This defines an optimum given the distribution of income; the amounts people would be willing to pay depend in part on their income. Thus, there may be a different optimum corresponding to every possible distribution of income.*

Optimum size is only one of many concerns of population policy and, in my opinion, is one of the least important for the United States. A given size can be achieved in a variety of ways, e.g., compulsory sterilization, economic incentives, euthanasia. Many people are likely to regard the question of the methods used to influence population size as far more important than that of size itself. Moreover, the composition of the population may be a critical variable. The number of coreligionists, bridge players, music lovers, or whatever, may be much more important to some than the total size of the population.

GEOGRAPHIC FACTORS

The geographic distribution of the population must also be considered. Most of the land area of the United States is very thinly

---

* The distribution of income may depend in part upon the population size.

populated. For instance, there are only nine states in the United States that have population densities higher than that of France, and France is not usually regarded as an overpopulated country. Furthermore, these nine states account for less than one-third of the United States' population.

It seems to me that many, if not most, states in this country suffer from having *too small* a population. That is to say, the cost of producing most goods and services and of satisfying most wants would tend to fall if their populations were larger. I realize that there are many costs associated with population growth, but let's not forget the benefits. Larger populations would enable many states to upgrade the quality of state and local government, improve educational and cultural programs and facilities, widen the range of choice among newspapers and TV stations, and in general provide many of the amenities— such as fine restaurants and good bookstores—that the inhabitants of thickly populated areas take for granted.

The location decisions that individuals make are based on consideration of private costs and benefits; the fact that other individuals may be affected, either favorably or unfavorably, tends to be neglected. In my view, the case for attempting to influence the geographic distribution of population in the United States is stronger than that for trying to control the total size.

POPULATION SIZE AND HEALTH

The health of any population depends upon genetic factors, environmental factors, and medical care. Other things being equal, the growth of population has favorable implications for genetic factors. A population can be too small from a genetic point of view but it is difficult to see how it could be too large. To be sure, allegations of a negative correlation between genetic stock and population size have been made, but these are critically dependent upon special assumptions regarding the source of the population increase. Such arguments bring us back to the question of population composition, not to that of size *per se*.

The major adverse implications of a large population for health are related to the impact of numbers on the environment. Overcrowding creates additional health hazards through pollution of air and water and the spread of communicable diseases. The latter is not, however, simply a function of population density. The number of persons per acre on New York's Park Avenue is thousands of times greater than it is on certain Indian reservations in the West, but the spread of communicable disease is a much more serious problem in the latter locale. Nevertheless, there is little doubt that, other things being equal, the larger the population the greater the risks to health.

With respect to medical care, the reverse is likely to be true. A population may be too small to permit specialization or may involve excessive travel to obtain care. For instance, the motor accident mortality rate across states is inversely correlated with population density. One important explanation that has been offered is the inverse correlation between population density and the length of time that elapses between the accident and the provision of medical and hospital care.

Consider hospital costs. It is well known that the smaller the population the greater the need for excess capacity in hospital beds and other medical facilities in order to provide for random fluctuations in illness and injury. Despite the large population of the United States, the problem of efficient hospital size is still an important one. Nearly all observers are agreed that there are economies of scale in the production of short-term general hospital services up to a size of at least 200 beds (and possible 500). However, at present, almost 40 per cent of the short-term patient days in the United States are provided in hospitals with fewer than 200 beds.

In general, the cost of producing medical care (adjusted for quality) goes down as population size increases. It may sometimes appear that costs increase with size, but this will usually be because of a failure to adjust for changes in quality or because more of the costs have become explicit in market transactions rather than being hidden in nonmarket services provided by family or neighbors.

If we try to strike a balance between the adverse effects of environment and the beneficial effects of cheaper and better medical care, what can we conclude about population size and health? In my view, the answer will vary depending upon the size and density of population under review. Health in New York City, for instance, would probably improve if the population pressure were reduced. The benefits from a better environment would probably more than outweigh any slight adverse effects on medical services. On the other hand, there are many towns and small cities in the United States where the improvement in medical services made possible by an increase in population would more than offset any slight deterioration in the environment.

My conclusion with respect to health is that in some parts of the United States the population is probably larger than socially optimal; in other parts it is surely smaller than would be desirable. Statements about the *total* size, without regard to distribution, are probably not very helpful.

Health Services and an Optimum Level of Population— Are We Part of the Solution or Part of the Problem?

Philip R. Lee

ABSTRACT

Sanitary services and modern medical practices have contributed to population growth by reducing mortality rates; but health services, through contraceptive control and fertility control, can make a major contribution to reducing the birth rate. Long-term solutions to present population problems will depend on research, on modifications of attitudes regarding family size and regarding legally-induced abortion, and on the development of a national population policy.

INTRODUCTION

The role of personal health services in our present population problems and their potential role in the solutions has long been a matter of dispute. There is, however, little question that adequate health services are now an essential element in the services required to enhance the quality of life for the individual citizen.

The subject has frequently been confused by the failure to differentiate family planning and population control, and the failure to define conception control, fertility control, and population control.[1]

Family planning has focused on conception control, utilizing medical (oral contraceptives, IUD) and nonmedical (condom, rhythm method) means. The purpose is to prevent conception. Fertility control is the prevention of births, using contraceptive methods as well as abortion. Population control is quite another matter and is dependent on the balance between fertility and mortality.

Health services may include both personal- and public-health services. Environmental control measures are often included in public-health programs. These will not be considered in this paper. Emphasis will be placed on the role of health services in contributing to our present population problems and their potential role in the solution of these problems.

WHAT ARE THE PROBLEMS?

Many of the ills of our present-day society are attributed to the rapid growth, the size, or the distribution of our population. Professor Roy Greep has argued that we are already feeling the effects of excess population: "Population pressure is felt in many aspects of our daily lives. We feel it in the morning traffic, in housing, in pollution of our air and water, in the destruction of our natural beauty and in the gradual erosion of individual freedom and the loss of privacy."[2] Many other analysts can be cited who believe we are already victims of excessive population growth and that the ill effects will intensify in the near future.

Problems there are, but can we really attribute them to the size of our population or its rate of growth? If we look at the Soviet Union or Australia, two countries with vast land areas in relation to population size, we find crowding, air pollution in industrial cities, and many of the same kinds of problems that plague us. The problems would appear to be more related to the distribution and the density of the population than its size or rate of growth.

The problems have become increasingly serious in our large urban areas. Writing about the problems in our cities, Tyler has offered the following diagnosis:

"What is the universal malady of cities? The disease is density. Where cities foresaw density and planned accordingly, the situation is bad but tolerable. Where exploding populations hit unready urban areas, they are in disaster. Where ethnic and political conflict add further disorder, the disease appears terminal."[3]

With overcrowding comes increased physical and mental illness, more crime and delinquency, and a loss of the personal identification with a neighborhood or a community that, until recent times, had been one of the characteristics of our society.

We are not only creating an increasingly ugly environment, but we are creating real and potential health hazards for ourselves and future generations. These include: the problems of air, water, and soil pollution; the extensive use of pesticides; the widespread use of food additives; and the growing use and abuse of drugs.

In a recent report on population growth and family-planning programs in the Far West, Jessup[4] described the problems facing that region due to rapid population growth. The most pressing problems include: housing, education, environmental pollution, the provision of health services, and the needs of special groups (e.g., American Indians) within the population.

One of the most striking population changes in this country has been in large urban areas, where there has been an immigration to the central cities by Negroes, Puerto Ricans, and other minority groups. Many of the poor and the elderly have remained in the central city while white middle-income families have moved to the suburbs.[5]

The change in the distribution of the population has affected far more than minority groups. Since 1920 the United States has changed from nearly half rural to a predominantly urban society. The 1960 census showed that almost 70 per cent of the population lived in communities of 2,500 or more. The trend continues.

We have noted major changes in other aspects of our population, particularly in the age distribution. Most noticeable has been the gradual increase in the number and percentage of the population aged 65 or over. In the past twenty years we have also seen a sharp rise in the number and percentage of children under the age of 18. The next twenty years will see a rapid increase in the number of women of childbearing age. This, in turn, will result in an upsurge in population, unless these women reduce their fertility.

Many of these developments have produced added strains on the available health services. Not only must two million more people be provided health services every year, but a number of special problems, directly or indirectly related to our rapid rate of population growth, migrations, and the changing age distribution within our population, must be dealt with effectively. Not the least of our problems is the provision of family-planning services.

HEALTH SERVICES AND POPULATION GROWTH

Before examining some of the medical and public-health problems related to our population size, growth, and distribution, I want to review some of the factors influencing population growth in the United States. Four factors seem to have contributed significantly to the growth of our population: (1) a rising standard of living; (2) immigration; (3) the application of sanitary measures to water supply, waste disposal, and food production, distribution, and preparation; and (4) the application of biomedical research advances through personal-health services and public-health programs such as mass immunization.

Improvements in the standard of living have had an impact on both the birth rate and the death rate. The importance of economic development, or an increase in per capita income, on fertility has long been debated. One school has contended that economic development and an improved standard of living promote fertility. Perhaps the foremost exponent of this view was Malthus himself. The predominant view today among many demographers and economists is that economic development inhibits fertility. In a recent paper, Heer[6] provided an interesting analysis that reconciles the apparently conflicting theories relating to economic development and fertility. He has postulated that economic development will increase fertility while the various other factors accompanying the process of economic growth and industrialization will inhibit it.

The application of sanitary measures has little direct effect on birth rate, but a profound effect on death rate. This is evident in an examination of birth rates and death rates in the United States during this century. The birth rate has fluctuated from one decade to another, while the age-adjusted death rates fell for the first half of the century. In the first decades of this century the birth rate was 30 per 1,000 population. The birth rate began to drop in the early 1920s and then declined rapidly in the 1920s and 1930s, when it reached a low of 18.4 births per 1,000 population. The birth rate rose rapidly between 1940 and 1947, reaching a peak of 26.6 births per 1,000 population. It remained relatively stable until 1957, when it began another decline, reaching a level of 18.5 in 1966. The crude and age-adjusted death rates in the United States fell steadily between 1900 and 1954, except for a sharp rise during the 1918 influenza epidemic. The age-adjusted death rate dropped most rapidly from 1937 to 1954, when it leveled off. The major reasons for the decline in the death rate prior to 1937 were, apparently, improvements in the standard of living and the broad application of sanitary measures. Medicine and public health played some part in these advances, but the declines were not related to any specific therapies available to physicians. The impact of biomedical science and its application in the practice of medicine began, according to McDermott,[7] after the introduction of sulfonamides in 1937. The most significant factor in the decline of the age-adjusted death rate between 1937 and 1954 was the application of antibiotics and chemotherapy to the treatment and control of infectious diseases.

Medical and scientific advances have not only had an effect on population growth, they have raised aspirations and modified the patterns of disease as well as the methods of care. The changes have contributed to rising demands for care and to rising costs.

THE CRISIS IN THE PROVISION OF HEALTH SERVICES

The provision of adequate, comprehensive health-care services has become a matter of growing concern: population growth, the rising economic and educational levels of the population, and the growth of private and public health-insurance or medical-care programs have placed a demand for services on physicians, hospitals, and other providers that continues to outpace the supply. New problems emerge as old ones come under control, costs rise rapidly, and adequate solutions seem to be in short supply. Indeed, the problems are such that the President of the United States has described the situation as one of impending crisis.

There are many dimensions to the problem, but basic to all of them is the fact that we have not invested adequately in the resources—research, manpower, facilities, and organization—essential to the task. Manpower shortages are evident, even in those areas of the country where supply appears to be more nearly adequate. At present we have a nationwide shortage of physicians that is estimated to exceed 50,000. Equally serious problems exist in nursing, dentistry, and in some of the allied health professions. Maldistribution creates even more serious problems for many people, particularly those living in the South, in rural areas, and in the poverty areas of our cities.

The National Advisory Commission on Health Manpower, in their report to the President in 1967, summed up the need:

"It is true that substantially increased numbers will be needed over time. But if additional personnel are employed in the present manner and within present patterns and systems of care, they will not avert or perhaps even alleviate, the crisis. Unless we improve the system through which health care is provided, care will continue to become less satisfactory, even though there are massive increases in costs and numbers of personnel."[8]

Although I share the view that we must improve the organization and delivery of health services, I do not believe that it will be accomplished without significant increases in the numbers of health personnel. In the face of continuing shortages of physicians and other health personnel and the growing demand for health care, I believe we must have a rapid and dramatic increase in the number of physicians in the country if we are to cope with the problems.

In addition to the investments needed to overcome the manpower shortages and the major changes required in the organization and delivery of health services, we must have new health policies responsive to the changing character and distribution of the population and the problems it faces.

SPECIAL PROBLEMS—ILLEGITIMACY AND EXCESS FERTILITY

The crisis in the delivery of health care has many manifestations. The number of women of childbearing age is expected to rise rapidly in the next ten years. At the present time, millions of women of childbearing age receive seriously inadequate health care. The two most sensitive indicators of health care—maternal and infant mortality—indicate that the poor, the minorities (especially the Negroes, Mexican-Americans, and American Indians), and those in rural areas do not receive adequate care.

A special problem is posed for unwed mothers. There has been a striking increase in the number of illegitimate births in the past twenty-five years, from 85,000 in 1940 to 291,200 in 1965.[9] One factor in this rapid rise may have been the advance of medical science which has produced effective chemotherapeutic and antibiotic drugs against venereal disease. There has been a sharp drop in sterility due to venereal disease during this same period. Many other factors undoubtedly contribute. One of the most important appears to be migration of the rural poor to the cities.

There are a number of health problems directly related to child-bearing, and these are accentuated for unmarried mothers because of their inadequate health care. The problems faced by the illegitimate child are often traceable to the inadequate prenatal and maternity care provided the mother. Unmarried pregnant women receive less prenatal care than married women and they are more likely to deliver their babies outside a hospital and without medical supervision.

A number of studies have evaluated the relationship among the number of pregnancies, the spacing of pregnancies, the age of the parents, and a variety of socioeconomic factors that influence the outcome of a pregnancy.

A woman is much less likely to carry an infant to full term after her fifth pregnancy. Fetal mortality for fifth-order births is almost twice that for second-order births, and it rises to three times the rate with sixth order and above.[10] Both infant mortality and mental retardation rates are higher than average for fourth and subsequent live births. These infants account for only about one-quarter of all live births, but for nearly half of all infant deaths and a larger proportion of infants born mentally retarded.

Spacing of pregnancies is also important. In a recent study in New York City it was found that the neonatal death rate of infants born one year or less apart is five times that for those births where the interval is two or three years.[7] Prematurity and immaturity have also been found more frequently where pregnancies are closely spaced.

Siegel has noted that increasing family size is associated with: "(1) Increased fetal, neonatal and postneonatal mortality rates, (2) higher prematurity rates, (3) less adequate prenatal care and more limited educational aspiration for their children, (4) increasing incidence of infectious diseases in parents and children, (5) poorer growth—both height and weight—among preschool and school children, (6) lower I.Q. scores among children, and (7) increased prevalence of selected diseases among parents."[11]

Maternal mortality and morbidity in the United States are affected by the inability to control fertility. For women aged 20 to 29, the mortality rate is two and one-half times as great for the fourth and higher parities as it is for parities one through three. Mortality also increases greatly with age. The overall rate for women over 40 years of age is seven times that for women under 20.[10,12]

Not only may the physical health of the infant or mother be impaired by excess fertility, but emotional problems may arise for the individual and the family. The problems faced by unwanted and illegitimate children have received some attention, and a considerable literature has accumulated relating family size, birth intervals, and birth order to a broad range of psychological and social problems.

Excess fertility has been a problem for women in all socioeconomic groups, but it has been a heavier burden on the poor because of lack of information about fertility and reproduction and the unavailability of family-planning services. In a study of fertility control in the United States, Campbell[13] noted that some families have more children than they want while others report failures in delaying conception for as long a period as desired. Couples experiencing either kind of failure comprised 56 to 58 per cent of the married population of reproductive age in 1955, 1960, and 1963. In 1963, more than 20 per cent of the couples reported failure to prevent conception after the couple had achieved the desired number of children.

In a more recent study, Ryder reports that nearly one-third of all married couples who intended to have no more children had at least one.[14]

According to the criteria developed by the Social Security Administration, in 1966, 21 per cent of women of childbearing age were poor or near poor, and only 15 per cent of these low-income women who were potential users of family planning services had adequate access to such services. It is small wonder that the fertility rate (births per 1,000 women 15 to 44 years of age) for poor or near poor women was 55 per cent above that for women not living in poverty.

We have been provided some insight into the reasons for this excess fertility in the studies by Beasley and his associates in New Orleans.[15] In a study of medically indigent, high-risk mothers they found an average of 4.9 pregnancies each, even though the women had a mean age of only 25.5 years. Over one-half of the women had already experienced more pregnancies than they originally wanted, three-fourths never wanted to become pregnant again, but over 50 per cent did not know that pregnancy results from the union of sperm and ovum and 90 per cent did not know when the fertile period occurred. Although many of the women used some form of contraceptive, the most effective medical methods were beyond their economic reach and were not provided in publicly-supported medical-care programs.

CONTRACEPTION, FAMILY PLANNING, AND FERTILITY CONTROL

Typical of the fragmented, categorical approach to health services has been our failure to provide family planning or birth control as part of comprehensive health services.

It now appears that as a result of private and public efforts, adequate contraceptive services will be available by 1974 or 1975 to all women of childbearing age who wish such services. In a period of fifteen years we have witnessed significant changes in public attitude, in governmental policies and programs, and in the availability of highly effective contraceptives. The impact of family-planning services on family size, the spacing of children, and the health and well-being of families are likely to be significant. We have already seen sharp declines in infant mortality rates among poor mothers provided such services. There is some evidence that birth rates will also decline when these services are widely available.

There has been a great deal of confusion about policies and programs because of the failure to differentiate between contraceptive control, family planning, fertility control, and population control. In the United States, the purpose of federal policies and programs has been to make family-planning or contraceptive-control services available. The basic purpose of these policies is to extend freedom of choice and equality of opportunity to all women who wish to control the spacing of their pregnancies or the size of their families. There has been no policy of fertility control or population control in the United States, but rather a family-planning policy.[16] The relevance of family-planning programs to population control has recently been questioned by Davis[17] and Blake.[18] Davis has focused some of the issues: "To acknowledge that family planning does not achieve population control is not to impugn its value for other purposes. Freeing women from the need to have more children than they want is of great benefit to them and their children and society at large. My argument is therefore directed not against family planning programs as such but against the assumption that they are effective means of controlling population growth."[17]

In the United States, federal policies have emphasized basic research on human reproduction, the development of effective, safe, and inexpensive methods of contraceptive control, and the extension of family-planning services to all who wish to use them.[16,19]

Recent changes in state laws, court decisions, and medical practice indicate that fertility control may soon become as important as contraceptive control. The principal means of fertility control other than contraception has been abortion.

Abortion has long been one of the most widely used methods of fertility control. In several countries where abortion is legal, such as Hungary and Japan, easy access to legal induced abortion has resulted in a number of abortions approaching or exceeding the number of live births. Also, population growth rates have been low.

In the United States, abortion has been illegal in some states for more than one hundred years. Its regulation has long been a matter of state law. In spite of the fact that abortion was illegal except to preserve the life of the mother, it was widely practiced in this country. The problem of illegal abortion has been, and remains, a major social and public problem. It has been estimated that between 500,000 and 1,000,000 illegal abortions are performed in the United States annually, with many maternal deaths and much maternal morbidity.

The medical, ethical, legal, and religious aspects of abortion have been extensively discussed in recent years[20] and the problems have received increasing attention by the public.

Two recent court decisions—one by the California Supreme Court[21] and another by a United States District Court judge in the District of Columbia[22]—may have a significant effect on current law if not on medical practice.

The Supreme Court of California held that the pre-1967 antiabortion law in California was unconstitutionally vague, considering the fact that it placed the physician in the untenable position of having an interest (fear of penalties) that prevented an unbiased determination of proper medical care for his patient. It also held that any strict antiabortion law, requiring a woman to risk high probability of death before abortion relief is granted, is unconstitutional because it improperly infringes upon the woman's right of privacy, liberty to choose whether to bear a child, and liberty to obtain proper medical assistance.

The California Supreme Court's decision also broadly construed the 1967 California Therapeutic Abortion Act as follows:

"Thus the test established is a medical one, whether the pregnant woman's physical and mental health will be furthered by abortion or by bearing the child to term, and the assessment does not involve considerations beyond medical competence. There is nothing to indicate that in adopting the Therapeutic Abortion Act the legislature was asserting an interest in the embryo." [21]

The judge in the District of Columbia case held that the District's sixty-eight-year-old abortion law was unconstitutional because the wording pertaining to preserving the life or health of a mother was too vague and because a woman has the constitutional right to determine whether she will bear a child. [22]

These decisions will undoubtedly lead to further test cases in those states with laws virtually identical to the pre-1967 California law.

The present pattern of practice in California is worth noting. The former antiabortion law was replaced in November, 1967. Before 1967, statewide there were 1.8 abortions per 1,000 live births. In 1968, there were 12 abortions per 1,000 live births, and in 1970 there were 172 abortions per 1,000. This does not tell the whole story. In San Francisco during 1970 there were 254 abortions per 1,000 live births, and in some Bay Area hospitals the number of abortions and live births run even. It is estimated that in 1971 there will be about 100,000 abortions and about 300,000 live births in the state.

Abortion laws and the patterns of medical practice are changing in many other states. Hawaii and New York have enacted two of the nation's least restrictive abortion laws in recent years.

The impact of these decisions about abortion by the courts, state legislatures, physicians, and patients remains to be seen. Will the number of legal abortions exceed live births in five to ten years? Will this result in dramatic changes in the birth rate in the United States in the next decade? Will present attitudes toward human life, pregnancy, and childbirth in our society be dramatically changed or undermined? Will we find new medical, social, and moral problems arising?

HEALTH SERVICES AND THE FUTURE OUTLOOK FOR POPULATION GROWTH

In spite of progress in family-planning programs and major shifts in attitudes, laws, and medical practice on fertility control, there very likely will be an upsurge of population growth in the next few decades because of the large number of women entering childbearing age (15 to 44). In the twenty years from 1965 to 1985 the number of women of childbearing age will rise by 58 per cent.[23] Unless these women reduce their fertility dramatically, with a resultant decline in the birth rate, there will be a significant increase in the number of births and an increase in our rate of population growth.

Present attitudes of men and women about family size, marriage, and the role of women indicate that significant changes must occur before birth rates or population growth rates are likely to decline. Numerous studies have shown that married couples in widely varying social and economic circumstances desire 3.3 children on the average. This norm, even if achieved through more effective birth control, will still result in a population in excess of 300 million by the year 2000. Another century of growth at the same rate would result in a population in the United States of over one billion people. Projections of this kind, even to the year 2000, imply major changes in many aspects of our society.

Although projections of population growth are fraught with danger, as many learned in the 1930s, it is evident that our population will continue to grow unless there are major changes in attitudes and policies in this country.

The third point of importance is that the demand for health services will continue to rise at a rate more rapid than the population. Health services can contribute to the solution, just as they are part of the problem. Health services have more to do with the rate of population growth than with the variety of other factors such as migration, distribution, and density. These latter have a major impact on the need for health services.

The question, at this time, is really not one of optimum population size, but whether or not it is feasible or advisable to achieve a zero rate of population growth in this country.

Many questions cannot be answered adequately at the present time because we do not have the facts nor have the consequences been fully evaluated. The proposals for social science research put forth by the Center for Population Research, National Institute of Child Health and Human Development, could provide much of the needed information in the next decade. The topics identified for special concentration include:[19]

1. Trends in fertility and related variables;

2. The antecedents, processes, and consequences of population structure, distribution, and change;

3. Population policies; and

4. Family structure, sexual behavior, and the relationship between childbearing patterns and child development.

The expansion of existing university population research and training centers and the establishment of new centers are crucial to the development of this mission-oriented research program.

The Presidential Advisory Commission on Population Growth and the American Future will also have to draw heavily on these centers for the studies it will certainly need. The Commission can contribute significantly to the public's understanding of our population problems and the policy alternatives before us if we are to achieve population control.

SUMMARY

Population growth in this country has contributed significantly to the profound social problems facing our society. Population migration and density contribute more to these problems than does the size of the population. Health services, sanitary measures, and economic and social development have all contributed to our population growth, primarily by their impact on mortality rates.

A number of health problems are associated with excess fertility and increasing family size: increased fetal, neonatal, and postneonatal mortality rates, increased maternal mortality, increased mental retardation or lower I.Q. among the children, increased incidence of infectious diseases among parents and children, and poorer growth among preschool and school children.

Health services, through contraceptive control and fertility control, can make a major contribution to reducing the birth rate. Major changes will have to occur regarding the status of women, marriage, and desired family size before full and effective use of these services is possible.

The rapid development of adequate and effective contraceptive control, or family-planning services, as an integral part of more comprehensive health care, will contribute to improvements in maternal, child, and family life, but it will not have a marked effect on population growth.

The most significant developments in the field of fertility control in the United States in recent years have been the legislative, court, medical, and personal decisions on legal induced abortion. It is too early to estimate the impact of these changes.

Long-term solutions to present population problems will depend on research, modification of attitudes, and the development of a national population policy.

Health services, while part of the problem, are also an integral part of the solution to our multiple population problems.

REFERENCES

1. P. M. Hauser, "Population: More Than Family Planning," *Jour. Med. Educ.*, 44, Part 2 (November, 1969), 20–29.

2. R. O. Greep, "The Population Crisis is Here," *The Pharos*, 31 (July, 1968), 94–100.

3. Gus Tyler, "Can Anyone Run a City?" *Saturday Review of Literature* (November 8, 1969), 22.

4. R. B. Jessup, *Profiles of Population Growth and Family Planning Programs in the West* (Washington, D.C.: Department of Health, Education and Welfare, 1968), pp. 1–39.

5. R. Farley and K. E. Tacuber, "Population Trends and Residential Segregation Since 1960," *Science*, 159 (March 1, 1968), 953–956.

6. D. M. Heer, "Economic Development and the Fertility Transition," *Daedalus*, 97 (Spring, 1967), 447–462.

7. Walsh McDermott. Testimony, hearings before the Subcommittee on Foreign Aid Expenditures of the Committee on Government Operations, United States Senate, Ninetieth Congress, second session on S. 1676, January 31, 1968, pp. 276–286.

8. *Report of the National Advisory Commission on Health Manpower*, Vol. 1 (Washington, D.C.: Government Printing Office, 1967), p. 2.

9. Alice C. Clague and Stephanie J. Ventura, *Trends in Illegitimacy*, National Center for Health Statistics, Series 21, Number 15 (Washington, D.C.: Department of Health, Education and Welfare, 1968), p. 90.

10. *Report of the Special Study Group on the Delivery of Family Planning Services* (Washington, D.C.: Department of Health, Education and Welfare, October, 1968), p. 53.

11. Earl Siegel, "The Biological Effects of Family Planning. A. Preventive Pediatrics: The Potentials of Family Planning," *Jour. Med. Educ.*, 44, Part 2 (November, 1969), 74–80.

12. R. L. Day, "The Influence of Number of Children, Interval Between Pregnancies and Age of Parents upon Survival of Offspring," *Advances in Planned Parenthood*, Proceedings of the Third and Fourth Annual Meetings of the Association of Planned Parenthood Physicians (New York: Excepta Medica Foundation, 1967), pp. 23–31.

13. A. A. Campbell, "The Role of Family Planning in the Reduction of Poverty," *Jour. of Marriage and the Family,* 30 (May, 1968), 236–244.

14. N. Ryder, "Rate of Unwanted Births is High, Professor Says," *The New York Times,* November 23, 1969.

15. J. D. Beasley, C. L. Harter, and D. V. McCalister, "Aspects of Family Planning among Low Income, 'High Risk' Mothers," *Advances in Planned Parenthood,* Proceedings of the Third and Fourth Annual Meetings of the Association of Planned Parenthood Physicians (New York: Excepta Medica Foundation, 1967), pp. 197–204.

16. P. R. Lee, "Population Policy, Family Planning and Public Health," Hilleboe Lecture, delivered before the 64th Annual Health Conference, Rochester, New York, June 12, 1968, p. 62; O. Harkavy, F. S. Jaffe, and S. M. Wishik, "Family Planning and Public Policy: Who is Misleading Whom?" *Science,* 165 (July 25, 1969), 367–373.

17. Kingsley Davis, "Population Policy: Will Current Programs Succeed?" *Science,* 158 (November 10, 1967), 730–739.

18. Judith Blake, "Population Policy for Americans: Is the Government Being Misled?" *Science,* 164 (May 2, 1969), 522–529.

19. *Report on Population and Family Planning Activities,* Department of Health, Education and Welfare. A report to the House Committee on Appropriations, prepared by the Office of the Deputy Assistant Secretary for Population and Family Planning, Office of the Assistant Secretary for Health and Scientific Affairs, February, 1969, pp. IV, 10–14.

20. R. E. Hall, "Abortion: A Non-Catholic View," in E. F. Torrey, *Ethical Issues in Medicine* (Boston: Little, Brown and Company, 1968), pp. 77–85; M. V. Viola, "Abortion: A Catholic View," *ibid.,* pp. 89–104; A. E. Hellegers, "A Doctor Looks at Abortion," Douglass Edward White Lecture, Georgetown University Law Center, March 16, 1966.

21. *People v. Belous,* in the Supreme Court of the State of California, Crim. 12739, filed September 5, 1969, p. 32.

22. "Abortion Law Voided; New Test Cases Seen," *American Medical News,* November 24, 1969, p. 3.

23. A. A. Campbell, "Control of Fertility in the United States," unpublished.

Note on the Demography of Poverty

Ezra Glaser

ABSTRACT

The relative magnitude of the "escape rate" from poverty and the differential fertility of low-income women will determine the balance between the welfare-dependent and the supporting population.

There are forces that tend to increase the relative numbers of poor persons in the United States population and there are forces that tend in the opposite direction.

In the most formalized and oversimplified version of this analysis, the population is conceived of as reacting to two differential systems:

1. The poorer segments of the population have a higher birth rate than the average. The differential increase is not offset by the higher infant mortality in these groups, nor do poorer survival rates in later years overcome the larger number of births. In the absence of other influences, this would lead to ever-increasing proportions of poor individuals for any fixed standard of poverty.

2. More people who are born into poor families "escape" from poverty (by any fixed standard, such as family income less than $3,000 per year) than suffer the opposite transition. This escape results from combinations of such factors as personal motivations and capabilities, favorable economic conditions, improved economic (and social) opportunity, education in general, specific programs directed at aiding the escape from poverty. In the absence of other influences, this trend would lead to an ever-smaller proportion of poor individuals in the United States. (The aged poor represent a special problem which is magnified by increased life expectancy at older ages. This group is relatively isolated from the economic and social upbringing of children, so it does not "pass along" its poverty and any attendant cultural deprivation to later generations.)

In these simple terms, the persistent dominance of one of these differential influences over the other would lead by convergence to a mostly-poor nation or one in which poverty is a minor problem. The consequences would be many and far-reaching, including a drastic unbalance in the size of the welfare-dependent population and the (economic) supporting population, in one direction or the other.

Two strategic questions emerge:

1. Even in the simplistic terms of this model, which way do the differentials seem to be drifting?

2. In what ways should the model itself be generalized by adding some more realistic structuring to the representation of poverty subpopulations, and how does this affect the outcome of (1) above?

The first question could be answered by developing data on differential reproduction of the poor and by estimating the "escape" rate from poverty. The 1970 decennial census should provide a basis for this, yielding birth rates by family income classes and the materials out of which survival rates could be developed for some subpopulations. Using older data, ". . . from 1960 to 1965, low-income women of childbearing age had an annual fertility rate of 153 births per 1,000 women. The rate for the rest of the female population was 98 births per 1,000."[1] This difference would be somewhat narrowed by higher mortality rates before the age of 45 (the conventionalized end of reproduction) among the poor.

The "escape" rate is difficult to measure.

. . . the crucial weakness of the poor family is its drastically reduced capacity to provide the resources and incentives that would enable its offspring to exit from poverty. We lack solid longitudinal data, but predictors of subsequent economic achievement—such as completion of high school—suggest that individuals raised in poor families have no better than a 2 to 1 chance of escaping poverty. The odds are worse if the child is reared in a large family that spreads its limited resources even more thinly. Children raised in poor families are far more likely (eight times more in some areas) than are their non-poor counterparts to drop out of school and thereby to lack the preparation for anything better than unskilled, marginal jobs. Persons raised in poor families also are far more likely to marry young and to have large families. Thus, lacking the resources to do otherwise, poor families create their own replacements.[2]

Much additional analysis would have to be undertaken before leaping to conclusions. If the poor reproduced at about 50 per cent greater rates than others, but two-thirds of them "escaped," there would seem to be grounds for optimism. A more developed model would have to take account of several factors: the better "escape" rates of families headed by an employed male (in our recent years of high economic activity); the correlation between poverty and many other disadvantaged conditions (physical disability, mental incompetence, emotional unbalance, etc.); the special problems of ethnic minorities. Finally, there is an evolution among those families that were precipitately urbanized during World War II with no preparation for their new surroundings; perhaps the next two generations will prove that at least some of the worst problems were symptoms of economic-social transition rather than permanent characteristics of the "vicious circle" of poverty.

REFERENCES

1. Wilbur J. Cohen, "A Ten-Point Program to Abolish Poverty" (adapted from a statement to the President's Commission on Income Maintenance Programs, September, 1968), *Social Security Bulletin*, 31, 12 (December, 1968), 5.
2. "Exits from Poverty for the Non-Aged Poor in the U.S." Unpublished paper of the Program Analysis Group on Exits from Poverty, Department of Health, Education and Welfare, August, 1968.

Whither the Urban Society?

Philip M. Hauser

ABSTRACT

Four developments have produced an urban crisis in our rapid transformation from an agrarian to an urban society: the population explosion; the implosion, i.e., the extremely rapid growth of metropolitan centers; the population displosion, which refers to the great heterogeneity of people who share not only the same geographic area but similar social-economic-political activities; and, finally, the accelerating tempo of technological change. It is necessary to add a new "Urban Bill of Rights" to the Constitution in order to keep our society viable.

The urban crisis will worsen in this decade, and all urban problems—physical, personal, social, economic, and governmental—will probably grow increasingly severe until the end of the century. There is no present indication that, during the 1970s, we will do very much to bring under control the acute and chronic problems plaguing our cities and threatening the viability of American society. Air and water pollution will continue to threaten health and life; housing supply and quality will remain inadequate; slums will not be eradicated;

air and surface traffic will continue to cause congestion; crime, drug addiction, alcoholism, and delinquency will continue at a high level; the revolt of our youth and blacks will no doubt not only continue but escalate; poverty will continue to remind us that we harbor grave systemic disorders; tax reforms and welfare provisions will continue to be inadequate—and so forth. In short, it can be anticipated that our cities will grow blacker and the suburbs whiter, the generation gap will increase, our politicians will continue in their well-worn paths, and social unrest undoubtedly will increase.

The United States is the world's most dramatic example of four developments transforming an agrarian to an urban and metropolitan society: population explosion, implosion, displosion, and the accelerating tempo of technological change.

Population explosion refers to the remarkable rate of population increase. Population implosion refers to the increasing concentration of people in relatively small areas. Population displosion refers to the increasing diversity of those who share not only the same geographic areas but also the same social, economic, and political activities. Technological innovations are self-evident.

The census in 1960 recorded a population in the United States of approximately 180 million; in 1970 a population of 205 million will probably have been recorded; by the year 2000 (with the second postwar baby boom) we can undoubtedly expect a population of more than 300 million.

In 1790, 95 per cent of the United States population lived in rural areas; we did not become an urban nation until about 1920. In 1960 the United States population was 70 per cent urban and 63 per cent metropolitan. It is likely that the 100 million we are likely to add to our population in the next thirty years will be urban, with about 80 per cent going into our metropolitan areas (places with 50,000 or more inhabitants and the counties in which they are located), which will probably swamp us before we can solve our present problems.

Our population comes from every corner of the globe. In 1900 only 51 per cent of the American population were native-born whites. The remaining 49 per cent were either foreign-born, children of immigrants, or members of the black and other races. In 1960, 30 per cent were still either foreign-born, children of immigrants, or members of the black and other races. We are indeed a polyglot nation; and we are in the midst of a black revolution. In 1910, 89 per cent of the blacks in the United States lived in the South. With World War I, the migratory movements of blacks from the South to the North began, accelerating with World War II. By 1960 the black concentration in the South had decreased to 60 per cent; now it is between 50 per cent and 60 per cent and will diminish to about 50 per cent in the 1970s. In the last fifty years, blacks in the United States have been transformed from 73 per cent rural to 73 per cent urban, and are now more highly urbanized than the white population.

As recently as 1960, 23 per cent of blacks 25 years of age and over were still functionally illliterate with little opportunity to achieve education beyond the fifth grade, unable even to read a newspaper with ease, and ill-prepared for life in metropolitan America. The black migration to urban areas with little but their strong backs (their national heritage!) gave them scant preparation to earn a living (no comparison to white immigrants landing on our shores, lacking education, skills, or language ability, but arriving when this nation was in the beginning process of building its physical plants, railroads, and highways). This, then, is the foundation of the population displosion in the United States.

To resolve the urban crisis the gap must be closed between the twentieth century technological, demographic world man has created and the nineteenth and prior century ideologies and institutions man has inherited.

The first step is to recognize the need to have an urban policy. The second step is to recognize that our federal constitution, in a number of respects, is outmoded.

A major need is for an Urban Bill of Rights to supplement the present Bill of Rights which was drawn in a rural agricultural setting, at a time when no one could anticipate the population explosion, implosion, displosion, and the great technological changes experienced since the founding of the United States.

This Urban Bill of Rights should include such fundamental things, necessary in the interdependent and highly vulnerable urban society, as economic opportunity and security, including assured employment and income flow; access to adequate education; access to an unpolluted environment; adequate housing; opportunity for health and longevity; and equality in the administration of justice. Especially significant would be a provision to make the interests of society paramount over those of the individual (which would in effect modify present provisions in our Constitution placing the rights of the person above those of society). As interpreted by the United States Supreme Court, present Constitutional provisions actually prevent urban areas in the nation from dealing effectively with organized crime, a problem afflicting our cities for more than fifty years. Finally, and perhaps most important, the new Bill of Rights must include the right to be free from the use of physical force in the resolution of conflicts of interest, domestically as well as internationally. On the home front this would, among other things, outlaw the use of force in the solution of labor-management strife—both the strike and the lockout—and require adjudicative means of settlement. Use of brute force to settle labor-management conflict is another survival from the past, generally injurious to the entire nation.

To deal with contemporary problems, both conservative and liberal approaches must be abandoned in favor of social engineering. The conservative turns to the past for present-day answers; the liberal too often manifests emotion, zeal, and determination—both approaches are hopelessly outmoded. The application of knowledge based on research to resolve problems—the social engineering approach—is what is needed to deal with social problems in the same way that physical engineering is utilized to solve physical problems and biomedical engineering (medicine and surgery) to meet biomedical problems. Society recognizes the role of the physical and biomedical engineer but has yet to recognize and accept the social engineer.

It took from 1750 to 1850, roughly, for the physical sciences to achieve respectability and acceptance; it required approximately the century from 1850 to 1950 for the biomedical sciences to acquire respectability and acceptance sufficient to enable the biomedical engineers—physician and surgeon—to apply knowledge to the solution of problems of health and life. It may take the century from 1950 to 2050 for the social sciences to gain comparable respectability and acceptance, permitting the social engineer to apply knowledge to the solution of our social problems.

Whether we shall remain a viable society to year 2050 is a moot question. It may well be that our present chaos will engulf and drag us down as a nation which achieved the miraculous in technology but was unable to adapt itself to the new world man created. The United States may well collapse and bring down most, if not all, of humanity. We do have the means to destroy ourselves; it is naive to assume that the use of these means is beyond the realm of possibility.

We also have within our grasp the means to deal with our problems in an effective manner, to create a world that is twentieth century in its social, economic, and political, as well as in its technological aspects.

The means to this lie in man's potential for rational behavior—in man's ability through science to acquire knowledge, and in his ability through engineering to apply knowledge to the solution of his problems.

PART III

The General Question of Optimum: Life Styles and Human Values

INTRODUCTION

The last group of papers deals with the question of an optimum level of population in a more general way. Walter O. Roberts leads off the discussion by stating his belief that an optimum level of population exists. He projects this optimum as a steady-state in ecological balance with the environment.

In a general methodological approach, Garrett Hardin makes clear that one should not confuse the existence of an optimum with its specification. Even though specification may be difficult, uncertain, or indeterminate, a set of optima may still exist. Plural optima imply choices and, therefore, a question of "taste." By means of a quasi-economic analysis, Hardin arrives at a figure of fifty million people, or perhaps less, as an optimum population for the United States. He points out that the well-known economies of scale demand large populations, but perhaps not even as large as fifty million. We have many examples of nations which have very adequate living standards, health services, environmental conditions—yet fewer people. The diseconomies of scale have perhaps not been investigated as thoroughly. For example, information management suffers as the number of people increases. Since the total number of possible relationships goes up as the square of their number, there soon comes a point when participatory democracy becomes very difficult. Transportation is affected in the same ratio, and pollution varies as some power function of population. Hardin feels it is important to maintain the concept of "growth" but to redirect it. Certainly, GNP is not an adequate measure of what is wanted, but perhaps something like "Net National Amenities" should be the index that we really ought to make grow.

Some of these thoughts, particularly relating to the transmittal of information and communication, are echoed in the remarks of John B. Calhoun. The remarks by Ezra Glaser underscore the need to have individual choice of life styles, and the need for an economic index based on the development of a suitable value system.

This line of thought is expanded in some detail in the paper by Lincoln H. Day. He rejects the usual economic criteria of the optimum as being either too narrow or sometimes actually misleading. It is clearly necessary to first develop better criteria under which to evaluate an optimum population. The optimum size has to be within the maximum set by either resource, ecological, or social limits. While one may not be able to specify this optimum, one can certainly specify the demographic characteristics of an optimum population since they would have to be those of a stationary population. Day suggests that a truly optimum population would have to have a negative growth rate in order that human numbers would stay in ecological balance with a steadily decreasing quantity of resources.

(This concept could well be developed further. For example, even with a declining population, one could achieve a "growth" of amenities, essentially by increasing productivity or through the use of accumulated capital.)

Joseph J. Spengler's paper gives a general overview on the subject of population optimum. Optimizing means maximizing a social welfare function. Spengler points out why the rate of population growth and the spatial distribution of population are significant: the former because it affects the age distribution; the latter because it introduces inefficiencies and excessive costs as when, for example, in 1960, nearly 30 per cent of the United States population occupied only .25 per cent of the land area. It would be good if there were feedback mechanisms which would bring the population to an optimum whenever a maladjustment occurred.

One must distinguish between size of economy and size of population. Only a few countries are large enough to permit their economies to have the advantage of scale. Small states are dependent on external exchange relations, but when these are operating well, they can draw on the outer environments of other countries and achieve economies of scale beyond the reach of small, closed economies.

Perhaps one should not ask whether further increases in population can be accommodated but, rather, do any net advantages flow from such increases to a country or to a city or to a metropolitan region. This requires an economic analysis in which, however, *all* of the costs must be considered, including items which are hard to quantify. We must also inquire into the distributional effects. Who gets the benefits? Who bears the cost? The beneficiaries of growth must compensate those on whom the costs are incident. The social costs of pollution will have to be internalized and charged to the polluter.

The power to decide on the growth and distribution of population is both dispersed and concentrated. Family formation (i.e., growth) is an example of dispersed decision-making power, but the formation of new cities which are based on industrial activities (i.e., distribution) is controlled by a very small number of major corporations. Ultimately, the number and distribution of people will be tied in with their desires for life styles.

This emphasis on life styles and human values is elaborated on by Margaret Mead. It may be difficult to shift from a traditional ethic which places a premium on large families to one which rewards those who have few or no children. One problem is to educate nations away from the syndrome of pure growth in terms of GNP. Perhaps they should be vying for progress which would be measured in terms of the closeness to a declared optimum level of population.

Until recently, population problems were thought to be those of the developing countries. Now, at last, we realize that the question "How many is too many?" applies to the developed countries also. What should be the basis for a rational public policy on population? Bernard Berelson reminds us that even if population growth were stopped immediately, our problems would not disappear: resources will be depleted; pollution will occur. But regardless of the ultimate, or even the optimal, population size, a lower rate of growth is desirable since it gives us a wider range of options for the future. He believes, in fact, that the optimum is better defined as a rate than as a size.

How to summarize the conclusions of these contributors?

Although one argues for a slight rate of growth and another for a slight decline of the present population, it is generally accepted that population will have to be stabilized: first, because the earth is finite and its resources limited; and, second, because the demand for natural resources creates an ever-increasing impact on the environment and threatens to destroy the stability of the ecosystem. Yet, the demographic facts of life make it plain that some further growth of population is inevitable—even if the birth rate were suddenly to be reduced to the (replacement) level which will eventually give a zero-growth population. In addition, social and political factors may delay the approach of a zero growth rate, thus allowing a still greater increase of population.

But it is important to realize that the crisis is produced not just by people but by their consumption of resources. Even if we achieved a zero-growth population, we would still have to work hard to make life more livable. (Of course, if the population grows, we well have to work even harder.) It is incumbent upon us then to learn how to reduce the environmental impact of population growth: by conservation of resources; by re-use and recycling; by a better distribution of people which reduces the extreme concentrations in metropolitan centers; but above all by choosing life styles which permit "growth" of a type that makes a minimum impact on the ecology of the earth's biosphere.

S.F.S.

There Is an Optimum Population Level

Walter Orr Roberts

We are asked, today, whether there is an optimum level of population for the nation and for the world. I am tempted to answer, "Yes, there *is* an optimum level of population. But that optimum is not any particular number." It's not just today's world population, or 75 per cent of today's population, or two-and-one-half times today's population. Rather, I'd say that the optimum is that level of population at which the growth of population has ended and society has firmly established its determination to live in harmonious balance with the environment.

In such a world, economic growth is no longer a goal. Reconstruction of the environment, protection of chosen areas as wilderness preserves, and enhancement of the quality of life everywhere become the major aims of human endeavor.

A major conceptual change is necessary, if we are to live in a world that is static in economic activity, population level, geographical frontiers, size of cities, and the like. But, as Bob Dylan has said, "The times, they are a-changin'." He also says, in somewhat more alarming fashion, "Get out of the way if you don't understand." Indeed, we are on a disaster course if we cannot adjust to the new values of a world like this.

Population growth has been a long-accepted feature of our national story. When the Pilgrims settled at Plymouth, the world population was estimated to be under 500 million. Two hundred years later it had not yet doubled, but had reached only about 900 million. Today, an additional 150 years later, population has nearly quadrupled to about three and a half billion. In the United States, our population was about 100 million in 1900. Today it is 200 million. By the end of this century it is likely to be at or above 300 million.

Roger Revelle graphically pictures the megalopolises of the future, where nearly everybody will be living, as long, narrow, super-cities formed by the spreading and coalescence of present cities—where the problems of water, air, and food supply, of removal of wastes, of transport and communication, and, above all, of maintaining life on a human scale will be of a magnitude never faced before in the history of mankind. The United States will be in reality, if not in legal form, a federation of cities, repeating on a giant scale the Greek city leagues.

There is another parallel with these ancient city-states. To the Greeks, the citizenry was distinguished from the barbarian hordes outside the city, where things were wild, uncivilized, and lawless. Today's danger is that the poorer parts of the old core city, as they grow deeper within the megalopolis, will become the domain, the compound, the prison of the lawless and the alienated. There is danger of impoverished, unrepaired, unswept, alleyed wildernesses within the greater cities, crowded with the poor, the idle, the angry, the children, and, those other ubiquitous urbanites, the rats. The core-city ghettos now exist. Will we simply build stronger the invisible walls against escape that are already there? Will we simply build walls to contain the threat, as ancient city-states built walls to protect the comfort and refinement of their power classes? I hope not. But the parallel is frightening!

I am, however, an optimist. The very science-technology that enables us to build jumbo jets, automobiles, off-shore drilling rigs can be used to control their hazards to our living space, to invent production-consumption-restoration cycles that do not insult the environment massively. We need to agree that it is a goal worthy of our highest dedication, and that we are prepared to pay the costs of achieving a harmonious balance with nature that will reward every citizen of the world-city, earth.

How to Specify an Optimum Level of Population

Garrett Hardin

The first step toward the solution of the problem of the optimum population is a methodological one. It is generally assumed, and sometimes said, that since we cannot (at present) uniquely specify the optimum, therefore there is no optimum (or that the concept of an optimum population is meaningless). This agnostic position is essentially based on a "burden of proof" argument.

The agnostic position confuses two matters: existence and specification. Because of the multidimensionality of the values involved in the population/well-being function, there must be many optima. Using the word "optimum" in the plural is contrary to popular usage, but is quite consistent with the usage of the calculus where one speaks of plural "maxima." In fact, the two concepts are related.

Given plural optima, the problem of choice among them reduces to one of choice among the value-functions that define the optima. Thus enter questions of "taste." In spite of the ancient maxim *de gustibus non disputandum est* history shows that there is, in the course of time, some diminution in the number of long-standing alternatives; but there is no reason to think that they will ever be reduced to one.

Given multiple defensible optima, how should a choice be made?

In so far as mankind is divided into numerous sovereignties and subcultures, different groups may choose different optima. With rigid sovereignties and parallel responsibilities, conflict may be avoided. A successfully monolithic state may, by definition, "agree" on a single optimum. The rest of mankind, in which we would no doubt prefer to include ourselves, must settle for some sort of suboptimization, or an uneasy equilibrium between incompatible optima. We will thus continue to struggle with the ancient problems of democracy and tolerant coexistence in a pluralistic state. In passing, it should be noted that all such problems are more easily resolved in less populous states. When we have sufficient elbow room we do not so keenly feel the sharp elbows of our variant neighbors.

The existence of a population optimum under any given set of values is readily demonstrated. We recognize that there are both economies of scale and diseconomies of scale. Focusing first on the former we note that Joseph J. Spengler in 1967 estimated that the economies of scale come substantially to an end at a nation-size of about fifty million. A complex modern machine like the automobile can be economically produced only by a nation of considerable size. The fact that Sweden, a nation of only eight million, produces two different makes of automobile that successfully compete in the international market suggests that Spengler's estimate errs, if at all, on the high side.

Passing now to diseconomies of scale, which have been criminally neglected in economic theory, we note their existence in several areas.

1. *Information management.* The democratic ideal is that each person should be able to exchange information (and opinions) freely with all other persons. The total number of possible relations between n people is $n(n - 1)/2$, which we can safely approximate by $n^2/2$ for large values of n. Simple democracy soon becomes impossible as population increases, because the number of communications needed to avoid misunderstanding goes up as the square of the number of people. The population of the United States increased from 5.3 million in 1800 to 180.7 million in 1960. This was an increase of 34 times. The number of possible relations between people increased approximately as the square of 34, that is, about a thousand times. The practical consequences of this increase can be put in various ways. The potential load of information per person increased a thousandfold. If each person protectively accepted only the same load, he had to become a thousand times more selective—that is, he had to risk ignoring a thousand times as much information input.

With population increase, participatory democracy becomes increasingly more impossible, and representation more remote. Increasingly more complex hierarchies must be devised. The individual must emotionally accept his personal political impotence. Supervision of the hierarchical structure becomes steadily more difficult; duplication and waste necessarily increase, and the probability of political catastrophe rises. Every increase in population size requires the renunciation of a larger proportion of the democratic ideal.

2. *Transportation.* In part, transportation is a form of communication, and so is affected by the square law of information load increase. This is not the whole story of transportation. Apparently, there is no general law of transportation, but the load is probably a power function of population size, with a power greater than unity. Thus, we are brought up against a diseconomy of scale once more. People already recognize that superhighways threaten to destroy the very cities they purport to serve. Despite all technological improvements, indefinite population increase means that we must ultimately give up the right of free movement.

3. *Pollution.* Natural recycling processes are capable of purifying air and water following many sorts of pollution. There may be threshold levels of pollution below which there need be no public concern. As pollution increases, however, the effort that must be expended to aid natural processes obeys some sort of power function. The irreversible eutrophication of heavily polluted lakes is evidence for this assumption.

4. *Natural resources.* The per capita share of each limited natural resource necessarily decreases with population size. The Grand Canyon is large, but not expansible. Wilderness can be enjoyed by only a few; the supply of it cannot be increased.

It should be noted that the economies of scale exhibited in the manufacture of artifacts increase the diseconomies of scale of per capita natural resource enjoyment. The cheaper automobiles and gasoline are (and the wealthier the people are) the greater is the population load of the national parks. During the last thirty years, while the United States population was increasing by a factor of 1.4, the use of the parks increased fiftyfold. Every increase in per capita wealth decreases the quality of the media of the world.

When all the economies and diseconomies of scale are brought together into a single system of accounting it is hardly conceivable that the optimum population of the United States will prove to be as great as fifty million. Not even the merits of urbanization require a large population—only local concentrations of the artists, artisans, philosophers, and scientists who are capable, under peculiar political and social circumstances that are poorly understood, of creating a distinctive "civilization." Athens, in its Golden Age, consisted of only a quarter of a million people, of whom almost half were slaves and only 40,000 were full citizens. The substitution of machine slaves for human slaves has surely reduced the critical size required for a great center of culture (given the right attendant circumstances) to considerably less than a quarter of a million.

Specifying what it is that we want to maximize is not yet possible. For years to come we will have to bring much thought, observation, and discussion to bear on this problem. Some plausible suggestions can, however, be made now.

It is certain that we do not want to maximize population size itself. The maximum number is achievable only by sacrificing all amenities to produce necessities—symbolically, by cutting down our redwood groves to plant potatoes.

Nor should we attempt to maximize the Gross National Product. First of all, the GNP increases (other things being equal) with population size, which we agree should not be maximized. Second, the GNP comprises not only all goods produced but also all services, including gambling and the cleaning up of pollution. All the costs of treating the sicknesses of an overcrowded society inflate the GNP. If these costs are power functions, as they undoubtedly are, with increasing population size the GNP comes to be increasingly a measure of the sickness of society rather than of its well-being.

What is desperately needed is an alternative statistic, which we might call the Net National Amenities (NNA). This would measure, among other things, not only such substantive goods as food and clothing, but also such genuine goods as music, art, solitude, wilderness, beautiful scenery, fresh air, and clean water. Billboards and advertising generally (with few exceptions) would be entered as deficits in the accounting of the NNA.

However, not even the NNA should be maximized. Surely, what we want to do is to maximize the per capita share of the NNA, which we might call the Per Capita Amenities (PCA).

The definition of the NNA (and its derivative, PCA) will surely be difficult to achieve, and to get accepted, but there are weighty reasons for getting on with this work immediately. A major religious idea of our time is the belief that perpetual growth is natural, healthy, and *right*. It is dangerous to simply destroy a religious myth without putting something else in its place. A myth by which people live is better modified than destroyed. It would be best if we continue to support the idea that growth is good, but seek to transfer the growth function from the Gross National Product to the Per Capita Amenities index. By successfully diverting public attention to the yearly progress of the PCA we can reaffirm our faith in growth and lay the groundwork for moving the population size in the direction of the optimum.

Transitory Population Optima in the Evolution of Brain

John B. Calhoun

ABSTRACT

For the past ten years I have been seeking to develop a logical basis for the future course of the human population as an outgrowth of evolution. My intent here will be to summarize the broad outline of my present insights. They indicate that man stands unique in being characterized by transitory world population optima along a path of his continual involvement in the evolution of a world brain enhancing the potentiality of the individual.

The descriptor term, brain, in normal usage refers to an assembly of interconnected neurons located at the anterior end of an individual animal. Functionally, brain denotes the storage, transfer, and transformation of information. Evolution of this biological brain implies increasing awareness of external conditions, and an enhancement of the integration of received information to produce more effective coping.

When *Homo sapiens* appeared on the scene as a clearly recognizable species, he reflected a long history of evolving biological brain. Paul MacLean[1] describes the progression of the evolutionary sequential components within the human brain. A basal portion, the "reptilian brain," governs instinctual behaviors relating to feeding, mating, and territoriality. Superimposed over this primitive brain, reflecting deeply ingrained ancestral memories, the paleomammalian brain provides an enhancement of plasticity of coping whereby emotions influence behaviors concerned with self-preservation, as well as preservation of the species. Finally, the neomammalian brain, overlaying the two earlier brains, brought in the ability to profit rapidly from experience and to extrapolate past experience into foresight for planning future action.

While these two strictly mammalian brains were evolving, a fourth brain gradually came into being. The stochastics of interaction among relatively solitary territorial mammals as they "sought" to make the most efficient utilization of resources led to loose clumpings of neighbors. Gradually, the selective value of collaborative action culminated in compact social groups, which on the average contained twelve adults along with associated immature progeny. [2] The human lineage lies along such an evolutionary course. These compact groups, evolved along the human lineage, represent the first development of brain external to the biological brain and may be designated as the first social brain. These four brains characterized man from his dawning as *Homo habilis* to the emergence of *Homo sapiens*.

Through this long period of about two million years, the biological brain and the body of the individual approximately doubled in mass, while the group size probably remained constant. It is my hypothesis that the average territory of a group remained unchanged during these two million years at about fifteen miles in diameter. Furthermore, very early in this period of human evolution all available land became occupied. This means that numbers remained constant while biomass very slowly doubled.

This constancy of numbers placed great stresses on evolving man, since he expressed reproductive capacities compatible with a continually increasing population. Each group would increase in size. Just before the group doubles in numbers, the rate of increase in frustration from crowding reaches a maximum and the normal course of events leads to a splitting of the group. Were there a nearby available uninhabited space, the group budded off would emigrate and settle in it. However, in the continuing situation where most territories were already inhabited, the only recourse open to an emigrating group was to attempt to supplant one already established.

Any group containing deviant members in the sense of larger body size, genetically or culturally enhanced technologies for mining resources, or more effective social brain would have a selective advantage. Through this process of one group being supplanted by another superior in technological capacities and creative talent, body and biological brain doubled in size, accompanied by comparable enhancement of the social brain which remained constant with regard to its contained elements, individual man.

This takes us to a time about 57,000 years ago when the technological capacities of *Homo sapiens* were such as to potentially enable him to double his numbers. And yet, the genetically built-in need to preserve his social brain at an N of twelve adults prevented him from fully exploiting this preadaptation. Increase in body and biological brain size no longer paid off. Man had arrived at a Rubicon of no longer being able to increase in numbers. Thus, as man emerged as fully *Homo sapiens,* from a biological point of view he had attained an optimum population and an optimum biomass in so long as he remained slave to his social brain of N = 12 adults in a social group.

The reason why he was thus held in slavery by his social brain, despite technological preadaptation for supporting a greater density, is readily apparent. Each animal in a group develops a unique set of behavioral characteristics. Thus, in a group where N = 12 there are $N(N - 1)/2$ or 66 different kinds of paired social bondings required for persisting social effectiveness. However, each new technological trait, whether of genetic or cultural origin, has a 1:1 relationship of the individual to his environment. In contrast, any change in a social trait will affect all 66 kinds of paired social bonds. In fact, it would appear that during the hundred million years of the slow evolution of this first social brain and its overlaying of the three biological brains, an extremely firm genetic basis has been acquired to implement its continuance. That is to say, there is a genetically built-in need for maintaining interactions with one's fellows to simulate that which would transpire in an essentially closed group of twelve adults.

Some time shortly before 40,000 years ago, this problem of simulation was first solved. By developing two clear-cut social roles, the group could double in size. Members of each role-defined social group gained most of their satisfactions from social life through interactions among their own kind.

With this transition biological man became human, and through successive elaboration of role-categories each individual could maintain his social transactions as if he were still living in a simple primitive group of twelve adults, despite the existing increase in density within the prior territory. Since this time, 40,000 years ago, each doubling of population has required half the time of the prior doubling. Each doubling has been accompanied by a doubling of conceptual space, that pool of information susceptible to formulation into concepts increasing the effectiveness of mining resources and defining social roles. By the continual discovery of this new kind of space, man has effectively maintained constant density despite increasing his numbers. At each doubling of population, when conceptual space has been adequately developed to provide adequate resources and a readjustment of the rate of meaningful interactions to that characteristic of biological man, the population is at an optimum. We are now approaching the tenth doubling, producing a thousandfold increase in population.

Each two doublings of population has produced a doubling of human potentiality, and a doubling of the facility with which information is stored, transferred, and transformed. Potentiality here means capacity to formulate information into concepts and utilize them. Each of these doublings of potentiality reflects the formation of a new level of social brain and has been accompanied by a major revolution in the way nature and man are viewed. So far, these revolutions include the Sapient, which transformed biological man into human man, the Agricultural, the Religious, the Renaissance, and the Scientific. We are now rapidly entering the Communication Revolution which, shortly after the turn of the century, will give way to the Compassionate Revolution. These latter two revolutions reflect the emergence of the last two social brains of the current era of human evolution.

Through this whole process of evolving social brains, their formation includes two generic categories of developments which facilitate the metabolism of information. Metabolism implies the storage, transfer, and transformation of information. The first category includes the whole range of prostheses from books to computers. The second category encompasses the linking of men into larger and larger socio-political unions. On the average, each doubling of population is accompanied by a coalescing of sets of seven neighboring such networks into a higher order union. Thus, each successive social brain is characterized by a socio-political union forty-nine times the size of the prior social brain. Continuation of this historical process of brain evolution will culminate in a total linkage of man into a single world union within less than a century, with a world population of about nine billion. This time and this population can also represent an optimum. However, once this optimum is achieved, it will simultaneously precipitate the major crisis of human evolution, one which will drastically affect the nature of possible later population optima.

To see why this is so requires consideration of two theoretical constructs, derived from my endeavors of the past few years,[3] to place population dynamics into an evolutionary perspective of the social use of physical and conceptual space:

A conceptual communication constant:

$$\mu'' = \frac{d''v''}{A''} \tag{1}$$

where d'' = potentiality of the average individual,
       v'' = a kind of conceptual velocity in the sense of accessibility to information ($v'' = p\ell$ as noted below), and
       A'' = total pool of available information (i.e., conceptual space).

At any population optimum, after the formation of a new social brain, $\mu'' = 1.0$. That is to say, there have been corresponding increases in d'', v'', and A''; and d'' and v'' are each equivalent to $(A'')^{1/2}$. Included in v'' are both prostheses, p, affecting the storage, transfer, and transformation of information, and linkages, ℓ, of people with people.

At the time when world union is attained, ℓ will be maximal since total linkage of mankind will have been consummated. Any further increase in the numbers, N, of man on earth will merely interfere with the functioning of the then eight social brains, and lead to a reduction of effective ℓ and a consequent reduction in v'', provided p remains static. Furthermore, since μ'' tends toward the equilibrium value of 1.0, d'' and A'' will also decline following any further increase in N beyond the optimum attained at the time of world union. Up to the time of the formation of the eighth social brain, represented by the Compassionate Revolution and World Union, ideomass $I = d''N$. Throughout all this forty millennia evolution of social brains, ideomass has been increasing far faster than N. At the culmination of this era of evolution, N will have increased two-thousandfold while ideomass, I, will have increased ninety-thousandfold. Once this degree of increase in ideomass has occurred, it will have reached a maximal value; Nd″ will have become constant. The world as a brain will have reached a peak of development, in so far as the total processing of information into utilizable concepts is concerned. The "carrying capacity" for ideomass will have been reached. Let I″ represent this carrying capacity value, then:

$$I'' = Nd'' \qquad (2)$$

Equations (1) and (2) represent my two basic hypotheses. From Equation (2) it is apparent that if N is maintained constant, d″ will also remain constant. Human potentiality will continue invariant and man will have entered a period of permanent cultural and intellectual rigidity.

However, it is possible for us to choose another course. We can elect, as our major goal, the continuing expansion of human potentiality: the increase of d″. To do so means that N must correspondingly decrease. Each further doubling of d″, accompanied by a halving of N, will introduce the completion of a newly evolved brain. Furthermore, each halving of N will denote a new transitory population optimum.

Pursuing this course of enhancing the potentiality of the average individual raises some interesting problems as to the nature of future stages of brain. $\mu'' = d''v''/A''$ will remain a constant equilibrium value of 1.0 at culmination of each new brain. Since d″ and A″ are both correspondingly increasing while N is decreasing, each individual person will become the focal point for the metabolism of more information. Each person can become such an increasing focal point only in so long as v″ also increases. Since $v'' = p\ell$, and ℓ will have already reached a maximal value, all further increases in v″ must derive from augmentation of the effectiveness of the p, prostheses to information metabolism.

With this perspective of past and future evolution, we may now evaluate the "population problem." In so far as evolving world brain is concerned, present population increase fits into the evolutionary pattern of each successive doubling requiring only half the time of the prior doubling. And yet, paradoxically, there is a population growth crisis with respect to the further development of human potentiality. At the transition point from a continually increasing to a continually decreasing population, the average number of young per female must reach a unitary value. Bringing about this degree of curtailment of the reproductive rate makes family planning much more important than simply required to attain a stationary population.

Even so, family planning is not the most critical issue in harmonizing population with evolution of brain. The measure of man reaches far beyond sustaining his biological body. At present, the realizable potentiality of the average individual should be thirty times that at the time of transition of biological man into man become human, 40,000 years ago. Population as a problem-posing factor in the sense of its biomass now represents only one-thirtieth of that posed by realizing the existing potentiality for conceptual development. Within less than a century this ratio of biomass to ideomass can shift to 1 : 45.

Maintaining transitory population optima thus places priority on enhancing the bonding among people and among institutions along with creation and utilization of prostheses implementing the metabolism of information. These objectives foster expansion of the potentiality of the individual. All other goals are subordinate. To realize this goal of expanding individual potentiality, which at the same time permits population optima, calls for establishing conscious evolutionary designing with maximum involvement of more effectively interlinked people and institutions.

REFERENCES

1. Paul D. MacLean, Alternative Neural Pathways to Violence," in Lary Ng (ed.), *Alternatives to Violence* (New York: Time-Life Books, 1968), pp. 24–34.

2. John B. Calhoun, "The Social Use of Space," in W. Mayer and R. VanGelder (eds.), *Physiological Mammalogy* (New York: Academic Press, Inc., 1964), pp. 1–187.

3. John B. Calhoun, "Space and the Strategy of Life" (Moving Frontiers of Science Lecture No. 3, at the Annual Meeting of the AAAS, Dallas, Texas, 1968), in A. H. Esser (ed.), *The Use of Space by Animals and Men* (New York/London: Plenum Press, 1971), pp. 329–387. "Promotion of Man" (presented at the Symposium on Global Systems Dynamics, University of Virginia, Charlottesville, Virginia, June 17–19, 1969), in E. O. Attinger (ed.), *Global Systems Dynamics* (Basel/München/New York: S. Karger, 1970), pp. 36–58. "Evolution of Work and Leisure; of Technocracy and Crearcracy" (presented before the Association for the Advancement of Psychotherapy at their Tenth Gutheil Memorial Lecture, New York City, November 2, 1969), URBSDOC No. 154; "Creativity and Evolutionary Design" (presented at the Conference on Religion and the Future, King of Prussia, Pennsylvania, November 22, 1969), URBSDOC No. 153, November 19, 1969.

Life Styles
and Value Systems:
Comments

Ezra Glaser

Many statements on the proper size of the planetary population proceed as though the ability to provide food is the only essential condition for a population to be considered "not-too-large." Hence, we turn to synthetic cellulose foods, protein derived from petroleum residues by bacterial action, the use of underwater vegetational growth from the continental shelves, etc. The unstated assumption is that the size of the population will be limited by food supply—even after these advances in food technology—before there is any other reason to regard the population as too great.

The point may be dramatized by burlesquing future civilization as a place where humans live the way chickens do on mass-production farms. Each person would live out his life in a small, temperature-controlled, air-conditioned cubby with limited mobility and almost no realization that there might be any other way to live.

The point is not that any particular style of living is better than the others but rather that there is value—possibly very great value—to the ability of each individual to have a wide choice of life styles.

In what sense and in what ways must the consideration of optimal planetary population take account of these values? Through vocations and avocations human beings engage in a fantastic variety of activities, including some that most of the population would never choose to engage in voluntarily. A naïve approach might be that for those activities enjoyed by very small fractions of the population (such as three-dimensional chess or playing ancient musical instruments), large populations would be an advantage. The larger the base number by which a very small percentage is to be multiplied, the greater the likelihood of arriving at a large enough handful of persons to engage in any activity, no matter how outlandish it might appear to the rest of us.

This model is too simple: it regards size of population as having no influence except as a vast reserve pool from which a few select individuals with the "right" characteristics might be drawn. Such, of course, is not the case. If the large-enough population is achieved only by substantial increases in traffic congestion and travel time, great increases in atmospheric impurities, noise, smells, bad-tasting water, dirty buildings, and the loss of the environment's natural beauty, the chess players and musicians might feel that they had made a poor trade.

These examples illustrate the dangers of proceeding on the assumption that value systems are not important because we have not been sufficiently attentive to realize their need or sufficiently ingenious to develop working models. Perhaps we need a type of planetary economics in which the principal burden would be the development of suitable value systems to support calculi that might deal with some of these problems which are now beyond quantitative treatment.

Without this kind of an approach it becomes difficult to do more than warn that educational services, social services, and a capability of obtaining satisfaction in personal living might break down well before the world population grew so large that it would be difficult to feed.

Concerning the Optimum Level of Population

Lincoln H. Day

ABSTRACT

There are three main problems in any consideration of population optima: problems of (1) measurement, (2) cultural difference and change, and (3) diversity of values.

Most efforts to determine population optima are seen as failing to take into account the great variety of human needs, and also as failing to appreciate the existence of ecological and social limits. In addition, their emphasis is on optimum *size* to the exclusion of optimum *characteristics*.

The usual economic criteria of the optimum are rejected as being either too narrow or, in some instances, actually misleading—and as almost invariably devoid of any consideration of limits. The existence of limits is seen as an essential element to any determination of the optimum: not only geographic and ecological limits, but also social limits. It is noted, further, that *population* is only one of three broad factors setting the limits on a people's opportunity to enjoy a high quality of life; the other two being: first, the *rate of consumption* of land, air, water, and minerals, and, second, the *use that is made* of those resources consumed.

Though the dependence of human well-being on the interplay of many diverse elements permits establishment of only very broad limits with respect to the *size* of an optimum population, there can be much more certainty about what the *characteristics* of such a population would be. Three such characteristics are noted: (1) low mortality, (2) a stable age and sex distribution, and (3) a secular growth rate of zero.

Such a population, whatever its ultimate size, would be what demographers term "stationary." Though older than the current United States population, its age structure would differ little from that of England or Sweden; and its dependency ratio would be lower. What life would be like in a society with such a population—given the limits established by its size—is seen to depend essentially on nondemographic variables.

The relationship of population size to human welfare has concerned men in all ages and in all kinds of societies.

"To the size of states," wrote Aristotle, twenty-three centuries ago, "there is a limit as there is to other things, plants, animals, implements; for none of these retain their natural power when they are too large or too small, but they either wholly lose their nature, or are spoiled. . . . [T]he best limit of the population of a state is the largest number which suffices for the purposes of life and can be taken in at a single view."[1]

Earlier in our own century, a native of the tiny Polynesian island of Tikopia explained the need for family limitation to the New Zealand anthropologist, Raymond Firth, in this manner:

"Families by Tikopia custom are made corresponding to orchards in the woods. If children are produced in plenty, then they go and steal because their orchards are few. So families in our land are not made large in truth; they are made small. If the family groups are large and they go and steal, they eat from the orchards, and if this goes on they kill each other."[2]

Any discussion of optimum population implies the existence of individual and social goals, the attainment of which is thought to be affected by the number and characteristics of the population. An optimum population is not a goal isolated from other social priorities, nor is it an end in itself. It is, rather, a means to the achievement of the conditions of life thought desirable. Thus, when we ask, "Is there an optimum level of population?" what we are really asking is: "What are the demographic conditions most conducive to some desired state of affairs?" Population is but one of the variables—albeit a most important one—to be considered in achieving an optimum environment for living.

There are three problems to contend with in any consideration of population optima: problems of measurement, of adjustment to cultural difference and change, and, finally, of diversity of values.

Problems of measurement are of two types. One derives from the fact of the causal interdependence of social phenomena. Because population is only one of several variables that can affect conditions of life, whether demographic characteristics are causally related to any particular set of circumstances is ordinarily impossible to determine in any but rather general terms. The measurement of specific relationships has been attempted. But even the most sophisticated of these attempts, such as Duncan's, some years ago, to determine to what degree the quality of life in American cities was a function of their size,[3] have foundered on the shoals of multiple causation. Any assessment of the role of population must invariably be hedged 'round by all manner of assumptions about "other things being equal."

In addition, it is virtually impossible to make any precise assessment of the *degree* of causal relationship with respect to demographic conditions. We may have a reasonably clear idea that country X would be better off with a smaller population, but we cannot know that it would be *8 per cent* better off with two and three-quarter million fewer inhabitants and but *4 per cent* better off with one and one-half million fewer. Nor can we know which of country X's inhabitants would gain the most, and which the least, from such an alteration in demographic conditions.

Determination of an optimum population is further impeded by the related facts of cultural change and cultural difference. At the time of Columbus, what is now the territory of the United States supported hardly more than a million people, and, because of the harsh conditions of life in many areas, may have seemed to some tribes to be overpopulated, even then. Yet, today, under remarkably different cultural conditions, it supports more than 200 times as many—and at a *material* level of living incomparably higher than that of the early aboriginal inhabitants.

Finally, there is the problem of values. Any definition of the optimum depends ultimately on one's values. To the problem of measuring the relationship between population and particular social conditions, and the difficulty of establishing absolutes in the face of cultural change and differences, must be added the diversity in human values about what ends are to be served by manipulating demographic factors. What, in short, are the criteria of an optimum population? Are they those of the nationalist who defines strength in terms of the numbers necessary to achieve some military objective? Those of the businessman who views babies as potential consumers of his product? Those of the wildlife fancier observing the progressive extinction of species? Each of these criteria is to some extent a product of, and relevant to, a particular cultural setting. The criteria of an optimum population, and the techniques by which to measure movement in the direction of this "optimum," are always to some degree particularistic and culture-bound.

Nevertheless, demographic factors are of such prime importance to human affairs that they must be taken into account, whatever the problems in doing so. In what follows, therefore, I should like to attempt at least a partial answer to that question that I have suggested may be essentially unanswerable: "What *is* the optimum population?"

Past efforts to determine the optimum can, I feel, be faulted on several grounds: first, the failure to think in terms of a wide variety of human needs; second, the failure to appreciate the ecological and social limits imposed by our finite planet; and third, the emphasis on consideration of optimum *size* to the exclusion of consideration of optimum *characteristics*. There can be, I think, much more certainty about what are the *characteristics* of an optimum population than there can be about its *size* alone.

Let me take as my goal for the optimum, something general enough to be agreed to by nearly everyone—something, for example, like "happiness" or "the good life" for all members of the society. In determining the bearing of demographic characteristics on "the good life" it is necessary to take both the *broad* view and the *long* view. The *broad* view of population and "the good life" involves recognition that human needs are complex and varied, and that they are different at different ages and at different steps of the life cycle. The environmental requirements of a 5-year-old are different from those of a 65-year-old; of an unmarried young adult different from those of his married counterpart. However, at all ages and all stages of life man needs more than food to be fully human. The cultivation of the whole person requires, also, serenity, dignity, order, leisure, peace, beauty, elbow-room—even though man can, on occasion, with his extraordinary powers of adaptability, become inured to severe deprivation with respect to one or the other of these needs, in much the way one can grow used to chronic pain. As Ansley Coale has written:

"It is my observation that the disadvantages of a larger population are seen most vividly by those who were born in an earlier era. Often the current inhabitants see nothing wrong with many of the changes that older citizens decry. I feel deprived by the disappearance of open land around Princeton. My children never miss it."[4]

This fluid nature of human values would seem, in fact, to constitute a major threat to any effort to block progressive deterioration in the quality of the environment. For there is a real tendency to adjust to debasement of the environment by being willing to settle for less; that is, by lowering our standards of the optimum for human society and individual well-being. Just as cultural change and difference affect a people's capacity for achieving particular results with a given population, so also do they affect a people's perception of what is desirable and of what is possible. An example of such change is the fact that Americans are now an overwhelmingly urban people, city-born and city-reared; and, moreover, that the major increases in our urban population now come much less from rural-to-urban migration than from the reproduction of urban dwellers themselves. This rising density of living and the increasingly smaller proportions of our population having any personal contact with rural life can hardly help but have repercussions for the views of Americans on the significance of human numbers for their way of life.

Most discussion of optimum population has been based on narrowly economic criteria of value. This is hardly surprising; economic conditions are more readily quantified, and data for them are more frequently collected. But for our purposes here, the economic criterion is a particularly misleading one, not only because of its implied assumption that economic growth invariably adds to the sum of human happiness, but also for its implied assumption that such growth can be endless, that the limits to economic development are essentially ones of technology and finance, not ecology and resources.

Using the broader criteria of human needs leads to the observation that there is no necessary connection between "the good life" and economic development. In a high-consumption society like our own, with a population of more than 200 million and limited space and resources, this relationship may, in fact, be almost a negative one in many respects: the greater the economic growth in *general* terms—as illustrated, for instance, by urban sprawl, highway construction, increased automobile usage, billboards, television advertising, and suburban power mowers—the greater the deterioration in the quality of life available to the individual, as he is deprived of community life, of peace and beauty, and suffers restriction of his access to outdoor recreation and to clean air and water. It is interesting to note, in this connection, that new appreciation of the costs of economic and technological growth is already being reflected in the development of new definitions of the optimum environment. The pioneering effort along these lines has come from Kenneth Boulding, himself an economist, who calls for change in our criteria of the good life from those of unlimited expansion to those of conservation, thrift, and careful husbanding of our resources instead.[5]

The broad view thus involves recognition that population size is not the only factor determining the quality of life or the relationship between man and environment. How a people experiences population size is mediated very largely through its cultural practices and standards. The chances for present and future generations to enjoy "the good life" thus depend on the interplay of *population size,* plus the *rate of consumption* of land, air, water, and minerals, plus the *use that is made* of the resources consumed. The interplay of these three factors sets the limits, but it does so, ordinarily, within a wide range of possible variation. We could halt population increase tomorrow and still consume our resources at ruinous rates. Whether this consumption of resources was wise or unwise in terms of immediate social utility, the rate of consumption could, itself, eventually result in hardship and chaos.

Taking the *long* view in determining the optimum level of population involves, first, recognition that posterity is relevant if for no other reason than that so many of us are going to survive long enough to experience the conditions formed by decisions taken in the present. An understanding of population dynamics forces us to think, even in terms of our own self-interest, well beyond the requirements of the present and the immediate future. A lot of posterity is already here. In the United States, for example, 85 per cent of us can expect to survive to the year 2000, and more than two-thirds to be around in the year 2015.* There is, thus, no need to appeal on the basis of as-yet-unborn children and grandchildren to impress upon us the necessity of having, in C. P. Snow's words, "an appetite for the future" when we consider the nature of population optima.

Moreover, population is not like water issuing from a tap—to be turned off at will when the desired level has been reached. To a unique degree, demographic conditions at any point in time are determined by what has gone on before. A pertinent illustration is the fact that even if, starting tomorrow, women were to have no more than two children apiece, total world population would continue to rise substantially for another two decades. Why? Because all the world's mothers for the next twenty years have already been born, and *the numbers* entering the childbearing ages are rising year by year. Concerning the United States, it has been calculated (assuming no change in the relative timing of childbirth) that, regardless of when reproduction declines to exact replacement level, the characteristics of the age structure will produce a continuation of population increases for a period of at least another sixty-five to seventy years.[6]

Finally, the long view requires that we acknowledge that this is a finite world: that population must, therefore, ultimately stop increasing and, in fact, that it may even need to decrease—particularly in a high-consumption society like our own—if we are to advance toward the goal of a good life for all.

* Estimated from United States Bureau of the Census, *Current Population Reports,* Series P-25, 381 (December 18, 1967), Table 16, and 434 (November 18, 1969), as follows:

a. Estimated population on January 1, 1970:   204,430,000
b. Estimated survivors to year 2000 from those born in years
   1966–1969:   15,280,000
c. Estimated survivors to year 2000 from those born before 1966:   156,560,000
d. Total (b + c):   171,840,000
e. Estimated per cent of January 1, 1970 population surviving
   to year 2000:   85%

---

a. Estimated population on January 1, 1970:   204,430,000
b. Estimated survivors to year 2015 from those born in years
   1966–1969:   14,900,000
c. Estimated survivors to year 2015 from those born before 1966:   124,580,000
d. Total (b + c):   139,480,000
e. Estimated per cent of January 1, 1970 population surviving
   to year 2015:   68%

But the limits we must work within are not all geographic or ecological. There are also social limits. Though I am reluctant to infer much about human behavior from the studies of behavioral anomalies resulting from crowding among Norway rats[7] and other species, it seems fairly obvious that there can arise such densities of human settlement as would result in a breakdown of those social relationships and patterns of individual behavior that are necessary to the continuation of human society, and even to the maintenance of individual life. Some suggestion of how greater human density can curtail social viability can already be gleaned from current experience of transportation and communication tie-ups, delays attending travel to work, the difficulties encountered in gaining access to recreation, in disposing of wastes, and so on. As society becomes more complex, its members become increasingly dependent upon one another even for the provision of essentials.

So far as optimum *size* is concerned, then, the dependence of human well-being on the interplay of many diverse elements permits us to set only very broad limits. Recognition of the facts of ecological, resource, and social limits sets the maximum number of people who can be supported, and thereby narrows the range; but there remains, nonetheless, a considerable latitude within which optimum size can be located.

However, as noted earlier, there is much less uncertainty about the demographic *characteristics* of an optimum population. If our goal is the good life for all members of society, it seems to me that an optimum population would have as its first characteristic a low level of mortality. I find it hard to imagine that death could be such a commonplace that it occasioned no sense of loss, no suffering—particularly when, as is the pattern in high mortality populations, it was so prominently visited upon infants and young children.

The second characteristic of an optimum population, it seems to me, would be a stable age and sex distribution. By definition, in such a distribution, there would always be the same proportion of the population reaching each age level: the same proportion reaching age 15, for example, in the year $n + 1$ as reached that age in year n; the same proportion reaching it in year $n + 10$ as in year $n + 9$. Such stability in age distribution obviously implies stability, as well, in annual numbers of births and in relationships among age-specific patterns of mortality. Because of general economic conditions, or the sheer numbers involved, it might still be difficult with such an age distribution to make adequate provision of school and other social services, and also of employment for new entrants into the labor market. But with a stable age distribution there would be no aggravation of these difficulties as a consequence of year-to-year fluctuations in the numbers succeeding to different age levels; no problems of the sort occasioned in the United States by the fact that for every three children born in 1945 there were more than four children born only two years later.

So far as stability of distribution by sex is concerned, such a condition, in combination with a stable age distribution, would, in a monogamous society like our own, minimize the likelihood of a person's being forced by demographic conditions to remain unmarried against his will.

The third, and final, characteristic of an optimum population would be a secular growth rate equal to zero. No population can increase indefinitely. As I have already noted, there are limits: limits to resources, to physical space, and to social space. Though these limits can be extended by changing the pattern of use of the environment and the pattern of behavior of individual members of society, there will be a point, even with the most judicious use of the environment and the most prudent pattern of human behavior, beyond which increases in population will result in declines in the quality of life.

In fact, in consequence of the existence of limits, one could argue that a truly optimum population would have a *negative,* not a zero, growth rate: a negative growth rate in order that human numbers—however efficient the use made of the environment—would be regularly brought into line with a steadily decreasing quantity of resources. Certainly, the period of growth—both economic and demographic growth—that we are currently experiencing can be little more than a tiny interlude in the history of mankind.

The kind of population I have been describing—one with a zero growth rate and an unchanging age and sex distribution—is a variant of what demographers term a "stationary population"; in this instance, a stationary population enjoying a low level of mortality. I have tried to show that such a population is desirable in the United States, first, because of the existence of geographic and ecological limits, and, second, because the size and complexity of our society already pose enormous difficulties for the adequate satisfaction of the wide variety of human needs.

Within the range of a stationary or declining population, the precise determination of optimum size becomes largely a matter of speculation and hunch, for, as already noted, the chances of living the good life depend on so much more than demographic variables. Nevertheless, I think we can say that the parameters of the optimum population level for the United States have surely been narrowed by the demographic behavior and pattern of resource-use of the past. Only by lowering the standards of human well-being, both here and abroad, could I envisage as optimum a population any more numerous than we are now. With our high proportion living in metropolitan areas and our rapid rates of consumption, I see little reason for concluding other than that the chances for present and future generations of Americans to enjoy the good life would have been greater had our increase stopped at the 150 million we numbered in 1950, instead of increasing another 37 per cent in the nineteen years since then. Certainly, our chances for the good life will be diminished less if our population increase ceases at, say, 250 million instead of going on to the 283 to 361 million forecast for the year 2000.[8]

I have had to speak here in rather general terms about optimum size because of the difficulties enumerated earlier concerning the determination of causal relationships involving demographic variables. But there is no need for such imprecision in discussing the age structure of the optimum population, for here the fact that the optimum has been defined as having the age structure of a stationary population permits us to work with model life tables. To ascertain the age structure of the optimum, in this particular instance, I have used the life table for the white population of the United States.[9]

There is no question that a stationary population would be an older population. With a life expectation at birth of some 71 years, the median age would be 37 as against 27 in the United States today. There would be about as many people over 60 as under 15, and the proportion 70 and over would be 63 per cent higher than at present.

However, this 63 per cent increase in the proportion 70 and over would involve an increase of less than four percentage points, going from 6.2 to 10.1 per cent. Moreover, dependency ratios would be substantially lessened. If we assume the "dependent" ages to be those below 18 and above 64, the number of "dependents" would be only 40 per cent of the total in the optimum population, compared with 45 per cent of the total in the United States population today. If, instead, we take the ages below 21 and above 69 as our "dependent" ages,* the proportion "dependent" drops to 37 per cent of the optimum population as against 47 per cent in the United States today.

About the other demographic characteristics of this optimum population—apart from natality and mortality, which have been established as low, and sex structure which, in the absence of unusual sex-specific mortality levels, can be taken as unchanging—there is nothing that necessarily follows from the conditions specified. Internal migration could be extensive or minimal. Marriage and, for women, childbearing could occur at a generally early age, or at a generally advanced age, and to nearly everyone, or to but a relatively small proportion. There could be either extensive or minimal differences in the numbers residing in rural areas, towns, cities, and urban agglomerations.

What life would be like in a society with this stationary population structure would depend essentially on nondemographic variables. Life could be meager or bountiful, violent or peaceful, miserable or happy. For any particular pool of resources, the demographic conditions posited here would only make the good life more attainable; they would not, in themselves, create it. Once the parameters of optimum population are established, the good life is more a function of social attitudes and policy than of any particular demographic characteristics.

I must note, however, that this observation about the variety of conditions of life possible in a stationary population is at variance with some current Western thinking. In fact, a major source of hesitancy about accepting the goal of a stationary population has to do with the changes in the age structure that it would entail. To some alarmists, such a shift in age distribution raises the specter of a society of graybeards in wheelchairs. A prominent economist, for example, has claimed not only that such a population would be less pleasing aesthetically, but that it "would not be likely to be receptive to change and indeed would have a strong tendency towards nostalgia and conservatism." [10] A French writer has characterized a stationary population (presumably one enjoying low levels of mortality) as "a

---

* This would be in recognition of two things: first, the longer periods of schooling and training characteristic of industrialized societies and, second, the fact that in at least one industrialized society (Sweden) the customary retirement age is 70—a result, perhaps, of the higher proportions in the upper age groups, and also of the generally good health these members of the Swedish population enjoy.

population of old people ruminating over old ideas in old houses."[11]

To answer these fears, I point out, first, that the age structure of a stationary population would, in fact, be little different from the age structures of Sweden and England today (see Table 1), populations hardly characterized by rampant decrepitude. As for the social consequences of an older population, we can hardly generalize from present social conditions and attitudes toward the aged. The current preference for youth and rapid change may itself be a reflection of our period of unrepressed numerical and technological expansion. The assumption that rapid change is invariably a desirable condition of human life may well yield to a greater appreciation of the value of stability and continuity with the past.

And what, moreover, about that supposed conservatism of the aged? "Conservative," "progressive," "reactionary," "radical"—these are loose terms, especially when removed from their specific referents. Were Hitler's youthful Brown Shirts "progressive"? Were the aged Townsendites "conservative"? Even if we know, ourselves, what

TABLE 1

Percentage Distributions by Age of the 1963 Population of England and Wales, the 1965 Population of Sweden, and the 1967 White Life Table Population of the United States *

Age	(a) 1963 England and Wales	(b) 1965 Sweden	(c) 1967 United States white life table	Ratios: a/c	b/c
0–9	15.5	14.0	13.7	1.13	1.02
10–19	15.0	15.1	13.6	1.10	1.11
20–29	12.6	13.8	13.5	.93	1.02
30–39	12.9	11.9	13.3	.97	.89
40–49	13.4	13.7	13.0	1.03	1.05
50–59	13.2	13.3	12.1	1.09	1.10
60–69	9.8	10.2	10.3	.95	.99
70–79	5.6	6.0	7.1	.72 {.79 .59	.77 {.85 .62
80+	2.0	2.1	3.4		

*United Kingdom and Swedish percentages calculated from N. Keyfitz and W. Flieger, *World Population* (Chicago: The Univ. of Chicago Press, 1968), pp. 508, 538; United States percentages calculated from United States Department of Health, Education and Welfare, *Vital Statistics of the United States, 1967*, Vol. II, *Mortality*, Part A (Washington: Government Printing Office, 1969), p. 5.4.

we mean by these terms, is the conservative on one issue invariably conservative on others? Recent nationwide public-opinion polls find the willingness to liberalize access to abortion *positively,* not negatively, associated with age.[12] Are these older respondents really demonstrating greater conservatism; are they really being "less receptive to change"?

In terms of the degree to which they seem willing to introduce changes in economic behavior, educational procedures, the status of women, and the like, the world's most conservative societies are those with the youngest—not the oldest—populations. To argue in terms of age is to commit the fallacy of misplaced emphasis, for how any group above the age of infancy behaves is essentially determined by its position in society, not its accumulation of years.[13]

To sum up: Population has to stop increasing sometime. This is both a physical and a social necessity. In terms of what it means for our options, both now and in the future, the sooner it stops, the better. Beyond this, whatever its ultimate size, I would claim it is better if that population's mortality levels are low and if year-to-year fluctuations in the numbers of births and deaths occurring to it are kept to a minimum. But whether this population will be living well or poorly will depend on much more than its size and composition. Size and composition will set the limits, but they will not, except at the very extremes, be the final arbiters of the quality of a people's life.

REFERENCES

1. Aristotle, *Politics,* Book VII, para. 4.

2. R. Firth, *We, the Tikopia* (2nd ed., London: Allen & Unwin, 1957), p. 491.

3. O. D. Duncan, in P. K. Hatt and A. J. Reiss (eds.), *Reader in Urban Sociology* (Glencoe, Ill.: The Free Press, 1951).

4. A. J. Coale, *Population Index* 34, 4 (1968), 471.

5. K. E. Boulding, in H. Jarrett (ed.), *Environmental Quality in a Growing Economy* (Baltimore: Johns Hopkins University Press, 1966).

6. T. Frejka, *Population Studies* 22, 3 (1968), 379–397.

7. J. B. Calhoun, *Scientific American* (1962).

8. United States Bureau of the Census, *Statistical Abstract of the United States 1969* (Washington, D.C.: Government Printing Office, 1969), Table 5, p. 7.

9. United States Department of Health, Education and Welfare, Public Health Service, National Center for Health Statistics, *Life Tables: 1959–61,* Vol. 1, No. 1 (Washington, D.C.: Government Printing Office, 1964), Table 4, pp. 14–15. (These are the most recent for single years of age.)

10. Coale, *op. cit.,* p. 471.

11. Quoted in *ibid.*

12. Gallup polls taken in August, 1962, December, 1965, and May and December, 1968; also the 1965 National Fertility Study, reported on in C. F. Westoff, E. C. Moore, and N. B. Ryder, "The Structure of Attitudes toward Abortion," *Milbank Memorial Fund Quarterly* (January, 1969), pp. 11–37.

13. See K. Davis and J. W. Combs, Jr., "The Sociology of an Aging Population," in *The Social and Biological Challenge of Our Aging Population* (New York: Columbia University Press, 1950).

Population Optima: Overview

Joseph J. Spengler

"If the world were not so full of people, and most of them did not have to work so hard, there would be more time for them to get out and lie on the grass, and there would be more grass for them to lie on."

> Don Marquis, in *The Almost Perfect State*.

When we think in terms of optima we take note of several conditions. We proceed upon the assumption that what a community of men seek may be ideally connected with the environment, natural and potential, of which they dispose. We recognize that we are caught up, each and all of us, in what might be a network of reciprocity—in what actually is a system of activities—with what takes place in any part affecting, for good or ill, what men can or may do in other parts. We do not now live in a world, if ever we did, in which any person or group can go it alone, be it in city, region, country, or (occasionally) world. All this has been amply demonstrated in the papers composing this volume. It is no longer possible, therefore, to do as the famous Lister was said to do, "smile . . . sweet with certainties."

OPTIMUM DEFINED

Optimizing is an analytical concept adumbrated long before Leibniz and his contemporaries believed they had discovered optimizing

288

processes at work in nature. Let us begin with a closed economy. In it we find what Herbert Simon[1] has called an outer environment, which may be said to consist in accessible space, time, and stuff, and an inner environment, which consists in the information, artifacts, and capacities for performance which enable communities of men to harmonize with their outer environment and employ it to serve their purposes. These purposes may be said to constitute the community's social welfare function, the function which they seek, or, as we sometimes say, ought to seek, to maximize. It may be expressed in aggregate terms or, as most of us would prefer, in per capita terms.

We may apply the concept of optimizing to anything involving the transformation of scarce inputs into outputs. Here we are concerned with its application to aggregations of populations, to those of nation-states, of regions, of cities, or of metropolitan areas.[2] We assume that if, as is often true, the optimum has been exceeded, curbing deviation from what is considered to be the optimum size of population is important because it conditions the magnitude of the social welfare function, maximization of which is sought. Within limits, a higher value is attainable when a population is larger than when it is smaller. A population is of optimum size when this welfare function takes on as high a value as is attainable, given man's outer and inner environments. Analytically, we might call the income optimum the Least Common Denominator of all the populations associated with the individual optimum-sized public and private plants composing our economy and polity and supplying the goods and services sought.[3]

The population growth rate may be too high even though the population aggregate is suboptimal in size. This rate is important for three reasons: it generates a relatively unfavorable age structure; it absorbs resources that could otherwise be used to augment welfare per capita, with the result that as much as 4 to 6 per cent of the national income may be required to support a 1 per cent per year rate of population growth; and it tends to intensify the forces making for maldistribution of population in space.*

* Were America's population growth rate to decline to zero from the rate of about 1 per cent per year, what would be the monetary savings associated with current child-bearing inclinations and plans? These savings would emerge slowly, but, in the end, at 4 per cent of GNP, would exceed $200 per year per capita of the then stationary population.

The population distribution in space is significant for two reasons: first, when aggregate population is excessive, distributing it optimally tends to reduce the costs associated with excessive size; and second, population distribution is more immediately subject to improvement than is population growth or size. It is essential, therefore, that a community not focus on size of population to the exclusion of its distribution in space, particularly when population is maldistributed (as is our own, among others, with 28.45 per cent of the 1960 population occupying about .25 per cent of the land area and about 30 per cent settled on about 99 per cent of the landed area).

Population maladjustment exists when the actual population is greater or smaller than optimum size; then the value of the social welfare index is lower than it would be, given a population of optimum size. There would, of course, be little or no problem if maladjustment were self-corrective; if, for example, passing beyond the optimum would produce a fertility-reducing feedback which would shortly halt population growth and thus avert gross deviation from the optimum level of welfare. Unfortunately, this feedback process is very weak, especially in the neighborhood of the optimum, under the conditions encountered in most societies. It would be ideal if such a feedback process could be built into societies, even in societies presently with populations quite beyond the optimum.

VARIABILITY OF OPTIMA

Defining an optimum satisfactorily presents theoretical and empirical difficulties, especially in a dynamic world. There is no unique unchanging optimum: man's outer environment is subject to change, in part because of what he does; his inner environment is also subject to change, usually in the direction of increasing his capacity to exploit the outer environment; and his welfare function—his budget of final wants—too, is subject to change, usually in an upward direction.

It is generally agreed, I believe, that John Stuart Mill underestimated this variability when, 122 years ago, he expressed the opinion that what then constituted an optimum population would not be increased by such changes as might take place in society. The massive inventions of the nineteenth and early twentieth centuries augmented both the size of states and the population magnitude of economic optimum size. Today, however, this process may be undergoing reversal under the impact of modern inventions, communication, computerization, probable change in number of employees per optimum size of plant, and growing demands upon amenities and surface and suprasurface space. What constitutes the optimum may be diminishing in size. The answer depends in part upon the content of the welfare function chosen for maximization. Mill had in mind the standard of life as he found it under then ideal conditions.

Before examining sources of variability in optima, three points are notable. First, one cannot assume, as some animal ecologists seem to imply, that the optimum for the human species is analogous to the optimum for an animal species. What is optimum for an animal species is determined almost entirely by circumstances exogenous to such species, affected as it is by predators, hosts, and subsistence, to all of which a species responds almost tropismatically. In contrast, what is optimal for a human population is determined both by circumstances external to this population and by changes which affect both the number of wants and the composition of its budget of wants. The human population may also modify its environments, especially its inner environment.

Second, distinction needs to be made between size of economy and size of population. In the contemporary world only a few states, together with their populations and average incomes, are big enough to permit their economies to reach levels of performance attainable in large economies. Small states are highly dependent, therefore, on their external exchange relations, or upon entering interstate cooperative arrangements, such as customs unions, when practicable.

Third, the role of past deviations of population size from optimum levels must not be exaggerated. After all, the great increase experienced in man's average income (as conventionally measured) over the past two centuries has been the result almost entirely of improvements in man's inner environment, traceable to scientific progress, innovations, and investment in physical and human capital which has made possible the exploitation of science and innovation.

Improvement in man's inner environment has affected his relation to his outer environment in two ways. (1) It has greatly increased the fraction of the outer environment of which he has been able to make use, and it has added to his outer environment, through space and similar programs, extraterrestrial environment on which he formerly could not draw effectively. Simple evidence of this is had in the fact that today man uses nearly all the elements whereas a century or more ago he used only a small number. (2) Man's use of his outer environment has subjected it to what may be called increasing economic entropy, and in addition has brought about its deterioration through pollution. He has extracted much of the utility potentially available in some of this environment and made other portions of it less contributive to his welfare. Up to now, however, he has gained, on balance, since he has brought into use more of the outer environment than he has rendered useless or less useful. This gain is more or less temporary, however, insofar as portions of the outer environment are depletable, since the depletable portion continues to be drawn upon, and increasingly as numbers and average consumption rise. Moreover, in proportion as weight is attached to water, natural amenities, accessible countryside, relatively pure air, and abundance of suitably situated space, the current deterioration of environment constitutes a diminution of the outer environment upon which man likes to draw.

Discussion of optimization at the national, as distinguished from the world, level entails consideration of international exchange relations, as has already been noted. For, international exchange augments, at least temporarily, the value of the outer environment of any particular country and the potential of its labor force. It may enable smaller countries to overcome some limitations of space and domestic markets by allowing them to draw on the outer environments of other countries and, thus, to achieve economies of scale beyond the reach of small, closed economies.[4] Few, if any, economies are completely closed, and some are quite open, drawing notably, as does the United States, on the outer environments of other economies. Such escape from local limitations is restricted in many instances, however, especially when economies short of appropriate outer environment are also short, as is India, of purchasing power wherewith to meet local shortages through purchases abroad. Ours is not One World, but a Divided World, the parts of which are but imperfectly connected by international exchange and grants. Moreover, even given good connections, great dependence on foreign supplies and markets tends to increase the vulnerability of an economy (e.g., Japan).[5]

Relevant also are patterns of consumption and changes therein. Suppose, for example, that the outer and inner environment are given. Then the optimum will turn on the content of the welfare function, on the budget of final wants whence flow, or are derived, the demands ultimately made upon components of the outer environment as well as upon the services of individuals. If the budget consists predominantly of the services of individuals, the optimum will tend to be larger than if it consists mainly of items into which components of the outer environment enter. It may pan out, of course, that even the services can be largely supplied by substitutes for man.

As a population becomes richer, the composition of the derived demand for components of the environment tends to change somewhat in composition. There will be a relatively large increase in the demand for space, amenities, and so on, and a smaller increase in the demand for food, etc.

COSTS, BENEFITS, POLICY

In view of the controversy always associated with what constitutes an optimum population, it may be preferable to ask the question: "Do any net advantages flow from further increase in the population of a country, or a city, or a metropolitan region?" We should not ask: "Can a further increase in population be accommodated?" This is simply the answer of the inverted Malthusian—the individual who thinks that a so-called Green Revolution has solved the population problem; or the reply of a Pangloss who prefers catching smallpox and then recovering from it to avoiding it in the first place (say) by vaccination. He prefers a pound of inferior cure to an ounce of healthy prevention.

We must also ask, "At what costs?" After all, life and growth are exercises in double-entry bookkeeping, requiring an accounting of both costs and benefits, always with the object in view of finding out if costs or gains are the larger. Measures taken to offset supraoptimal population size or growth, even when seemingly effective, may impose costs relatively invisible in the short-run but emergent in the long-run. Representative would be adverse effects attendant upon excessive use of chemical fertilizers, dependence upon DDT or other persistent pesticides or herbicides, and pollution costs which tend to accompany increasing use of both fossil fuels and nuclear energy.

We must inquire also into the distributional effects of population growth. Who gets the benefits? Who bears the costs? Even if the benefits could be said to exceed the costs, growth is not warranted unless the beneficiaries of growth compensate those upon whom the costs are incident, fully and to the satisfaction of the latter. National as well as urban population growth needs to be stripped of unearned increments and unearned profits.

We must look at *all* costs. Those who fail to take all costs into account present distorted pictures of what is taking place. They only allow for some costs and some returns, and then infer that policies are good if there is a balance in favor of returns thus defined. We need complete national income accounts, accounts that record *all* costs and *all* gains. For only then can we tell if, in the aggregate, a policy is good. We cannot tell this from current Gross National Product data. As Mishan observes, growth policy is "a mass flight from reality into statistics."[6] It is not easy to assess all costs. What figure, for example, should be put upon anomie generated by life in crowded high-rise urban rabbit warrens masquerading as apartments—sequelae to population concentration following on the heels of continuing population growth. We can, however, learn to cost evil as well as virtue, at least approximately.

REWARDS, PENALTIES, INCENTIVES

There is need to reorient the world of rewards and penalties, incentives and disincentives incident either upon persons of reproductive age or upon those who tend to benefit from population maladjustment of various sorts.[7]

Illustrative of the former case is the need to correct for the impact of discrimination against woman, upon her position in the world of affairs, and hence upon her view of reproduction. Ours is still a man's world. Woman is discriminated against in our society and in most, if not all, other societies. Her overriding alternative may therefore appear to her to be marriage and motherhood, a function she alone remains able to perform. If all discrimination against woman were removed, other activities would tend to absorb a portion of the time, energy, and skill which she currently devotes to marriage and motherhood, with the result that average family size would be reduced. For, in a world attaching less weight to family formation and family size and more to woman's freedom and the quality of children reared, average family size would tend to be lower, and there would be greater emphasis upon quality instead of upon quantity of children.

Illustrative of the second case is the need, in so far as feasible, to make *all* the costs of growth—of population, city-size, Gross National Product, and so on—incident upon those responsible for these costs. To this principle there is one qualification, however, namely, that its execution not disadvantage children brought into this world. Effectuation of this principle, even as qualified, entails greater understanding than we currently have of the effective use of economic incentives. Creative thinking, together with experience, will generate the required knowledge.

What is actually done turns on how men choose, on the values and cost-benefit relationships giving rise to their choices. For today's choices condition tomorrow's options. If we have gotten off the optimum path, one leading to a society in which material welfare is accessible to all, but compatible with the preservation of a healthy and self-sustaining physical, social, and ideational environment, it is because too many unwise choices were made in the past. Too much scope has been allowed to processes which appear to be stochastic in character and carry men along Markov paths, seemingly of their own choosing. Underlying these tendencies is a very high degree of specialization, unbalanced by salutary coordination of the sort potentially associated with thinking and planning in terms of much more inclusive systems than have shaped thought and action in the past. We are, therefore, greatly in need of information respecting the generation, confirmation, and harmonization of man's choices in the recent past as well as in the present. Given enough such information, errors of the sort made yesterday should prove avoidable or remediable at least in part. For, when such information is available, penalties and rewards can be embedded in new institutional matrices and thus made to give almost automatic, self-correcting direction to relevant human behavior.

The power to decide issues pertinent to the growth and distribution of population is both dispersed and concentrated. Illustrative of dispersed decision-making power is that relating to family formation. Illustrative of concentrated decision-making power is that relating to the distribution of population in space. A small number of corporations, ultimately governed by 10,000 to 15,000 key executives, determine over the longer-run where much of America's population must live. Over one job in five is directly controlled by 750 corporations which also determine where are manufactured the intermediate products of which they make use. These corporations could easily establish 600 cities, each with an economic base for something like

100,000 to 200,000 inhabitants. These cities would be capable of absorbing our unavoidable population growth, possibly over 100 millions, and thus of easing the pressure upon our present large cities—cities increasingly better known for their crime rates than for their industrial or artistic contributions.[8] Indeed, were every employer required to pay a portal-to-portal wage or salary, redistribution along these lines would get under way quite rapidly.

Ultimately, the degree to which numbers are controlled and distributed optimally will turn on the pattern of wants that becomes regnant. Unfortunately, man is capable of adapting himself to extremely unattractive styles of life. For example, had Tom Sawyer a great grandson, the latter might well be happy on "pot" in a noise- and pollution-ridden central-city habitat; or his tastes might, on the contrary, have been those acceptable to an Aristotle or an Aquinas. The task confronting searchers after optima will consist in part, therefore, in giving appropriate shape to men's tastes, expecially to those of taste-setters and those preferred by taste-formers and manu-facturers—in (as Walter Lippmann might say) inducing in the heads of enough men similar pictures conducive to the realization of population optima. For this there is some basis for optimism if Americans are as other-directed as David Riesman asserts.[9] They must, however, as Elizabeth Hoyt suggests,[10] set in motion a suitable chain of choices, since otherwise, as G. L. Stebbins infers from man's natural history, he will continue to stumble "from one morass of maladjustment, misery, and partial destruction to another similar quagmire."[11]

REFERENCES

1. H. A. Simon, *Sciences of the Artificial* (Cambridge, Mass.: M.I.T. Press, 1969), Chap. 1.

2. P. S. Dasgupta, "On the Concept of Optimum Population," *Review of Economic Studies,* 36 (1969), 295; Daniel Price (ed.), *The 99th Hour* (Chapel Hill: University of North Carolina Press, 1967); Horace Miner (ed.), *The City in Modern Africa* (New York: Frederick A. Praeger, Inc., 1967); Harvey Leibenstein, *A Theory of Economic-Demographic Development* (Princeton: Princeton University Press, 1954); A Sauvy, *Théorie générale de la population* (Paris: Presses Universitaire de France, 1952).

3. J. J. Spengler, "Aspects of the Economics of Population Growth," *Southern Economic Journal,* 14 (1947–48), 233.

4. Manuel Gottlieb, "Optimum Population, Foreign Trade and World Economy," *Population Studies,* 3 (1949), 151.

5. E.g., see Leon Hollerman, *Japan's Dependence on the World Economy: The Approach toward Economic Liberalization* (Princeton: Princeton University Press, 1967).

6. E. J. Mishan, *The Costs of Economic Growth* (New York: Praeger, 1967).

7. Spengler, "Population Problem: In Search of a Solution," *Science*, 166 (1969), 1234; Harold Frederiksen. "Feedbacks in Economic and Demographic Transition," *Science*, 166 (1969), 837.

8. Spengler, "Population Pressure, Housing, and Habitat," *Law and Contemporary Problems*, Spring (1967), 191; and "Drift to the City," *South Atlantic Quarterly*, 67 (1968), 611.

9. David Riesman et al., *The Lonely Crowd* (Garden City, New York: Doubleday & Company, Inc., 1954).

10. Elizabeth Hoyt, *Choice and the Destiny of Nations* (New York: Philosophical Library, Inc., 1969).

11. G. L. Stebbins, "The Natural History and Evolutionary Future of Mankind," *American Naturalist* 104 (1970), 125.

Human Values and the Concept of an Optimal Level of Population

Margaret Mead

ABSTRACT

The concept of an optimal level of population, optimal for a given country at a given period, provides a useful way in which the need for a shared ethic for population control can be demonstrated. A desirable ratio between adults and children, in terms of the given degree of technological advancement, education, urbanization, and rates of infant survival and expectation of life, can be stated comparatively and noninvidiously, and be revised periodically without the need for dramatic reversals.

The concept of an optimal level of population for any given society at any given period of history lends itself exceedingly well to the construction of a universal ethic of population control. It is essential to develop such an ethic. Living as we do in one world, reacting to the same newscasts and the same photographs of infants dying for lack of food or care, we need to have an ethic which can involve us all: rich crowded countries and rich empty countries; poor crowded countries and poor underpopulated countries. No proposal for population control which considers that some country, because it is richer or presently has more space, can exempt itself from the effort to stop the population explosion, can possibly be satisfactory. Equally, no ethic that does not take into account those human factors which have operated in the past—the hope for immortality, the need for heirs, the need for support in old age, the validation of maleness and femaleness—can hope for success. Throughout history, almost all societies have, most of the time, been geared to population increase, and so reared their children that most men and women would want to have children; would, indeed, have as many children as possible, as a protection against the danger of population decrease and diminution of group identity because—due to the high infant death rate—many had to be born so that a few would survive. The sudden realization that the medical revolution has reversed this situation and that now, still, many are born but many fewer die has come at a time when contemporary human societies cling to values attuned to scarcity although there is an overabundance of infants and young children. To shift from this traditional ethic to one which places a premium on having few children or no children at all, which rewards the childless, the late marrying, and the unmarried, even while those who are alive to make the change still hold deeply to the older ethic, is very difficult indeed.

The use of the concept of an optimal level allows us to make cross-national and cross-cultural statements in a way that using simple quantitative data on rate of increase or decrease does not. If simple decrease or increase figures are used, then nations inevitably compare rates of growth, and many people become frightened at the idea that they are falling behind, for fear that in the long run they may disappear as viable communities. If, however, instead, the question is raised "Have you an optimal level of population now?" and comparisons are made on the basis of success in attaining an optimal level (in terms of complex ratios among resources, space, level of technological and agricultural development, rates of immigration and emigration, and, perhaps most important of all, the *ratio* between adults and children) then countries may vie with each other in reaching the optimal population level for themselves at a given moment in history. As Socialist countries report the success of their five-year plans, the plans themselves being complex and peculiar to each nation, figures in United Nations reports would be stated in terms of approximations to declared optima. For this, the Gross National Product is obviously too narrow a concept.

In considering an optimal ratio between adults and children it is possible to recognize that the countries which are most out of balance are the very modern and affluent and the very technologically backward and poor. In the technologically backward countries, with few educated specialists of any sort, the burden on every adult and trained person is tremendous. It is the enormous number of children under fifteen that weigh down the adults—themselves ailing from lack of childhood medical care and adequate nutrition—who must somehow get the country organized and care for the children. In very rich, technologically advanced countries, just because they are so advanced, the possibilities of what can be done for each child, by trained, educated, attentive adults, is enormous. With the lowered infant death rates, many more vulnerable children are saved, and much more delicate remedial work has to be done, to strengthen, reeducate, and provide for the handicapped. The amount of parental, pedagogical, and medical time needed is much greater. Also, with increased urbanization and rapid social change, it is no longer possible for a reasonably adequate pair of parents to bring up eight or ten children and provide good models for them, as was once done on the farm; nor is it possible for a relatively untrained teacher to succeed by merely replicating the methods by which she herself was taught. Each child, successfully reared, eyes and teeth and ears cared for, creatively educated, peculiarities diagnosed and allowed for, involves an increasing amount of adult time.

Countries somewhere in the middle range, less technologically advanced, not so crowded, not so pressed, with a moderate infant survival rate so that the number of vulnerable children has not reached such proportions, may be able to tolerate a lower ratio of adults to children than either the very advanced or the very poor countries.

The optimal level will be different, but it will not be stated in terms of special privilege; it will not invoke accusations of excessive self-satisfaction, because it will be stated as part of a complex set of relationships. Furthermore, as conditions change and peoples lose or gain a place on the world market, as some new development, like the discovery of natural gas in the Netherlands, is made, the optimal level can be readjusted without any dramatic or internationally embarrassing revision of commitments or national goals.

If we are to work out a solution to the population explosion, the human factor will be terribly significant—especially if we hope to avoid governmental coercion because there seems no hope of voluntary adjustments. The rise of the mass media has given us the power to send news around the world swiftly. If we can send the news about population so that it can be heard by all, in palatable terms of ratios and optima, we may be able to make it.

Toward a Policy for an Optimum Population

Bernard Berelson

These are the population years. What was a disregarded and somewhat esoteric academic specialty only a short time ago has become a "burning issue" with great medical, religious, economic, and political ramifications. The "population problem" is more and more acknowledged to be consequential—indeed, is constantly being redefined into increasingly serious proportions. A few years ago the prototypic "population problem" was too rapid population growth in the developing world—i.e., India. Today there has been added the too-high cost of population growth in the developed countries, with regard to its ecological and environmental consequences—i.e., the United States.

As illustrations of concern over the optimum, in different settings, witness these recent statements:

In November 1966, an all-Union symposium was held which discussed the questions of the Marxist-Leninist theory of population movement. . . . The participants of the symposium came to the conclusion that it is high time to take off the signal "forbidden" from a notion like optimum population. . . . The development of the population is submitted to the overwhelming impact of socio-economic relations, but it is in a dialectic, mutual interaction with the development of the society, which permits to raise the inevitable question concerning the optimal type of reproduction. It has, however, no common features with the bourgeois-apologetic theories of optimum which aim at replacing class conditions by the ratio of the number of inhabitants to the resources; thus they do not differ essentially from the Malthusianism which is as old as the world itself.[1]

How many Britons is best? The Institute of Biology has a nose for topicality. Last year, it devoted its annual symposium to biology and ethics; this year it set its speakers to grapple with the theme of "the optimum population for Britain." The issue neatly segregated the social scientists into the hawkish camp, which saw no danger in Britain's present rate of population growth, and the biologists and politicians into the legion of doves, which believes that Britain is already overpopulated. The symposium, which was held in London on September 25 and 26, produced a resounding democratic victory for the doves. . . . The intellectual victory, however, fell to the hawks by an equally large margin. Whether the hawks are right is quite another matter.[2]

Each generation seems to assume that the demographic circumstances it is experiencing will persist and tries to formulate population policies to insure that they won't. During the 1930's social scientists, noting that fertility had been declining for more than a century in the United States and for 50 or 60 years or more in most of the wealthier European countries, and observing that, although natural increase was still positive for most of these populations, current fertility was below replacement and the intrinsic rate of increase was negative, foresaw a declining population in the near future. . . . These circumstances and trends led some alarmists to speak of incipient race suicide, and others to deplore the supposed dysgenic effects of especially low fertility among the educated and wealthy. . . . Today, after some 20 years of fertility well above the pre-World War II levels, it has become fashionable to explain almost every national failure or shortcoming by rapid population growth—the ugliness and hopelessness of slum life, wasteful and irritating traffic jams, unemployment and delinquency among the disturbingly large fraction of adolescents who drop out of school, the pollution of air and water, and the disappearance of the natural beauty of our country behind a curtain of billboards and under a blanket of kleenex and beer cans.[3]

So the questions "how many is too many, and why?" are being asked, and the community of related specialists are called upon to provide, if not answers, at least guidance toward the answers. Against the background of this Symposium, then, I briefly offer six propositions that, taken together, are intended to provide a basis for the rational determination of public policy.

1. Population, being people, is involved in all human problems, but not all our problems derive directly and substantially from population size or population growth in the sense that demographic factors provide the easiest or the earliest remedies. Many of our deplored and deplorable social problems would not disappear if population growth stopped now. The greater multipliers of undesirable consequences have been technological development and economic productivity, and the associated desire for GNP or per capita income or affluence. A distinguished American demographer recently wrote:

> It is clear that the consumption of non-renewable resources is not proportional so much to total population as it is to total expenditure (total income). Gross national product is also gross national consumption (and, since what goes up must come down, gross national excretion). In the interests of man's limited patrimony, the governments of the less developed countries (those with meager GNPs) should be sending AID missions to the wealthy nations. Thus the perils of the population explosion, so-called, would still exist even if populations were stabilized, but we would then be forced to ascribe those perils to the production explosion. . . . The Doomsday thesis, and the associated insistence on a zero rate of growth, seem to be a simple-minded misunderstanding of the nature of the long run problem—which is indeed the same ecological problem man has always faced.[4]

In any case, population factors are responsible for enough, but they are not responsible for everything. (Sartre observed in *No Exit* that "Hell is other people," and in that setting there were only three people, not three-and-a-half billion!) There are two lessons here: we should not get distracted from working directly on the disturbing conditions themselves, e.g., pollution, by seeking a demographic panacea; and we should not get distracted by incomplete or inadequate diagnosis of what the problem is—technological development or economic affluence as against population growth, or population distribution as against population growth. In each pair, the former may be more the villain than the latter.

2. We cannot foresee the demographic future very well—as past predictions show only too well—but we do seem to be caught in a rather narrow range of current issues in at least four respects: (a) historically (the narrow band of population growth between two long-run eras of little growth); (b) demographically (big enough for the division of labor that leads to affluence and other values, the stimulation of the cities, etc., but not too big to be manageable); (c) resourcewise (unless nuclear energy, through fusion, will provide us with everything we want); and (d) politically/administratively (we have relatively few years to deal with the great problems). And underlying all of this is lack of information and knowledge with regard to the technology of the future as well as the demography. Therefore:

3. We would do well to keep our choices as open as possible for two important reasons: the danger of miscalculation and the range of options we owe to succeeding generations. In general, the tighter the environmental constraints, the more hazardous the human journey. Hence, prudence dictates caution—what if the pessimists are right?—plus our moral obligation to be sure to give the next generations better and more choices than we received. On this score, incidentally, we have not done too badly, since the younger generation now has more choices than any generation in the history of the world. In this connection, affluence may at some point conflict with numbers of people. So far, when the world has had to choose it seems to have chosen affluence, i.e., the developed world and its lowered fertility, Therefore:

4. Regardless of the ultimate or even the optimal size, we can agree on the desirability of a lower *rate* of growth—in the United States and in the developing world. Indeed, the optimum itself is better defined as a rate than a size. Anyway, we do not need to know the ultimate value, only the direction in which it will be found. Today, that direction is a lowered growth rate. But in the United States we can hardly realize a nongrowing population for decades: as has been shown, the lowest we can realistically get is 40 per cent more people over the next five to seven decades.[5] Thus, if nongrowth is needed now, or very soon, we should have started decades ago—at just about the time the demographers had us worrying about a declining population!

5. In any case, those are the easier questions: What? and the answer is down; Why? and the answer is because of safety and options and the quality of life; When? and the answer is now or "as soon as possible." The hard question is How? For that too, and the human values it represents, is part of any optimum, and a particularly difficult part since values change over time. In other words, the means are equally involved in policy answers with the ends. And the *how* refers not just to growth but, in the United States, perhaps even more to distribution. So *how* are we to get to the goal (which itself contains respect for human freedom and dignity) with personal freedoms safeguarded and not too readily relinquished for hypothetical values of the remote or even the near future?[6] *How* are we to get there with political acceptability under democratic processes? *How* are we to get there with implementable policies? So far we have tried to do two things—provide services and provide information and education on consequences. In the end, of course, it is the people's choice: that is, the trade-offs they want to choose between children and other values, individually and collectively.

6. So, by way of conclusion: Is there an optimum level of population? There is an optimum, but it is a rate, not a size. The rate should be determined sequentially through time relative to the demographic impact on other factors and vice versa, and determined democratically on the basis of full information and free behavior, with special consideration to our responsibility to later generations (the open options). Thus, the issue is more process than substance. And, as guide to policy, knowledge is the basic resource—scientific knowledge and public knowledge.

REFERENCES

1. A. Ya. Boyarski and D. I. Valentei, in Egon Szabady (ed.), *World Views of Population Problems* (Budapest: Hungarian Academy of Sciences, 1968), 49–50.
2. *Nature,* 224 (October 4,1969), 8–9. (And note that the designation of hawks and doves is opposite that used in this country.)
3. Ansley J. Coale, "Should the United States Start a Campaign for Fewer Births?" (Presidential address at the 1968 Annual Meeting of the Population Association of America), *Population Index,* 34, 4 (October–December, 1968), 467–474 (Office of Population Research, Princeton University).
4. From a personal memorandum by Norman B. Ryder, Veblen Professor of Sociology, University of Wisconsin, March 1, 1969.
5. Tomas Frejka, "Reflections on the Demographic Conditions Needed to Establish a U.S. Stationary Population Growth," *Population Studies,* XXII, 3 (November, 1968), 379–397.
6. For a discussion, see Bernard Berelson, "Beyond Family Planning," *Science,* 163 (February 7, 1969), 533–43 (abridged version); *Studies in Family Planning,* 38 (February, 1969).

Appendices

INTRODUCTION

The appendices contain material judged to be useful and interesting to the reader, but somewhat peripheral to the volume itself. They include a description of the Symposium which led to the volume, information about the authors, plus several substantial appendices.

The setting up of a National Commission on Population Growth and the American Future is an event of major significance, and marks the official recognition by the United States government of the interdependence between population and government policies, particularly as they relate to resource and environmental programs, tax policies, urban and economic development, and programs of health care, education, and social welfare.

One of the principal methods of influencing population development is through family planning, an activity into which governments have entered only slowly and recently. Private organizations have largely carried the burden and pioneered in this area, both here and abroad. The world-wide survey of the state of family planning programs by Dr. B. Berelson, President of the Population Council, is therefore of direct relevance.

Professor Manfred Kochen of the University of Michigan deals with the optimum size of new cities. The subject is important for two reasons. For nations or for the world itself, there may also be an optimum population level for a city. While the analogy cannot be carried too far, it is interesting to examine the methodology that might be used to optimize a city to see what relevance it has to the rather different problem of the optimum size of a country's population. Secondly, one of the important ways of reducing the environmental impact of population growth may lie in achieving a better distribution of population. This means building new cities or expanding existing small population centers so as to slow down the growth of megalopolises with their attendant diseconomies of traffic snarls, pollution, and the whole range of other urban problems.

The final appendix, by the editor, describes a possible approach for determining an optimum population level (or rather—*levels*) which is based on a particular method for defining the "optimum." But within the context of the definition it may be possible to show that a certain range of population levels can result in the highest quality of life for the maximum number of people.

SFS

AAAS Symposium: Is There an Optimum Level of Population?

Arranged by S. Fred Singer

MONDAY, DECEMBER 29, 1969

9:00 A.M.   Physical Factors
        Chairman: ROGER REVELLE (*Center for Population Studies, Harvard University*)

Nonrenewable Resources
    PRESTON E. CLOUD, JR. (*Department of Geology, University of California, Santa Barbara*)
    HARRISON BROWN (*Foreign Secretary, National Academy of Sciences*)
    JOSEPH L. FISHER (*President, Resources for the Future, Inc.*)

Energy
    ALVIN M. WEINBERG (*Director, Oak Ridge National Laboratory*)
    CHAUNCEY STARR (*Dean, School of Engineering, University of California, Los Angeles*)
    H. LANDSBERG (*Energy and Mineral Resources, Resources for the Future, Inc., Washington, D.C.*)

Environmental Quality
    S. FRED SINGER (*Deputy Assistant Secretary, Department of the Interior*)
    WALTER O. ROBERTS (*President, University Corporation for Atmospheric Research, Boulder, Colorado*)
    CHRISTIAN DE LAET (*Secretary-General, Canadian Council of Resource Ministers, Montreal, Canada*)

2:00 P.M.   Biological Parameters
        Chairman: Garrett Hardin (*University of California, Santa Barbara*)

Food
    LESTER R. BROWN (*Senior Fellow, Overseas Development Council, Washington, D.C.*)
    WILLIAM PADDOCK (*Author, Washington, D.C.*)

Health Services
    PHILIP R. LEE (*Chancellor, San Francisco Medical Center, University of California*)

JOHN H. KNOWLES (*Director, Massachusetts General Hospital*)

VICTOR R. FUCHS (*Vice President for Research, National Bureau of Economic Research, New York*)

Fundamental Biological Problems

    H. BENTLEY GLASS (*Academic Vice President, State University of New York, Stony Brook*)

    BARRY COMMONER (*Center for the Biology of Natural Systems, Washington University*)

    HAROLD A. THOMAS, JR. (*Center for Population Studies, Harvard University*)

TUESDAY, DECEMBER 30, 1969

    9:00 A.M.   Social-Personal Factors

        Chairman: BERNARD BERELSON (*President, The Population Council, New York*)

Educational Services

    WERNER Z. HIRSCH (*University of California, Los Angeles*)

    NORMAN GLASS (*Institute of Ecology, University of California, Davis*)

Social Services, Demographic and Psychological Factors

    EZRA GLASER (*Director, Division of Statistical Information and Studies, United States Office of Education*)

    LINCOLN DAY (*School of Public Health, Yale University*)

    JOHN B. CALHOUN (*National Institutes of Health, Department of Health, Education and Welfare*)

    JOSEPH SPENGLER (*Department of Economics, Duke University*)

    PHILIP M. HAUSER (*University of Chicago*)

    1:30 P.M.   Panel Discussion

        Chairman: ATHELSTAN SPILHAUS (*President-Elect, AAAS*)

    BERNARD BERELSON, PRESTON E. CLOUD, JR., GARRETT HARDIN, MARGARET MEAD (*American Museum of Natural History*), and S. FRED SINGER

    We have become increasingly aware of the fact that a population problem exists not only in some of the less-developed countries but right here in the United States. This fact has become most apparent in our overcrowded cities where traffic, pollution, and social pressures are producing concern—to name but a few problems. President Nixon has called for the establishment of a Commission on Population Growth and the American Future, thus recognizing the importance of the problem at the highest governmental level. But before policies can be fully developed, it is necessary to understand goals more completely. Is there an optimum level of population for the United States, for example? What do we mean by "optimum" and how does this concept depend not only on the level but also on concentration and rates of growth? Traditionally, food has been considered as the important limiting factor on a growing population, but there are many other limiting factors which may be more relevant in a particular situation. It is important to understand the relationship between a given factor, such as environmental quality or health services, and the demographic parameters which describe the population. It is important also to develop a methodology which allows one to make predictions and to model what will happen. We need to understand also the interaction between various factors. Out of such discussions and studies comes a better understanding of the implications of population growth to the quality of life, and, therefore, an important body of information which can form the basis for setting policies for governmental and private actions.

There are quite a few charming vignettes of the Symposium which can never be adequately conveyed in a volume of published papers—questions, comments, interruptions, and *faux pas*.

For example, a student group which wanted to take over the Symposium distributed handbills saying: "Is There an Optimum Level of Population?—Ask a stupid question, get a stupid answer!" They soon became involved in the spirit of the discussion, however, and cheered the speaker who declared that "our ethical obligation is to pass on more options to the next generation." They laughed when our present system of meat production was described as a "giant welfare state run for the benefit of cows," and when one of the speakers who was proposing post facto contraception came up with "post facto conception."

Quite naturally, the discussion moved on to what needs to be done to control population growth. The speaker who espoused legalized abortion as a measure against "enforced pregnancy" was cheered and the slogan "Dilution is the solution to pollution" was booed. There even was formed an *ad hoc* group called STOP—which stands for Society Towards Optimum Population. Buttons were distributed by ecological action groups, with a picture of the earth and the slogan "Love It or Leave It." The Zero Population Growth group had one that read "Jesus Was an Only Child."

It was interesting to see that the young students in the audience had so much in common with the speakers, many of whom were two generations older. But occasionally the gap showed: for example, when the point was raised to the panel (all aged 45 and over) that zero population growth would produce a population with median age of 40, the panel's reaction was, "Well, what's wrong with that?"

APPENDIX B

About the Authors

BERNARD BERELSON is President of the Population Council in New York City. He received his B.A. from Whitman College, his M.A. from the University of Washington, and his Ph.D. from the University of Chicago, where he specialized in communication research and the behavioral sciences, and later taught and served as Dean. For seven years he was Director of the Behavioral Sciences Program of the Ford Foundation; then again returned to the University of Chicago where he conducted a study of graduate education in the United States under a grant from the Carnegie Corporation. After a brief period as Director of the Bureau of Applied Social Research at Columbia University, he joined the Population Council. Among other publications he is co-author of *Human Behavior, An Inventory of Scientific Findings.*

HARRISON BROWN, Foreign Secretary of the National Academy of Sciences, is Professor of Geochemistry and Professor of Science and Government at the California Institute of Technology. He holds honorary degrees from the University of Alberta, Canada, Rutgers University, and Johns Hopkins University, and has received the Annual Award in Pure Science from the AAAS, the American Chemical Society's Annual Award in Pure Chemistry, and the Lasker Award. In addition to many scientific papers on meteorites and cosmogony, he is the author of *Must Destruction Be Our Destiny?* and *The Challenge of Man's Future,* and co-author of *Years of the Modern, The Next Hundred Years, A World Without War,* and *The Cassiopeia Affair.*

314

LESTER R. BROWN, a Senior Fellow with the Overseas Development Council in Washington, D.C., was formerly Administrator of the International Agricultural Development Service where he coordinated the Department of Agriculture's program to increase food production in developing countries. He has received the Department of Agriculture's Superior Service Award and the Arthur S. Fleming Award (both in 1965), and has been cited by the United States Jaycees (1966) for his work on the world food problem. He is author of *Man, Land and Food, Increasing World Food Output,* and, most recently, *Seeds of Change,* on the Green Revolution.

JOHN B. CALHOUN is a psychologist with the National Institute of Mental Health at the National Institutes of Health in Bethesda, Maryland. He received his B.S. at the University of Virginia, and his M.S. and Ph.D. at Northwestern University. His special field of interest is ecological behavior.

PRESTON CLOUD, Professor of Biogeology of the University of California, Santa Barbara, has taught at several major universities. He served as Chief, Paleontology and Stratigraphy Branch, United States Geological Survey, from 1949 to 1959. He has received the A. Cressy Morrison Prize of the New York Academy of Sciences, the Rockefeller Public Service Award, and the Distinguished Service Award and Medal of the Department of the Interior. He is a member of the National Academy of Sciences and currently serves on the Board of Directors of the International Oceanographic Foundation, and the All-University of California Natural Resources Advisory Committee. He is an associate editor of the *American Journal of Science* and of the *Journal of Space-Life Sciences,* and is editor and co-author of the books *Resources and Man* and *Adventures in Earth History.*

BARRY COMMONER is professor of Biology and Director of the Center for the Biology of Natural Systems at Washington University in St. Louis. An active investigator into the physico-chemical basis of biological processes, he holds his baccalaureate from Columbia College and his doctorate from Harvard University. He has held several distinguished academic posts, and has received the Newcomb Cleveland Prize of the AAAS and several honorary degrees. Active on AAAS committees, in 1967 he was elected to the Association's Board of Directors. He is a founder of the St. Louis Committee for Environmental Information, Co-chairman of the Scientists' Institute for Public Information, and serves on the advisory board of *Science Year* and the Editorial Board of *The World Book Encyclopedia*. His book, *Science and Survival,* deals with the threats to human survival of modern technological changes.

LINCOLN H. DAY is Chief of the Demographic and Social Statistics Branch, United Nations Statistical Office. Formerly, he was Associate Professor of Public Health and Sociology at Yale University. He holds his B.A. from Yale, and his M.A. and Ph.D. from Columbia University. He has taught sociology at Mount Holyoke College, Princeton University, and Columbia, has been a Research Associate at Columbia's Bureau of Applied Social Research, and a Visiting Fellow in Demography at the Australian National University. The author of numerous research papers in demography and sociology, he is also co-author of two books, *Too Many Americans* (with Alice Taylor Day) and *Disabled Workers in the Labor Market* (with A.J. Jaffe and Walter Adams).

JOSEPH L. FISHER is President of Resources for the Future, Inc., in Washington, D.C., a nonprofit research and educational foundation concerned with the development of natural resources. He has his B.S. from Bowdoin College, his M.A. from George Washington University, and his Ph.D. from Harvard University. He served for six years as economist and executive officer of the Council of Economic Advisers, Executive Office of the President, has taught at several universities, and has consulted widely on resource development. He is co-author of two books, *Resources in America's Future* and *World Prospects for Natural Resources,* and numerous professional articles.

THEODORE C. FOIN, JR., a Research Associate at the University of California, Davis, received his B.A. from Stanford University and his Ph.D. from the University of North Carolina at Chapel Hill. He is presently involved in the Environmental Systems Group as a postdoctoral fellow.

VICTOR R. FUCHS, a graduate of New York University, holds his doctorate from Columbia University and has taught at both schools. Currently he is Research Vice-President of the National Bureau of Economic Research, Professor of Economics and of Community Medicine of the City University of New York, and a member of the President's Committee on Mental Retardation and a number of other advisory panels of the Department of Health, Education and Welfare. He is the author of scores of articles in professional and popular journals and of five books, the latest of which is *The Service Economy.*

BENTLEY GLASS, who is currently Academic Vice-President and Distinguished Professor of Biology at the State University of New York at Stony Brook, and whose teaching career spans thirty-five years, holds his A.B. and M.A. from Baylor University and his Ph.D. from the University of Texas, as well as many honorary degrees. He has served as President of the AAAS, the AIBS, the American Society of Naturalists, the American Society of Human Genetics, and Phi Beta Kappa. He is currently President of the National Association of Biology Teachers. He has chaired the Atomic Energy Commission Advisory Committee on Biology and Medicine and served on, among others, the National Academy of Sciences Committee on the Genetic

Effects of Atomic Radiation. He is the author of two dozen texts and scientific books and of over 200 scientific, professional, and general articles.

EZRA GLASER is currently Director of the Division of Statistical Information and Studies of the National Center for Educational Statistics, Washington, D.C. He served in the Bureau of the Budget for eleven years, in the National Bureau of Standards as Chief of the Computer Applications Section, and as Acting Deputy Assistant Secretary of Health, Education and Welfare. He was President of the Washington Statistical Society and Vice-President (for Statistics) of the AAAS. He has published articles on operations research, computer systems, and statistical organization.

NORMAN R. GLASS is a Research Associate at the University of California, Davis, Operations Manager of the Environmental Systems Group, and a consultant to the RAND Corporation. He received his A.B. and Ph.D., both in zoology, from the university. His professional interests lie in the areas of systems analysis, of biological processes, population biology, human ecology, and fisheries and resource management.

R. PHILIP HAMMOND, Director of the Nuclear Desalination Program at the Oak Ridge National Laboratory, has his B.S. from the University of Southern California and his Ph.D. from the University of Chicago. He was twice a member of the United States delegation to the Geneva Conference on the Peaceful Uses of Atomic Energy, an exchange visitor to the U.S.S.R. desalination facilities in 1964, five times a member of IAEA special panels on nuclear desalination, and since 1965 an alternate member of the USAEC-Mexico-IAEA Study Team. He wrote the article on atomic energy in the 1964 edition of the *Encyclopaedia Britannica,* and is the author of numerous publications and patents in such fields as evaporator and reactor design, economics of desalination, economics of nuclear power, advanced reactor fuels, and many others.

GARRETT HARDIN, B.A. University of Chicago, Ph.D. Stanford University, is Professor of Biology at the University of California, Santa Barbara campus. He has been a Ford Fellow at the California Institute of Technology, a visiting professor on the Los Angeles and Berkeley campuses of the University of California, and Willetts Visiting Professor at the University of Chicago. In addition to his textbook, *Biology: Its Principles and Implications* (in its fourth edition), he is editor of *Population, Evolution, and Birth Control, 39 Steps to Biology,* and *Science, Conflict and Society,* and author of *Nature and Man's Fate.*

PHILIP M. HAUSER is currently Professor of Sociology, Director of the Population Research Center, and Director of the Chicago Community Inventory, all at the University of Chicago, from which he received his M.A. and Ph.D. For nine years he was Chairman of the University's Department of Sociology, and has served as statistical advisor to the governments of Burma and Thailand, Acting Director of the United States Census, a Director of the Social Science Research Council, Chairman of the Advisory Panel on Integration in Chicago Public Schools, member of the Illinois American Negro Emancipation Commission, and Director of the Task Force on Education of the White House Conference to Fulfill These Rights, in addition to other distinguished posts. He has been active on the editorial staff of technical journals and is author or co-author of a dozen books.

WERNER Z. HIRSCH is Professor of Economics and Director of the Institute of Government and Public Affairs at the Los Angeles campus of the University of California. He received his Ph.D. from the University's Berkeley campus. He is consultant to the RAND Corporation, the Bureau of the Budget, and the International Institute for Educational Planning (Paris), and is a member of the International Institute of Public Finance, the International Association for Research on Income and Wealth, the National Academy of Sciences' Outdoor Recreation Research Group, and Resources for the Future's Committees on Urban Economics and Regional Accounts. He has published half a dozen books, including *The Economics of State and Local Government* and *Spillover of Public Education Costs and Benefits*.

JOHN H. KNOWLES, General Director of Massachusetts General Hospital in Boston, Research Associate to the Program on Technology and Society, Harvard College, and Professor of Medicine, Harvard Medical School, holds his A.B. from Harvard College and his M.D. from Washington University School of Medicine. He has received numerous professional and civic awards, including the Howard McCordoch Book Prize in Pathology and the Conjoint Prize in Internal Medicine, and has served as editor on several professional journals.

MANFRED KOCHEN is Professor of Information Science and Urban Regional Planning and Research Mathematician at the Mental Health Research Institute, The University of Michigan. He received his B.A. from MIT, his M.A. from Columbia, and his Ph.D. in applied mathematics from Columbia. Dr. Kochen was at the Institute for Advanced Study from 1953 to 1955 and at the IBM Research Center from 1955 to 1960. He is the author of *Some Problems in Information Science* (Metuchen, N.J.: Scarecrow Press, 1965), *The Growth of Knowledge* (New York: Wiley, 1967), and *Integrative Mechanisms in Literature Growth* (soon to be published by Greenwood).

CHRISTIAN DE LAET has been, since 1964, permanent Secretary-General of the Canadian Council of Resource Ministers, an intergovernmental coordinating agency in natural resources development, established and financed jointly by the federal and the ten provincial governments of Canada. He is a member of the World Health Organization expert committee on environmental health, and various *ad hoc* study groups in resources management and has been visiting lecturer at universities in Canada and the Netherlands. Mr. de Laet is a member of the National Research Council's Associate Committee on Scientific Criteria for Environmental Quality, and he has recently been elected to the New York Academy of Sciences.

HANS H. LANDSBERG is Director of the Resource Appraisal Program of Resources for the Future in Washington, D.C., where he specializes in analysis of the future adequacy of resources, including minerals and energy. He has served in the United Nations Relief and Rehabilitation Administration and, in connection with the National Power Survey, on two successive technical advisory committees of the Federal Power Commission. He is currently a member of the Editorial Advisory Board of *Technological Forecasting*. Among his books are *Natural Resources for U.S. Growth, Resources in America's Future* (with L. L. Fischman and J. L. Fisher), and *Energy in the United States* (with S. H. Schurr).

PHILIP R. LEE, Chancellor of the San Francisco Medical Center of the University of California, received his A.B. and M.D. from Stanford University, and his M.S. from the University of Minnesota. He has served as Assistant Secretary for Health and Scientific Affairs for the Department of Health, Education and Welfare, and Director of Health Services of the Office of Technical Cooperation and Research of the Agency for International Development, among other medical and advisory posts. He is the author of half a dozen textbooks on health care, population problems, and health manpower and the impact of the environment.

MARGARET MEAD, presently Curator Emeritus of Ethnology at the American Museum of Natural History, Adjunct Professor of Anthropology at Columbia University, and Chairman and Professor in the Social Sciences Department of the Liberal Arts College, Lincoln Center Campus, Fordham University, obtained her B.A. from Barnard College and her Ph.D. from Columbia. Her first field expedition, in 1925, led to *Coming of Age in Samoa*, followed by *Growing Up in New Guinea*, a study of the Admiralty Islanders, revisited and described in *New Lives for Old*. Among her most recent publications are *The Small Conference: an Innovation in Communication* (with Paul Byers) and *Culture and Commitment: A Study of the Generation Gap*. She is currently President of the Scientists' Institute on Public Information and the World Society of Ekistics.

WILLIAM C. PADDOCK, since 1965 a Washington, D.C., based consultant in tropical agricultural development, earned his Ph.D. at Cornell University. After serving as Assistant Professor of Plant Pathology at Pennsylvania

State University, Professor of Plant Pathology at Iowa State University, and Director of the Iowa State College-Guatemala Tropical Research Center in Antigua, Guatemala, he joined the International Cooperation Administration as head of the Guatemalan Corn Improvement Program, followed by five years as Director of the Panamerican School of Agriculture. In 1962 he returned to the United States as head of Latin American affairs for the National Academy of Sciences. He is co-author of *Hungry Nations* and *Famine—1975*.

WALTER ORR ROBERTS, President of the University Corporation for Atmospheric Research in Boulder, Colorado, received his A.M. and Ph.D. from Harvard University and holds honorary Doctor of Science degrees from several colleges and universities. In charge since 1940 of the High-Altitude Observatory at Climax and Boulder, he was also, for nine years, Director of the National Center for Atmospheric Research. A member of many professional societies and scientific panels, he has served the AAAS as Chairman of the Board of Directors, President, and Chairman of the Committee on Public Understanding. He is a Trustee of the Max C. Fleischmann Foundation, the C. F. Kettering Foundation, and Amherst College.

S. FRED SINGER, now Professor of Environmental Sciences at the University of Virginia, has served as Deputy Assistant Secretary for Scientific Programs in the Department of the Interior in Washington, D.C. He received a Ph.D. from Princeton and an honorary D.Sc from Ohio State University. A geophysicist, he has alternated between university and government positions. He has been a university dean and has also served as first Director of the U.S. Weather Satellite program. His research and publications include atmospheric and space physics, oceanography, and a special interest in the origin and early history of the Earth-Moon system. Currently, his major concern is environmental quality and its relation to resource use and population. His most recent book is titled *Global Effects of Environmental Pollution*. He has recently been elected to the Committee on Council Affairs of the AAAS and serves as chairman of the AAAS Committee on Meetings.

JOSEPH J. SPENGLER is presently Director of the Duke University Population Studies Program and a member of the Duke faculty. He received his A.B., A.M., and Ph.D. from Ohio State University. He has been President of the American Economic Association, the Southern Economic Association, and the Population Association of America, and Vice-President of the AAAS. He has taught internationally, specializing in population and resource problems, and economic and social theory. He is author, editor, or co-editor of ten books and of many articles on economical, sociological, and political subjects. His newest book is *Indian Economic Thought: A Preface to Its History.*

CHAUNCEY STARR, Dean of the School of Engineering and Applied Sciences of the University of California, Los Angeles, received both his E.E. and his Ph.D. from Rensselaer Polytechnic Institute. He has been President of North American Aviation's Atomics International Division. He is a frequent speaker on the applications of nuclear energy, and has published many related articles in technical journals. He belongs to a score of professional organizations, is Vice President of the National Academy of Engineering, and was chairman of its Committee on Public Engineering Policy.

HAROLD A. THOMAS, JR., Gordon McKay Professor of Civil and Sanitary Engineering at Harvard University since 1956, is a member of several professional societies, and has published more than fifty articles in engineering journals. He has served as consultant to the Department of Health, Education and Welfare, the Department of Defense, and the Atomic Energy Commision. Since 1954 he has pioneered in applying systems analysis to the problems of resource development both in the United States and abroad.

KENNETH E. F. WATT, Professor of Zoology and Research Systems Analyst in the Institute of Ecology of the University of California at Davis, holds a B.A. from the University of Toronto, a Ph.D. from the University of Chicago, and an LL.D. from Simon Fraser University. He was the recipient of the Entomological Society of Canada's Gold Medal, and the Wildlife Society's Fisheries Ecology and Management Award, and has served in the statistical research division of the Canada Department of Forestry, and Department of Agriculture, and the Ontario Department of Lands and Services. In addition to several dozen technical articles and book chapters and three books in preparation, he is the author of *Ecology and Resource Management* and *Systems Analysis in Ecology.*

ALVIN M. WEINBERG is Director of the Oak Ridge National Laboratory of the United States Atomic Energy Commission. He holds his B.S., M.S., and Ph.D. degrees from the University of Chicago and honorary degrees from several Universities. In 1960 he received the Atoms for Peace Award and the E. O. Lawrence Memorial Award (for his contribution to nuclear reactor theory), and in 1966 received the University of Chicago's Alumni Award. He has served on or chaired several government panels, the Council of the National Academy of Sciences, and the President's Task Force on Science Policy. He has devoted much of his life to the peaceful applications of nuclear fission.

APPENDIX C

Commission on Population Growth and the American Future

MESSAGE FROM THE PRESIDENT OF THE UNITED STATES RELATIVE TO POPULATION GROWTH*

JULY 21, 1969.—Referred to the Committee of the Whole House on the State of the Union and ordered to be printed.

To the Congress of the United States:

In 1830 there were one billion people on the planet earth. By 1930 there were two billion, and by 1960 there were three billion. Today the world population is three and one-half billion persons.

These statistics illustrate the dramatically increasing rate of population growth. It took many thousands of years to produce the first billion people; the next billion took a century; the third came after thirty years; the fourth will be produced in just fifteen.

If this rate of population growth continues, it is likely that the earth will contain over seven billion human beings by the end of this century. Over the next thirty years, in other words, the world's population could double. And at the end of that time, each new addition of one billion persons would

* Ninety-first Congress, first session, House of Representatives Document No. 91–139.

not come over the millenia nor over a century nor even over a decade. If present trends were to continue until the year 2000, the eighth billion would be added in only five years and each additional billion in an even shorter period.

While there are a variety of opinions as to precisely how fast population will grow in the coming decades, most informed observers have a similar response to all such projections. They agree that population growth is among the most important issues we face. They agree that it can be met only if there is a great deal of advance planning. And they agree that the time for such planning is growing very short. It is for all these reasons that I address myself to the population problem in this message, first to its international dimensions and then to its domestic implications.

In the Developing Nations

It is in the developing nations of the world that population is growing most rapidly today. In these areas we often find rates of natural increase higher than any which have been experienced in all of human history. With their birth rates remaining high and with death rates dropping sharply, many countries of Latin America, Asia, and Africa now grow ten times as fast as they did a century ago. At present rates, many will double and some may even triple their present populations before the year 2000. This fact is in large measure a consequence of rising health standards and economic progress throughout the world, improvements which allow more people to live longer and more of their children to survive to maturity.

As a result, many already impoverished nations are struggling under a handicap of intense population increase which the industrialized nations never had to bear. Even though most of these countries have made rapid progress in total economic growth—faster in percentage terms than many of the more industrialized nations—their far greater rates of population growth have made development in per capita terms very slow. Their standards of living are not rising quickly, and the gap between life in the rich nations and life in the poor nations is not closing.

There are some respects, in fact, in which economic development threatens to fall behind population growth, so that the quality of life actually worsens. For example, despite considerable improvements in agricultural technology and some dramatic increases in grain production, it is still difficult to feed these added people at adequate levels of nutrition. Protein malnutrition is widespread. It is estimated that every day some 10,000 people—most of them children—are dying from diseases of which malnutrition has been at least a partial cause. Moreover, the physical and mental potential of millions of youngsters is not realized because of a lack of proper food. The promise for increased production and better distribution of food is great, but not great enough to counter these bleak realities.

The burden of population growth is also felt in the field of social progress. In many countries, despite increases in the number of schools and teachers, there are more and more children for whom there is no schooling. Despite construction of new homes, more and more families are without adequate shelter. Unemployment and underemployment are increasing and the situation could be aggravated as more young people grow up and seek to enter the work force.

Nor has development yet reached the stage where it brings with it diminished family size. Many parents in developing countries are still victimized by forces such as poverty and ignorance which make it difficult for them to exercise control over the size of their families. In sum, population growth is a world problem which no country can ignore, whether it is moved by the narrowest perception of national self-interest or the widest vision of a common humanity.

International Cooperation

It is our belief that the United Nations, its specialized agencies, and other international bodies should take the leadership in responding to world population growth. The United States will cooperate fully with their programs. I would note in this connection that I am most impressed by the scope and thrust of the recent report of the Panel of the United Nations Association, chaired by John D. Rockefeller III. The report stresses the need for expanded action and greater coordination, concerns which should be high on the agenda of the United Nations.

In addition to working with international organizations, the United States can help by supporting efforts which are initiated by other governments. Already we are doing a great deal in this field. For example, we provide assistance to countries which seek our help in reducing high birth rates— provided always that the services we help to make available can be freely accepted or rejected by the individuals who receive them. Through our aid programs, we have worked to improve agricultural production and bolster economic growth in developing nations.

As I pointed out in my recent message on Foreign Aid, we are making important efforts to improve these programs. In fact, I have asked the Secretary of State and the Administrator of the Agency for International Development to give population and family planning high priority for attention, personnel, research, and funding among our several aid programs. Similarly, I am asking the Secretaries of Commerce and Health, Education, and Welfare and the Directors of the Peace Corps and the United States Information Agency to give close attention to population matters as they plan their overseas operations. I also call on the Department of Agriculture and the Agency for International Development to investigate ways of adapting and extending our agricultural experience and capabilities to improve food production and distribution in developing countries. In all of these international efforts, our programs should give further recognition to the important resources of private organizations and university research centers. As we increase our population and family planning efforts abroad, we also call upon other nations to enlarge their programs in this area.

Prompt action in all these areas is essential. For high rates of population growth, as the report of the Panel of the United Nations Association puts it, "impair individual rights, jeopardize national goals, and threaten international stability."

In the United States

For some time population growth has been seen as a problem for developing countries. Only recently has it come to be seen that pressing problems are also posed for advanced industrial countries when their populations increase at the rate that the United States, for example, must now anticipate. Food supplies may be ample in such nations, but social supplies—the capacity to educate youth, to provide privacy and living space, to maintain the processes of open, democratic government—may be grievously strained.

In the United States our rate of population growth is not as great as that of developing nations. In this country, in fact, the growth rate has generally declined since the eighteenth century. The present growth rate of about one percent per year is still significant, however. Moreover, current statistics indicate that the fertility rate may be approaching the end of its recent decline.

Several factors contribute to the yearly increase, including the large number of couples of childbearing age, the typical size of American families, and our increased longevity. We are rapidly reaching the point in this country where a family reunion, which has typically brought together children, parents, and grandparents, will instead gather family members from *four* generations. This is a development for which we are grateful and of which we can be proud. But we must also recognize that it will mean a far larger population if the number of children born to each set of parents remains the same.

In 1917 the total number of Americans passed 100 million, after three full centuries of steady growth. In 1967—just half a century later—the 200 million mark was passed. If the present rate of growth continues, the third hundred million persons will be added in roughly a thirty-year period. This means that by the year 2000, or shortly thereafter, there will be more than 300 million Americans.

This growth will produce serious challenges for our society. I believe that many of our present social problems may be related to the fact that we have had only fifty years in which to accommodate the second hundred million Americans. In fact, since 1945 alone some ninety million babies have been born in this country. We have thus had to accomplish in a very few decades an adjustment to population growth which was once spread over centuries. And it now appears that we will have to provide for a third hundred million Americans in a period of just thirty years.

The great majority of the next hundred million Americans will be born to families which looked forward to their birth and are prepared to love them and care for them as they grow up. The critical issue is whether social institutions will also plan for their arrival and be able to accommodate them in a humane and intelligent way. We can be sure that society will *not* be ready for this growth unless it begins its planning immediately. And adequate planning, in turn, requires that we ask ourselves a number of important questions.

Where, for example, will the next hundred million Americans live? If the patterns of the last few decades hold for the rest of the century, then at least three quarters of the next hundred million persons will locate in highly urbanized areas. Are our cities prepared for such an influx? The chaotic history of urban growth suggests that they are not and that many of their existing problems will be severely aggravated by dramatic increase in numbers. Are there ways, then, of readying our cities? Alternatively, can the trend toward greater concentration of population be reversed? Is it a desirable thing, for example, that half of all the counties in the United States actually lost population in the 1950's, despite the growing number of inhabitants in the country as a whole? Are there ways of fostering a better distribution of the growing population?

Some have suggested that systems of satellite cities or completely new towns can accomplish this goal. The National Commission on Urban Growth has recently produced a stimulating report on this matter, one which recommends the creation of 100 new communities averaging 100,000 people each, and ten new communities averaging at least one million persons. But the total number of people who would be accommodated if even this bold plan were implemented is only twenty million—a mere one-fifth of the expected thirty-year increase. If we were to accommodate the full 100 million persons in new communities, we would have to build a new city of 250,000 persons each month from now until the end of the century. That means constructing a city the size of Tulsa, Dayton, or Jersey City every thirty days for over thirty years. Clearly, the problem is enormous, and we must examine the alternative solutions very carefully.

Other questions also confront us. How, for example, will we house the next hundred million Americans? Already economical and attractive housing is in very short supply. New architectural forms, construction techniques, and financing strategies must be aggressively pioneered if we are to provide the needed dwellings.

What of our natural resources and the quality of our environment? Pure air and water are fundamental to life itself. Parks, recreational facilities, and an attractive countryside are essential to our emotional well-being. Plant and animal and mineral resources are also vital. A growing population will increase the demand for such resources. But in many cases their supply will not be increased and may even be endangered. The ecological system upon which we now depend may seriously deteriorate if our efforts to conserve and enhance the environment do not match the growth of the population.

How will we educate and employ such a large number of people? Will our transportation systems move them about as quickly and economically as necessary? How will we provide adequate health care when our population reaches 300 million? Will our political structures have to be reordered, too, when our society grows to such proportions? Many of our institutions are already under tremendous strain as they try to respond to the demands of 1969. Will they be swamped by a growing flood of people in the next thirty years? How easily can they be replaced or altered?

Finally we must ask: how can we better assist American families so that they will have no more children than they wish to have? In my first message to Congress on domestic affairs, I called for a national commitment to provide a healthful and stimulating environment for all children during their first five years of life. One of the ways in which we can promote that goal is to provide assistance for more parents in effectively planning their families. We know that involuntary childbearing often results in poor physical and emotional health for all members of the family. It is one of the factors which contribute to our distressingly high infant mortality rate, the unacceptable level of malnutrition, and the disappointing performance of some children in our schools. Unwanted or untimely childbearing is one of several forces which are driving many families into poverty or keeping them in that condition. Its threat helps to produce the dangerous incidence of illegal abortion. And finally, of course, it needlessly adds to the burdens placed on all our resources by increasing population.

None of the questions I have raised here is new. But all of these questions must now be asked and answered with a new sense of urgency. The answers cannot be given by government alone, nor can government alone turn the answers into programs and policies. I believe, however, that the Federal government does have a special responsibility for defining these problems and for stimulating thoughtful responses.

Perhaps the most dangerous element in the present situation is the fact that so few people are examining these questions from the viewpoint of the whole society. Perceptive businessmen project the demand for their products many years into the future by studying population trends. Other private institutions develop sophisticated planning mechanisms which allow them to account for rapidly changing conditions. In the governmental sphere, however, there is virtually no machinery through which we can develop a detailed understanding of demographic changes and bring that understanding to bear on public policy. The Federal government makes only a minimal effort in this area. The efforts of state and local governments are also inadequate. Most importantly, the planning which does take place at some levels is poorly understood at others and is often based on unexamined assumptions.

In short, the questions I have posed in this message too often go unasked, and when they are asked, they seldom are adequately answered.

COMMISSION ON POPULATION GROWTH AND THE AMERICAN FUTURE

It is for all these reasons that I today propose the creation by Congress of a Commission on Population Growth and the American Future.

The Congress should give the Commission responsibility for inquiry and recommendations in three specific areas.

First, *the probable course of population growth, internal migration, and related demographic developments between now and the year 2000.*

As much as possible, these projections should be made by regions, states, and metropolitan areas. Because there is an element of uncertainty in such projections, various alternative possibilities should be plotted.

It is of special importance to note that, beginning in August of 1970, population data by county will become available from the decennial census, which will have been taken in April of that year. By April 1971, computer summaries of first-count data will be available by census tract, and an important range of information on income, occupations, education, household composition, and other vital considerations will also be in hand. The Federal government can make better use of such demographic information than it has done in the past, and state governments and other political subdivisions can also use such data to better advantage. The Commission on Population Growth and the American Future will be an appropriate instrument for this important initative.

Second, *the resources in the public sector of the economy that will be required to deal with the anticipated growth in population.*

The single greatest failure of foresight—at all levels of government— over the past generation has been in areas connected with expanding population. Government and legislatures have frequently failed to appreciate the demands which continued population growth would impose on the public sector. These demands are myriad: they will range from pre-school classrooms to post-doctoral fellowships; from public works which carry water over thousands of miles to highways which carry people and products from region to region; from vest pocket parks in crowded cities to forest preserves and quiet lakes in the countryside. Perhaps especially, such demands will assert themselves in forms that affect the quality of life. The time is at hand for a serious assessment of such needs.

Third, *ways in which population growth may affect the activities of Federal, state and local government.*

In some respects, population growth affects everything that American government does. Yet only occasionally do our governmental units pay sufficient attention to population growth in their own planning. Only occasionally do they consider the serious implications of demographic trends for their present and future activities.

Yet some of the necessary information is at hand and can be made available to all levels of government. Much of the rest will be obtained by the Commission. For such information to be of greatest use, however, it should also be interpreted and analyzed and its implications should be made more evident. It is particularly in this connection that the work of the Commission on Population Growth and the American Future will be as much educational as investigative. The American public and its governing units are not as alert as they should be to these growing challenges. A responsible but insistent voice of reason and foresight is needed. The Commission can provide that voice in the years immediately before us.

The membership of the Commission should include two members from each house of the Congress, together with knowledgeable men and women who are broadly representative of our society. The majority should be citizens who have demonstrated a capacity to deal with important questions of public policy. The membership should also include specialists in the biological, social, and environmental sciences, in theology and law, in the arts and in engineering. The Commission should be empowered to create advisory panels to consider subdivisions of its broad subject area and to invite experts and leaders from all parts of the world to join these panels in their deliberations.

The Commission should be provided with an adequate staff and budget, under the supervision of an executive director of exceptional experience and understanding.

In order that the Commission will have time to utilize the initial data which results from the 1970 census, I ask that it be established for a period of two years. An interim report to the President and Congress should be required at the end of the first year.

Other Government Activities

I would take this opportunity to mention a number of additional government activities dealing with population growth which need not await the report of the Commission.

First, increased research is essential.—It is clear, for example, that we need additional research on birth control methods of all types and the sociology of population growth. Utilizing its Center for Population Research, the Department of Health, Education, and Welfare should take the lead in developing, with other federal agencies, an expanded research effort, one which is carefully related to those of private organizations, university research centers, international organizations, and other countries.

Second, we need more trained people to work in population and family planning programs, both in this country and abroad.—I am therefore asking the Secretaries of State, Labor, Health, Education, and Welfare, and Interior along with the Administrator of the Agency for International Development and the Director of the Office of Economic Opportunity to participate in a comprehensive survey of our efforts to attract people to such programs and to train them properly. The same group—in consultation with appropriate state, local, and private officials—should develop recommendations for improvements in this area. I am asking the Assistant to the President for Urban Affairs to coordinate this project.

Third, the effects of population growth on our environment and on the world's food supply call for careful attention and immediate action.—I am therefore asking the Environmental Quality Council to give careful attention to these matters in its deliberations. I am also asking the Secretaries of Interior, Agriculture, and Health, Education, and Welfare to give the highest priority to research into new techniques and to other proposals that can help safeguard the environment and increase the world's supply of food.

Fourth, it is clear that the domestic family planning services supported by the Federal government should be expanded and better integrated.— Both the Department of Health, Education, and Welfare and the Office of Economic Opportunity are now involved in this important work, yet their combined efforts are not adequate to provide information and services to all who want them. In particular, most of an estimated five million low income women of childbearing age in this country do not now have adequate access to family planning assistance, even though their wishes concerning family size are usually the same as those of parents of the higher income groups.

It is my view that no American woman should be denied access to family planning assistance because of her economic condition. I believe, therefore, that we should establish as a national goal the provision of adequate family planning services within the next five years to all those who want them but cannot afford them. This we have the capacity to do.

Clearly, in no circumstances will the activities associated with our pursuit of this goal be allowed to infringe upon the religious convictions or personal wishes and freedom of any individual, nor will they be allowed to impair the absolute right of all individuals to have such matters of conscience respected by public authorities.

In order to achieve this national goal, we will have to increase the amount we are spending on population and family planning. But success in this endeavor will not result from higher expenditures alone. Because the life circumstances and family planning wishes of those who receive services vary considerably, an effective program must be more flexible in its design than are many present efforts. In addition, programs should be better coordinated and more effectively administered. Under current legislation, a comprehensive state or local project must assemble a patchwork of funds from many different sources—a time-consuming and confusing process. Moreover, under existing legislation, requests for funds for family planning services must often compete with requests for other deserving health endeavors.

But these problems can be overcome. The Secretary of Health, Education and Welfare—whose Department is responsible for the largest part of our domestic family planning services—has developed plans to reorganize the major family planning service activities of his agency. A separate unit for these services will be established within the Health Services and Mental Health Administration. The Secretary will send to Congress in the near future legislation which will help the Department implement this important program by providing broader and more precise legislative authority and a clearer source of financial support.

The Office of Economic Opportunity can also contribute to progress in this area by strengthening its innovative programs and pilot projects in the delivery of family planning services to the needy. The existing network of O.E.O. supported community groups should also be used more extensively to provide family planning assistance and information. I am asking the Director of the Office of Economic Opportunity to determine the ways in which his Agency can best structure and extend its programs in order to help achieve our national goal in the coming years.

As they develop their own plans, the Secretary of Health, Education, and Welfare and the Director of the Office of Economic Opportunity should also determine the most effective means of coordinating all our domestic family planning programs and should include in their deliberations representatives of the other agencies that share in this important work. It is my intention that such planning should also involve state and local governments and private agencies, for it is clear that the increased activity of the Federal government in this area must be matched by a sizeable increase in effort at other levels. It would be unrealistic for the Federal government alone to shoulder the entire burden, but this Administration does accept a clear responsibility to provide essential leadership.

For the Future

One of the most serious challenges to human destiny in the last third of this century will be the growth of the population. Whether man's response to that challenge will be a cause for pride or for despair in the year 2000 will depend very much on what we do today. If we now begin our work in an appropriate manner, and if we continue to devote a considerable amount of attention and energy to this problem, then mankind will be able to surmount this challenge as it has surmounted so many during the long march of civilization.

When future generations evaluate the record of our time, one of the most important factors in their judgment will be the way in which we responded to population growth. Let us act in such a way that those who come after us—even as they lift their eyes beyond earth's bounds—can do so with pride in the planet on which they live, with gratitude to those who lived on it in the past, and with continuing confidence in its future.

RICHARD NIXON

THE WHITE HOUSE, *July 18, 1969*

THE PRESIDENT'S REMARKS UPON SIGNING THE BILL TO ESTABLISH THE COMMISSION MARCH 16, 1970*

LADIES AND GENTLEMEN:

We have asked you in this room because the Cabinet Room is presently being redecorated.

The purpose is to sign the population message. I shall sign the message and then make a brief statement in regard to it.

First, this message is bipartisan in character as is indicated by the Senators and Congressmen who are standing here today. This is the first message on population ever submitted to the Congress and passed by the Congress. It is time for such a message to be submitted and also the time to set up a Population Commission such as this does.

Let me indicate very briefly some of the principles behind this population message.

First, it will study the situation with regard to population growth both in the United States and worldwide.

Second, it does not approach the problem from the standpoint of making an arbitrary decision that population will be a certain number and will stop there. It approaches the problem in terms of trying to find out what we can expect in the way of population growth, where that population will move, and then how we can properly deal with it.

It also, of course, deals with the problem of excessive population in areas, both in nations and in parts of nations, where there simply are not the resources to sustain an adequate life.

I would also add that the Congress, particularly the House of Representatives, I think, contributed very much to this message by adding amendments indicating that the Population Commission should study the problems of the environment as they are affected by population, and also that the Population Commission should take into account the ethical considerations that we all know are involved in a question as sensitive as this.

I believe this is an historic occasion. It has been made historic not simply by the act of the President in signing this measure, but by the fact that

---

* From *Weekly Compilation of Presidential Documents,* week ending Saturday, March 21, 1970.

it has had bipartisan support and also such broad support in the Nation.

An indication of that broad support is that John D. Rockefeller has agreed to serve as Chairman of the Commission. The other members of the Commission will be announced at a later time. Of all the people in this Nation, I think I could say of all the people in the world, there is perhaps no man who has been more closely identified and longer identified with this problem than John Rockefeller. We are very fortunate to have his chairmanship of the Commission and we know that the report he will give, the recommendations that he will make, will be tremendously significant as we deal with this highly explosive problem, explosive in every way, as we enter the last third of the twentieth century.

I again congratulate the members of the House and the Senate for their bipartisan support. I wish the members of the Commission well.

NOTE: The President spoke at 10:16 A.M. in the Roosevelt Room at the White House. Mr. John D. Rockefeller 3d was present for the ceremony.

As enacted, the bill (S. 2701) is Public Law 91–213. For an announcement of the signing of the bill, see the following item.

ANNOUNCEMENT OF SIGNING OF BILL ESTABLISHING THE COMMISSION

The President today approved a bill establishing a Commission on Population Growth and the American Future (S. 2701).

The purpose of the Commission as proposed by the President in a message to Congress on July 18, 1969, will be to study the various aspects of the projected growth of the population of the United States between now and the year 2000.

The Commission will be composed of two members each from the Senate and the House of Representatives and not more than 20 members appointed by the President. An interim report is required after 1 year of study and a final report to the President and the Congress after 2 years.

The Commission is charged with studying the probable course of population growth, the resources of the public sector necessary to deal with population growth, and the impact of population increases on the environment and on the activities of Federal, State, and local governments.

The bill was sponsored in the Senate by Karl Mundt of South Dakota and John McClellan of Arkansas.

In addition, the President is announcing the appointment of John D. Rockefeller 3d of New York City as Chairman of the Commission on Population Growth and the American Future. Rockefeller, 63, is a graduate of Princeton University, was the founder of the Population Council in 1962, and serves as the chairman of the board of directors. He is chairman of the Rockefeller Foundation, chairman of the Lincoln Center for the Performing Arts, and a trustee emeritus of Princeton.

He served with the State-War-Navy Coordinating Committee during World War II, and as Special Assistant to the Under Secretary of the Navy. He was a member of the Dulles Mission to Japan in 1951.

Rockefeller received the Albert Lasker Award of the Planned Parenthood Federation in 1961, and is a recipient of the Order of the British Empire. He has been a leader in bringing the subject of domestic and international population growth to the attention of the American people. In this connection, he served as Cochairman of the President's Committee on Population and Family Planning in 1968.

APPENDIX D

The Present State of Family Planning Programs*

Bernard Berelson

My assignment is to appraise the present state of family planning programs: where do we stand? where do we go from here? In my view, the present state is impressive, frustrating, uneven, inadequate, and doubtful or unknown; the prospects are simultaneously promising and dubious. In the remainder of this paper I shall seek to justify these adjectival conclusions.

But first, a few words about the nature of the task and its difficulty. By "family planning programs" we mean deliberate efforts, typically governmental in funding and administration, to provide birth-control information and services on a voluntary basis to the target population, to the end of lowered fertility (among other objectives, e.g., maternal health, child health, reduced resort to nonmedical induced abortion). Given that task, the inherent difficulties are so numerous and so great as to make it seem virtually unsolvable (which indeed it may be, by some definitions of "solution").

There are *political* difficulties: lack of convinced and informed will within

* This paper was prepared for the Conference on Technological Change and Population Growth at the California Institute of Technology, May, 1970.

I am indebted, as always, to Dorothy Nortman of the Council staff for her good help in the preparation of this paper. I asked her for many hard-to-get data and she was able to provide most of them, for which thanks are due and hereby given.

A small portion of this material was used in a presentation I made at an OECD meeting of donor and recipient organizations in the population field in November 1969.

the government, fear of political liabilities in promoting the program, governmental instability, ethnic competitions, resistance to perceived neo-colonialism, concern with military power.

There are *bureaucratic* difficulties: "standard operating procedures," jealousy of any new and popular program, a widespread bureaucracy to be activated, the press of other business upon already overburdened staffs.

There are *organizational* difficulties: lack of trained personnel to run the program, thin channels of communication to the people, lack of a medical infrastructure to attach the program to, the occasional opposition or indifference of the professional medical community, dispersal of population into many small villages, the heavily rural complexion of the society.

There are *economic* difficulties: costs of the program, the competition for funds with the going establishment, the requirements of finance ministries.

There are *cultural* difficulties: the weight of tradition, the inertia of high fertility built into the family system over centuries, the lack of popular education, the subordination of women, early marriage, high marriage rates.

There are *religious* difficulties: active in some places and passive in others, and meant to influence both the people and, perhaps even more, the government.

There are *personal* difficulties: illiteracy and ignorance, the ancestral need for sons, the social-security need for sons, social pressures toward parenthood, the superstitions and customs attached to menstruation, the sensitivity of sex-related behavior, peasant resistance to change, the invisibility of social support on so private a matter, remoteness of rewards.

There are, finally, the difficulties of *sheer size:* tens of countries and each a new venture, hundreds of staff directors to be recruited and trained and located effectively, thousands of clinical facilities to be established and operated, a few hundred thousands of staff workers to be recruited and trained and located effectively, a few hundred millions of individual couples to be informed and served, many hundred millions of births to be averted, * billions of dollars needed.

---

* For example, by a rough calculation and simply to indicate order of magnitude, 1.125 billion births to be averted between 1970 and 2000 in the entire developing world (including Mainland China), to get from a birth rate of forty to twenty or, with anticipated declines in mortality, from a growth rate of 2% to 1%. If the developed world reached a net reproduction rate of one by 2000 and the developing world got there by 2050, the world's population would be stable in 2100 at about fifteen billion.

When the matter is put that way, one would only stand in awe of the problem were it not for the heavy consequences—for the individual child, for the family, for the community, for the developing nations, for humankind. We are undertaking a virtually unprecedented effort at deliberate social change of a very great magnitude. So again: where do we stand? where do we go from here?

WHERE DO WE STAND?

Let us begin our appraisal by evaluating the record against seven criteria: needs, magnitudes, comparative programs, costs, targets, trends, and fertility effects.

§ BY NEEDS

There are four ingredients at need (aside from money): the political will at the top to support the effort; the interest and motivation among the people to accept the practice; the technology for application in the individual case; and the organization to implement the policy by bringing the technology to the service of the motivation. Where do we stand on them, compared with, say, 1960?

With regard to *political will,* there are two basic points. The first is that, in the past decade, there has been what can only be described as a great upsurge in awareness, interest, and policy determination on "the population problem" on the part of policy makers. In 1960, only three countries had antinatalist population policies (all on paper), only one government was offering assistance, and no international assistance organization was working on family planning. In 1970, nearly twenty-five countries on all three developing continents, with 67 per cent of the total population, have policies and programs; and another fifteen or so, with 12 per cent of the population, provide support in the absence of an explicitly formulated policy (see Table 1); five to ten governments now offer external support (though only two in any magnitude); and the international assistance system is formally on board (the UN Population Division, the UNDP, WHO, UNESCO, UNICEF, FAO, ILO, OECD, the World Bank, plus regional offices).* Even if some of this development is merely international fashion or response to funding opportunities, it is still a truly historic development: a large one and, as Table 1 shows, a very recent one.

The second point is that in many cases this achievement is still more apparent than real, more word than deed. A policy is not a program, and

* Also worth noting on the international front is the lessened impact of the two major ideological disputes over population/family planning centered on Marxism and Roman Catholicism.

APPENDIX D   : : 339

TABLE 1

Governmental Policy on Family Planning in
Developing Countries

Population Size (in millions)	Policy and/ or Program	Support but No Policy	No Support, No Policy
400 and more	China (1962) India (1952, reorganized in 1965)		
100–400	Pakistan (1960, reorganized in 1965) Indonesia (1968)		
25–100	Philippines (1969) Thailand (1970) Turkey (1965) United Arab Rep. (1965) South Korea (1961) Iran (1967)	Nigeria (1969)	Brazil Mexico Burma
15–25	Morocco (1965)	Colombia (1967)	Ethiopia North Vietnam South Vietnam Congo, Democratic Rep. Afghanistan Sudan
10–15	Taiwan (1964) Ceylon (1965) Nepal (1966) Kenya (1966) Malaysia (1966)	Venezuela (1965)	Algeria Peru North Korea Tanzania
Less than 10	Ghana (1969) Tunisia (1964) Puerto Rico (1969) Singapore (1965) Jamaica (1966) Trinidad and Tobago (1967) Mauritius (1965)	Chile (1965) Cuba (?) Ecuador (1968) Dominican Republic (1967) Hong Kong (1956) El Salvador (1967) Dahomey (1969) Honduras (1965) Nicaragua (?) Costa Rica (1968) Panama (1969) Gambia (1969) Barbados (1967)	Africa— 26 countries Asia— 19 countries Latin America— 7 countries

a lightly held policy can hardly even be called a policy. So, in several of the favoring countries, and, indeed, in a few of the favoring international organizations, a question arises about the strength of the will to effect fertility decline: Do they really mean it?

With regard to *interest and motivation,* we have assembled a great deal of survey evidence in the past decade, contravening earlier belief, to the effect that there is some degree of interest among the people, even among illiterate and uninformed villagers. Knowledge about the matter is scant, but attitudes are generally favorable; the interest is in stopping rather than in spacing (the latter is a more sophisticated form of family planning that came later in the West as well); the wanted number of children is larger than in the modernizing world but smaller than couples now have; the better educated and the better off, typically in the cities, are further along in this aspect of modernization as they are in all others; and the proportion who want no more children now rises sharply with the number already had (see Figure 1). Thus, at least by verbal profession, there does seem to be a market for family planning in the developing world—not overwhelming in demand but not trivial either.

With regard to the *contraceptive technology,* we are much better off than in 1960 but still not really well off. We have the contraceptive pill, which has worked well in the developed countries but not well in the developing (and which is presently suffering from medical doubts). We have the IUD, which has in a relatively few years become the single best contraceptive method (reversible) for the developing world; it illustrates how technology matters in this field, not only in itself but indirectly, too, in stimulating development of the organization to deliver services. We have better methods of sterilization and abortion. We have much more research aimed at discovering and testing out better methods—better forms of IUDs, a "once-a-month" pill, a chemical abortifacient, a "morning-after" pill, an injection, or an implant.

With regard to *organization and administration,* we have made at least a start wherever there are favoring policies and have made impressive progress in a relatively short time where the will has been strong. But, overall, organization and administration has been and remains a problem. The programs are usually located in health ministries, which typically are not strong in developing countries. There are administrative weaknesses— not least the burden of frequent administrative changes—and bureaucratic obstacles. The record by country shows a wide range of performance simply in getting in position to carry on a program. How ready are the countries to deliver information and services, as indicated by their capability to reach the target population? This is not an easy question to answer reliably and systematically but a rough estimate can be made based on the distribution of personnel and facilities (see Table 2). The range is about as great as it

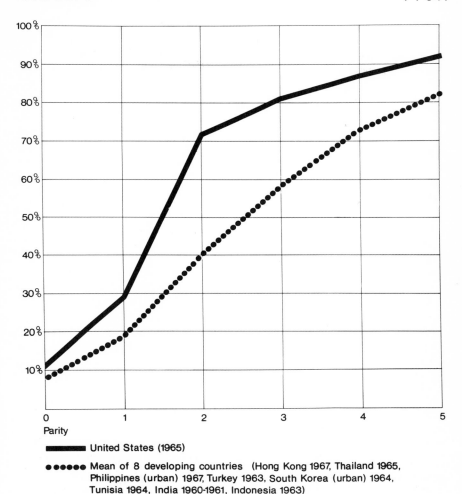

United States (1965)

●●●●●● Mean of 8 developing countries (Hong Kong 1967, Thailand 1965, Philippines (urban) 1967, Turkey 1963, South Korea (urban) 1964, Tunisia 1964, India 1960-1961, Indonesia 1963)

FIGURE 1
Percentage of respondents not wanting more children, by parity.

can be, even within the category of official policy, and the median is only about 50 per cent. There is a slight correlation between capacity and duration—the programs in the higher countries are two or three years older than in the lower ones—and, in several of these countries, there is a sharp disparity between the urban and rural capacities, to the disadvantage of the latter. Overall, the distribution does show that many countries with favorable policies on paper lack programs in the actual fact. Thus, even

TABLE 2

Estimated Organizational Capacity of Programs to Reach
Target Population with Family Planning Information
and Services

From 85% to 100%:	
Ceylon	95*
Singapore	95
Taiwan	95
South Korea	90
From 55% to 85%:	
Pakistan	75
U.A.R.	75
Kenya	70
India	65
From 25% to 55%:	
Malaysia	50
Thailand	40
Tunisia	40
Iran	40
Colombia	35
Dominican Republic	30
25% and below:	
Chile	25
Salvador	25
Venezuela	25
Turkey	15
Indonesia	10
Morocco	5

*What the tabulation says, for example, is that approximately 95% of the target popula-
tion in Ceylon is in principle reachable by the organized program. The estimate of organizational capacity to reach the target population is based on the proportion of facilities and
personnel in place of the target. Two factors have an important influence on this capacity:
(1) the target ratio of population to facility-personnel, and (2) the extent to which facilities
and personnel capable of providing services already exist in the country when the program is
adopted. These estimates do not evaluate the quality of the target itself nor the extent to
which existing facilities and personnel are actually in use. They are only estimates of organizational capacity based on the targets set by the program administrators.

the mandated effort has actually been carried out only in a limited number
of cases, usually the more advantaged ones—which has led a highly knowledgeable observer to say that the family planning effort, like Christianity,
has not failed, it just has never been tried. In several settings, it is more
correct to say that family planning has not really been implemented than
to say that once implemented it cannot be effective.

And the consequence in program effectiveness is reasonably clear (see

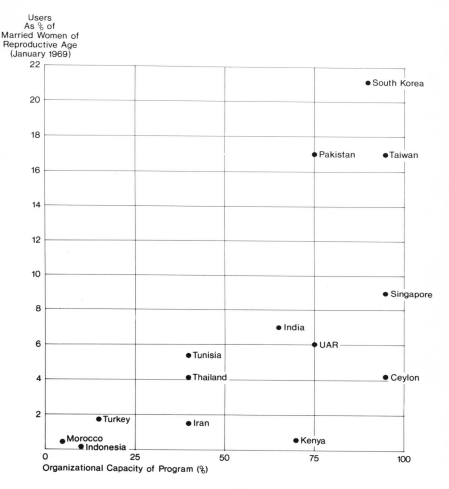

Users
As % of
Married Women of
Reproductive Age
(January 1969)

FIGURE 2
Relation of organizational capacity of program and achievement in use of program contraception.

Figure 2): there is a good correlation between capacity and actual achievement, as measured by the proportion of married women of reproductive
age (MWRA) who were contraceptive users from program sources in January, 1969. And there are ready explanations for individual countries off the
trend: Kenya, Ceylon, and the U.A.R. have incorporated family planning
into their general medical services, but more by fiat than by fact, and
Singapore has three times as many users in the private sector. But on the

whole—and this is an important and encouraging point that, among other things, speaks to the "reality" of existing motivation—effort does pay off.*

§ BY MAGNITUDES

In the developed world, almost all contraceptive practice (that is, contraception involving supplies or services) derives from the private sector; in the developing world, more contraception depends on the governmental programs, thus attesting to the importance of the efforts under consideration. Even here, however, the private sector is by no means insubstantial. By the best available estimate, something over half the current users of family planning services in a number of developing countries are provided contraception through the public programs, but with a wide range (see Table 3). The median in these countries is nearly a 60/40 public/private ratio, so both are clearly important.

As a rough estimate of the magnitudes involved, note the proportion of all MWRA covered by supplied contraception (Table 4). That, of course, does not include rhythm or *coitus interruptus* on the one hand or abortion or sterilization on the other, in which case the proportions rise to approxi-

* My colleagues William Seltzer and Dorothy Nortman properly point out that Figure 2 does not take account of the time/effort factor in programs. A revised and complementary attempt along these lines is presented as an appendix to this paper.

TABLE 3

Percentage of Family Planning Services and Supplies
Provided to Current Users by the Program (January 1969)

India	87%
South Korea	84%
Ceylon	76%
Tunisia	66%
U.A.R.	60%
Malaysia	57%
Turkey	57%
Thailand	56%
Taiwan	53%
Iran	50%
Kenya	50%
Morocco	40%
Singapore	24%

NOTE: Adapted from Table 12 in "Population and Family Planning Programs: A Factbook," *Reports on Population/Family Planning*, 2 (December, 1969), pp. 46–48.

TABLE 4

Estimated Users of Supplied Contraception in the World
(Excluding Mainland China, Soviet Union, and Eastern Europe)

	(*In Millions*)			*Rough Estimate of Proportion of Eligible Population (MWRA)*
	Private Sector	*Public Sector*	*Total*	
Developed countries	30–35	2–2.5	32–40	30%
Developing countries	4–5	6–6.5	10–12	5%
Total	35–40	8–10	42–52	12%

NOTE: In the developed world, the major methods are the pill and the condom; in the developing world, the major methods are the IUD and the condom.

mately 75 per cent in the developed world and perhaps 25 per cent in the entire world. In the absolute, it is almost certainly true that abortion and sterilization together account for far more averted births in the developing world than all the methods of supplied contraception combined. As someone has observed, we should never forget the psychological attractiveness of a single-act certainty over a multiple-act probability.

As to magnitude of supplied contraception, the national programs in eighteen developing countries have actually provided family planning to about 15.3 million acceptors, or about 10 per cent of the total MWRA (with a range of .3 per cent to 45 per cent, individually given below *). This has been done over an effective program life for these eighteen countries of four years, on the average. Is that achievement to be considered "only" or "fully"?

§ BY COMPARATIVE PROGRAMS

How have family planning programs done as compared to public health programs at a similar age of development—appreciating that all the public health programs have been aimed at the universally accepted goal of death control and illness control whereas in the case of family planning both ends and means are often in question. A colleague of mine who has had considerable experience in such matters concludes:

I know of few, if any, newly started public health programs which have been so widely accepted and implemented, in so many developing countries within a

* Ceylon (6%), Chile (22%), Colombia (4%), Dominican Republic (7%), Hong Kong (45%), India (9%), Iran (1.5%), Kenya (7%), Malaysia (6%), Morocco (.8%), Nepal (.3%), Pakistan (13%), Singapore (37%), South Korea (42%), Taiwan (31%), Thailand (6%), Tunisia (10%), Turkey (2%).

period of so few years, or have in general progressed as well as has family planning since about 1963–64, indicating the time when large-scale reasonably effective control programs became possible both technologically and financially.

—and he compares public health programs in environmental sanitation and, thereby, control of some of the infectious and parasitic diseases: smallpox, venereal disease, tuberculosis, and leprosy. He goes on:

> There is no doubt that malaria control programs have achieved a great deal of success in recent years, but we have to bear in mind the many steps and the length of time which were required to achieve this success and even today the problem is far from solved. . . . Given a similar stage in the development of national programs, those for population control suffer little, if any, by comparison.[1]

In both cases, in public health and family planning, a good proportion of the ultimate effect has come and will come from nonprogrammatic factors like improvement in nutrition or a shift toward modernization. In any case, this seems an instructive comparison with what would appear to be the easier job of improving the health of a community.

§ BY COSTS

Are such programs economic? Are the returns worth the costs? There is a rough consensus among economists that an averted birth, viewed strictly from the economic standpoint, is worth at least one to two times the annual per capita income (or, say, 100 to $200) in a typical developing country. How much have these programs actually cost? In absolute figures, the answer is: not very much. National efforts cost only a matter of cents per capita (see Table 5)—a median around 5¢ which translates into about 30 to 35¢ per MWRA. Internal program costs in the established programs in Korea and Taiwan range around $3.00 per acceptor and $5.50 per current user. The most comprehensive and sophisticated analysis of costs in this field, recently completed,[2] finds that a "couple-year-of-protection" (CYP) costs

TABLE 5

Governmental Allocations for Family Planning Programs
(latest available year, usually 1969)

Per Capita, in U.S. Cents	Countries
Less than 2	Indonesia, Kenya, Morocco, Nepal
2–4	Iran, Turkey
5–8	Malaysia, South Korea, Taiwan, U.A.R.
9 or more	India, Pakistan

roughly the same amount across countries (especially when differences in per capita income are taken into account):

Chile, 1968	$6.95
South Korea, 1968	4.36
India, 1968	3.10
Pakistan, 1967	2.79
Taiwan, 1968	2.21

As a rough order of magnitude, assume three to four CYPs for one averted birth—in which case the cost-benefit ratio for family planning ranges from 1 : 10 to over 1 : 30. Another recent study on India found a much higher ratio of return (present value of monetary saving) accruing from averted births to the cost of averting them, in the order of 60 : 1.[3]

§ BY TARGETS

How have the programs done when measured against their own targets? This straightforward question is not easy to answer: absence of data, non-continuity between the targeted category and the data, unspecificity of the target, imprecisions of temporal interpolation. But for ten programs we do have (or can derive) the needed information, and again the range is extremely wide, from above target to far from it (see Table 6). Moreover, the proximity to target is closely related to the degree of effort expended on the program (as indicated in Table 2). Naturally, any interpretation must be weighed against the requirement of the target itself, which in the case of Singapore, for example, is particularly severe.

§ BY TRENDS

Here again the picture is mixed (see Figure 3). A few countries still appear to be building the program (Chile, Thailand, Turkey) but more seem to have hit a plateau of acceptance (Ceylon, Hong Kong, South Korea, Taiwan, Tunisia, and Singapore). The data are not clearly available from India and Pakistan but a plateau is probably indicated there as well. The interpretation partly depends upon absolute levels of performance—increases cannot be sustained indefinitely—but the situation does require attention, especially since the demands of the next years will not decrease in most countries. And not one program started since 1965 has really been "successful."

§ BY FERTILITY EFFECTS

The effect on the birth rate itself is the ultimate test, and at the same time a very difficult one to appraise because of technical problems—lack of decent data on the birth rate, inability to separate out the program's impact from a whole welter of other factors, inability to handle the program's indirect effects (What happens outside the program but as a result of

TABLE 6

Achievement of Family Planning Programs Compared to
Targets (end of 1968)*

Country	Program Target	Conversion to Users/Acceptors by End of 1968	Percentage Achieved by End of 1968
South Korea	From 1962–1971, 1.8 million IUDs 150,000 sterilizations In 1968, 171,000 orals	1,080,000 IUDs 90,000 steril. 171,000 orals	113%
Taiwan	600,000 IUDs in 5 years, by mid-1969	540,000 IUDs (for June, 1969)	93%
Pakistan	5 million users by 1970	4 million users	83%
India	CBR from 41 (1965) to 25 (1976)	10 million users	66%
Malaysia	Natural growth from 3% (1966) to 2% (1985)	90,500 users	60%
Ceylon	750,000 acceptors in 10 years, by 1975	225,000 acceptors	44%
Singapore	CBR from 32 (1964) to < 20 (1970)	82,000 users	37%
Turkey	2 million acceptors by 1972 (from 1965)	800,000 acceptors	17%
Morocco	CBR from 50 (1965) to 45 (1972)	114,500 users	10%
Dominican Republic	CBR from 48 (1967) to 28 (1977)	54,000 acceptors	10%

*To convert birth or growth rate targets into family planning acceptors or users by the end of 1968, total population was projected from the initial target year to 1968 and the number of women of reproductive age was projected at the initial growth rate. The crude birth rate (CBR) targeted for 1968, as applied to the projected 1968 population, yielded the target births for 1968, and total births divided by the number of MWRA projected for 1968 yielded the 1968 general fertility rate to meet the target. By assuming this GFR to be a weighted average of no fertility for users and the base-line fertility for nonusers, MWRA were dichotomized into users and nonusers. The procedure is considered to yield findings of a reasonable order of magnitude.

program activity?), inability to handle the so-called substitution effect (What would have happened in the absence of a program?), inability to assess credit for accelerating declines as against "causing" them. But there are some pieces of evidence:

An analysis conducted for OECD on "the demographic impact of family planning in developing countries" concluded that the programs ac-

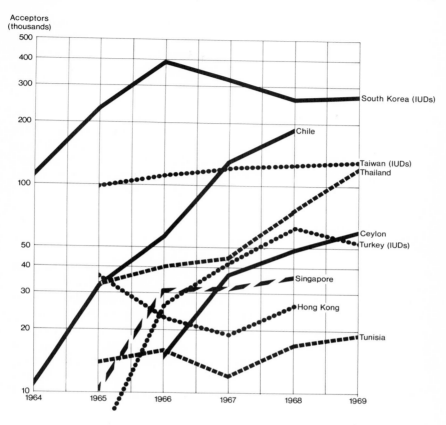

Acceptors
(thousands)

FIGURE 3
Trend in annual acceptors, by country (all program methods,
unless method specified).

counted for 2.3 million averted births in 1968, or a decrease of "1.3 points, or approximately 3%, off the birth rate" of 43.8 (excluding Mainland China). The analysis rests on several assumptions, naturally, and yields what the author calls a "very limited success"—though that impact could also be reasonably interpreted as a substantial one indeed.[4]

In Hong Kong the crude birth rate has been falling for a decade, from about thirty-five to about twenty. According to a sophisticated analysis, "the 1961–1965 period contrasts with 1965–1967. . . . Most of the earlier decline probably can be attributed to changes in age and marital status distributions (particularly the former); but almost none of the recent birth rate decline is due to these factors. Almost all of the 15 per cent decline in the birth rate in 1966 and 1967 can be attributed to a genuine decline in the fertility of married women. . . . The 1965–67 declines occurred at a time and in age patterns which make it plausible to interpret the change as due to a significant degree (but certainly not entirely) to the activity of the Hong Kong Family Planning Association. . . ."[5]

In South Korea the crude birth rate fell about ten points during the 1960s, by best estimate, due partly to increasing age of marriage, partly to increased use of induced abortion (at least an estimated 20 per cent of 1968 pregnancies), partly to a contraceptive program that has reached nearly 50 per cent of the MWRA, and partly to increased urbanization and industrialization (women in the labor force).[6] On the effect of the large IUD program alone, one analysis credits it with a decline in the crude birth rate of about 10 per cent.[7]

In Taiwan, the birth rates in local areas are significantly related to program acceptances, even beyond the influence of nonprogram factors;[8] and in another careful study, the decline in fertility among IUD acceptors was over thirty percentage points greater than among their matches.[9]

In Tunisia, a detailed analysis concluded that contraceptive usage (about two-thirds from the program) accounted for about a third of the decline of the birth rate for 1968, or about 1.5 points or 3 per cent (with later marriage and change in age structure accounting for the remainder of the estimated 5-point decline).[10]

The evidence is not full or finally convincing, but it is beginning to come in and to show a moderate but still heartening result in the desired direction. With less stringent data on program impact on information, attitude, and acceptance, it does carry a certain plausibility.

Finally, by way of summarizing record and prospect, what is to be defined as "success" or "failure" in this field? What is the required goal and when is it to be reached? As a personal offer for consideration, let me mention four reasonable goals, in order of decreasing demand, and measure our chances against each of them.

If the goal is zero growth by the year 2000, then I am confident the goal will not be reached in the developing world, and probably not in the developed world either.[11] We have noted the tremendous task of bringing the growth rate in the developing world down to 1 per cent, let alone zero—averting over a billion births in thirty years. In any case, we are just beginning to see a fascinating historical phenomenon in the countries now closest to zero growth—a phenomenon that has the characteristics of what psychologists call an approach-avoidance conflict, in individual behavior: the farther one is from a goal the better it looks, but the closer one gets to it the less attractive it becomes. Psychologists know that an approach-avoidance conflict is a stable one; that is, it is very hard to resolve. So if zero growth within the next few decades is "absolutely necessary," whatever that means, then we may be in for a dark future.

Second, if the goal is to take 1 to 1.5 points off the growth rate in the developing world in the next twenty years, or, say, fifteen to eighteen points off the birth rate, then it seems to me we have a differential chance at that. My own view is that in the favored countries—those with higher literacy and popular education, with good communication channels, with a decent medical network—this goal can be reached. In the middle countries, my answer would be perhaps, depending upon how fast general development moves ahead and how markedly the contraceptive technology improves in the intervening period. In the unfavored countries, the answer may be no, or close to it.

Third, if the goal is to bring about the ultimate fertility decline faster than it would otherwise occur, by a nontrivial number of years, then, on the evidence of South Korea, Taiwan, Singapore, Japan, and selected places in India and Pakistan, we probably have a decent chance to gain a few decades on what would occur to fertility in the absence of such programs, particularly if the subject countries have the will to do so.

And, finally, fourth, if the goal is to get organizationally ready to do the job more effectively whenever circumstances truly permit, then the prospects seem good indeed, since we have already moved some distance toward that goal.

WHERE DO WE GO FROM HERE?

If that is where we are, what is ahead? Here it is convenient to distinguish between *within* family planning and *beyond* family planning. The former refers to efforts to lower birth rates directly by seeking to extend effective family planning on a voluntary basis by provision of services and information (including persuasion to the small-family norm). The latter refers to efforts to lower birth rates indirectly by instituting social or economic measures that would themselves influence people toward diminished fertility.

§ WITHIN FAMILY PLANNING

There are several things that can be done that should make a difference:

1. *Full, continuous, and informed implementation of mandated programs:* As suggested above, we need to do what we know needs to be done. There is not a going program that cannot be significantly improved in management—most by a good deal. We know what the common improvements are: better training; better supervision; better informational programs, including population, in the schools; better fiscal arrangements; fewer bureaucratic controls; more experimentation for feedback into program; far better evaluation, and so on. Indeed, perhaps the first need is for the field to get its own house really in order: that in itself could make a substantial difference. This is not the place to go into the specifics, but the fact is that the present policies are not being pursued energetically, systematically, or fully, and doing so would seem to be one of the best places to go from here.

2. *Improvements in contraceptive technology:* The contraceptive technology is better than in the past, but by no means good enough. A logistically easy, effective, simple, one-time, reversible, trouble-free, culture-free, doctor-free, coitus-free, inexpensive technique would make an important difference, especially now that the means of delivering the technique is available or in process of being built up (thanks partly to the most recent technological development, the IUD).

3. *Extension of the means for fertility limitation:* Beyond contraception but within family planning is legalized, medically supervised induced abortion. This is a sensitive subject but an important one. Legalized abortion now exists in several countries in varying degrees of liberality and appears to be increasingly acceptable (viz., India and the United States). Illegal, nonsupervised abortions are common throughout the world—literally millions a year by best estimates—and, indeed, represent the stimulating factor for contraceptive programs in Latin America. Probably nowhere has abortion been legalized for demographic reasons, but it has always had a demographic effect. * Indeed, someone has said that while some contraceptive programs have failed, all abortion programs have succeeded, in the double sense that they have had large numbers of acceptors, wherever suitably available, and have made a demographic difference. Here again, if countries find this an acceptable means of population limitation by their own standards, the technique becomes critical since medical doctors are insufficiently available where they are most needed; hence, a nonsurgical means of terminating pregnancy is needed.†

* As in the well-known case of Japan, for example, and the lesser-known case of Rumania, where stringent restrictions on abortion suddenly introduced in November, 1966 (along with some pronatalist social measures) resulted in a birth rate a year later over two and one-half times greater (34.2 as against 13.4, now down to the mid-to-low 20s).

† Christopher Tietze has shown, with regard to medical safety, that "in terms of the risk to life, the most rational procedure for regulating fertility is the use of a perfectly safe, although not 100 per cent effective, method of contraception and the termination of pregnancies resulting from contraceptive failure under the best possible circumstances, i.e., in the operating room of a hospital," in his "Mortality with Contraception and Induced Abortion," *Studies in Family Planning,* 45, (September, 1969), pp. 7–8. Here are the data:

4. *Extension of the urban postpartum concept:* Whether it is the highest point of motivation for family planning or not (and it may well be), certainly a very good time for family planning advice and services is the immediate postpartum period. A demonstration program including over 125 hospitals in the developing world has had good results, including reaching younger women, but there are another 350–400 hospitals of some size potentially available. The extension is desirable on all grounds, including the involvement of medical schools and the medical community. A current estimate is that the maximum cost of institutionalizing family planning in all such hospitals would be about forty million dollars over a ten-year period.

5. *Extension of the postpartum concept to the rural areas:* The postpartum program is now essentially limited to the cities of the developing world, since that is where the delivery institutions are. But the large proportion of the population is rural. The idea is to provide some degree of MCH care plus family planning to every pregnant woman in the society (out of humanitarian and medical concerns, not just demographic). A feasibility study is now in process in eight to ten countries to see what such an effort would require in people, training facilities, physical facilities, transport, and all the rest, including money. Preliminary data suggest costs in the range of about 50¢ per capita per year.

6. *Incentive programs:* Several countries have used payments to programmatic workers, from the field to the doctor's office, to promote and/or effectuate family planning on a piecework or bonus basis. By incentives is meant payments directly to the target population for initiating or practicing contraception or for periods of nonbirth. To a large extent, especially for those with deferred payments, such plans are put forward as surrogate for the social-security value of children or sons. A number of such schemes have been proposed[12] but for various practical reasons none has yet been tried in the field. To my mind, their potential value is limited, but some experience should be gathered wherever feasible and acceptable.

7. *The private sector:* Here there are two possibilities. First, we have seen (Tables 3 and 4) that the private sector is an important part of the distribu-

---

Illustrative Annual Rates of Pregnancies and of Deaths Associated with Contraception, Pregnancy, and Induced Abortion per 100,000 Women of Reproductive Age in Fertile Unions

	Pregnancies	Deaths
1. No contraception, no induced abortion	40,000–60,000	8–12
2. No contraception, all pregnancies aborted out of hospital	100,000	100
3. Ditto, aborted in hospital	100,000	3
4. Highly effective contraception	100	3
5. Moderately effective contraception, no induced abortion	11,800–13,000	2.5
6. Ditto, all pregnancies aborted out of hospital	14,300	14.3
7. Ditto, aborted in hospital	14,300	0.4

tion of contraception to people in the developing world. There is a great
reservoir of talent and energy in that sector that could in principle contribute
to the legitimate extension of the practice. It would be good to find ways
to encourage private industry along this line. * Second, there are industrial
pathways that could be utilized (as they have been in Japan)—the tea estates
on the Indian subcontinent, the agro-industrial estates in the Philippines,
and similar enterprises with credibility and a service network among large
numbers of people.

§ BEYOND FAMILY PLANNING

There are other ways to attack "the population problem" than by direct
promotion of family planning, ways in which the primary motive power
comes from social factors that in turn promote fertility limitation. Where
do we go on them?

1. *Development—social, economic, educational, informational, health:*
There is no doubt but that general development would have an effect on
birth rates: industrialization and a rising standard of living (for people
always seem to choose affluence over fertility, within the family and within
the nation); popular education (by making the future real, and hence making
any kind of planning sensible); nutrition and health (by lowering infant and
child mortality, in the absence of which lowered fertility is unlikely); mass
communication (by making it possible to reach the masses with a message);
and attitudinal modernization in general (by breaking up the traditional
cake of custom in which high fertility is imbedded). No real question about
all that. There are, however, two questions: can development come fast
enough, given the population burden? and, is investment in that route better
in cost-benefit terms than investment in family planning itself? The first
is at best problematic. As for the second, the population/family planning
budget in most countries is less than 1 per cent of the national development
budget and would appear to be better invested, from the standpoint of
development, where it is: that 1 : 99 mix is preferable to 0 : 100. With regard
to popular education, for example, the family planning budget would buy
one more day of school in Taiwan and Singapore, two and one-half days
in Ceylon, and seven to nine days in South Korea, Pakistan, and India.[13]
Presumably, the family planning program is doing more for fertility decline
than those extra hours in school would do.

2. *Tax and welfare benefits and penalties:* Here again, a number of paper
proposals have been made but few have been effected in practice: withdrawal of maternity benefits, withdrawal of family allowances, withdrawal
of large-family requirements for public housing, tax on births after a given

* For some suggestions to this effect, see Alfred Sollins and Raymond Belsky,
"Commercial Production and Distribution of Contraceptives," *Reports on Popula-
tion/Family Planning,* 4 (June, 1970).

number, tax benefits for the smaller family, withholding of educational benefits, pensions for parents of small families as a social-security measure. Most social welfare systems now in effect have a certain pronatalist cast, but at best it is doubtful that they have had a pronatalist effect. The current proposals vary in detail but all seek to turn the system in an antinatalist direction. Here are a few instances: Singapore's opening of public housing to couples with few or no children; Singapore's imposing a much larger fee for delivery of the fourth and subsequent child in the major governmental maternity hospital; removal of maternity and tax benefits in Pakistan; consideration in the U.A.R. of restricting educational and subsidy benefits to the first two children; consideration in Iran of a revision of the child benefit plan to decrease the amounts for later children; a proposal in Malaysia to limit maternity benefits to the first three children; a proposal in Colombia (defeated twice) to obligate girls for social service after their schooling; incorporation of population or family life materials into the school curriculum in a few countries. It is too early to say whether such measures are or, since most are still proposals, would be, demographically effective. In any case, as population pressures grow, countries may move further in this direction, when they can, but not only are there ethical issues (e.g., protecting the child from the penalty) and political problems, but the practical problems are enormous. As has been said, if a country could administer such complex systems for demographic ends, it probably would not need to do so in the first place.

3. *Shifts in social institutions:* Such basic changes can be seen as part of general development and hence desirable as basic underpinning to fertility decline. At bottom, they involve the emancipation of women, in one way or another. The first mode usually advanced is to delay the age of marriage from around the current 16 to, say, 20 (as currently being considered, for example, in the U.A.R. and some other African countries). This would have a worthwhile effect on the birth rate, at least in the short run, but the problem is how to bring it about, since passing a law, while good, is not sufficient where the problem is greatest. Another mode is the promotion of female participation in the nonagricultural labor force: again, worthwhile, and possible in limited situations (currently in the urban areas of Korea), but difficult to implement in the typical rural areas of the developing world.

4. *Coercion:* Proposals are being seriously made by responsible men that "the population problem" is too great to be left to the inevitable failure of voluntary contraception, that the right to free individual choice of numbers of children does not exist, because of what the economists would call the neighborhood effects, and that the "privilege" to reproduce can be, and at present must be, limited by the state to a level acceptable for the society as a whole. Again, plans have been put forward, but apart from other obstacles—ethics, administration, technology—there is no political climate for such an enterprise.

It is, I think, fair to say that the field has been diligently looking for something to do "beyond family planning"—something practicable and ethical, economical, and with some chance of effectiveness, even on an experimental or demonstration basis. On the whole, we have not found it, and we continue our search.

At the same time, it is worth noting that whatever else one does in order to effect the necessary fertility decline, either in general development or in measures other than family planning, some means of contraception is required as instrument. * If age of marriage is raised or popular education extended or employment of women promoted, contraceptive practice is still required to make those favorable conditions fully responsive in fertility behavior. So if this movement, in the long view of history, turns out to have provided only the instrument, with all the engine power coming from the developmental or social structural side, that still will have been a major contribution and will bring about the decline faster than otherwise. And if family planning is not "enough," what *is* that can be done? The empirical question remains as to how the same amount of money and effort could have a greater demographic impact, given the realities, and most of us in the field are looking for an answer.

CONCLUSION

In summary, then, where we stand is indicated by my initial adjectives. The present state of family planning programs is:

impressive, in that a great deal of program development has occurred in a very few years, and with relatively small resources, both personnel and funding; indeed, a great social movement has been instituted, against formidable obstacles and without any major political disruptions, in an historical eyeblink;

frustrating, in that many things that we know need to be done and are in principle do-able are simply not being done, because of lack of will or bureaucratic limitations or personality conflicts or lack of funding or some other unworthy reason;

uneven, in that a few countries have been able to achieve important targets and sustain the forward movement, even to the point of suggesting that they may reach a take-off point in the foreseeable future, whereas others have been unable to do so or have not really tried (and the same can sometimes be seen within a country, as in India where the performance by states varies by a factor of at least three,[14] and by different areas of program operation);

* As Spengler himself says in the last sentence of his article in the December 5, 1969, *Science,* "the arrangements cannot succeed unless the means of control family size are widely available and very cheap in relation to the incomes of the masses" (p. 1238).

inadequate, not only in that "the population problem" has not been "solved" by family planning programs in most of the countries at issue, but also, and more realistically, in that the efforts in several key countries are not adequate to the requirements of the task; and, finally, *doubtful or unknown,* in that we simply do not know how well or badly things are going in several places for lack of a proper system of evaluation, fed back to guide the administration of the program (let alone the lacunae deriving from the difficult and still-unsolved technical problems of measurement).

And the prospects are simultaneously:

promising, in that awareness of consequences is still growing, the technology is likely to improve and/or expand, the programs are gaining both acceptance and experience, effort has been shown to matter, and the momentum is still running in this direction though not so strongly as in the mid- and late-sixties, and in that anything done now makes the task easier later on, other things equal, because of the group support engendered and the subsequently averted births of currently averted births, and in that "the speed of (the demographic) transition, once firmly begun, has accelerated over time"; * and

* Dudley Kirk, "Natality in the Developing Countries: Recent Trends and Prospects," in S. J. Behrman *et al.* (eds.), *Fertility and Family Planning: A World View* (Ann Arbor: University of Michigan Press, 1969), p. 85. In a later paper in the same work (Dudley Kirk and Warren Sanderson, "The Accelerating Decline of Fertility in the Demographic Transition") there is the following remarkable tabulation, showing that the later the reduction of crude birth rates began, the less time it took to go from 35 to 20:

Years Historically and Presently Required for Countries to Reduce Annual Crude Birth Rates from 35 to 20, 1875 to Present[a]

Period in Which Birth Rate Reached 35 or Below	Number of Countries	Number of Years Required to Reach Birth Rate of 20		
		Mean	Median	Range
1875–1899	9	48	50	40–55
1900–1924	7	39	32	24–64
1925–1949	5	31	28	25–37
1950–	6	23	23	11–32

[a] Countries included are: 1875–1899: Austria, Australia, England and Wales, Finland, Italy, Netherlands, New Zealand, Scotland, United States; 1900–1914: Argentina, Czechoslovakia, Germany, Hungary, Japan, Portugal, Spain; 1925–1949: Bulgaria, Poland, Rumania, U.S.S.R., Yugoslavia; 1950– : Ceylon, Chile, Hong Kong, Puerto Rico, Singapore, Taiwan. The initial and terminal dates were determined by 3-year averages rounded to 35 and 20 respectively.

The authors also "suggest that the threshold for fertility reduction is itself changing over time, i.e., a lower level of socio-economic development than was historically necessary in Western Europe is now required to 'trip off' the same fertility reduction" (p. 8).

dubious, in that the problem itself is terribly resistant, the positive results tend to be concentrated in the more favorably situated countries where traditional fertility patterns are beginning to break up under social pressures; we may be hitting a plateau of effort and results at the same time that we encounter more women in the reproductive ages as an echo effect of the post-war baby boom, and the measures beyond family planning are unlikely to be helpful in the short run.

We are thus in a mixed position that is difficult to appraise with confidence. With so much having gone on in so many places in so few years, we do not altogether know where we now are. We are trying to digest our experience to date, to assimilate it, to balance the achievements and the shortfalls, to appraise alternatives even as we seek to advance beyond what we now do. Nor do we lack for critics on all sides: politicians who suspect the whole enterprise of impure motives; international civil servants who think the whole "population problem" has been oversold; financial supporters who want more results; program administrators who want more freedom; self-interested operators who seek to turn the family planning movement to their own ends; demographers who feel the effort has become captured by the medical men; medical men who feel the effort has been captured by the demographers; social scientists who say that family planning will never work in the absence of deep structural changes; doctors who say it will never work in the absence of a complete medical infrastructure. If one does not close his eyes and ears, as of course he should not, then he is beset with conflicting and usually unrealizable advice, and derives only a little comfort by rationalizing that he seems to have a position somewhere near the "norm of the middle."

All of this leaves us, so to speak, in the "Yes, but . . ." stage. Since this great effort is a continuum of challenges, there is always a convenient location for critics: whatever we have been able to do, there is always something beyond that we have not done. Do we measure initial acceptors reasonably well? Yes, but we cannot get good continuation rates. Did we demonstrate something in Taichung? Yes, but that's only one city. Do we have an impressive program in Taiwan? Yes, but Taiwan isn't India. Is the IUD an improvement over earlier contraceptives? Yes, but the removal rate is high. Is there now a much larger investment of personnel and funding in this field? Yes, but it is not enough. Is family planning itself worthwhile? Yes, but it ought to go on within the health context; or Yes, but it really needs stronger social measures to succeed. Did a program have a fertility effect? Yes, but it would have happened anyway. Given the nature of the effort and the many specialized interests with an investment therein, there need be no cause for surprise in such responses—and, as I have tried to suggest, the reality includes sufficient material to justify both the "Yes" and the "but."

What do we now need? As starters, we need three things—and there is not much room for substitution: all three are needed. We need the will, expressed in governmental action, to do the job with appropriate means. At present, if I am not badly mistaken, there is a discontinuity of will between the donor and the recipient agencies: they do not fully share the common objective of population control. The irony is that, with a few exceptions on each side, the donors are more committed than the recipients, yet it is the latter who must do the job. The one cannot substitute its will for the other's. Presumably, enough is shared so that together they can, if they will, usefully get on with the task.

We need funding. For family planning alone, a good deal can be done for five to ten cents per capita per year, properly applied. But greater funding is needed for going the medical route via extension of the MCH infrastructure throughout the society and perhaps for some of the social measures beyond family planning. Large sums could probably be well used over the years, but not immediately—and especially not in the absence of strong will. *

Third, we need time. Given the will and the funding, better programs are likely to be forthcoming with better results, whether or not they "solve the problem." But in the nature of the case, this appears to be a task not for years but for decades, and it is well to remember that we are barely past the middle of the first one. In my judgment, the honeymoon is over, and donors and recipients alike need to settle down to the hard and difficult task of being partners over the longer run.

Where are we and where are we going? The advances of these few years appear to be novel for programs of this magnitude and delicacy, perhaps even unique, and are certainly not to be discounted. At the same time, we must recognize that they are largely, in themselves, the infrastructure—less the job itself than getting ready to do the job. It is a necessary step but not a sufficient result. We could end up, five to ten years hence, sharply ahead, moderately ahead, about where we now are, or moderately back, in a relative sense—probably not sharply back but quite possibly not really knowing. Where we end up depends on what we do now and in the interim.

The development of national family planning programs was a truly historic innovation of the 1960s. The full outcome is still in the balance.

---

* As a rough order of magnitude, the averted births needed to cut the birth rate in half in the developing world (excluding Mainland China), at a cost of $25 each, would come to about $1 billion a year. Today's allocation, both internal and external, is about $200 million.

Surely every medicine is an innovation, and he that will not apply new remedies must expect new evils, for time is the greatest innovator; and if time, of course, alters things to the worse, and wisdom and counsel shall not alter them to the better, what shall be the end?

—Francis Bacon, *Of Innovations*

APPENDIX

As noted in the footnote (page 344) associated with Figure 2, Seltzer and Nortman estimated the personnel-years per 1,000 MWRA in each program by the procedure shown in the table to the right and in Figure 4.

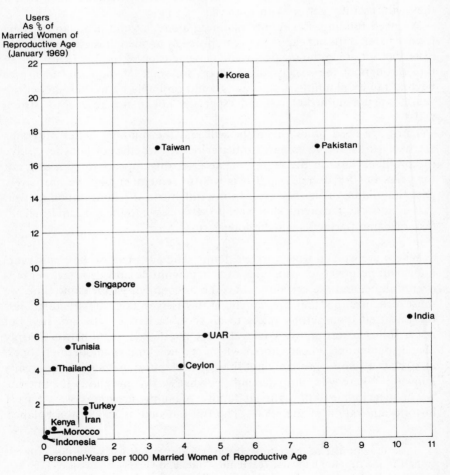

FIGURE 4
Relation of program personnel to achievement.

Estimate of Personnel-Years Put Into National Family
Planning Programs by the End of 1968

Country	Starting Year[1] (1)	No. of Personnel (1968 or 1969)[2] (2)	MWRA (000) 1969[3] (3)	Personnel-yrs. Factor[4] (4)	Personnel-yrs. Thous.[5] (5)	y Users as % MWRA (6)	x Personnel-yrs. per 1,000 MWRA (7)
Ceylon	1965	3,234	1,700	2	6.7	4.2	3.9
India	1964	513,000	96,000	2	1,000.0	7.0	10.4
Indonesia	1968	691	20,000	1/2	0.3	0.1	0.02
Iran	1967	5,000	4,300	1	5.0	1.5	1.2
Kenya	1966	300	2,000	3/2	0.5	0.6	0.3
Korea	1961	3,800	4,500	6	22.8	21.2	5.1
Malaysia	1966	230	1,600	3	0.69	3.4	0.4
Morocco	1965	173	2,600	2	0.35	0.4	0.1
Pakistan	1964	52,000	20,000	3	156.0	17.0	7.8
Singapore	1965	96	290	4	0.38	9.0	1.3
Taiwan	1964	1,400	1,700	4	5.6	17.0	3.3
Thailand	1967	1,300	4,400	1	1.3	4.1	0.3
Tunisia	1964	218	650	2	0.44	5.4	0.7
Turkey	1965	4,500	5,600	3/2	6.8	1.7	1.2
U.A.R.	1965	8,500	4,600	5/2	21.2	6.0	4.6

[1] "Population and Family Planning Programs: A Factbook," *Reports on Population/Family Planning*, 2 (December, 1969), Table 6.

[2] *Op. cit.*, Table 7.

[3] *Op. cit.*, Table 4.

[4] Based on columns 1 and 2 and judgmental value of trend in personnel build-up.

[5] Column (2) × column (4).

REFERENCES

1. From a memorandum by Dr. Richmond K. Anderson, Director of the Technical Assistance Division, Population Council, January, 1969.

2. Warren Robinson, *A Cost-Effectiveness Analysis of Selected National Family Planning Programs* (University Park: The Pennsylvania State University Press, December, 1969).

3. George B. Simmons, *The Indian Investment in Family Planning* (Ph.D. dissertation, Department of Economics, University of California at Berkeley, June, 1969).

4. *The Development Centre Report on Population,* Chap. IV (Paris: OECD, October, 1969).

5. Ronald Freedman *et al.*, "Hong Kong: The Continuing Fertility Decline, 1967," *Studies in Family Planning,* 44 (August, 1969).

6. Hi Sup Chung, "The Korean Family Planning Program: Achievements, Problems and Prospects," paper prepared for a meeting of the Southeast Asia Development Advisory Group Population Seminar, New York, December 19–20, 1969.

7. John Ross, "Woman Years of Use, Cost-Effectiveness, and Births Prevented by the Korean National Program." (Unpublished manuscript, utilizing Potter's methods, June, 1968.)

8. Freedman *et al.*, *Family Planning in Taiwan* (Princeton: Princeton University Press, 1969), pp. 338–39.

9. L. P. Chow *et al.*, "Taiwan: Demographic Impact of an IUD Program," *Studies in Family Planning,* 45 (September, 1969), pp. 1–6.

10. Robert J. Lapham, "Family Planning and Fertility in Tunisia," *Demography,* 7 (May, 1970).

11. Even a Net Reproduction Rate of 1 in the United States now would not bring zero growth to this country by the end of the century. See Tomas Frejka, "Reflections on the Demographic Conditions Needed to Establish a U.S. Stationary Population Growth," *Population Studies,* 22 (November, 1968), pp. 379–97.

12. For a general review, see Bernard Berelson, "Beyond Family Planning," *Studies in Family Planning,* 38 (February, 1969). As later examples, see Ronald G. Ridker, "Synopsis of a Proposal for a Family Planning Bond," in *SFP,* 43 (June, 1969); Ismail Sirageldin and Samuel Hopkins, *Family Planning Programme: An Economic Approach,* preliminary memorandum, April, 1969; and Joseph J. Spengler, "Population Problem: In Search of a Solution," *Science,* 166 (December 5, 1969), pp. 1234–1238.

13. Gavin Jones, "How Much Education Could be Bought with Family Planning Budgets?" Population Council memorandum, July, 1969.

14. See Morrie K. Blumberg, "Indian Family Planning Progress and Potential: The 1968–1969 Program," Population Council memorandum, January, 1970.

APPENDIX E

On Determining Optimum Size Of New Cities

Manfred Kochen *
University of Michigan

ABSTRACT

Starting with a search for a rationale underlying the population ceilings that are specified when new towns are planned, we found that no single, simple optimization criterion has theoretical validity. We explored the implications of population bounds imposed by finite "portal" capacity of a growing city, of minimizing the response time for services to citizens, of central place theory. After analyzing a number of such criteria and methods for calculating optimal size, we investigated tradeoffs between them. We found that, if there is an overriding criterion, it is maximizing that aspect of quality of life which derives from social culture, of which cities are the main source and site. The growth of social culture necessitates face-to-face contacts, the creation of I-Thou relations which can in principle not be reproduced by the most sophisticated telemedia reproduction of remotely located communicants, and that is a major reason why people flock together in cities. To ensure at least the survival of cultural man, we urge the creation of new cities with an economic base in the knowledge industry—new "four-year college" towns— with the primary purpose of providing test vehicles of in vivo social-political

* AUTHOR'S NOTE: The valuable comments and suggestions of K. W. Deutsch, W. Everett, and R. Crickman helped considerably to improve this paper.

innovation, fostering the development of the idea of a "learning" plan in place of master plans, and of a stronger underlying theoretical foundation, including a deeper scientific yet humanistic conceptualization of a "city."

1. INTRODUCTION

This paper discusses various methods and some criteria for optimizing the size of developing urban units and the tradeoffs between these criteria. The question is of importance because of the need for a rationale underlying the population ceilings which are selected when new cities are planned. The underlying analyses may also help build the theoretical underpinnings for national or regional growth policies. The difficulty of formulating this into a meaningful problem is to find an adequate compromise between the great complexity of the reality we would like to capture and what we can do with available analytical capabilities.

Doxiadis[20] suggests that "dynamic cities have no optimum size, but only an optimum speed of growth; the optimum size city is a myth." Many planners agree with this. On the other hand, the distaste of searching for optima might be the reaction to an inadequate conceptualization of "city." We are concerned with the concept of an urban unit or atom that serves as the building block for new cities, and this concept has yet to be explicated. The area, density, and population of such a unit may be meaningful planning variables to be evaluated only after we have a clearer notion of the "smallest city," "quartier," or "ward."

What is a city? Its roots go deep.* What do a group of white houses shimmering on the Mediterranean coast or a cluster of gabled towers or an island of wooden settlements in the middle of a wheat field have in common? They all provide services. The city is a trade center for the long reach and also an area in which multiple, aggregable, and responsive services can be provided to the area residents. It can be a central place where capital-intensive, high-quality, and specialized services can be concentrated and afforded, each located so that a visitor can conveniently reach one facility from another during a single trip.

Even if an optimum population ceiling for a new town could be derived, there would surely be more than one optimum, and the set of optima would vary with proximity to existing cities, natural barriers, etc. It may be more realistic to search for upper and lower limits on growth rate of population density distribution, and revise estimates or first approximations to these according to a "learning" algorithm. As steps toward developing such an

---

* Urbanization started about 10,000 years ago, at the end of the human revolution, when hominids had achieved upright posture, bipedal gait, the use of hands for manipulating, carrying, and manufacturing generalized tools, *plus* language.[29]

algorithm, we present in this paper some results obtainable by analyzing simple mathematical models of extreme cases. These deal with the implications of a few plausible optimizing criteria and the tradeoffs between them.

It is our central thesis that the city is a source of emerging culture, enabling us to make the rate at which we learn to cope with problems be at least equal to the rate at which we generate new problems.* An overriding optimization criterion is maximizing that aspect of the quality of life which is due to the kind of social culture made possible by cities, and this includes the advance of problem-solving capabilities.

2. WHAT IS A NEW CITY UNIT?

Why do people flock together? And why does too great a density seem objectionable as demeaning the quality of life? At the current rate of population growth in the United States,† the *equivalent* of a city the size of Dayton—about ¼ million—is likely to be built every month[64]. Most of this natural increase of 3 million Americans per year will further swell the existing urban population, which is already such that one-half of all Americans occupy 3 per cent of the land and one-fourth live in the ten biggest cities.[25] This may take place without adherence to a plan, or this urban growth may be faster than most current plans can be implemented.

But a small fraction of the population increase may be in the settlement of new towns. Estimates vary from 15 per cent[64] to 2 per cent, the actual figure for housing construction in the New Towns Policy of Great Britain.‡[45] Even if only 2 per cent or 60,000 Americans per year settle in new towns, it means building a new city the size of Dayton every four years.

There are, at present, over two dozen new United States towns under development or in planning and many times that abroad.[50,35] This excludes towns like Oak Ridge or Los Alamos and includes Columbia, Maryland, Reston, Virginia, and Welfare Island in New York City's East River. The last is perhaps the most exciting and recent plan because of the opportunities for in vivo experimentation to assess cost-savings, new forms of refuse

---

*The wise use of computers based on reasonably realistic and powerful models[46,12,13,20,61,2] may speed up the process of planning and plan management, but the main sources of delay are political, legal, and social; getting approval for a development plan is still the longest single delay.[62] One country planner, for example, has to deal with twenty-six planning boards, each of which is "advisory."

† Projections to the year 2000 vary from about 250 million to 320 million, and 60 million over 30 years or 3 million per year may be a serviceable approximation to reality.[19]

‡ From H. Finger, Assistant Secretary, HUD, Panel on Technology and Design for New Cities and Towns, AAAS Symposium, Dec. 29, 1970.

disposal and transportation (articulated electric buses), new forms of modular construction, and the creation of a mixed-income, integrated, urban society which enriches rather than demeans the quality of human life.* Planned by the New York Urban Development Corporation (which is planning two other new towns as well)[48] for 20,000 people, it is to provide, by 1976, 5,000 dwelling units distributed as follows: 20 per cent high-income, 25 per cent middle-income, 25 per cent moderate, 30 per cent low-income including 10 per cent elderly.

Whatever the definition of "city," it is now widely accepted that "city"-size distribution is truncated log-normal;[16] previously it was believed to be the rank-size distribution,[28] which is a crude approximation to the log-normal. The number of "cities" with a population of x or greater varies approximately as Ax^{-1} (or somewhat more generally as Ax^{-a}) where A is the population of the largest city in the sample. Thus, if $A = 12 \times 10^6$, for NYC, and $x = 6 \times 10^6$, then the number of cities having populations not less than 6×10^6 should be ($12 \times 10^6/6 \times 10^6$) or 2; i.e., the city with 6×10^6 people is of rank 2 (e.g., Los Angeles). The rank-size distribution is shown in Figure 1. No two large cities have the same size, but there are numerous small towns of the same size. About 30 per cent of the world's population lives in cities of 20,000 or more, 13 per cent in cities of at least 100,000, and 4 per cent in cities of a million or over. Since new towns necessarily start small, we might expect them to begin life about as equally as other growing organisms. They may continue to grow and eventually fall into the city-size distribution. Cities also have a finite lifetime.

Economic geography is the source of an important basis for analyzing the formation of cities: central-place theory, as developed by Christaller, Berry, and others.[4,5,14,15,55] Services are assumed to be aggregated in a central place for the convenience of customers in a surrounding "hinterland," who "batch" their needs so that they can be satisfied in one occasional or periodic trip. Certain simple goods and services could be obtained in the nearest "hamlet," but less simple ones would require a trip to a larger town with more variety of business-types, more establishments. This implies a hierarchy of central places, such as is observed. Figure 2 tabulates, for comparison, three hierarchies that may help in the search for the smallest unit we would be willing to call a city (in the sense of "civitas" rather than "urbs," which refers to physical form). Christaller's "town," for example, has fifty kinds of business, one hundred establishments, and attracts people from anywhere in a hexagonal region from up to 8 miles away; his "small city" of 6,000 would have ninety kinds of business spread over 350 establishments with a 20-mile reach into a total population (market) of about 20,000 with about $15 million (1960 figures) per year. It would provide "full convenience"

* From A. Yarmolinsky, AAAS Symposium, Dec. 28–30, 1970.

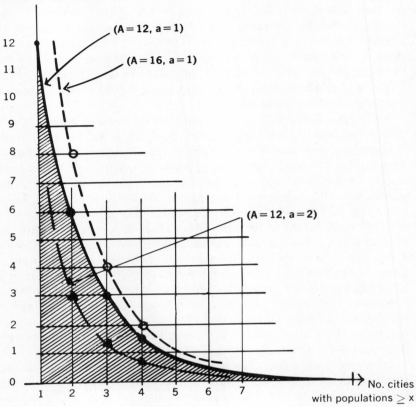

FIGURE 1
The skew distribution of people in cities.

including city government, luxury stores, shoe and clothing stores, movies, cars, etc. K. Fox,[24] taking account of the automotive revolution which increased the speeds and reachable distances known in horse and buggy days by a factor of 10, and considering also the generally rectangular road network in much of the United States, has used a diamond rather than hexagonally shaped regions and discovered that the United States consists of about 500 functional economic areas of 100,000 to 500,000 residents. This would correspond to what we called a "city" in Figure 2.

We conjecture that necessary and sufficient conditions for maintaining a quality of life built on at least the level of social culture attained so far are social organizations at our level 5 or higher (Figure 2), probably at a

Level: (ours)	Due to Christaller-Berry Name	Pop.	Due to Doxiadis Name	Pop.	Our Synthesis Name	Pop. Range	Social Unit
0	None		Man Room	1 2	Private space	1	Individual
1	None		Dwelling	4	Dwelling unit	2–7	Nuclear family
2	Hamlet Village	100 500	Dwelling group Small neighborhood	40 250	Floor, building Block, neighborhood (dep. on density)	40–300	Community
3	Town	1,500	Neighborhood	1,500	Precinct	1,500–7,500	
4	Small city	6,000	Small town	9,000	Ward (5 precincts)	10,000–50,000	
5	Regional city Regional metropolis	60,000 250,000	Town Large city	50,000 300,000	City (5 wards)	50,000–500,000	
6	National metropolis	1,000,000 (or more)	Metropolis Conurbation, etc.	2,000,000 14,000,000	Metropolis (5 cities)	1,000,000 & over	

FIGURE 2
Hierarchy of Urban Spaces

density exceeding 2,000 people per square mile, We defer our arguments for this to Section 5. At this point, we note that a city is, among other things, a concentration in one place of spatially aggregable services. Sewage and water supply are obvious instances of aggregable services, as are public health and secondary education, while specialized research centers are not so aggregation-prone. In many United States urban areas, however, many aggregation-prone services were developed separately, ad hoc. They often did not fit together and furthered detachment of political life from other daily concerns, to low political participation, to low salience. This malaise appeared as the Tammany (political bossism) and technocracy syndrome, with public service agencies seen as unresponsive. On the more economic side, it is argued * that a "city" or market area of less than 50,000 does not provide enough of a population base to lure industry, and Neutze[53] argues that for concentrated populations over 500,000, external diseconomies begin to outweigh internal economies of scale.

Berry[4] has shown, in a recent extension of central place theory, that in developing countries the distribution of population over space tends to shift from one of primacy—where there is just one major city in which much of the population is concentrated—to one of rank-size (Figure 1). Though we may question why rank-size (or more accurately truncated log-normal) is desirable or representative of a high quality of life,[43] the emergence of more cities of various sizes would seem to imply an advance in social culture, civilization. Israel, for example, adopted in 1948 a master plan for developing new towns to lessen the impact of population growth. An excellent recent report[1] of the results strongly supported this shift from primacy to rank-size. The population was redistributed from 57 per cent in the Tel-Aviv Metropolitan area in 1948 to 53 per cent in 1967; Haifa's share dropped from 21 per cent to 16 per cent. This occurred during a period of enormous growth due to immigration; most of the new town settlers were from Africa and Asia, and many left the new towns for Tel Aviv, Haifa, or Jerusalem after several years. This is in accord with Morrison's[52] findings that the settlers of a new town are likely to be young people with a history of frequent moves, likely to move again. (In the United States, about one in five changes residence annually, and one in fifteen migrates across a county line.) But, contrary to the planners' goals that the new towns would be only regional service centers to the surrounding region, these new towns had economic bases in either agriculture or industry and belonged to two parallel hierarchies.

It is noteworthy that not one of the new towns in the United States is

* Private communication from D. Shelton, of the Metropolitan Fund, Inc., December 20, 1970.

economically self-sufficient. Most are satellite towns. Two are towns-in-towns. Columbia, Maryland, for example, was started in 1965 and planned for a population ceiling of 120,000 to be reached by 1980; in 1970, there were about 25,000 people and thirty kinds of business, with General Electric scheduled to locate a plant there to employ 12,000.* The Rouse Company, a joint venture of Howard Research & Development Company and Connecticut General Life Insurance Company, developed Columbia—at an initial cost† of $23.5 million for 28 square miles and from $80 to $100 million to date, of which $40 million is in land—in order to plan and build an entire city, respect the land, provide an environment favorable to the growth of the individual and family, and *make a profit*.[62,63] It was expected to clear a profit in about a decade. It is being built in "village" increments of 10,000 to 15,000, of which three have been built in the first five years. Possibly, an economic base to make Columbia self-sufficient may emerge, but the proximity of Washington and Baltimore provides insurance if this does not happen.

The numerical estimates discussed above suggest that a new city unit might be chosen, as a working hypothesis, as what can be profitably‡ built in a decade, providing for a population in the 50,000 to 500,000 range at level 5 in Figure 2, with at least 100 industries and 350 establishments, at least a forty-mile reach, a variety of housing[25] such as that on Welfare Island, and with some degree of autonomy. The most aggregable services might be under the jurisdiction of a municipality, with the somewhat less aggregation-prone services under jurisdiction of a ward; the least aggregation-prone could be decentralized to maximize responsiveness.

* Private communication from Mr. Hoppenfeld, December 1970.

† Recent federal legislation for insurance loans at premiums of .75 per cent has encouraged the submission of over sixty applications, of which five were accepted by the end of 1970. One was for a city of 110,000 south of Chicago, one for 77,000 in Maryland, one for 50,000 near Minneapolis. A ceiling of $650 million which HUD can insure at one time implies that if a city of 250,000 requires a ten-year loan of about $50 million for initial land purchases, then $(10 \times 50)/650 = 1/1.3$ city/year or one new city every 7.7 years could be built with such financing, roughly 4 per cent of the population increase.

‡ The people of the United States are not likely to embrace large-scale master planning. The black community[36] is especially likely to reject the concept of "new cities" if blacks believe it to be a diversion of resources and leadership from solving the problems of existing cities. Loans from public funds might, at best, be expected for new towns that can serve as test vehicles for innovations, such as Welfare Island. Congress may encourage this.[35] Hence, optimal growth, size, mix, etc., of new cities—even their existence—may be primarily determined by our ingenuity in attracting private investment capital, individual entrepreneural geniuses, and leadership.

3. SOME CRITERIA FOR CALCULATING CITY SIZE

In this section we present a few models using different optimizing criteria to calculate city size to show the inadequacy of considering any one simple criterion by itself. We would also like to convey to the reader the possibility of approaching urban studies with the same sense of wonder, excitement, playfulness—and initial naïveté—which characterizes the spirit of science.

We could classify the criteria according to whether requests for services (and goods) are client-initiated or server-initiated. In the first class are minimization of response time (total time elapsed between a request and its satisfaction) and optimal utilization of batch time (the time allotted to a weekly downtown "shopping" spree). Analyses to minimize response time and maximize responsiveness to the client connect with decentralization theory.[37] Optimizing batch time connects with central place theory. In the second class of technocratically operated, server-initiated services such as epidemic control, public education, etc., one criterion is to maximize utility for the greatest number of clients; another is to maximize safety, health, resistance to damage.

We do not follow this classification exhaustively, but indicate a small sample of two analyses.

§ 3.1 PORTAL CAPACITY AS A LIMITING FACTOR

Consider first a highly oversimplified model of a city for the purpose of showing the importance of picking optimizing criteria. Let us compute maximum rather than optimum size. Another procedure leads to a minimum size, and optimum size must lie between the minimum and maximum. Asking for the biggest a city can be is somewhat analogous to asking how big an animal could * get. This suggests exploring the analog of a well-known relation between surface area, through which metabolic exchange has to occur, and volume.[44,70]

Consider, then, a rectangular city (a bit like Manhattan) of dimensions $D \times W$ miles. See Figure 3. Suppose that this city's material inputs and outputs flow through as many channels as there are streets traversing the city's boundaries; that the city has a uniform residential, work, and play density, organized into square blocks of size d miles on a side. The number of streets (channels) traversing the boundary—let us call them *portals*—is $2(D + W)/d$. The number of blocks is DW/d^2, if streets took up no space.

---

* By contrast, asking how big an animal like a pig *should* get might involve criteria like minimizing the amount of feed per dollar of pork, maximizing the price per pound of pork, etc. The optimum size of man, on the other hand, if at all meaningful, is perhaps determined by how size relates to the organization of his nervous system (if it does).

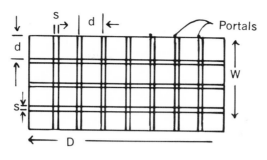

FIGURE 3

In fact, they occupy from 33 to 47 per cent of a city's area, and the number of blocks would, more realistically, be ($\frac{2}{3}$ DW/d^2). Let s be the width of a street. Then the number of blocks is DW/(d + s)^2. Now let:

p= density, in people per square mile (about* 10^4)[11]

w_i = number of pounds per day to supply a person with water, food, fuel (about 10^3)[71]

w_o = number of pounds per day of outflow per person in sewage and refuse (about 10^3)[71]

 C = capacity of a portal, in trucks per minute (about 1)

 c = capacity of a truck, or hauling unit, in pounds (about 20,000)

 T = time to load and unload a hauling unit, in minutes (about 100)

 t = average time (minutes) from one intersection to another (about $\frac{1}{2}$)

In this simplest case, it takes pd^{2}w lb./day to support a block (here $w_i = w_o = w$), and pDWw [d/(d + s)]^2 lb./day to support the city. But all the portals can pass (only) 10^3Cc[2(D + W)/d] lb./day, assuming about 1,000 min./day and full capacity use of each portal. Thus, the city's size D,W cannot exceed the limit given by:

$$dpDWw \left(\frac{d}{d + s}\right)^2 \le 2Cc\,(D + W) \times 10^3 \qquad (1)$$

If D = W (a square city), then D $\le$ (4,000C/pwd) $\times$ [(d + s)/d]^2. With the approximate estimates suggested above, D $\le$ (4 $\times$ 20,000/$10^4 \cdot 10^3$) $\times$ [(d + s)^2/d^3] $\times$ 10^3 or D $\le$ (8/d)[(d + s)/d]^2 mi., d + s = .05 mi.† (20

---

* It varies from 3,000 in towns like Columbia, Maryland, to 75,000 in mid-Manhattan. By definition of "urbanized area,"[28] p $\ge$ 2,000, and the average urban density is p = 8,000 people per sq. mi.

† This, plus [d/(d + s)]^2 = $\frac{2}{3}$, implies that, approximately, s = .2d, and if s + d = 250 ft. = 1.2d, then d = 204 ft., s = 46 ft., or about eight 6-ft. lanes including two sidewalks.

blocks/mi.), then $D \leq 240$ and its population cannot exceed 567 million, an upper bound not yet approached by any urban area but close to the thirteenth item in Doxiadis' fifteen-level hierarchy, an "urban region." Clearly, a long, thin* city could meet the requirement of inequality (1) far better than a square city. Indeed, if the ratio of length to width W is r, $r = D/W$; then, since $[d/(d + s)]^2 < 1$

$$W < \frac{2,000Cc}{pwd} \frac{1 + r}{r} \tag{2}$$

With the above estimates for C, c, w, and d, neglecting s, this is $W \leq (8 \times 10^5/p) \times (1 + r)/r$, and population cannot exceed pDW or p(rW)W or $64 \times 10^{10}[(1 + r)^2/pr]$. This is approximately $(64 \times 10^{10}/p) \cdot r$, for very large r. A megalopolis 10 miles wide and 300 miles long has $r = 30$, and its population could not exceed $(1920/p) \times 10^8$ people, which is about 100 million at an average (low) density of 2,000 people/sq. mi. and 10 million at 20,000 people/sq. mi. (By the year 2010, the New York metropolitan area could be as large as 30 million people at an average density of 24,000 people/sq. mi.)[67]

§ 3.2 STREET CAPACITY AS A LIMITING FACTOR

Let us, however, look at how many moving trucks are in the city at one time. Suppose that, on the average, a truck passes $D/2d$ blocks going into and out of a square city. Neglecting its (slow) speed of motion, it will spend at least $(D/2d)t$ minutes at intersections plus T minutes loading/unloading, assuming no congestion. We assume that during each minute $(4D/d)C$ trucks enter, and that many also leave the city. During the $(D/2d)t + T$ minutes the first truck to enter the city spends inside, $(4DC/d)[(D/2d)t + T]$ more trucks enter before this first truck leaves. With the above figures, and $D = 10$ miles, this figure is 120,000 trucks. Note that it increases as $(D/d)^2$; for $D = 20$ miles, it is 320,000 trucks on the city's $2 \times 20 \times 400 = 16,000$ miles of roads, or twenty trucks/mile or one on each side of a block. If we increase D to 150, which is not wholly unrealistic but far below the theoretical maximum of 240, we get about 630 trucks per block-side (about 250 ft. long), and if we allow no more than 25 ft. from the front end of one truck to that of the next, we would need seven lanes with complete congestion. Going above this would drastically reduce what is left of our block below the two-thirds we assumed. Moreover, as s increases, so does portal capacity C, allowing more trucks to enter per unit time and increasing congestion even more.

---

* Young cities actually grow like star-shaped figures with newer settlements strung out along commuter lines radiating from the center. This gives maximum perimeter for a given area. But newer access routes tend to be built between the star's tentacles into the center, filling the spaces to fill out the city into a convex shape.

Clearly, capacity of transport facilities is a more limiting factor than portal capacity if material flow is by truck over roads. The city would become a gigantic parking lot of moving cars (like the Los Angeles freeways during rush hours) long before its area outweighs its boundary capacity. This is analogous to the problem of designing a skyscraper; with increasing height a greater fraction of each floor must be devoted to circulation: elevators, heating, plumbing. Moving much of the circulatory functions of a city underground would make more than two-thirds of the city available for enhancing the quality of life more directly.

Most of the 1,000 lb. for the daily support of each citizen that flows in and out of the city is water, which would, of course, not be delivered by truck but by subterranean pipe. * Fortunately pipe capacity increases as the square of pipe diameter, and with foresight deeper layers of pipe or tube networks can meet the needs of an indefinitely expanding population. In sum, whether or not "portal capacity" is a limiting factor depends on technological decisions made as the city develops.

§ 3.3 OTHER LIMITING FACTORS

Note that air pollution from car exhaust, which accounts for about 65 per cent of all unburned hydrocarbons, will also increase as D^2. In the absence of devices for reducing such air pollution, intolerable levels may be reached at an even smaller value of D than that specified by street capacity. Nor have we mentioned the use of cars for travel between work, play, and residential sites; this internal circulation system would interfere with the external circulation system, and long before the paralysis of acute congestion † sets in, the inconvenience of local travel would set an even lower maximum on D.

Similar relations between needed and available capacity as a function of D hold for communications. It is well-known that the number of potential telephone connections increases as the square of the subscribing population served by a network. As a city grows, each network can become a subnet of a larger network, such as the telephone, telegraph, radio, and TV nets; more exchanges are added; and enormous control problems must be solved.

We have, of course, vastly oversimplified. In reality a city has many superposed circulatory networks: one or more pipeline networks for water, for sewage, for gas, for electricity. Our considerations suggest subterranean

---

* We should really distinguish between *portal* capacity and *pore* capacity. The former permits transport of people and items that do not circulate continually, analogous to the body's cavities; the latter are analogous to membranes in a biological system.

† This is not only a lock-in of traffic that cannot move. It is manifested by an increase in accident rate and by insufficient adaptiveness in case of emergencies.

conveyor tube networks for all the other items to be circulated, much as proposed by A. Spilhaus in his most stimulating article.[65] Even roads should be subterranean, with traffic in perpendicular directions at different levels, and clear separation between pedestrians, bicyclists, cars, trucks, rail traffic, water traffic, and air traffic.

To get lower bounds on the size of a city, we should examine the life cycles and metabolism of the larger ecosystem containing a city.[49] People in a city generate some of the energy to sustain cycles such as the treatment of sewage or a balanced water-food economy. What is the critical number of people necessary to make such cycles resource-preserving? The requirement that such cycles have some stability, or controlled "wobble,"[17] may help determine the maximum population that a given region can support.

4. TRADEOFFS BETWEEN SOME OPTIMIZATION CRITERIA

Planning is a dynamic process. Underlying it should be a scientific and humanistic basis. Insofar as planning requires prediction, its scientific foundation must enable us to assert and check valid claims about the future. There is now no scientific basis for city planning so complete as to provide a riskless rationale on which to base fairly certain predictions about the consequences of planned acts. It will at best take decades before such a firm basis is developed.

But we cannot wait. J. Platt[58] has likened man's state to that of the first space-bound rocket on its launching pad during countdown. If we make it, we enter a new and better era. We can make it if we act appropriately now. We can shape our future.[59] His reasons for believing that the forces of history are converging at a critical incendiary point within the next few decades stem from the observation that the growth curves of all the major technologies—medicine, transportation, defense, computers, communications, etc.—will be leveling off soon, reaching their natural limits in a decade or two, but before then, the danger of multiple crises combined with our very slowly growing capability to respond is an explosive mixture.

We must act now, despite lack of adequately developed underpinnings. To paraphrase Medawar: We are not yet qualified to prescribe for the welfare of our grandchildren; present skills suffice for present ills. We can set *tentative* long-range goals—e.g., ultimate population size for a new town—but we must take actions with reasonably predictable short-term consequences (two to fifteen years). These actions will provide the basis for revised plans and predictions. Their consequences allow us to learn, to grow a knowledge base for continually improving planning. The most important things to learn are priorities to assign to various optimization criteria and their systemic properties: how optimizing according to one criterion affects performance according to the other criteria. Nor can certain non-renewable resources like coal and oil be committed for very long periods. This suggests that we develop the concept of a "learning" plan and train some planners accordingly. This is a plan that is so flexible that it can be revised quickly and responsively in order to adapt to the relevant facts, constraints, and criteria as these unfold as a result of the actions taken.[38,30,51]

The consequences of uncontrolled growth, without any urban plan, are well-known. Master plans can be equally disastrous. For example, Ciudad Guyana in Venezuela[61] was planned in 1960 to reach a population of 200,000 by 1975, but unexpected mass influx of rural jobless doubled these estimates and created immediate social problems of major dimensions. These forced delays and revisions in implementing a plan. Planning an economic base began with a first approximation, which had to be corrected as soon as better data emerged; computers helped incorporate these corrections fast enough. Here, however, is the first tradeoff facing a planner: planning for a long-range objective, e.g., toward a major advance in the national economy versus planning to provide short-range benefits to "unplanned" urban residents with immediate, urgent needs.

What are some of the possibly conflicting criteria? We have already examined some we would call circulatory. Others are primarily economic, viewing the city as an enterprise exporting certain services or goods.[68,34] Yet others stress the city's role as a political unit, asking for optimal density and size for self-government,[16] or socio-cultural criteria,[18,33,23] or criteria of physical and mental well-being.[21,66,10]

§ 4.1 FORMULATION OF GOALS

The first tradeoff appears in the very statement of the problem. We buy clarity at the expense of capturing the realism and essence of the problem. To say that a city enhances the quality of life because it offers options from a coordinated diversity of services, housing, jobs, social contacts, recreation, and culture is a step toward clarity, especially if we can characterize these diversities with variables, specify in mathematical terms the constraints that interrelate them, and formulate an optimization problem. We could thus conceive of designing a suburban super-shopping center—with mobile or fixed libraries, museums, churches, theaters, and professional offices on the site— which meets these specified conditions and criteria. But we might still prefer the downtown area of an inner city. Why? Because there is a mixture of old and new, a sense of history, a mixture of rich and poor, etc.? If it matters enough, we could build those qualities into a suburban "super-shopping center" too. Still, we might not *feel* the same quality of life in such a center as we would in a stroll through, say, Amsterdam (an example of a "new city" which was planned). Why? Perhaps we can only know but not explicate.

Perhaps the closer we get to capturing the heart of what in a city enhances the quality of life, the less we can explicate and analyze it to mathematically derive recommendations for planning.

Yet, as scientists, we must try to explicate, to analyze, to experiment, to explain.

§ 4.2 COST MINIMIZATION

Consider again a $D \times W$ rectangular city, as in Figure 4, with uniform density distribution of dwellings. For simplicity, assume that $s = 0$. We wish to compute n, the number of service facilities (e.g., food stores) at separate locations that minimizes total cost. Let $n = n_D n_W$, with $n_D/D = n_W/W$. Hence, $n_D = (D/W)n_W$ or rn_W using again r as the length-to-width ratio, and $n = rn_W^2$. In addition to the variables defined in Section 3.1, let:

ℓ = the number of requests, trips, or transactions per person per month (about 10)

K = the cost, in \$/mo., of operating a facility (about 50,000)

v = the speed, in mi./hr., at which users reach a facility (about 10)

c = the cost of the user's time, in \$/hr. (about 3)

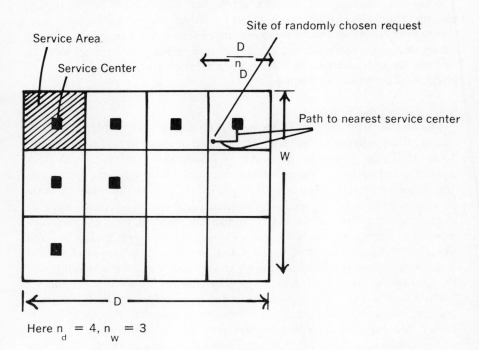

Here $n_d = 4$, $n_w = 3$

FIGURE 4

We divide our $D \times W$ rectangle into n square service regions. The side of such a square is W/n_w mi. But $n_w = (n/r)^{1/2} = (nW/D)^{1/2}$. Hence $W/n_w = W(nW/D)^{-1/2} = (DW/n)^{1/2} = (A/n)^{1/2}$ where A is the area of the city. We assume a service facility to be centered in each square service region, and each resident goes to the facility in his region. His average "east-west" distance from the center line is $\frac{1}{4}$ of the side of the square, or $\frac{1}{4}(A/n)^{1/2}$. The average "north-south" distance is the same, and the total average "Manhattan" distance from his residence to the center is $\frac{1}{2}(A/n)^{1/2}$; the average round-trip distance is $(A/n)^{1/2}$ mi. At v mi./hr., this will take $1/v(A/n)^{1/2}$ hr., ignoring time spent at the facility; it will cost him $(c/v)(A/n)^{1/2}$ \$/trip or request. With a population density p and a total area A, there are Ap users generating $Ap\ell$ requests monthly costing $(pc\ell/v)A^{3/2}n^{-1/2}$ \$/mo. to the users. The cost of operating n facilities is nK \$/mo., assuming no economies of scale.*

The value of n that minimizes total cost to operators and users, which is

$$nK + \frac{pc\ell}{v} A^{3/2}n^{-1/2} \tag{3}$$

can be estimated by viewing this as a differentiable function of n, setting its derivative with respect to n equal to 0, and solving for n. This gives:

$$n \doteq A\left(\frac{pc\ell}{2Kv}\right)^{2/3} \tag{4}$$

The service area per center is $A/n = (pc\ell/2Kv)^{-2/3}$. If this area is not to exceed that of a hexagon with an outer radius of 7 mi. (which amounts to about a half-hour's travel), or about $36\sqrt{3} \doteq 62$ sq. mi., then we can get a lower bound on population density p. It is $p \doteq 2Kv/62^{3/2}c\ell \doteq 2 \times 50,000 \times 10/(500 \times 3 \times 10) \doteq 76$ people/sq. mi. with the numbers assumed above. Compare this with the average United States density of about 70 people/sq. mi. (The density in France is, by contrast, 235 people/sq. mi.)

Of course, dwellings are not distributed uniformly over an area. It is more likely[11] to decrease (in one dimension) with radial distance R from the center as e^{-kR}. There are also many more variables and economies of scale that need to be included. One small example of this will suffice. If a region is to be served by n rather than 1 facility (neighborhood groceries versus a supermarket), the monthly cost to run each one of the n will be higher than K_1/n, where K_1 is the monthly cost of running a 1-facility service; if economies of scale did not favor the supermarket and the n facilities were equivalent to the one central facility costing $\$C_1$/mo., then each of the n would

---

*This also assumes that the cost does not depend on the number of people per month served by one center, which would decrease as n^{-1}.

cost exactly $K_n = K_1/n$ \$/mo. But suppose that $K_n = K_1/n \times b^n$, where $b = 1$. Instead of Equation (3), we now have to find the n that minimizes

$$nK_n + \frac{pc\ell}{v} A^{3/2}n^{-1/2} = K_1 b^n + \frac{pc}{v} A^{3/2}n^{-1/2} \qquad (5)$$

Differentiate this with respect to n, set to 0, and get

$$n^{5/2}b^{n-2} = \frac{\ell pc A^{3/2}}{2vK} \qquad (6)$$

to be solved for n. We can solve it if $b = 1$, when

$$n = \left(\frac{pc\ell}{2vK}\right)^{2/5} A^{3/5} \qquad (7)$$

The average round-trip distance, $(A/n)^{1/2}$, increases as $(2vK_1/pc)^{1/5}A^{1/5}$. Let us estimate $v = 10$ mi./hr., $K_1 = 50,000$ \$/mo., $p = 10,000$, $c = \$3$/hr., $\ell = 1$. If we wish to keep the round-trip distance below 7 mi., then $[2 \times 10 \times 5 \times 10^4/(10^4 \times 3)]^{1/5}A^{1/5} \leq 7$ or approximately $2A^{1/5} \leq 7$ or $A \leq (7/2)^5 = 150$ sq. mi. This gives an upper limit* of $1\frac{1}{2}$ million on population.

Suppose we assume, as in prior papers[37] toward a theory of decentralization, that the utility of a service to a client varies as R/T \$/per request that he is willing to pay, where T is the total response or turn-around time between his request and its satisfaction. Here R is what he would be willing to pay, in \$/request, for a service characterized by a 1-hour turn-around time. It is the value of the client's time and may be related to his "quality of life." The *net* utility to the total client-centered system is

$$U = (R/T)L - nK - LcT$$

where L is the total number of requests per month the system has to service and n,K,c is as before; also, $T = D/4nv$ for a one-dimensional model and $(1/v)A/n$ for a two-dimensional model with uniform load distribution. Also as before, we can let $L = Ap\ell$.

Regarding U as a differentiable function of n, we can determine which value of n maximizes U by setting

$$\frac{dU}{dn} = 0: \frac{dU}{dn} = \frac{d}{dn}\left(\frac{RLv}{A}n^{1/2} - nK - \frac{ALc}{v}n^{-1/2}\right)$$

$$= \frac{RLv}{2A}n^{-1/2} - K + \frac{ALc}{2v}n^{-3/2} = 0$$

* Doxiadis[20] might argue that no upper bound on A is implied because v, the speed of transportation, is increasing. Some increases are possible, but there are fundamental upper limits (far below the speed of light!). As Platt shows[58], we are approaching the natural limits very rapidly.

This is a cubic equation in $x = n^{-1/2}$, $ax^3 + bx - K = 0$, plotted in Figure 5. The effect of increasing b is simply to decrease the root x or to increase the value of n maximizing U. Thus, if a, which is ALc/2v, is constant, then increasing b or RLv/2A favors decentralization. For fixed b, increasing a also increases n (decreases x, the place where the curve for a fixed b intersects the x-axis in Figure 5). Thus, increasing L, the total number of requests per month, favors decentralization; if ℓ and p, the population density, stay constant, then increasing population, or increasing A, which is the populated area, favors decentralization.

In the above argument, n measures pluralization and dispersion, and these are only two aspects of decentralization. In a series of studies toward a more general and realistic theory of decentralization,[37] K. W. Deutsch and the author have also begun to examine three other aspects of decentralization: functional specialization, customization, decisional decentralization. These are published elsewhere.

But there will be demand for a mix of facilities, from a few very large, costly, and more centralized ones that pass economies of scale on to the user and provide him with a wider range of higher-quality services to numerous smaller, more limited, but highly responsive local facilities.

Several tradeoffs are implicit in this discussion: (a) maximizing responsiveness at the expense of optimizing the benefits from economies of scale, services of higher quality and of greater variety; (b) stressing the develop-

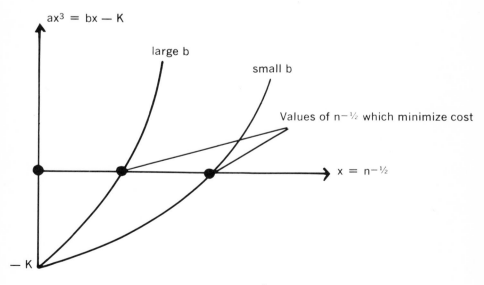

FIGURE 5

ment of income-elastic services (e.g., private cars rather than public transportation) at the expense of stress on meeting the needs of the less privileged and on environmental quality (e.g., air pollution, congestion); (c) stressing the greater organizational efficiency of centralized nets at the expense of the greater autonomy and reliability of polymorphic, decentralized structures.

Nearly all considerations about urban density and size in the literature are economic.[57] Much of this literature focuses on the size. It is generally accepted that a developing city needs receipts from exports to finance the purchase of what it needs for economic development.

Another proposed economic criterion for city size distribution is maximization of national income, either GNP or GNPC (per capita). Neutze[53] argued that regional centers of about 500,000 people should be developed in New South Wales and Victoria, Australia, because at this size many firms that could be diverted from Sydney would find their greatest profits in cities of about that population, and prefer a city of that size; more firms and families would suffer than gain from growth beyond this size. This might lead to maximizing GNP at the expense of GNPC, since most of the growth in GNP comes from the wealthier half of the population and in turn benefits them the most. If there is a rich-poor gap, economic growth without measures to change this gap may tend to widen it. Too many large cities from which most of the growth of GNP is distributed and where, also, the rich-poor gap is greatest, might rather increase the growing gap in GNPC between rich and poor. The criteria of maximizing GNP may be traded against criteria of income equalization, for which various "liberation" movements are agitating.

Doxiadis[20] argues that neither municipal efficiency nor organizational aspects serve as criteria for optimization because ratios between age groups, technical and managerial abilities are constantly changing. Yet there are fundamental limits to individual human capacities that may at least help set bounds on urban growth rates. Thompson[68] argues that management may be the scarce factor in urban growth. Above a certain critical level—he guesses about 250,000 on the ground that only two United States cities in the $\frac{1}{4}$- to $\frac{1}{2}$-million population range experienced any absolute declines between 1950 and 1960—managerial inefficiency and increasing costs of public services lead to diseconomies. Neutze[53] presents some data that weakly support this: the percentage of an Australian city's total expenditure in 1957 that was spent on administration increased as the city was increased in steps of 25,000 as follows: 9.9 per cent for cities of less than 25,000 people; 7.8 per cent for the 25,000 to 50,000 range; then 7.4 per cent, 6.5 per cent, 6.0 per cent, and 8.6 per cent. The latter figure was for Sydney, the only city over 150,000 in 1957. Assuming that the 8.6 per cent is representative despite the sample of one, and that Australia is also representative, then cities in the 125,000 to 150,000 range may have the greatest efficiency. * But efficiency as a criterion can be traded against the criterion of creative vitality. In too small a city, while very efficient, the probability of an entrepreneurial genius or job-creator arising and staying in the city may be too low for new ideas, new jobs, and exciting new projects to maintain a high morale. According to deSolla Price,† there is persuasive historical evidence that, within a factor of 2, eminence occurs about once in a thousand people, genius about once per million. Allowing for a dozen eminent candidates from which to choose, city size should be no less than 10,000 for the emergence of eminent leadership needed for self-government.

§ 4.3 GEOGRAPHIC AND TECHNOLOGICAL CRITERIA

Historically, cities were located at break-points or key nodes of a transportation net. This should be of less importance in planning future new towns. The design of transportation nets, such as jet routes and pipelines, could follow rather than precede the building of new towns. Transportation speeds and efficiencies may be approaching natural limits. But there are still many technological options in transportation systems for greatly increasing the fraction of the country in which it is cost-effective to locate cities. It is not that technology removes prior constraints, such as proximity of water supply, navigable waterways, etc., but replaces the old constraints by new ones, which, generally, give the designer more options.

More important, however, is the trend toward greater relative concern with communication and control than with energy and matter.[26] Concentrated population density distributions must provide not only for the production, circulation, and consumption of material goods, but also of energy, and this has implications for energy or power (e.g., electricity, heat) networks. But the design of these can also follow the design of a network of new cities. There are even fewer of the above natural constraints on these than there are on the design of material flow nets. Most important are communication and control networks which are, as yet, most free of constraints.

By the end of this century, we might expect the economic base for half the new towns to be in the (tertiary) knowledge industry. As we shift from primary (e.g., mining, agriculture) through secondary (e.g., manufacturing)

---

* Everett (private communication) suggests that different styles of management are characterized by different functional shapes (all inverted bell shapes) relating the fraction of city expenditures on administration as a function of population. The minimum may be at a lower population level for one style than for another. Yet the larger city has the greater chance for spawning a manager with the most cost-effective style.

† Private communication, Dec. 29, 1970.

to tertiary (e.g., services) industries, we are now witnessing a rapid growth among the services toward those having to do with information processing. By 2000, half of our GNP is expected to be in the knowledge industry: education, computer applications, automatic control systems, entertainment, etc.[47] While traditional tertiary industries[27] were capital-extensive, these will become capital-intensive. What does this imply for settlement patterns? Whereas operatives during the industrial revolution had to be physically present in a materially based factory, this is no longer the case for automated plants that can be remotely controlled. Indeed, it is desirable to keep men and machines apart except at special "symbiotically designed" interfaces. Tele-transport, tele-control, and multi-media tele-transmission channels should be considered in planning new cities. The trend is toward poly-morphic computer networks with a hierarchy of stores, from a few very large, slow (10^{12} bits or more) semi-centralized ones to numerous widely dispersed smaller but fast stores, connected through a variety of selector channels to numerous control units, processors, and a wide spectrum of terminals, ranging from very costly sophisticated ones to ubiquitous ones like a tele-phone handset. Though future organizations could become primarily a subnetwork within a larger net rather than a set of physical plants shared by employees, this is not likely for deeper reasons discussed in the next section.

A basic tradeoff appears here. The criterion of using an expensive com-munications/control system in a most cost-effective way involves balancing idleness and congestion of key components. Only recently, with time-sharing, has the value of the user's time been drawn into the total systems analysis. Still, there are those who want their own "private" system over which they have complete control; for example, each white-collar worker may wish office furniture and equipment such as a telephone extension even though he uses it very little. Fuller utilization of terminals and perhaps more expensive units are gained at the expense of convenience to each user.

In central place theory,[4,5,14,15,55] the basic criterion is to minimize the effort by consumers in visiting a marketplace regularly. Less frequent, longer trips in which the shopper batches many activities are presumed to be most cost-effective for him. This assumption implies that as many services as the visiting shopper might wish to utilize in one trip should be clustered together, making each conveniently accessible to the other. In an important sense, a shopper batches at the expense of satisfying his needs immediately after he recognizes them. For example, in the classical (Christaller's) formulation, a farmer needing a fuse would be willing to travel as far as the nearest "town" (pop. of 1,500, fifty kinds of business, 100 establishments) up to 8 miles because he could not get it in the nearer "village" or "hamlet"; he would not just stop what he is doing to get the fuse, but combine this with other needs, for, say, banking and dry cleaning, into his weekly trip to town.* How much more convenient it would be if he could call and get delivery within an hour. While it may not be cost-effective to have a distributed system of hardware depots for phone-order teleporting automated delivery, this is more feasible for stored information.

Two necessary conditions for the observed hierarchical structure of central places are: (1) The market area for a good or service supplied by a supplier located at a point is bounded from above, because people must travel to the point and will not spend more than a certain time doing so (Doxiadis says 10 minutes).[20] (2) It is bounded from below to provide enough buyers enabling the supplier to make a profit.

In the knowledge industry (e.g., entertainment, education, etc.), it might seem that sizable markets could extend over wide areas, ranging far from the locus at which the item is produced or "broadcast." Consumers need not travel to the point of delivery. Hence there need be no upper limit on the market area. Why then should services be centralized at a point to service a surrounding region? Why should anyone remain in the hinterland, batching his needs for servicing by larger central places rather than live there in the first place?

The "areas" provide a service for the "points" in return for the services to the areas emanating from the points. Areas are sources or reservoirs of raw materials (ores, wood fibers), life-support materials (water, oxygen, fruits and vegetables, grazing lands, fish), energy (lakes act as thermostats), and require custodians to some degree. To provide a person with 3,200 calories a day—the average American use—for one year takes $\frac{1}{2}$ acre if it were all bread, 2 if it were all milk, and 10 if it were all beef. †[42] The dramatic increase in the number of acres that can be managed by one area custodian with automation is well-known. Thus the total proportion of man-hours spent on *work* in areas rather than at points should be decreasing. The proportion spent on *play* may be increasing. But the residential density distribution should show increasing concentration in urban centers.

§ 4.4 OTHER CRITERIA

A plausible criterion is that each resident minimize the total time elapsed from the first experience of a "problem-state" to the first experience of

---

* Of course, his weekly "shopping spree" serves an important mental health function and means of social contact, communication. The farmer may go, even if he has no business in town, simply to stroll, mix, "celebrate."

† The possibility of eventually manufacturing food, synthetic fibers, and construction materials through use of nuclear fusion reactors further supports belief in decreased dependence on areas and decreased demand for area custodians, up to limits imposed by basic ecological cycles.

satisfaction. By a problem-state, I mean a state in which a challenging *task* or *opportunity* presents itself. A fuse blows, and the resident experiences the need for a new fuse. He may not find it convenient to batch buying a fuse with other purchases in his next trip to town. Or, he meets an acquaintance on the street corner, who, he discovers, has just like himself wanted to buy a $30,000 boat but had only $15,000 for this purpose. On a street corner with only 10 man-hours per year, he could hardly expect such a fortuitous encounter. The opportunity to purchase a boat jointly with an acquaintance is also a problem-state.

The desire to minimize total response time would cause people to live in physical proximity to one another. Two primary needs, sex and child-rearing, which are functions of the family in most of our present culture, imply that members of the nuclear family live within the same 500 to 5,000 square feet. This dwelling *area* has "mobility" in the sense that many families move from one dwelling to another while the family's dwelling area stays constant or increases.

An amusing exercise is to apply a variant of Equation (4) to estimate the "optimum" number of United States families from the cost-effectiveness viewpoint. We have proved that if the locations of two people anywhere in a D × D square are independent and uniformly distributed over the square, then the average horizontal distance between them is D/3. Similarly for the average distance in the perpendicular direction. Suppose that, on the average, 2D/3 miles need to be traveled for the two to meet at v = 3 mi./hr. The optimal number of "centers"—each family member of a family—to cope with about $\ell = 1,500$ interactions/month is given by

$$n = \left(\frac{Pc\ell A}{3Kv}\right)^{2/3} \tag{8}$$

where P is the total United States population in nuclear families, say 150 million, c is the value, say $3/hr. of a family member's time, and K is that value in $/mo., while A is the United States area, about 3.6 million sq. mi. Thus

$$n \doteq \left(\frac{150 \times 10^6 \times 3 \times 1,500 \sqrt{3.6 \times 10^6}}{3 \times 500 \times 3}\right)^{2/3} \doteq 41 \times 10^6 \text{ families}$$

implying about $150/41 \doteq 3.6$ members per family.

Included in the 500 to 5,000 sq. ft. of dwelling space for the nuclear family are at least 40 to 100 sq. ft. to ensure the privacy of each member, what Chermayeff-Alexander[10] consider the lowest level in the urban hierarchy of spaces. Note the correspondence with our level 0 of Figure 2. Though the analogy is tenuous, there is some evidence from experiments with overcrowding among rats that when density exceeds a certain limit, the apparent "information overload" has dramatic and negative social consequences, such as vast rise in infant mortality rate due to neglect, among the rats.[8] The *option* of *both* privacy and access to other family members is most important. The private dwelling area, like the family dwelling, also has mobility.

Clearly, minimizing total response time for such needs (problem-states) as sex and child-rearing, also requires that the average time for one family member to reach another, $\sqrt{a}/3v$ hr., where a is the family dwelling area, should be minimum (less than 10 min.) but not so small as to cause overcrowding or no option for privacy. But minimizing response time for interaction with nuclear family members does not necessarily also minimize response time for interaction with friends, neighbors, co-workers, playmates. Indeed, there may be major tradeoffs, and an overriding principle which orders the various optimization criteria by priorities becomes predominant.

5. CITIES AS CENTERS OF CULTURE AND THE QUALITY OF LIFE

One might think that as various technologies soar to their natural limits of capacity in the next two decades, the need for people to "huddle" would decrease. Quite the contrary may occur. Are there functions which could not, *in principle*, be performed by remote communication? There are many reasons for the necessity of face-to-face rather than telemedia contact (no matter how sophisticated or with what fidelity tele-phone, tele-vision, tele-touch, and tele-smell could simulate a reproduction of a remote correspondent) other than sex and child-rearing at the family level. Team play (e.g., football), parties, and intellectual cross-fertilization by two "minds at work" (despite the impressive promises of the on-line intellectual community at MIT[56] and Stanford[22]) appear to necessitate face-to-face contact. Indeed, the more certain kinds of contacts and transactions can be effected remotely, the greater the importance of the essential face-to-face contacts. For example, the more we use our options of enjoying concerts, via records and the home radio-TV, the more we also seem to need mingling with other concert-goers at a live performance. Or, the more we watch sports on TV, the more we turn out in the cold at a huge stadium to feel part of a colorful, traditional sports crowd that we can join in cheering; and the more often, easily, and conveniently we can reach our co-workers, subordinates, or superiors by telephone or mail, the more we seem to want to set up committees or staff meetings, seminars, etc. Professors, scientists, and scholars spend more time away from their home base than in previous times, despite the latest innovations in information processing and communications technology. Finally, despite—or because of—our ability to widely extend our social contact choices by telemedia, an empty sidewalk or street corner, an empty store, or lack of parties epitomizes loneliness.

There are far deeper and important criteria for "huddling" than mini-mizing the total response time of *specialized* service facilities. These may be the main reasons why people flock together in cities. Let us examine them further with a view to connecting them with population density distribution over space.

The most important reason for face-to-face contact is the experiencing of I-Thou relations.[6] Man can in principle represent his environment, by forming models and theories, so that he can take increasingly effective actions, perhaps even without limit. This means that, with the passing of decades and centuries, he can recognize and cope with an increasing variety of problem-states. By a problem-state I mean a recognized task or opportunity for action likely to result in improved quality of life that was not thought of before, as explicated elsewhere.[38] Many of the problems requiring just one problem-solver have been solved, and future problem-states are those requiring cooperative (i.e., social) problem-solving.

The growth of the sciences, particularly modern Big Science,[60] is the result of cooperative problem-solving, via social enterprise. So are technological developments such as space travel and, of greater relevance to new city planning, nuclear fusion reactors, desalinization, rigid polyurethane foam as new building material. Moreover, our key problems of how to design and manage the complex institutions necessary for modern health and governmental services, for example, are almost entirely organizational, requiring cooperative problem-solving. In coping with mental health problems, current trends are toward dealing with communities rather than individuals, providing an example of team problem-solving of social problems. Perhaps, the well-planned city contains the seeds of a cure for its own malaise.

In certain species, if the individuals are too far apart, the low likelihood of mating threatens species survival. Family-organized species such as lions and men are safe in this regard. But in modern man, survival and further growth of accumulated *culture* are equally essential for the survival of *cultured man*. Let us view social culture as a level of advancement in civilization, as a state characterized by relative progress in the arts due to a refinement of taste, in science due to understanding, and in statecraft due to "wisdom." The social process for the transmission of culture is education, in its broadest sense. This necessitates face-to-face contact. "Only he can educate," said Martin Buber,[7] "who stands in the eternal presence; he educates by leading them into it." Essential to this process is the creation of an I-Thou relation, of an *awareness* by a person in the role of teacher that the person in the role of learner is like himself for his awareness. Higher level cooperative problem-solving necessitates such I-Thou relations, such awareness on the part of each team member about his partners being like himself in their ability to use their awareness of their own abilities, including the ability to think. Though a telemedia-transmitted reproduction of a remotely located partner might be extremely realistic, it is unlikely to confuse the recipient's *awareness,* that he confronts a reproduction versus his belief (mistakenly) that he is face-to-face with the original; at the same time, too, the remotely located partner would also have to mistakenly believe that he is face-to-face with his "viewer." Considerable experience and controlled experimentation with educational innovations have led to the conclusion that, despite the optimism and considerable progress of enthusiasts for computer-aided instruction,[39,44] face-to-face contact is essential for genuine education and the transmission of culture.

Still another reason for the importance of face-to-face contacts is the inconvenience and non-spontaneity of having to *schedule* remote telemedia contacts. Like batching, this decreases total response time between awareness of a problem-state and its partial resolution through contacts.

Education, in the deep and broad sense intended above, is not necessarily synonymous with schooling.[32] Nonetheless, schools do provide for face-to-face contact. After the nuclear family, the school is a large unit in a hierarchy, which shares with the family the function of socializing and educating the young. Children travel to and from school, and should not have to spend more than 10 minutes per trip, whether by bicycle, foot or other means. What is the optimum size of a school district? If we use our previous estimate for v, 3 mi./hr., then the distance to the school should not exceed $\frac{3}{6} = \frac{1}{2}$ mi; assuming hexagonal (space-filling) districts (following Christaller), this is an area of about $\frac{3}{8}$ sq. mi. At a density of 8,000 people/sq. mi., a school district comprises about 3,000 people, with about 500 students (from kindergarten to high school) per school. This is about the size of what we called a precinct, level 3, in Figure 2.

Between the 2- to 7-member nuclear family and the 3,000-people school district might be one, perhaps two units of urban aggregation. Let us assume just one and call it a "community,"* as in Figure 2. The head of a nuclear family has responsibility, matched by authority, to provide for basic needs of food, shelter, sex, and affection. The head of a community, by contrast, has responsibility for solving only one class of several more specialized classes of problems: work, play, worship. A family is governed by rules, but a community is governed by the rudiments of law, by a constitution. If the pairs in a family have 1,500 interactions per month with such short response times as necessitate face-to-face contact, the members of a community need to meet less frequently and can schedule their meetings. The leader of a community unit, like any manager, cannot keep up with and coordinate the activities of many more than ten people, varying from two to fifteen. The number of players in a sports team, soldiers in a squad, members in

---

* "Quorum" might be a better name for the smallest community.

the smallest religious congregation, employees in a work group or department, or members in a committee is around ten. Thus, there may be ten families in the smallest community, or about forty people.

Suppose each family representative in a community belongs to seven groups (e.g., a work group, a play group, a religious group, a political group, and three social circles). Suppose these seven groups are not so unconnected as to comprise $70 - 7 = 63$ different acquaintances, nor so cliquish as to comprise only ten people. If belonging to two groups to which a given person P belongs were statistically independent events, then the expected number of people (common acquaintances of P) in both of two quorums containing P would be $100/n$, where n is the size of the population from which the quorum members are drawn. Independence is not a plausible assumption, because knowledge that P is in social circle C, for example, would make it more probable that P is also in a certain other social circle C' which overlaps with C than the knowledge that P is not in C. Also, if n is too large, then P has many diverse contacts in his group, with each of whom there is a low frequency of contact, perhaps too low for sufficient reinforcement of the relation to occur; if n is too small, even if independence holds, P is in too narrow a clique, contacting the same few people over and over, and perhaps missing many new ideas and viewpoints that a broader circle of acquaintances could bring.

Communities need meeting places that are within 10 minutes of commuting time from the members' residences. Offices, cafés, parks, bars, golf courses, sports courts, sanctuaries (chapels), plazas, and key street corners[33] (sidewalk spots) could be good meeting places. Since community meetings are scheduled, the 10 minutes is not total response time, and central place theory should apply. This would lead to a hierarchy of such central places.

After the meeting place would come sites for facilities of community services, such as police, fire fighting, first aid, mail, and utilities. Let us call them *community* centers serving a larger region.

The precinct, which we discussed before as a school district of 3,000, would also provide schools, hospitals, markets, theaters, courts, and specialty shops of a quality that could not be supported by a smaller region. At an urban population concentration 50,000, which occupies about 4 sq. mi., or a 2 by 2-mi. square, we could afford to build and maintain public circulatory networks, libraries, power plants, larger parks and lakes, regional information processing and communication centers.

Why does a person P wish to live in a city? If it is to improve some quantity q(P) which we shall call the quality of his life, according to his personal value judgments, then we can still assume that three factors specify q(P):

1. The range of choices among goods and services pertaining to safety, health, convenience, economy, and amenities[9] that help him cope effectively and efficiently in a variety of problem-states.

2. A partial ordering of this set of options that reflects priorities of survival value, of humanism, of culture.

3. An algorithm enabling P to choose "wisely" among these options in different problem-states; this means selecting that good or service which maximizes his enjoyment-effort ratio subject to constraints which ensure that the potential for enjoyment by contemporary or future others does not fall below certain limits. *

Clearly, q(P) depends on the level of culture in P's time and the extent of his exposure to that culture through "education" in the sense of our discussion. Residence in a city can optimize this exposure by maximizing the likelihood of face-to-face contacts leading to I-Thou relations. This likelihood increases with the population up to a point, beyond which social fragmentation sets in. When fragmentation leads to suburban growth instead of new towns in the central place hierarchy or something at least equivalent,[3,33] the result may be further social disintegration evidenced by rising crime rates and other signs of physical and mental deterioration. Over half the residents of large cities consider crime their chief urban problem.†
While studies on the incidence of psychiatric disorder in the population at large show no correlation with the size of a city—it is about 20 per cent in rural and urban regions alike[10,21,66]—they have established a strong connection with the degree of social integration of a community.

6. CONCLUSIONS

In planning new cities, using a simple criterion to specify an optimal eventual population limit does not appear possible or necessary. Different criteria for optimizing or bounding city size yield different results. Optimizing according to one criterion can cause very poor performance according to another criterion. Which criteria predominate and which are limiting factors depend on the action taken. These in turn depend on the kind of decision-making citizens who are attracted to the new city.

Who the first settlers of a new city will be is therefore the most important determinant of its future growth and the quality of life it offers. They will create the climate which attracts later settlers, and their combined decisions will determine criteria for optimum size and quality. An even more important determinant than the initial settlers is the learning process accompanying the city's growth, by which new settlement and behavior emerge that may eventually lead to a size and quality independent of the initial settlers.

---

* As discussed previously, such attempts at explication are incomplete. Left out are the feeling or knowing that this city is pleasant but this one isn't, though we cannot make "why" precise.

† From *Inner City Problems: The View from the Inside*, Center for Urban Studies, University of Michigan, Dearborn, 1968.

Cultural levels are such emergent, systemic properties of a growing city which make cities both the sources and loci of advancing civilization.

Insofar, then, as there is an overriding criterion governing new city planning, it is to optimize the advance of social culture by education toward wisdom.[46] This implies optimizing the chances for contacts[18] leading to I-Thou relations among individuals. The optimum growth rate of a new city is then such that the rate of increase in quality of life (ability to recognize and cope with problem-states by wise utilization of a wide range of cooperative problem-solving services) is not less than the rate at which such problems increase. This implies providing such services (and goods) as maximize total benefit-cost figures, where "total" means stress on satisfying the complete need of the service's users while yet considering the motives and costs of the service provider. The total response time between the user's first awareness of need for service and delivery of a satisfactory response should be minimized, and the inconvenience to the user of scheduling or batching his use of centralized services should be taken into account. This implies effective, responsible decentralization. For governmental services, it means decision-making close to the need and the action, participatory democracy, and somewhat centralized intelligence.

More concretely, for a front-end investment in (1) acquisition of a site at which housing, jobs, and access are feasible, and (2) the development of utility systems, roads, schools, libraries, public, commercial, and communication facilities to have short-term profitability, it is necessary to create a cultural environment above a certain level at the outset. There may be a level of investment, or rather a policy of investments over time, for which the returns per dollar are maximum. This appears to be a researchable question, answers to which may be most useful for new town planning.

The best course is to develop what we have called "learning plans," by in vivo experimentation with, not on, settlers of an innovative new town and by building a theoretical framework at the same time.

APPENDIX:
SUGGESTIONS FOR NEW TOWN PLANNING

1. Plan at least one city with primary economic base in the knowledge industry. Possible product service: a novel kind of national news service, exported to entire nation. Receipts from these and associated exports should be over half the city's total production. Products include a variety of telemedia terminals, channels, controllers, stores. Services include: synthesis and repackaging of information to meet needs of decision-makers, beyond and in addition to reporting and interpreting news, high-level question-answering (now partly done by "Dear ——" columns, but intended to bring to bear all resources of an up-to-the-day information center); editorial feedback beyond letters to editor, more like continual opinion polls, referenda; "courses" and other exposure to culture; matching people.

2. Include cultural amenities at the very start to attract rapid in-migration of critical-size initial settler community. This should have the flavor of a special pioneer community, such as the Peace Corps. The example of how "rock music" caused the instantaneous assemblage of a city-sized community at Woodstock may have something to teach.

3. Grow rapidly, with (a) the population at any time large enough to divert, and keep enough businesses and entrepreneurs from competitive cities but not so big as to risk social disintegration, instability; (b) the rate of population increase being fast enough to keep investors happy but not so fast that the rate at which problems arise outstrips the rate at which the city's problem-solving capacity is growing.

4. Introduce automation to decrease rather than increase variance in income distribution.

5. Plan for expansion in all three dimensions. Consider vertical under-shafts that can be deepened if lower subterranean layers of circulatory networks must be added. Have all non-human circulation underground except air and water travel. Conceivably jet runways could be partially underground too, to confine and control that source of air pollution. Have VTOL and helicopter pads on inner-city rooftops.

6. Plan all construction for finite life, using materials that can be recycled, e.g., polyurethane. The research, development, and manufacturing of these materials plus the service of material circulation and dwelling assembly should be a local industry, intended increasingly for export.

7. Within 3 to 7 years, try to have at least ninety kinds of business, spread over 350 establishments, mostly related to the initial knowledge industry (e.g., electronics, optics, banking, theaters, etc.), and characterized by experimentation with new technologies, organizational innovations, creative leadership. Try to attract within that period an initial settler population of about 20,000 with a large proportion of intelligent, energetic young people and a smaller fraction of retired professionals to serve as consultants. Aim for an annual sales volume of about $25 million, and a cumulative capital investment of about $100 million over that 3- to 7-year period. Consider locating the city in the West, far from other cities, and not as a central place providing services to a surrounding region.

8. Make it primarily a test vehicle for innovations from which we can add to knowledge that can be applied more generally, like the Welfare Island project. It would differ in that it is not a town-in-town, perhaps not even a satellite, but a city based in the knowledge industry aiming for economic and political autonomy. Assume that it will attract a young, transient population. Perhaps consider it part of a chain of "college" or "vanguard" cities, with Vanguard City I populated by undergraduates, Vanguard II by another four-year transient population, etc.

REFERENCES

1. D. H. K. Amiran and A. Sachar, *Development Towns in Israel*. Report from the Hebrew University, Jerusalem, 1970.

2. G. O. Barney, "Understanding Urban Dynamics" (clarified exposition of J. Forrester's *Urban Dynamics and Synthesis of Critiques*). Urban Dynamics Series Working Paper D-1480, MIT, Cambridge, November, 1970.

3. B. J. L. Berry, "Research Frontiers in Urban Geography," in P. M. Hauser and L. F. Schnore (eds.), *The Study of Urbanization*, pp. 403–430.

4. B. J. L. Berry, *Geography of Market Centers and Retail Districts* (Englewood Cliffs, N.J.: Prentice-Hall, 1967).

5. B. J. L. Berry and F. E. Horton, *Geographic Perspectives on Urban Systems* (Englewood Cliffs, N.J.: Prentice-Hall, 1967).

6. Martin Buber, *I and Thou* (New York: Scribner, 1958).

7. Martin Buber, *A Believing Humanism* (New York: Simon & Schuster, 1969), p. 101.

8. J. B. Calhoun, "Population Density and Social Pathology," *Scientific American,* February, 1962.

9. F. S. Chapin, *Urban Land Use Planning* (Urbana: University of Illinois Press, 1965), p. 25.

10. S. Chermayeff and C. Alexander, *Community and Privacy* (Garden City, N.Y.: Doubleday, 1965).

11. B. Chinitz, "New York: A Metropolitan Region," *Scientific American,* September, 1965, p. 134.

12. A. E. Cochran, *M.E.T.R.O.—Apex: A General Description*. Report of Environmental Simulation Lab, University of Michigan, Ann Arbor, 1970.

13. J. P. Crecine, *A Dynamic Model of Urban Structure*, Rand Report P-3803, March, 1968.

14. M. F. Dacey, "A Probability Model for Central Place Locations," *Annals Association of American Geographers,* 56, No. 4 (December, 1966), pp. 550–568.

15. M. F. Dacey, "The Geometry of Central Place Theory," *Geografiska Annalen,* 47 B (1965), pp. 111–124.

16. R. A. Dahl, "The City in the Future of Democracy," *The American Political Science Review,* 61, 4 (December, 1967), pp. 953–970.

17. E. S. Deevey, "General and Urban Ecology," in L. J. Duhl (ed.), *The Urban Condition* (New York: Basic Books, 1963), pp. 20–32.

18. K. W. Deutsch, "On Social Communication and the Metropolis," in L. Rodwin (ed.), *The Future Metropolis* (New York: George Braziller, 1961), pp. 129–143.

19. A. Downs, "Economic Investment in Alternate Forms of Urban Growth"; also "Creating the Institutional Framework for Encouraging New Cities," in *Regional New Towns* (Detroit: Metropolitan Fund, 1970), pp. 44–51, 98–104.

20. C. A. Doxiadis, "Ekistics, the Science of Human Settlements," *Science,* 170, No. 3956 (October 23, 1970), pp. 393–404.

21. L. J. Duhl, ed., *The Urban Condition* (New York: Basic Books, 1963).

22. D. C. Engelbart, *Study for the Development of Human Intellect Augmentation Techniques* (Menlo Park, California: SRI Report, February, 1969).

23. E. G. Ericksen, *Urban Behavior* (New York: Macmillan, 1954).

24. K. A. Fox, "Population Redistribution among Functional Economic Areas," unpublished paper presented at AAAS Symposium, December 30, 1970.

25. R. M. Gladstone, "Does Building a City Make Economic Sense?" *The Appraisal Journal,* July, 1966.

26. G. Hardin, *Science, Society and Conflict* (Readings from *Scientific American*) (San Francisco: Freeman, 1969), p. 86.

27. P. Harrison, "Canberra—Case Notes on a New Town," *Planning 1965,* p. 270.

28. P. M. Hauser and L. F. Schnore, *The Study of Urbanization* (New York: Wiley, 1967), pp. 5–9.

29. C. Hockett and R. Ascher, "The Human Revolution," in P. Shepard and D. McKinley, *The Subversive Science: Essays Toward an Ecology of Man* (Boston: Houghton Mifflin, 1969), p. 19.

30. A. Hormann, *Planning by Man-Machine Synergism,* SP-3484. SDC Report, 2500 Colorado Avenue, Santa Monica, California, March 31, 1970.

31. J. C. Hudson, "Diffusion in a Central Place System," *Geographical Analysis,* January, 1969, pp. 45–58.

32. I. Illich, *Celebration of Awareness* (Garden City, N.Y.: Doubleday, 1970).

33. J. Jacobs, *The Death and Life of Great American Cities* (New York: Random House, 1961).

34. J. Jacobs, *The Economy of Cities* (New York: Random House, 1969).

35. B. L. Johnson, "The Economics of New Innovative Cities in the Arid West," plus private communication, December 30, 1970. Paper presented at the AAAS Symposium, December 30, 1970.

36. L. Johnson, Statement in *Regional New Towns* (Detroit: Metropolitan Funds, 1970), p. 124.

37. M. Kochen and K. W. Deutsch, "Toward a Rational Theory of Decentralization," *American Political Science Review,* September, 1969.

38. M. Kochen, *Cognitive Learning Processes* (Edinburgh Univ. Press, 1970).

39. M. Kochen, "Information Science and Computer Aids in Education," *Proceedings of the Sixth Annual National Colloquium on Information Retrieval,* Medical Documentation Service, Philadelphia, 1969.

40. M. Kochen, "Stability in the Growth of Knowledge," *Journal of the American Society of Information Science,* July, 1969. See also Kochen (ed.), *The Growth of Knowledge* (New York: Wiley, 1967).

41. Department of Housing and Urban Development, *New Communities: A Bibliography* (Washington, D.C., December, 1969).

42. H. H. Landsberg, *Natural Resources for U.S. Growth* (Baltimore: Johns Hopkins Paperbacks, 1964), p. 32.

43. C. Levin, "Determinants of Size and Spatial Form of Urban Area," *Papers of Regional Science Association, 22* (Budapest, 1968), pp. 7–28.

44. W. K. Linvil, Report on Workshop on "Urban-Regional Problems: New Communities for the Year 2000." International IEEE Convention, March 26,

1970, (particularly remarks by D. Alpert on the PLATO System for automated instruction at the University of Illinois for its impact on the urban-regional problem).

45. R. Llewelyn-Davies et al., "New Cities—A British Example: Milton Keynes," *Regional New Towns* (Detroit: Metropolitan Fund, 1970), pp. 108–113.

46. I. S. Lowry, *Seven Models of Urban Development: A Structural Comparison,* Rand Report P-3673, September, 1967.

47. F. Machlup, *The Production and Distribution of Knowledge in the U.S.* (Princeton, N.J.: Princeton University Press, 1962).

48. R. E. McCabe, "New York State Role in Metropolitan and New Town Development," *Regional New Towns* (Detroit: Metropolitan Fund, 1970), pp. 72–74.

49. R. L. Meier, private communication. See also *Communications Theory of Urban Growth* (Cambridge, Mass: MIT Press, 1962).

50. Metropolitan Fund of Detroit (from R. Reynolds, *Ann Arbor News,* Sunday, December 6, 1970, p. 47, col. 2).

51. M. Minsky, "Steps Toward Artificial Intelligence," *Proceedings Institute of Radio Engineers* 49 (1961), pp. 8–30.

52. P. A. Morrison, "Implications of Migration Histories for Moral Design." RAND Report P-4342, April, 1970; also "Urban Growth, New Cities and 'The Population Problem,'" Rand Report P-4515-1, December, 1970.

53. G. M. Neutze, *Economic Policy and the Size of Cities* (Canberra: Australian National University, 1965).

54. S. Nordbeck, "The Law of Allometric Growth," in discussion paper no. 7, Michigan Inter-University Community of Mathematical Geographers, June, 1965.

55. J. D. Nystuen and M. F. Dacey, "A Graph Theory Interpretation of Nodal Regions," *Papers and Proceedings Regional Science Association,* 7 (1961), pp. 29–42.

56. C. F. J. Overhage and R. J. Harman, "The On-Line Intellectual Community and the Information Transfer System at MIT in 1975," in M. Kochen (ed.), *The Growth of Knowledge* (New York: Wiley, 1967), p. 77.

57. A. H. Pascal (ed.), *Contributions to the Analysis of Urban Problems,* Rand Report P-3868, August, 1968.

58. J. Platt, "What We Must Do," *Science,* 166 (November, 1969), pp. 1115–1121 (also, private communication).

59. J. Platt, "How Men Can Shape Their Future," *Futures Magazine,* March, 1971.

60. Derek De Solla Price, *Little Science, Big Science* (New York: Columbia University Press, 1963).

61. L. Rodwin, "Ciudad Guyana: A New City," *Scientific American,* September, 1965, p. 122.

62. W. G. Rouse, "Significant Principles Guiding the Planning and Development of Columbia," *Regional New Towns* (Detroit: Metropolitan Fund, 1970), p. 78.

63. W. G. Rouse, "Practical Aspects of New Town Development," *Regional New Towns* (Detroit: Metropolitan Fund, 1970), pp. 114–116.

64. S. F. Singer, "Reducing the Environmental Impact of Population Growth," *Science,* 170 (1970), p. 223.

65. A. Spilhaus, "The Experimental City," *Science,* 159, no. 3816 (February 16, 1968), pp. 710–715.

66. L. Srole, et al., *Mental Health in the Metropolis* (New York: McGraw-Hill, 1962). (The startling results are that in a random sample of midtown Manhattan residents who were examined for psychiatric disorders by contemporary methods, only about 20 per cent are diagnosed "well," while about 20 per cent are considered to be "impaired," the remaining 60 per cent ranging from "mild to moderate symptom formation." Leighton has found this 20 per cent incidence of psychiatric disorder to be culture-independent and to increase even more in socially disintegrating communities.)

67. G. Taylor, *The Doomsday Book* (London: World Publishers, 1970).

68. W. Thompson, *Preface to Urban Economics* (Baltimore: Johns Hopkins Paperbacks, 1965), p. 24.

69. R. White, "Economic Assessment of Large-scale Projects," *The Appraisal Journal,* January, 1969, p. 360.

70. L. L. Whyte, *Hierarchical Structures* (New York: American Elsevier, 1969), p. 208.

71. A. Wolman, "The Metabolism of Cities," *Scientific American,* September, 1965, p. 180. (It takes 1,200 lb./day to supply each citizen with water, 4 lb./day of food, and 20 lb. of fuel. This totals 1,224 lb., which we take to be about 10^3. Each person generates 1,000 lb. of sewage [suspended solids], 4 lb of solid refuse, and about 2 lb. of air pollutants, which we neglect.)

FOR FURTHER READING

Berry, B. J. L. "The Geography of the U.S. in the Year 2000," *Ekistics* 29, no. 174 (May, 1970), p. 339.

Duncan, Otis Dudley. "Social Organization and the Ecosystem," in Robert E. L. Faris, ed., *Handbook of Modern Sociology.* Chicago: Rand McNally & Co., 1964, pp. 36–82.

Duncan, Otis Dudley, Scott, W. R., Lieberson, S., Duncan, Beverly, and Winsborough, H. H. *Metropolis and Region.* Baltimore: Johns Hopkins Press, 1960.

Myerson, Martin, ed. *The Conscience of the City.* New York: George Braziller, Inc., 1970, 397 pages.

Morrill, Richard L. *The Spatial Organization of Society.* Belmont, Calif.: Wadsworth Publishing Co., 1970.

Murphy, Raymond. *The American City: An Urban Geography.* New York: McGraw-Hill, 1966.

Perloff, Harvey S., and Wingo, Lowdon, Jr., eds. *Issues in Urban Economics* (Based on a paper presented at a Conference, Baltimore; published for resources for the future). Baltimore. Johns Hopkins Press, 1968, 668 pages.

Sjoberg, Gideon. *The Pre-Industrial City: Past and Present.* New York: Free Press, 1965.

Troxel, Charles Emery. *Economics of Transport.* New York: Rinehart, 1955.

APPENDIX F

Governmental Policies and Optimum Population Levels: Outline for a Study

S. Fred Singer

The purpose of the study is to explore different approaches and to develop a methodology which will allow a calculation of "optimum levels of population." The discussion will be specialized to the United States, but the methodology should be broad enough to handle other countries, including less-developed countries. The study will be based on economics, but with major inputs from the areas of technology, natural resources management, environmental effects, and demography.

The general approach will be to develop an *index for quality of life* (IQL) and to maximize this index as a function of level and distribution of population. The technique consists of a reshuffling of national income accounts so as to be able to go from the Gross National Product (GNP) to IQL, plus a careful discussion of what is and what is not to be included. The second part of the study consists of a projection of IQL as population level increases and as population distribution changes, under the assumption of various technologies, particularly as these relate to water use and the consumption of minerals, energy, and other natural resources. One would expect that as economic growth continues, an increasing fraction of expenditures would be for the diseconomies produced by population growth.

This study should be useful by providing a rational base for governmental policies regarding population, both in the United States and abroad. Another application of the study is to *technology assessment,* by measuring the impact on economic well-being through the introduction of new technologies. Therefore one can gauge the necessary and desirable investments in certain new technologies.

INTRODUCTION

In recent years the question of population has moved to the center of the stage and has become also a concern of the federal government. The establishment of the National Commission on Population Growth and the American Future, in March 1970, and the passage of the Family Planning Services and Population Research Act, in December 1970, have put the government in a position where policies directly affecting the growth of population may soon come into being.

This is not to say that government policies have not affected population in the past, but usually this has been a by-product rather than a deliberate attempt to influence growth or distribution of population. Yet every government policy does have an effect, directly or indirectly, on population growth and distribution. During the last century, the policies of opening up the West made possible the large migration within the United States and also attracted many additional immigrants. In more recent years, agricultural policies and urban policies may have led to the large migration from rural areas to the cities. (In fact, the very success of our agricultural technology has led to a reduction of the agricultural working population from something like 80 per cent to our present 5 per cent.) Then there are economic policies, investment policies, and tax policies, all of which have an impact; for example, mortgage policies and special subsidies for veterans and other groups have had an effect upon the development of housing and population distribution, but also on family size and population growth.

In turn, the growth and distribution of population have important consequences. People consume resources prodigiously—or rather they transform them into wastes. Therefore, with an ever-growing population and an ever-increasing standard of living, there has come a vastly increased use of natural resources and, of course, a vastly increased level of pollution. Pollution has been particularly pronounced in urban areas. There the density of population has become so large that the additional disamenities of crowding, of traffic snarls, and of all kinds of urban problems, from drugs and crime to noise, have produced an increasing economic burden not only for the residents of the particular city but for the nation as a whole. We thus conclude that governmental policies influence population growth and distribution, but these in turn may have consequences which run counter to the intended effects. We have here a classic problem of feedback which calls for systems analysis. In order to understand and predict the effects of policies, we need to establish first an adequate data base and a model.

One of the most important questions we need to ask is what is the most desirable level and distribution of population. What is the optimum or ideal for a country like the United States? Do we want more people or less people? If we are going to set up far-reaching policies, we need to be fairly sure that the directions are really desirable. Instead we find that policies are proposed, or at least discussed, without an adequate understanding of their impact, or even without a clear definition of their goals. Most people, particularly those who live in crowded environments, would opt for not much further increase in population. Many even believe that our population should be smaller and that this would result in a better life for all of us. A few believe that we should keep on increasing. Some argue for an immediate zero population growth—ZPG—while others feel that only a slowdown is desirable. Most of these reactions are intuitive. Clearly, we would like to have some rational analyses to back up our policies.

DEFINING AN INDEX FOR QUALITY OF LIFE (IQL)

It should be clear at the outset that any quantitative result about optimum population depends on the assumptions, and especially on how one defines "optimum." A pragmatic approach is to work up a definition to which reasonable people can agree, calculate the corresponding optimum level, and then parameterize the situation by varying the definition to see how the result changes. This approach can establish just how sensitive the actual result is to the definition.*

The first step, then, is to arrive at a suitable definition for "optimum." What are the criteria for such a definition? It should be (1) acceptable; (2) unambiguous; and (3) operational, i.e., it should incorporate a method of calculation.

One definition often proposed defines optimum as the "highest quality of life for the largest percentage of population." This puts the burden on defining "quality of life," and on devising a yardstick for measuring it. In our society, where material comforts are important and contribute to what people perceive of as happiness, a loose definition might be "having as much money as possible left over after taking care of the basic necessities, and having the necessary time and opportunities for spending it in a pleasant way." It means also having the maximum range of choices for a way of

---

* It is clear that optimum is not synonymous with maximum; in fact, the optimum level should be well below the maximum sustainable population level. This is in sharp contradistinction to, say, the raising of cattle where optimum, from the rancher's point of view, means the level which will result in a maximum financial yield.

life. This definition, however, might not be acceptable to a society living a monastic kind of life.

The definition just given satisfies our criteria reasonably well. It tells you how to measure quality of life in terms of dollars by calculating the potential consumption and assigning a monetary value to free time. Specifically, then, one starts by examining the national income accounts, which aggregate the output of the nation, to see which items, and to what extent, they contribute to an index of quality of life (IQL). One includes amenities, such as leisure time, which are not counted in the GNP; one subtracts items that enter into the GNP, but are really disamenities and do not contribute to quality of life. Among the most important are pollution control costs and increased costs of distribution in crowded urban areas.*

DEPENDENCE OF IQL ON DEMOGRAPHIC PARAMETERS

Once the IQL has been defined, we can go back into the historic record, trace its variation, and analyze its dependence on demographic parameters. In general, each item which enters into the IQL will show a quite specific dependence on population distribution, income, and age. We will discuss here three specific examples within the broad general categories of goods, services, and government expenditures to illustrate the complexity of this dependence.

1. The cost of *consumer goods* depends on wages, rents, the amount of capital invested in producing the goods, and on the costs of the input material—which includes manufactured goods but also primary resource items such as minerals, energy, water, and air. (By tracing back the manufacturing steps we arrive, of course, at only primary items, including agricultural commodities.) The costs of the primary resource items depend on their level of exhaustion in the case of non-renewable resources such as fuels, and also on the costs of maintaining environmental quality.

Natural resources are limited and the capacity of the environment to absorb wastes is limited. As a consequence, the environmental costs rise not only faster than population, but faster even than the amount of pollution released to the environment, which itself is roughly proportional to the GNP. In a very rough way, therefore, one can see that the natural resource and environmental costs must increase faster than the GNP itself and thus occupy a larger and larger fraction of GNP—and of GNP per capita. Fortunately, it is rather low right now, with the environmental costs less than 1 per cent of GNP. Approximately 0.5 per cent of GNP is devoted

---

* An interesting approach, which suggests how to include interpersonal factors (such as status and love) in a definition of IQL, comes from the work of Uriel G. Foa, *Science,* 171 (1971), 345.

to municipal waste collection and disposal, and the rest to all of air and water pollution abatement. But this situation cannot be maintained, e.g., as mineral supplies become exhausted and lower grade ores have to be mined, or as the capacity for waste absorption of the air and water becomes stretched to the limit, especially since the water supply itself is finite.

It is important to understand how all of these costs change as the level of population or distribution of population changes. This requires a rather complete study for each resource area to determine the availability of the resource, the probable demands, the environmental effects produced in obtaining the resource, and the costs incurred in maintaining environmental quality. The data base for this effort has not yet been assembled. It is clearly necessary to prepare it and, if possible, publish and disseminate it widely, so as to make it available to many people who can use it. The data themselves are dispersed among several government agencies and many experts. However, we are currently assembling the information in separate chapters, each for a basic resource area. This work leans on the classic study on the adequacy of natural resources for the United States, entitled *Resources in America's Future, 1960–2000*, conducted by H. H. Landsberg, L. L. Fischman, and J. L. Fisher of Resources for the Future. Our present effort goes over similar ground, but pays particular attention to the costs of protecting environmental quality, relates the overall costs to demographic parameters, and calculates the change in IQL.

2. *Educational services* is an example of an item which does not involve the consumption of resources, does not create pollution, but is strongly determined by demographic parameters. It can also be influenced by new technology. Total national expenditures for education have been rising sharply, from 1.8 per cent of GNP in 1943 to 7.1 per cent in 1968, increasing nearly linearly with time at the rate of 0.2 per cent per year. These expenditures cannot increase indefinitely; therefore, one must carefully analyze the reasons for the increase. A large part may be due to the fact that a larger fraction of the population is now covered by educational services. Secondly, the quality and extent of education have increased. Finally, also, the efficiency may have suffered. One question to be investigated is: When will saturation be reached; i.e., when will everyone in the United States be able to obtain an adequate level of education? At that point, national educational expenditures should be reasonably predictable in terms of demographic parameters. One must also investigate the impact of new technologies which would tend to lower the costs of instruction or the preparation of educational materials. In principle, the costs per capita should diminish as the size of population grows, since this would allow spreading of the cost for the preparation of such educational material. But another alternative is likely to take its place, namely an improvement in the diversity and choice of educational and cultural experiences as population rises. In either case, there will be a rise in the IQL.

3. The final example is *space research*. Clearly the cost of exploring Mars should not depend on the level of population. Therefore, the larger the population of taxpayers, the lower the per capita cost. Other examples in this category are expenditures for scientific research, medical research, and, interestingly enough, expenditures for defense. However, each item will make a different positive or negative contribution to the IQL, which must be discussed in detail.

With these three examples we illustrate how we would go about revising the Department of Commerce–Department of Labor model of GNP projection into one of predicting IQL. We would also construct a model in which the IQL depends explicitly on three major demographic parameters: geographic distribution, income, and age.

Once the model has been developed and programmed so that it can be quickly "exercised" on a high-speed computer, it is then possible to apply various external conditions and observe their results. In the simplest case, we would let the model develop according to the demographic forecasts of the Census Bureau, which are also used by the Department of Commerce. In addition, however, one would examine specific government policies and determine their effects upon demographic parameters, or upon the costs of any of the components which go to make up the IQL (see chart on page 404). One could also examine the effects of new technologies and thereby have a quantitative tool for technology assessment. As an example, one could examine the development of a non-polluting automobile engine which might reduce environmental costs of transportation by perhaps $6 billion per year. Or one could examine the consequences of an effective desulfurization of fossil fuels which could reduce environmental costs nationwide by perhaps $2 billion per year. A breakthrough in the desalination of seawater could improve the water supply situation in the arid Southwest and make possible settlements in areas that are now without water. Clearly there is no limit to the runs that can be made once a mathematical model is developed and found to be acceptable. It might then become an important tool for testing the effects of proposed governmental and private policies before they are put into operation.

ACKNOWLEDGMENTS

This appendix, written in February 1971, is an outgrowth of the earlier symposium paper (see pages 156 to 172) which explores the environmental costs of a growing population in a preliminary way, and concludes that these costs will form an increasing fraction of the GNP. The more detailed

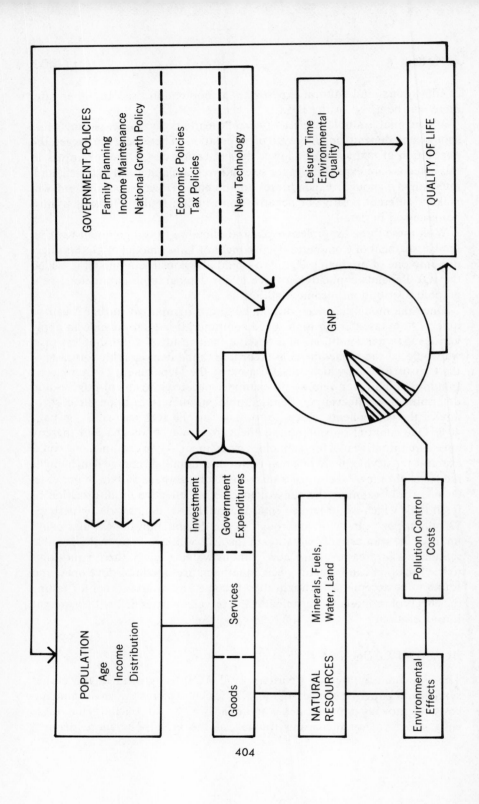

assessment of these costs was carried out in 1970 with the help and counsel of so many experts that I cannot list them individually.

I want to acknowledge the research assistance by Mrs. Barbara Burke, Mrs. Penny Brooks, and Mr. Richard Prendergast, as well as financial assistance to them by the Population Council.

FOR FURTHER READING

I am not aware of any quantitative work dealing with optimum level of population. The subject is, of course, discussed from many different points of view, mostly qualitatively, in many of the papers of the present volume. It has also been highlighted in the report of the National Goals Research Staff of the White House issued on July 4, 1970, and entitled "Towards Balanced Growth: Quantity with Quality" (pages 39–61).

The need to develop an index for quality of life was stressed throughout the Symposium and especially in the papers of Preston Cloud (page 8) and Garrett Hardin (page 260). A pioneer attempt toward a quantitative definition for a measure of economic welfare has been given by William Nordhaus and James Tobin in a report for the National Bureau of Economic Research, December, 1970.

There are many papers and books which discuss the relationship between population, natural resources, and environment. I have found the following to be helpful:

Hans H. Landsberg, *Natural Resources for U.S. Growth* (Johns Hopkins Paperbacks, 1964).
Committee on Resources and Man of the National Academy of Sciences, *Resources and Man* (W. H. Freeman and Company, 1969).
Ansley J. Coale, "Man and His Environment," *Science,* 170 (1970), 132–136.

EPILOGUE

Is There an Optimum Level of Population?*

In earlier and simpler days, this question would not have stirred up much philosophical concern. Each clan, each tribe, each nation was absorbed with survival in its fight against a hostile environment and hostile neighbors. And "optimum" meant making the population as large as possible so as to have as many kinsmen, as many workers, as many warriors as possible. "Be fruitful and multiply" says the Bible. And for good measure, Genesis grants man dominion over all beasts and over all the earth, to subjugate and exploit its resources.

Somehow this no longer rings true. Machines have taken over from human labor, and automation is gradually replacing the human brain where creativity and judgment are not needed. Wars are now fought with weapons of mass destruction, and a large population may no longer be the asset it once was. This new outlook seems to have arisen early in the Industrial Revolution. In 1848, John Stuart Mill wrote: "After a degree of density has been attained, sufficient to allow the principal benefits of combination of labour, all further increase tends in itself to mischief, as regards the average condition of the people."

But this question of "optimum" has to be looked at again—in

*This essay appeared in abridged form in the *Washington Post*, February 22, 1970.

today's terms. In the present volume this concept has been thoughtfully examined from many different points of view. And the consensus is that not only does the question make sense—but it may even be possible to develop methods to arrive at an answer. "Optimum" is defined as that condition which results in the best quality of life for the population as a whole.

That there is an optimum of some sort is intuitively obvious. Think, for example, of a city: If it is too small, then we cannot afford advanced schools, medical centers, symphony orchestras, and baseball clubs; and if the city becomes too large, then other problems arise which in very real terms lower the quality of life—traffic snarls, noise, reduced access to outdoor recreation.

But intuition is a poor way to answer such an important question. For example, many people somehow feel that the optimum has been passed. Yet when pressed on the point, they can rarely express these feelings in a quantitative manner but base them on impressions concerning local crowding, pollution, parking problems, and so on. Then there are also people—not many to be sure—who feel that we can comfortably support a much greater level of population, that the United States can feed five to ten times the number we now have, and that all of this expansion can be handled simply by better organization. Production of food is probably not a limiting factor—at least not in the United States. However, there are other factors that may be much more pertinent.

The central questions then are the following: Where is the trade-off between quantity of people and quality of life? Which of the many parameters that are important to quality of life provides a real constraint, a real hard upper limit on the level of population? It is immediately obvious that *level* of population is not the only parameter; it may not even be the major parameter. *Rate* of growth needs to be considered. *Distribution* of population may be even more important. Perhaps we should build new cities, far away from the metropolitan areas of the East Coast and the West Coast, and take advantage of modern technology to liberate us from the traditional concepts of establishing human settlements.*

---

* The magnitude of the United States population problem becomes graphically apparent when we keep in mind that we are now growing at the rate of 3 million a year. A new city the size of Dayton or Tulsa, about 250,000 people, is required every month. Of course, this increase is added on to the existing overcrowded cities, which are simply expanding. A number of brave attempts have been made to build satellite cities which are located near major urban centers. But in most cases this does not really solve the regional traffic and pollution problems; it simply diffuses them.

A better distribution of people is an absolute necessity and will ameliorate many of the problems which are produced by a growing population—perhaps for a few decades. But it cannot by itself solve the long-range problems. Even with a perfect distribution of population there comes a point where something goes out of balance. It is as if we were driving an old car and putting our foot on the gas to increase its speed to greater and greater values. What will go wrong first? Will the tires blow out before the engine blows up? Will a wheel come off before the transmission gives out? In the population problem we also want to know what will be a limiting factor. For example, running out of metals or oil has very little to do with the distribution of population; it is the level of population and total consumption that matters. On the other hand, social and urban problems, problems of health care and of pollution, are very closely tied to the concentration of population, as well as to the level.

DIAGNOSING THE PATIENT

A systematic analysis of these and other relevant factors has never been attempted. We are still in the exploratory phase of the problem. What we would like to do, ideally, is to find out what constitutes an optimum, say for the United States, so that we can define a national goal for population policies on a rational and scientific basis—we first want to diagnose the state of the patient and discover his illnesses, before prescribing the medicine.

The present volume was not designed to present an action program, but merely to open up a wide-ranging discussion. Our purposes were modest: not to state an actual number which purports to be the optimum level, but rather to discuss the ingredients, factors, and methods to use in making such an analysis.

First of all, does it make sense to talk about optimum levels of population, or optimum rates of change, or optimum concentrations—are these concepts meaningful and useful? I hope that the collection of papers, essays, and discussions in this volume has answered this rather fundamental question positively, so that we can go on now to ask: What methods do we use to determine this optimum level or optimum rate of growth or optimum concentration, whether it be for a city, a region, a country, a continent, or the world?

One way, and perhaps the best way, to make this kind of analysis is to look at the Gross National Product and ask the following question: What happens to the various sectors of the GNP "pie" as population, population concentrations, and levels of consumption increase? What happens to the part of the pie that we call disposable income and essentially refers to the amount that is left over from the paycheck after all of the "necessities" have been taken care of? It is that fraction which is somehow related, although not perfectly, to what we call quality of life. Once we pass the "optimum," then the Gross National Product may well rise as the population increases in number, but the quality of life of the average person will get worse.

For example, if the population becomes too large, then metals and fuels might become scarce, and the cost of water would also rise. But health services and educational services—if properly managed— might actually improve with a larger population. Interestingly enough, defense and space expenditures would occupy a smaller fraction of the GNP pie. For it costs no more to defend a 300 million population of the year 2000 with superweapons than it does to defend a 200 million population of today. And exploration of the planetary system won't cost more just because the population rises.

On the other hand, the quality of the environment does depend on population levels and on GNP. The beer cans; the junked cars; the mounting stacks of newsprint, packages, bottles; the wastes from mining operations and from agriculture—all of these rise. Air pollution, which is almost a direct result of the number of automobiles and of the production of electric power, and water pollution increase in close correlation with GNP, and perhaps a little faster. And the cost of achieving and maintaining a clean and healthy environment rises even faster, so that, as GNP rises, an increasing fraction of GNP would have to be devoted to pollution control. We are therefore back to a quasi-Malthusian equation. A "modern Malthus" would say that pollution will get us in the end, if something else doesn't do us in first.

THE "POPULLUTION" PROBLEM

How do we meet this problem of "popullution." I coin this term because I find it hard to separate population and pollution. To pull us out of this situation, we must look not only to technology, but also to the social sciences because the attitudes and customs of the people and their institutions are involved here. Technology has its ups and downs, of course, as the public looks at it. First-order effects are always widely hailed; technical discoveries produce more goods more cheaply and lead to higher standards of living. We have air-conditioning, for example, which certainly increases "welfare." But it consumes tremendous amounts of electricity and produces secondary effects, e.g., the waste heat from electric power generation, which are undesirable, as are the secondary effects of many other technologies. These side effects result in pollution of the environment and degradation of our quality of life. We therefore have to develop further technology to overcome the unwanted by-products of our primary technology.

In fact, without the "technological fix," the situation might become hopelessly expensive. It is the technological fix that allows us to reclaim waste water economically and clean it up so that it can be re-used for all purposes. It allows us to halt the deterioration of lakes and even restore them. It allows us to replace the internal combustion engine with an inherently low-pollution engine. It allows us to extract the sulfur from coal during combustion so that the atmosphere will not be polluted with sulfur oxides. Once we have caught up with the pollution backlog which has accumulated because of the neglect and apathy of past generations, then the costs of control will drop to a much lower level.

The biggest technological advance that we can look forward to is the development of electric power from nuclear fusion—the controlled hydrogen bomb. Research teams in the United States, in Europe, and in Russia are racing toward this goal. It is too early to tell if or when any of them will succeed. But if they do, then it will be a "whole new ball game." The dimension of the population problem will change as well, but only in the sense of postponing the inevitable confrontation with the facts of life for a few more years.

But perhaps this is the respite which is required before we can all become convinced of the seriousness of the problem. Perhaps a better distribution of population and technological fixes will postpone the day of reckoning. In the meantime, we might still learn how to change our attitudes and customs, even our institutional arrangements—to accept recycling and re-use of water, of metals, and of other raw materials, to practice conservation of resources and lands. We might learn to redirect growth away from wasteful production to more essentials and more services—all of it designed to provide a better quality of life throughout. Above all, it may give us that vital span of time in which to learn how to set up policies for the control of population growth.

Few will question the need for immediately slowing growth by reducing fertility. It is the wisest course to follow, even if we are not certain where the optimum lies, since a population control program may take decades to produce significant impacts. In the meantime, it is in the less-developed countries, with their high rates of growth, that the situation is particularly serious. For example, in Latin America, where the rate is 3 percent per year, the present population of 280 million would increase by over 140 percent by the year 2000. In the same thirty-year span, the world population would double from 3.5 up to about 7 billion.

Whether or not the predicted famines and other disasters will actually occur, the danger signals of unlimited population growth are here for all of us to see. Most of us prefer to see them in other countries, but they are just as real in the United States, although they look different.

Professor René Dubos, in a recent editorial in *Science,* reminds us that all ecological systems, in the long run, achieve a state of equilibrium. Societies like ours which are highly industrialized have been in a state of disequilibrium for several decades. We have been overusing and abusing our resources and environment. Furthermore, ecological instability is increasing at such an accelerated rate that ecological disasters are inevitable if the present trend continues.

Garrett Hardin has pointed out how very difficult it is psychologically to really believe that a disaster is impending. "How can one believe in something—particularly an unpleasant something—that has never happened before?" This must have been a terrible problem for Noah. Can't we just hear his "cornucopian" compatriots: "Something has always happened to save us." Or "Don't worry about the rising waters, Noah; our advanced technology will surely discover a substitute for breathing." Could *we* respond to a crisis that has never been faced by mankind? Would *we* build the Ark today if we could predict the flood? Unfortunately, the Bible doesn't tell us much about Noah's psychological trials and tribulations. But if it was wisdom that enabled Noah to believe in the "never-yet-happened," we could use some of that wisdom now.

A much better perspective of the state of human affairs, and of the prospects for the future, can be obtained if the events with which we are concerned are regarded on a time scale of some tens of thousands of years. On such a scale, the quantities whose growth with respect to time we have been considering—the world's human population, the consumption of energy per capita, the development of water power, and the exploitation of the energy from fossil fuels—would all plot as curves with such uniform similarities as to be almost indistinguishable from one another. The curve of human population, for example, would plot as a nearly horizontal line just above zero for the entire period of human history until the last thousand years or so. Then a barely perceptible rise would begin and, as the present is approached, the curve would turn abruptly upward and rise nearly vertically to the present world-population figure of about 3.5 billion.

Looking into the future on the same time scale, M. King Hubbert, writing in *Resources and Man,* concludes:

. . . assuming that a catastrophic event such as the near annihilation of the industrialized world by thermonuclear warfare can somehow be avoided, the physical realities discussed in this book dictate that the curve of human population must follow one of three possible courses: (1) It could continue to rise for a brief period and then gradually level off to some stable magnitude capable of being sustained by the world's energy and material resources for a long period of time; (2) it could overshoot any possible stable level and then drop back and eventually stabilize at some level compatible with the world's resources; or (3) finally, as a result of resource exhaustion and a general cultural decline, the curve could be forced back to a population corresponding to the lowest energy-consumption level of a primitive existence.

The one type of behavior for this curve that is not possible is that of continued and unlimited growth. To see that limits do exist, one need only consider that if the present world population were to be doubled but 15 more times, there would be one man for each square meter on all of the land areas of the Earth, including Antarctica, Greenland, and the Sahara Desert. And at the present rate of growth, this would require but 525 more years.

It now appears that the period of rapid population and industrial growth that has prevailed during the last few centuries, instead of being the normal order of things and capable of continuance into the indefinite future, is actually one of the most abnormal phases of human history. It represents only a brief transitional episode between two very much longer periods, each characterized by rates of change so slow as to be regarded essentially as a period of nongrowth. It is paradoxical that although the forthcoming period of nongrowth poses no insuperable physical or biological problems, it will entail a fundamental revision of those aspects of our current economic and social thinking which stem from the assumption that the growth rates which have characterized this temporary period can be permanent.

SFS

Index